The McGraw-Hill Environmental Auditing Handbook

The McGraw-Hill Environmental Auditing Handbook

A Guide to Corporate
and Environmental
Risk Management

L. LEE HARRISON, Editor in Chief
Editor, Environmental Audit Letter

McGRAW-HILL BOOK COMPANY
New York   St. Louis   San Francisco   Auckland
Bogotá   Hamburg   Johannesburg   London   Madrid
Mexico   Montreal   New Delhi   Panama   Paris
São Paulo   Singapore   Sydney   Tokyo   Toronto

Library of Congress Cataloging in Publication Data
Main entry under title:

The McGraw-Hill environmental auditing handbook.

Includes index.
1. Pollution—Economic aspects—United States—Addresses, essays, lectures.   2. Environmental impact
analysis—United States—Addresses, essays, lectures.
I. Harrison, L. Lee.
HD69.P6E58   1984   363.7'31   83-13559
ISBN 0-07-026859-2

1 2 3 4 5 6 7 8 9 0   DOC/DOC   8 9 8 7 6 5 4

ISBN 0-07-026859-2

The editors for this book were Harold B. Crawford and Mary
Farrell, the designer was Karin Batten, and the production supervisor was Sally Fliess. It was set in Baskerville by Achorn Graphics.

Printed and bound by R. R. Donnelley & Sons Company.

TO RUTH AND JUSTIN

Contents

Contributors

Joseph P. Barzotti, Supervisor of Environmental Auditing, Environmental Auditing Staff, General Motors Corporation, Warren, Michigan

Michael F. Basta, Supervisor of Environmental Auditing, Pennsylvania Power & Light, Allentown, Pennsylvania

Mitchell H. Bernstein, Attorney, Skadden, Arps, Slate, Meagher & Flom, Washington, D.C.

Karen Blumenfeld, Manager, Regulatory Reform Staff, Office of Policy & Resource Management, U.S. Environmental Protection Agency, Washington, D.C.

Nancy S. Bryson, Acting Assistant Chief, Environmental Defense Section, U.S. Department of Justice, Washington, D.C.

Robert W. Cutler, Manager, Regulatory Audits, Olin Corporation, Stamford, Connecticut

Mark P. Denbeaux, Professor, Seton Hall Law School, Newark, New Jersey

Maryanne DiBerto, Consultant, Center for Environmental Assurance, Arthur D. Little, Inc., Cambridge, Massachusetts

George S. Dominguez, President, Springborn Regulatory Consultants, Enfield, Connecticut

Stuart E. Eizenstat, Attorney, Powell, Goldstein, Frazer & Murphy, Washington, D.C.

John T. Funkhouser, Director, Center for Environmental Assurance, Arthur D. Little, Inc., Cambridge, Massachusetts

David C. Garrett III, Attorney, Powell, Goldstein, Frazer & Murphy, Atlanta, Georgia

J. Ladd Greeno, Senior Consultant, Center for Environmental Assurance, Arthur D. Little, Inc., Cambridge, Massachusetts

Mark Haddad, former Manager, Regulatory Reform Staff, U.S. Environmental Protection Agency, Washington, D.C.

Stephen W. Hamilton, Attorney, Skadden, Arps, Slate, Meagher & Flom, Washington, D.C.

L. Lee Harrison, Editor, *Environmental Audit Letter*, New York, N.Y.

Gilbert S. Hedstrom, Consultant, Center for Environmental Assurance, Arthur D. Little, Inc., Cambridge, Massachusetts

Jesse W. Hill, Attorney, Powell, Goldstein, Frazer & Murphy, Atlanta, Georgia

William C. Hope, Sun Information Services, Radnor, Pennsylvania

Walter J. Huelsman, Partner, Environmental Services, Coopers & Lybrand, Washington, D.C.

William G. Kelly, Manager, Environmental Services, Atlantic Richfield Corp., Los Angeles, California

Robert E. Litan, Attorney, Powell, Goldstein, Frazer & Murphy, Washington, D.C.

Angus Macbeth, Attorney, Bergson, Borkland, Margolis & Adler, Washington, D.C.

Jeffrey G. Miller, Attorney, Bergson, Borkland, Margolis & Adler, Washington, D.C.

James T. O'Rourke, President, Industrial Division, Camp, Dresser & McKee, Boston, Massachusetts

John Palmisano, Director, New Reforms Project, Regulatory Reform Staff, U.S. Environmental Protection Agency, Washington, D.C.

James A. Rogers, Attorney, Skadden, Arps, Slate, Meagher & Flom, Washington, D.C.

Myra L. Tobin, Managing Director, Marsh & McLennan, New York, N.Y.

Preface

A growing number of major corporations—Allied, Olin, Atlantic Richfield, General Motors, and Pennsylvania Power & Light, to name a few—have active environmental auditing departments. And at least five states—New York, New Jersey, Pennsylvania, North Carolina, and Michigan—have set up pilot programs to explore the benefits of environmental auditing. For maximum benefit to the environment and for maximum support from both public and private sectors, however, these efforts need to be backed by a national program.

Such a national approach—perhaps beginning with a test to see whether firms with their own auditing programs are more apt to be in compliance than those without such programs—could help to move government and industry away from the destructive and costly adversarial system of regulation that exists now. Participation in such a program should be voluntary, and there should be some reward for companies that develop successful auditing programs and maintain a high level of compliance because of them. Licensing of new facilities could be speeded, and inspections and paperwork could be lessened. But the threat of on-site inspection should never be removed entirely, lest the impetus for establishing rigorous environmental auditing programs go with it. The EPA would benefit by being able to aim its enforcement resources where they would be likely to do the most good—at companies without an auditing program.

Admittedly, under such a national program, companies with approved auditing programs would have to be granted some measure of protection from prosecution for violations that their own auditors found, as long as such problems were corrected within a reasonable time. Without such protection, the fear of having internal documents subpoenaed during a legal proceeding might be enough to force a chief executive to quash any notion of internal environmental auditing.

But if the goal of our society is to preserve the environment while encouraging economic development—rather than to punish violators—then the problems of developing a national environmental auditing program are surmountable. Industry, however, will have to realize that environmental auditing is its own best hope for rational enforcement of environmental laws and push for such an expanded program.

Along with the development of efficient compliance procedures and better relationships with regulatory bodies, environmental auditing, at the very least, can offer a corporation better community relations: Just knowing that a company has such a program may make a community feel that the company is a responsible neighbor. On a more essential level, however, environmental auditing might also keep a corporation out of bankruptcy court through early detection of an environmental problem.

But no environmental auditing program will be effective without the active support of top management. The program must have the imprimatur of the chief executive, and all personnel must understand that their company takes environmental auditing seriously. Who knows, as a side benefit, a strong environmental auditing program might even help the chief executive sleep at night!

It was to increase public and private understanding of environmental auditing that I undertook this handbook project. If it only increases the *dialogue* about risk management and environmental protection, then I believe reason will prevail and the book will have succeeded.

L. LEE HARRISON

The McGraw-Hill
Environmental
Auditing
Handbook

P A R T

1

INTRODUCTION

Environmental Auditing: A New Risk-Management Tool

Lee Harrison
Editor in Chief

O ver the last few years, spurred on in part by the Environmental Protection Agency's own regulatory reform effort, corporations have developed a process by which they can verify their compliance with environmental laws and regulations. The process, differing in form from company to company and generally called "environmental auditing," has gained favor with a large number of major industrial and manufacturing corporations across the country and is now spreading throughout the entire private sector.

In its strictest form, environmental auditing can resemble an all-out financial audit for detecting fraud, similar to those conducted by the Securities and Exchange Commission and other regulatory agencies. A company choosing this route might bring in outside consultants to take samples of air and water emissions, bore wells to check for toxic substances leaking from landfills, and check all data against existing company reports.

Yet environmental auditing can also function as an ongoing, comprehensive management information system to alert top corporate officials to potentially devastating risks associated with company operations before major harm is done to people or to the environment. This approach also can serve as an early warning system, identifying any number of product safety hazards and hidden liabilities posed by acquisition targets as well as by off-site suppliers and jobbers.

In essence, risks faced by corporations are of two kinds. First, there is the risk of fines and imprisonment of top officials for failure to comply with rules and standards set forth by EPA and other regulatory bodies, both federal and state. Second, there are the as-yet unidentified risks—perhaps unidentified even by federal and state agencies—which can cause immense damage to the corporate treasury and reputation before they are resolved. By developing an environmental auditing program (or perhaps combining two separate environmental and risk-management programs) that is broad enough to deal with both kinds of risks, corporations can have at their disposal an effective tool with which to manage risk.

Example A major chemical company brought in an outside audit consulting firm to review its operations' compliance with environmental regulations. The company assumed that the audit consultant would review in detail the company's manufacturing and waste-control operations, which it did. But the consultant also inquired as to the existence of any jobbers—small companies performing specific manufacturing tasks for the corporation. There were none, but one small company did provide a special service for the corporation. It bagged one of the corporation's pesticides in an unusually large bag for one large customer with special needs, something the chemical company could not handle. Since the jobber only bagged the pesticide, no one had thought to examine the entire operation. However, upon inspection, the audit consultant found that the jobber used the same facilities to bag pet food as to bag the pesticide. Red flags went up, and the bagging operation ceased before any harm was done. But had it gone on, contamination of the pet food could have resulted, and the chemical company could have sustained massive financial losses as well as damage to its reputation. The hazard-identification nature of the consultant's audit procedure probably saved the corporation many times the cost of the audit.

Example Two workers at a large manufacturing facility in rural Pennsylvania were apprehended by state environmental authorities as they dumped toxic chemical waste at an abandoned site near the plant. The workers were participating in a plantwide cleanup in preparation for a visit by senior corporate management later that same day. Yet officials at the home office of the company insisted that the men were acting without the authority or knowledge of company management and in violation of plant procedures for handling waste chemicals. Somehow those procedures had broken down, and company officials were forced to negotiate a consent decree with state environmental authorities, resulting in a payment of $20,000 in civil and criminal fines.

These examples are not unique. Such situations develop quite easily in a large corporation that deals with hazardous products and waste products. Yet managers are responsible under the law for their operations, so their response to such risks must come in the form of surveillance. Managers must be confident that there are adequate controls in place to ensure that corporate environmental policies are followed; and surveillance, in the form of environmental audits, can provide that assurance.

Cases like these have shown corporate managers that they must combine environmental and risk-management programs (which are often dispersed or segregated) into an effective risk-management operation. It is the purpose of this handbook to serve as a basic reference work, providing the information you need to set up your own environmental auditing program or to measure your current program against those of other companies.

The next two chapters in this section of the handbook provide a background on the need for and the development of environmental auditing. Chapter 2 provides in detail a description of the legal, financial, and health problems caused Allied Corporation by its association with a jobber (not the company in the example above, but a case not entirely dissimilar), while Chapter 3 gives the theoretical foundations of environmental auditing and examines the question: Why conduct an environmental audit?

Part 2 of the handbook sets forth the risks in terms of noncompliance with environmental, health and safety, Securities and Exchange Commission, and product-liability law that United States corporations face. Most of the chapters are written by lawyers with broad experience in government, some as prosecutors, but they did not write *for* lawyers. We have aimed this book at the corporate executive who is responsible for setting corporate policy, assuming that he is not a lawyer but that he is at least familiar with the penalties posed by noncompliance with such laws and regulations.

The last three chapters in Part 2 require special mention, because, unlike the earlier chapters, they do not deal with specific regulations that are more or less straightforward. Product liability, for instance, is continually developing as the body of case law grows. Each new decision—be it on the female hormone DES or something as recent as Tylenol—changes the law. And Chapters 10 and 11 of Part 2—the former on the current situation and the latter providing a historical perspective—may force you to consider new roles for your environmental auditing team.

The last chapter in Part 2, "Acquisition and Divestiture," opens up an entirely new role for environmental auditing. How many corporate acquisitions would have been canceled if hidden liabilities in the form of abandoned waste sites or unsafe product lines were known ahead of time? As the author of this chapter notes, no stone is left unturned in examining a takeover target's financial pluses and minuses, but only rarely is an environmental auditor brought in to assess the likelihood of unstated environmental risks.

Similarly, corporations with many different operating divisions might do well to examine, through environmental auditing, the risks associated with staying in certain businesses. Perhaps some risks are not worth taking, given what they bring to the bottom line each year.

Part 3 is what this handbook really is all about—conducting an environmental audit—and you will read about it from several perspectives: those of the professional auditor, the consulting engineer, the insurance broker, and four major corporations. It is necessary to present these various views because environmental auditing is so new. Unlike financial auditing, which has been in existence since the first business was established, environmental auditing is a recent phenomenon. There is no standard-setting board, so any number of approaches are considered acceptable. Much has to do with a corporation's culture and philosophy. These environmental auditing programs have been developed to deal with a body of environmental, health, and safety regulations that are themselves in a state of flux. Accordingly, the approaches to environmental auditing presented here will, without a doubt, evolve over time.

As with Part 2, the last three chapters in Part 3 deserve a special word. Chapter 8 of Part 3 presents the result of a survey of corporations that have environmental audit programs. Each corporation was asked about the report prepared as a result of any given audit: who got the report, its purpose, degree of complexity, etc. The results will be of interest to readers who are concerned about presenting a clear picture of a corporation's compliance situation without creating additional risks and liabilities as a result of the report itself.

Chapter 9 of Part 3, a discussion of alternative approaches to environmental auditing, examines the forces that shape auditing programs and aims to help the corporate executive in sorting out the choices in developing such a program.

The last chapter in Part 3 explains the efficiencies that can result from using a computer to organize and report the thousands of pages of compliance data required by current regulations.

Perhaps the greatest fear that strikes corporate executives ruminating on the advantages and disadvantages of environmental auditing is the loss of confidentiality of any report generated by an audit. Chapter 1 of Part 4 deals at length with this subject and will probably be the best-read chapter in this handbook. Chapter 2 of Part 4 tells you how to size up your current auditing program vis-à-vis those of your competitors. Environmental auditing, as mentioned earlier, is an evolutionary process. Not only are audits themselves changing and becoming more sophisticated, but the laws they measure compliance against also are changing constantly. You are, in essence, shooting at a moving target from a moving platform, and it is a good idea to see what others are doing as a way of measuring your own success.

Part 5 presents the Environmental Protection Agency's perspective on environmental auditing. To date, the agency has opted only to "endorse, analyze and assist" in the development of corporate and state environmental auditing programs. The reasons for that decision and what it means are presented here.

Each part of this handbook has been written to provide a different perspective on this new discipline we call environmental auditing. The whole should give a three-dimensional view of the state of the art to aid you in developing an effective corporate risk-management tool.

What an Environmental Audit Can Help You Avoid: The Case History of Kepone

Angus Macbeth
Jeffrey G. Miller
Bergson, Borkland, Margolis & Adler

In June 1975, Dale Gilbert, a Hopewell, Virginia, chemical worker, went to his doctor with the shakes—dizziness and trembling. Unsure of the cause, the doctor shipped a sample of Gilbert's blood to the Center for Disease Control in Atlanta, which analyzed it as having a high level of Kepone, a DDT-like pesticide. Within days, Life Science Products, the Kepone manufacturing company where Gilbert worked, was closed. The tests at the Center for Disease Control had rung the bell of a major health alarm for the Kepone workers and their families and a major environmental alarm for Chesapeake Bay and the James River estuary. The events they precipitated also caused a financial and public relations disaster for Allied Chemical Corporation—one of the largest chemical companies in the nation—for whom the Kepone was being manufactured by Life Science Products.

When Virginia state inspectors went into the Life Science Products Kepone plant, they found the granulated pesticide littering the work places of the plant and seven workers so acutely ill that they had to be hospitalized at once. Before the state health department could serve a closing order, Life Science Products shut its plant down. In all, thirty people were hospitalized with tremors, blurred vision, and loss of memory, and the community was afire with fear of sterility and cancer. Fishing in the James River from Richmond down to Chesapeake Bay was banned for both sports and commercial fishermen.

This was the end of Allied Chemical's production and marketing of Kepone. Kepone had been developed by Allied 25 years before and had been used in forty household products to control insects, although most of it was shipped abroad. Allied had produced the pesticide at Hopewell for many years, and in 1974 it had spun off the operation to Life Science Products, a firm put together by employees leaving Allied. Allied entered into a "tolling" agreement with Life Science, a common device in the chemical industry by which risky or troublesome chemicals are given to a subcontractor for redelivery after processing. The inspectors' visit was the beginning of investigations and lawsuits which went right past Life Science to Allied.

Shortly after the state's inspection of the Life Science plant, regional officials of the Environmental Protection Agency (EPA), who had become aware of the employee sickness through the media, entered the investigation. Life Science had already come under EPA's scrutiny by claiming that a loophole in pesticide-shipping regulations exempted Kepone. In addition, EPA was examining the failure of Hopewell's sewage treatment plant. When EPA discovered that an ailing sewage treatment plant worker had developed symptoms similar to those of the sick employees at Life Science, the agency conducted tests at the treatment plant. It discovered that the plant had failed because its biological digesters had been destroyed by Kepone. The matter was serious enough to require action, and EPA sent letters to Allied Chemical requesting its files on Kepone.

Allied Chemical's initial response to EPA disclaimed responsibility for Kepone because it was manufactured by Life Science and Allied was only a customer of Life Science. EPA, however, combed through information provided by the city, the state, and Allied Chemical to discover that Allied Chemical had manufactured and discharged Kepone prior to the existence of Life Science. Moreover, it had failed to disclose the existence of Kepone in its discharge in a Clean Water Act (CWA) discharge-permit application to EPA. This discharge of 150 gallons per day for 940 days eventually led to a criminal indictment, guilty plea, and sentencing.

THE COST OF POLLUTION

Congress did not ignore the growing clamor along the James. In January 1976, Allied went through 4 days of hearings before a Senate subcommittee on Kepone and the Hopewell disaster. A parade of horrors was spread across the media. One typical Kepone worker told the subcommittee: "I couldn't drink a cup of coffee without spilling it on my clothing, and when I walked, I sort of bounced." There were suggestions that families had been contaminated and injured by Kepone clinging to the clothes that plant workers wore home and that the fears and complaints of plant employees had been brushed aside by the bland assertion that Kepone was "harmless to humans."

Investigations, indictments, and lawsuits from every quarter followed:

- A federal grand jury indicted Allied on 1094 counts of violating the pollution laws. After protestations of innocence, Allied pleaded no contest to 940 counts covering the time prior to the advent of Life Science, when Allied had been directly discharging Kepone and its employees had not been accurately reporting its activities to the government. Allied was fined $13.2 million, a sum the judge reduced to $5 million after Allied gave $8 million to an independent environmental foundation.

- Virginia and the city of Hopewell sued, and Allied settled by paying them $5.25 million for damages.

- Approximately fifty Kepone workers and their families sued. The settlements in these cases were not made public, but the first round of settlements involved nineteen workers and their families, including Dale Gilbert, who said he was "very well pleased" with the settlement. It was later estimated that this group of suits was settled for close to $3 million.

- Commercial fishermen and the seafood industry sued. After a considerable period of legal maneuvering, Allied settled with 180 plaintiffs in these cases in 1980. These settlements were also secret, though they probably involved much less in payment than did the worker injuries.

- The Securities and Exchange Commission (SEC) sued for failure to disclose material environmental information and liabilities to investors. This was the SEC's first foray into environmental disclosures, and its settlement with Allied probably would have been more onerous if the commission had not been looking at such issues for the first time. Nevertheless, in settling the suit Allied agreed to investigate its environmental risk areas which were of significance to prudent investors in the company's stock and to follow a policy of keeping the corporate management fully informed of environmental risks and uncertainties.

Beyond all this damage, Allied has clearly had other major costs—a stockholder's suit, legal fees, the costs of advertising campaigns to repair its image, insurance problems, even the expenditure of $934,000 to raze the Hopewell plant to the ground. As the president of the company's chemical unit put it, Kepone "knocked out any degree of respectability we had." Partly as a result of all this, the company dropped "Chemical" from its name. It is now the Allied Corporation.

There is no doubt that internal controls and checks by Allied would have avoided most of the public damage and massive liability that the company suffered. Allied itself argued to the Senate subcommittee that in the plants which it directly controlled with strict health and safety rules, there were no cases of Kepone poisoning. Allied even answered the indictment by complaining that the regulatory agencies had not done the job they should have in inspecting the plants—there had been a worker complaint to the Occupational Safety and Health Administration—and the company suggested that the grand jury should have looked harder at that failure.

Today Allied has an extensive surveillance program involving not only pollution control and occupational health but, in addition, plant safety and product safety. In 1977 Allied hired a major management consulting firm to design and implement an environmental audit program. There is a corporate environmental staff of about 20, and 400 employees are engaged in environmentally related work at Allied's operations. Allied instills effective managerial attitudes by teaching appropriate environmental response through the discussion and evaluation of hypothetical cases. A few hundred thousand dollars of prevention is worth $25 million of cure.

Kepone is, of course, a dramatic case and an uncommon one, but it illustrates effectively the range of interlocking liabilities that effective internal control of a company's operations can prevent or mitigate: violations of criminal and regulatory law, claims for damages and injury from private parties, and missed opportunities for managerial or financial improvement. Moreover, it raises the question of how to cope with liabilities outside the corporation's doors. Environmental auditing is one of the best tools for addressing these liabilities.

THE ENVIRONMENTAL AUDIT SOLUTION

The environmental audit is a flexible mechanism which may be designed to meet a number of management needs. In its most straightforward form, the audit analyzes a company's present compliance with federal, state, and local environmental regulation. For instance, it checks whether the company has all required environmental permits, makes all required reports accurately and promptly, and disposes of all hazardous wastes properly. But an audit can go much farther. By taking split samples and analyzing them in different laboratories, it can check on whether inside and contractor laboratories are providing accurate analyses of wastes. It can be used to examine past practices such as hazardous-waste disposal which may present future liabilities. It can address future control requirements to see whether they are adequately provided for in the corporate budget. In addition to searching for possible liabilities, the audit can be used for more positive management goals: cost savings by fully exploiting efficiencies at all plants; accurate pricing of acquisitions by discovering their hidden liabilities; and reducing the cost of insurance or self-insurance.

An audit is basically a close study and analysis of the environmental practices of a corporation directed toward well-defined goals: regulatory compliance, liability risk reduction, cost saving, efficiency of operation, or some other corporate aim. It goes without saying that to be truly effective the audit must be followed by action. What the audit provides is the knowledge necessary for intelligent action—a way to avoid the kind of trouble Allied found itself in.

Financial and Managerial Opportunities

The Kepone disaster was in large measure the result of bad miscalculations by Allied on financial and managerial opportunities. Life Science was a captive supplier run by Allied's former employees. Although the issue of Allied's civil liability for Life Science was never fully litigated, Allied made major payments on claims it could have argued were Life Science's responsibility. Given this liability, which Allied had not audited or otherwise anticipated in advance, its calculation of the value of the Life Science deal was way off—the net profit on Kepone never exceeded $600,000 a year. Had Allied audited the extent of its liabilities, it would quickly have seen how shortsighted was its response to this apparent business opportunity. Auditing an ostensibly independent operation may not normally be feasible, but the economic or corporate relationship that plausibly gives rise to liability is also likely to provide the leverage to allow some auditing or review procedure. Particularly in the hazardous-substance field, what one's business allies do should be closely examined.[1]

A more typical example of business choices improved by auditing is Allied's experience *after* it initiated its surveillance program and discovered that, instead of installing expensive new equipment to control discharges of calcium chloride at its fluorocarbon plant in Louisiana, a market could be developed for the commercial sale of the material for use in oil drilling liquids. Cost savings make up the largest and perhaps the most important category of opportunities that may be missed without an environmental audit program. Savings come in many guises, and identifying them requires an alert eye moving through the company's operations on a regular basis. An obvious example is the transferral of ideas from one facility to the next. Cost savings achieved at particular facilities—by using process changes rather than adding control equipment, by using wastes as raw materials or fuel instead of treating them, or by economies in the equipment, operations, and materials used for pollution control—can be multiplied if transferable to other facilities. Joint treatment of specialized wastes by several facilities may create economies of scale.

If conducted over time, audits will lower the cost of environmental impairment liability insurance or self-insurance—not least by building the positive managerial attitude that risk assessors look for in determining whether a company is actively working to limit its risks and liabilities. Audits may aid financial planning and costs by enabling future environmental controls to be phased in rationally with other capital expenditures. Auditing potential acquisitions can prevent the acquisition of unforeseen environmental liabilities.

The Keene Corporation bought a small company making asbestos insulation products in 1968 and since then has been deluged with suits by workers claiming damages for having contracted asbestosis. The chairman of Keene has publicly regretted the day he wasn't "smart enough not to spend $7 million to buy [the small company] and the unforeseen pack of troubles that eventually resulted." Since defendants are generally liable for what they knew or should have known, a careful audit procedure at the time of purchase might have repaid the cost to Keene many times over.

Other opportunities that can be missed without environmental auditing are of more general management benefit and not as easily quantifiable. The exposure of corporate headquarters environmental personnel to field operations personnel in an intense and helpful manner in an audit program can strengthen the environmental department. The use of field personnel to assist in auditing other facilities can broaden their experience and perspectives. These opportunities for improved management are important by-products of the auditing process.

Criminal Liabilities

Auditing clearly would have lessened Allied's exposure to criminal prosecution, since comparing actual plant discharges with those allowed by permit (or local rule) is an obvious first step in checking for regulatory compliance. But at the same time it must be recognized that audits are not a cure for criminal liability when a company discovers that its employees have lied to the government in reports or knowingly operated in violation of environmental requirements. An apology is not always enough. Some familiarity with prosecutorial policies will show the value of auditing.

Most violations of federal environmental statutes are subject to both civil and criminal sanctions. The only statutory distinction drawn between the two for prosecutions is normally that criminal sanctions are for knowing or willful violations. Knowing or willful violations can result from management decisions to continue operating facilities which miss deadlines for installing pollution control equipment or whose pollution control equipment continually fails to meet emission or discharge limitations. Such violations, spanning the range from gross to insignificant, can all be criminal as well as civil.

The factors normally considered by prosecutors in determining whether to enforce in these situations and whether to seek administrative, civil, or criminal remedies include (1) the extent of environmental or public health damage, (2) whether the violation and damage have been or are being terminated, and (3) the cooperativeness or recalcitrance of the violator. Indeed, Department of Justice policy requires that, in determining whether or not to prosecute criminally, federal prosecutors consider the degree of culpability of a potential defendant and the availability of noncriminal alternatives such as civil suits or some rehabilitative program by which the defendant does not enter the criminal justice system.[2] Corporations that audit their compliance with environmental laws, take prompt corrective action when needed, and report both fully to regulatory agencies exhibit good faith and minimize the extent of violations and resulting damage. In combination, these factors make criminal prosecution less likely. Indeed, depending on the prevailing state of federal enforcement philosophy, they may make any enforcement sanctions unlikely.[3]

Perhaps the greatest significance of an audit program in avoiding criminal liability is its effect on corporate personnel. It impresses on them that corporate policy really is to comply with environmental laws and that employees participating in violations of environmental requirements will not prosper in the corporation. This will in itself discourage conduct that could lead to prosecutions.

The mere existence of a corporate audit program should particularly discourage the practice of false record keeping and false reporting. This is significant for criminal liability, because cases of this type constitute a large portion of the environmental criminal docket. Moreover, false reporting by individuals in the corporation can create criminal liability for their superiors and for the corporation itself. The federal prosecution of the Sewer Committee of Little Rock, Arkansas, is a good example. The superintendent of the Little Rock sewage treatment plant repeatedly submitted false discharge monitoring reports to the authorities. The reports, required under the CWA, document compliance with the pollution-discharge limits set under the statute. Although none of the committee's five members were aware of the superintendent's illegal practice, both the committee and the plant superintendent were convicted of criminal violations because the sewer committee had authority over the superintendent and was responsible for his actions.[4] An environmental audit conducted independently by or for the sewer committee could have discouraged this behavior or could have detected and stopped it at an early stage, avoiding prosecution or lessening the likelihood of prosecution of the committee.

Criminal liability will be an increasing reality over the next few years. The Department of Justice has repeatedly stated its willingness to prosecute environmental crimes, has offered the services of the Federal Bureau of Investigation in investigating them, and has prodded the EPA to increase prosecutions by hiring trained criminal investigators. Despite budget cutbacks in 1981 and 1982, EPA hired such investigators for the first time, set up a viable criminal investigation program, and committed itself to developing an increased number of criminal cases.[5]

To be of value an audit must be thorough and well thought out. A well-conducted audit by Allied would not have helped in the Kepone case if it had not looked beyond what the people at the plant had told the government. Moreover, there are criminal cases in which audits would be of no benefit: violations which are the result of a conscious management decision or which result from the acts of those who had conducted or supervised the audit.[6] Indeed, an audit may make matters worse if it brings violations to the attention of management and the corporation then ignores the facts that are before it. Less obvious reckless disregard of the facts is sufficient to convict in cases involving financial audits, and the same would surely apply in the environmental context.

Regulatory Liabilities

Allied is not alone in being the subject of SEC actions for failure to disclose material environmental information. Both United States Steel Corporation and Occidental Petroleum Corporation were investigated by the SEC and charged with failure to disclose potential environmental liabilities; resulting settlements included environmental audits.[7]

Such investigations may have serious consequences. The Occidental investigation grew out of and contributed to successful efforts by Mead

Corporation to resist a takeover bid by Occidental. Mead alleged that Occidental had failed to disclose the significant environmental liabilities of its subsidiary, Hooker Chemical. One of those liabilities was Hooker's toxic waste dumps at Love Canal. The publicity resulting from these efforts and the information and documents produced during the SEC investigation probably contributed in real but intangible ways to the subsequent commencement and prosecution of federal and state civil cases against Occidental to force cleanup of Love Canal and three other hazardous waste sites near Buffalo, New York. The combined requests for penalties in the cases are in excess of $45 million, and the remedial actions sought could well cost more than $200 million.

Of course, what companies normally seek to avoid through the use of environmental audits are administrative and civil enforcement actions for violations of statutory requirements. A good example is the case of the Ironstone Division of Dayton Malleable, Inc., which failed to treat its discharges of foundry wastes to the Ohio River by July 1, 1977, as required in its CWA permit issued by the state of Ohio. Plans for the treatment facility were submitted 3 months behind schedule and were incomplete. Construction began 19 months behind schedule, and final compliance was not achieved until 15 months after the final deadline. The state trial court assessed a penalty of $493,000, comprising small amounts to redress harm to the public health and to recover the economic benefit of delayed compliance and a substantial amount for the apparent indifference of corporate management to achieving compliance with the law in a timely manner. Dayton Malleable appealed the penalty as excessive, but the Ohio Court of Appeals (with four states filing amicus briefs in support of Ohio) found that the record showed that "DMI was insensitive to the regulatory scheme. . . . The considerable delays in achieving compliance with the permit were clearly unjustified."[8] (Although upholding the trial court in its approach to setting the penalty, the court of appeals did reverse it on the number of days on which violations had been established.)

A timely environmental audit would have determined that planning and construction of pollution control equipment were required and would have questioned whether adequate provision had been made. The court of appeals concluded that the company's management was its own business, but it also noted that "given a legislative policy favoring environmental laundering, many businesses will be required to change and so may DMI in the future."[9] It is clear from the opinion that a management attitude evidenced by a good audit program and the prompt corrective and reporting actions that accompany it would have made a penalty of this magnitude inappropriate even if some violations had occurred.

Audits can assist management in reducing the number of violations that occur and in reducing the likelihood of significant penalties for those that do occur by promptly detecting, remedying, and reporting them. Even during periods of aggressive enforcement, EPA has taken good-faith efforts to comply into account in determining whether to file suit and in determining penalty amounts.[10] In the more relaxed enforcement climate of 1981 and 1982, there was serious discussion of forgoing potential remedies against companies that undertake auditing programs meeting specified criteria. Whether such a policy will become a reality and, if it does, its extent and duration are speculative. But however this trend develops, the good faith of potential defendants will inevitably be considered by regulators in making enforcement decisions, and good audit programs are hallmarks of good faith.

Tort Liabilities

In an increasing number of cases private parties are making claims for bodily injury and property damage—torts—based on pollution or some form of environmental exposure or damage. It is important to recognize the relation of these cases to those brought by the government. The testimony, documents, and other information which the government collects from defendants and witnesses through discovery when it is preparing for trial in enforcement cases may well be available to private plaintiffs. Hooker found this to be true when it sought to prohibit disclosure of information it provided to the government in the Love Canal cases. The court, recognizing that disclosure could be detrimental to Hooker in the private tort cases which were based on the same pollution as the government's case, refused Hooker's request:

> Use of the discovery fruits disclosed in one lawsuit in connection with other litigation . . . comes squarely within the purposes of the Federal Rules of Civil Procedure. . . . This is particularly the case in lawsuits where the resources available to the parties are uneven. Individuals who are plaintiffs might have a most difficult time extracting information, whereas powerful litigants such as the United States and the State might find it relatively easier to compel production.[11]

Such piggybacking will be very helpful to private parties where the government undertakes vigorous discovery. At Love Canal it could be devastating to Hooker, where 1400 plaintiffs have brought 600 lawsuits seeking a total of more than $2 billion in damages. Even allowing for plaintiffs' puffery, the cases represent serious litigation and underscore the importance of not arousing the government to persistent and determined efforts at civil enforcement. It may well be that Ralston Purina's recent guilty plea to a CWA indictment for discharging hexane, a solvent, which subsequently exploded in the Louisville sewers, was motivated in part by a desire not to have the government present its grand jury evidence at a public trial.[12] Once disclosed, this evidence could have been used by private plaintiffs in tort suits with millions of dollars in claims arising from the same sewer explosion.

The theories of negligence or failure to warn of dangers or strict liability for ultrahazardous activities on which environmental and toxic tort cases can be based are numerous, and this is not the place to review them. It is apparent that properly designed and executed environmental audits can limit a company's exposure to a broad range of common-law damages by preventing potentially damaging situations from arising and by identifying damaging situations that do occur and promptly correcting them. Even the most naive auditor should have been able to spot the desperately sick workers in the Kepone plant. And by using an environmental audit as further evidence of due care and reasonable action, a company may overcome inferences of negligence. Indeed, lack of environmental auditing itself may be viewed as an element of negligence as more companies develop auditing programs, following the doctrine in the case of the tugboat *T. J. Hooper*, that reasonable care may require practices not yet in common use.[13]

A strong note of caution is required here. Audits which are primarily designed as regulatory compliance audits will do an incomplete job of lessening exposure to potential tort liability. Much past and present business activity in unregulated areas that could be responsible for damages would be missed in a regulatory compliance audit. An expanded audit program, therefore, incorporating principles of risk analysis, is necessary to deal effectively with such liabilities. Moreover, carelessly drafted and overly conclusive memoranda developed in the course of an audit would be useful ammunition in the hands of a good plaintiff's attorney. The process and content of an audit need to be carefully watched so that inferences of negligence or recklessness cannot be unfairly drawn from the audit documents.

CONCLUSION

The criminal, regulatory, and common-law tort liabilities that can be avoided by environmental audits are well documented in legal casebooks and in the press. With increasing criminal prosecutions by the federal government and the awakening of the plaintiff's bar to environmental torts, reported examples can be expected to increase steadily in the years to come. Financial and management opportunities forgone in the absence of environmental audits are more difficult to document but no less real.

Environmental audits can be of significant benefit in avoiding these liabilities as well as lost opportunity costs. Audits, however, are not panaceas. They will do little more than they are designed to do. An audit designed to monitor regulatory compliance will not comprehensively identify potential tort liability. The first task of a corporation considering auditing is to identify its objectives carefully and design its audit program to meet them. Conducting the audit may present problems of maintaining corporate morale while assuring that a thorough and accurate review of practices and policies is made. Questions of what may be kept confidential within the corporation may well arise, and there may be the embarrassment of thoughtlessly written memoranda that are powerful ammunition in the hands of an opposing trial attorney or a government investigator. Audits may uncover unpleasant situations that must be resolved. Frequently they must be coupled with prompt responses to and correction of problems discovered. Response action is also necessary to take advantage of cost-saving possibilities discovered. Environmental audits can provide the knowledge and analysis that are necessary for informed and effective action, but it is the corporate officers and their advisers who remain responsible for deciding what action to take. The buck stops in the same place.

1. At the same time, the power to audit another enterprise's environmental practices may itself increase the risk that joint liability could be inferred. There are no neat or easy answers.

2. Department of Justice, *Principles of Federal Prosecution*, pp. 5–14.

3. Even for remedying highly publicized hazardous-waste-site problems, EPA at present considers voluntary disclosure a factor in deciding whether to enter an out-of-court settlement instead of a judicial consent decree. See "Guidance on Hazardous Waste Site Settlement Negotiations," Dec. 18, 1981, from William A. Sullivan, Jr., enforcement counsel, to regional counsels, regional enforcement division directors, and regional Superfund coordinators.

4. *United States v. Little Rock Sewer Committee*, 460 F. Supp. 6 (E.D. Ark. 1978); *United States v. Ouelette*, No. LR-CR-77-97, 11 E.R.C.1350 (E.D. Ark. 1977). See also *United States v. Olin Corp.*, 465 F. Supp. 1120 (W.D.N.Y. 1979) (conviction of corporation and employees directly responsible for submittal of falsified water-pollution-monitoring reports); *United States v. City of New Albany* (S.D. Inc. 1978), 9 *Envir. Rep.* (BNA) (digest) (conviction of city and sewage treatment plant superintendent for submittal of falsified discharge-monitoring reports which the superintendent prepared for the signature of the mayor).

5. See statement of James Moorman, assistant attorney general for lands and natural resources, in 1978, and that of Attorney General Benjamin Civiletti, in 1980, both quoted extensively in "White Collar Crime: Environmental," 18 *Am. Crim. L. Rev.* 345, 369, nn. 1718, 1719 (1981). The statements emphasize criminal prosecutions for

violations involving endangerment of public health and falsification. They also emphasize prosecution of responsible corporate officials. Recent statements by both EPA and Department of Justice officials indicate no abandonment of this thrust; see *Inside EPA*, p. 13 (Nov. 13, 1981), and 12 *Envir. Rep.* 895 (Nov. 20, 1981). EPA's new criminal policy and structure are reported verbatim in *Inside EPA* (Dec. 4, 1981) and *Inside EPA Special Supplement*, pp. 1–4. The effort is directed from the Office of Enforcement Counsel in Washington by a small staff of investigators and prosecutors. It is executed by twenty-five trained investigators operating out of four area offices but responsible to headquarters. They concentrate on violations (1) resulting in substantial harm; (2) evidencing serious recalcitrance; and (3) involving falsification, concealment, or destruction of information and records. See also "Memorandum on Criminal Enforcement Priorities from EPA Associate Administrator Robert M. Perry," 13 *Envir. Rep. Cur. Dev.* 859 (BNA); "EPA General Operating Procedures for the Criminal-Enforcement Program," 13 *Envir. Rep. Cur. Dev.* 1042 (BNA).

6. The Little Rock and New Albany cases cited in footnote 4 are examples of this. If audits had been conducted internally, they would have been conducted by or under the supervision of persons responsible for the violations. A more celebrated case was *United States v. FMC*, in which the corporation and employees in its counsel's office and environmental department were charged with false reporting of conditions at one of its plants. Had the corporation conducted an internal audit, the same persons might have supervised or participated in the audit of that plant. This pitfall may be avoided if auditors report to the board of directors rather than to management.

7. *In re U.S. Steel Corp.*, Exchange Act Release No. 16223, Sept. 27, 1979; *In re Occidental Petroleum Corp.*, Exchange Act Release No. 16950, July 2, 1980.

8. *State v. Dayton Malleable, Inc.*, 11 E.L.R. 21026, 21029 (Ohio Ct. App. 1981).

9. Ibid.

10. Good-faith efforts to comply reduced the priority for enforcement against potential defendants and obviated it entirely in some cases during EPA's drive to prosecute major dischargers which had missed the 1977 CWA deadline for meeting initial treatment levels. See "Setting Priorities for Enforcement Actions Concerning July 1, 1977 Violations," June 3, 1977, memorandum from Stanley W. Legro, assistant administrator for enforcement, to regional administrators. Good faith was also taken into account as a factor mitigating penalties in EPA's initial penalty policy. See "Settlement of Section 309(d) Enforcement Cases for Monetary Amounts," June 3, 1977, memorandum from Stanley W. Legro, assistant administrator for enforcement, to regional administrators. Subsequently this was recast negatively; i.e., bad faith became a factor in increasing penalties. See "Civil Penalty Policy," April 11, 1978, from Marion B. Durning, assistant administrator for enforcement. The significance of this difference may have been masked in practice, since evidence of good faith often decreased the likelihood of success at trial, and that, in turn, mitigated the penalty sought in settlement.

11. *United States v. Hooker Chemicals & Plastics Corp.*, 16 E.R.C. 1268, 1272 (W.D.N.Y. 1981).

12. *New York Times*, Dec. 31, 1982.

13. 60 F.2d 737 (2d Cir. 1932). In this tort casebook classic, Judge Learned Hand of the United States Court of Appeals held a tugboat to be unseaworthy because it lacked a radio receiver, although radio receivers were not yet generally used in the industry. They were, however, known, reliable, and inexpensive, and their use could have prevented the loss of barges by early warning of an upcoming storm. The relevance of audits to this doctrine is obvious.

The Growth and Evolution of Environmental Auditing

John T. Funkhouser
J. Ladd Greeno
Center for Environmental Assurance
Arthur D. Little, Inc.

Although it is evolving rapidly, environmental auditing is still a young enough discipline that the phrase itself connotes a wide range of practices, some modeled closely after a financial audit, some with a strong emphasis on risk, and others less rigidly defined—perhaps more like an assessment or professional opinion than a conventional audit.

Certainly the diversity reflects not only the absence—as yet—of industrywide or professional standards but also the fact that each corporation's reason for auditing will be quite different, depending on the company's business, leadership, and management philosophy and, accordingly, the goals and objectives selected for its overall environmental management program.

Despite these differences, almost all companies have had compliance in mind as they developed audit programs. The rapid growth in environmental, health, and safety regulations, particularly during the late sixties and seventies, prompted companies to devise systems to check whether the company was indeed complying not only with regulations but with the company's own environmental policies.

Many companies that initiated environmental auditing to deal directly with compliance are finding that as it becomes more sophisticated the program and the reasons for it become more complex. For example, the relationship between auditing and the management and control system

—the system of controls and mechanisms that are in place to ensure compliance—is obviously important. A company's reason for auditing could reasonably shift from verifying compliance to verifying that the system which ensures compliance is operating correctly. Similarly, some companies use their environmental management systems to focus on reducing potential risks, a decision which, in effect, forces them to look beyond their auditing programs.

THREE PHASES OF ENVIRONMENTAL MANAGEMENT

In the broadest terms, there is a progression in corporate objectives for developing an environmental management system. One facet of this progression is a broadening of the scope of the problems the company chooses to address.

Phase 1

In the earliest stages, a company's environmental management efforts are characterized by the desire to stay out of trouble. The program is intended to solve the immediate and most pressing problems and to avoid the burdensome costs of environmental incidents. The responsibility for environmental management, for the most part, lies at the plant level, with engineers and technical personnel who have been instructed to address only the "necessary" laws and regulations—those which leave no room for interpretation—and the most significant hazards.

Because there are no (or very few) corporate standards and procedures for recording and monitoring environmental data or for conducting operations in an environmentally acceptable manner, this early, or phase 1, audit program is actually more of an assessment or a judgment regarding the plant's potential environmental problems.

At a certain point it becomes apparent that staying out of trouble is not enough, and management begins to see that the lack of procedures for dealing with environmental matters reduces the efficiency of operations in the long run.

Phase 2

The firm then moves into the second phase, that of managing for compliance. This shift may stem from management's desire to do what is prescribed by the law—albeit no more—or a desire for operational confidence that the company will do its best to avoid significant environmental incidents. It begins to develop a system of policies and procedures to ensure compliance—the underpinnings of a management and control system. With standards to audit against, those directing the audit program can begin to test or verify the compliance status. The program becomes concerned with more than the necessary laws and the most significant hazards. With the desire to stay in compliance, management has broadened its objectives to address all laws and regulations. It has also moved to respond to the need for a management system for compliance.

Phase 3

Phase 2 may typify the majority of firms with audit programs, but increasing numbers of firms—those in phase 3—cite another reason for developing environmental auditing and management programs: they wish to identify and manage hazards that are not yet regulated.

A phase 3 company believes that its auditing program should be part of the corporation's broader risk-management program. Management continues to audit for compliance but also to help identify unknown risks; it wishes to avoid surprises. With these objectives, the shape of the system changes. The program becomes formalized at corporate, division, and plant levels; moreover, functional activities—air pollution, hazardous waste, health and safety, for example—are integrated at all three levels. In addition, a highly specific management and control system is in place or being developed.

In addition to auditing for all the reasons of phase 2, a phase 3 company seeks to identify unanticipated hazards that could have material impact on the corporation. Finally, the audit program is designed to verify not just compliance but also the management and control system.

The reasons for auditing, then, shift somewhat as the overall environmental management program advances. The problems addressed by auditing widen; management attention, which may be minimal in the early stages, becomes more focused on both the systems that protect the company and the need to reduce future risks.

Not all companies develop audit programs in such a well-defined progression. Some never adopt the phase 1 attitude of simply staying out of trouble and move directly to phase 2, staying in compliance. Others believe that a compliance approach is adequate to protect the corporation and are not interested in staying ahead of the pack, looking for risks that are not yet identified. Within each phase, companies envision a wide range of goals and objectives for their audit programs.

FROM MANAGEMENT ASSURANCE TO RISK MANAGEMENT

In more detail, then, what are some specific reasons for developing and conducting an audit program?

Assuring Management

Many companies want to provide assurance to top management and the board of directors. Quite simply, any significant auditing program exists because the board of directors and/or top management believe corporate environmental protection is important and necessary. The exception may be the phase 1 audit program, which is less developed and lacks the management involvement that is key to the development of the more advanced programs. However, in phase 1 and 2 programs it is essential to understand management's reasons—at the heart of which is a desire for assurance—for initiating an environmental auditing program.

For instance, the board of directors is charged with protecting the interests of the public and the company's stockholders. It follows that board members want assurances that they are directing an organization which is a good corporate citizen, and which is also controlling costs to protect stockholders' interests. Auditing, then, can serve to assure the board that no unforeseen material risks have been identified.

In practice, that need has proved to be an important factor in establishing audit programs. A study of auditing practices conducted by the Center for Environmental Assurance indicated that three of seventeen companies interviewed named the board of directors as one of the primary driving forces behind their program's existence.[1] In some cases, an environmental incident had brought fines and penalties as well as a dramatic loss of public support for the corporation. The board, in effect, was asking for assurance that environmental risks would be reduced and that such incidents would not occur in the future.

Top management must manage the corporation within the prescribed policy of the board. Moreover, the chief executive officer (CEO) is charged with managing the organization efficiently, profitably, and responsibly. In this context, therefore, any environmental management system is in place to support the needs of the CEO.

Perhaps one of the most frustrating outcomes, from the CEO's point of view, is knowing that corporate management has developed sound environmental policies and then learning that these have not been followed throughout the organization. The result can be an incident that, according to corporate policies and procedures, never should have happened. An auditing program that is integrated throughout all levels of the organization can help assure top management that its mandate is being followed—that is, that operations are completely consistent with policy.

Verifying Compliance

Companies conduct environmental audits for some of the same reasons they perform financial audits. The obvious difference is that the financial audit is governed by definite standards and procedures; the environmental audit is still largely a self-initiated, individual company effort. Nevertheless, a rather involved definition can be applied to both functions: Auditing, in its most common sense, is a methodical examination, involving analyses, tests, and confirmations, of local procedures and practices leading to a verification of their compliance with legal requirements, corporate policies, and accepted practices. More simply stated, management is looking for a methodical means of verifying compliance. And an audit, whether financial or environmental, provides such a means by checking that:

- All important matters are disclosed.
- Management's accounting—or environmental—procedures are in accord with generally accepted practices.
- Practices have been followed consistently.

In addition, the auditor is interested in company policies and procedures as well as building in checks to verify that personnel are doing the job as expected.

A few firms, in fact, are convinced that the financial audit is the correct model. These companies turn to their internal auditing departments to initiate, direct, and conduct the audit program. The focus of one such program, as described in the auditing survey of the Center for Environmental Assurance, is to ascertain the accuracy of data reported to regulatory and other government agencies; all audit team members have auditing rather than only technical backgrounds.

Companies also audit because management views the audit as a way to obtain assurance that the firm is in compliance with applicable rules and regulations. As mentioned previously, this objective is implicit in nearly all auditing programs, with the exception of phase 1 companies. An audit program offers the systematic checking of procedures needed by companies which, in a relatively short time, have had to comply with a complex web of regulatory requirements from a host of agencies at the federal, state, and local levels.

In all likelihood, a multidivisional manufacturing company would have to satisfy regulations regarding product safety, air and water pollution, waste disposal, and worker health and safety, to name just a few areas. In fact, the director of one corporate auditing program interviewed for the audit survey estimates that each year his company submits nearly 4000 government reports.

Financial concerns are sometimes named as a related reason for environmental auditing. Although many companies regard compliance efforts as an unprofitable expenditure, they view auditing as an efficient means of assuring compliance. Some environmental managers also point out that since auditing helps reduce overall risk—and resulting potential penalties—it actually helps the corporation save money. The financial implications are also mentioned when a firm considers acquisitions. One manager who participated in the Center for Environmental Assurance survey noted that the auditing program helped determine the compliance costs that would be assumed by acquiring a specific company.

More often, however, the need to comply with regulations is the key point. Yet when top management or the environmental manager speaks of auditing for compliance, it is important to make one distinction. A compliance-oriented program can detect risks that are both known and regulated, but it does not necessarily detect risks beyond this. It is the risk-management program, with auditing as a component, that helps detect the unregulated and unanticipated risks.

Verifying Management and Control Systems

Auditing also helps verify that the systems designed to detect and manage problems are operating as planned. The management and control system has already been referred to as the system of controls and mechanisms in place to ensure compliance. Specifically, the system includes three elements: a written statement of plant-level controls specifying minimum standards and regulations, methods for collecting data which will then be measured against these standards, and a reporting system which indicates areas of smooth operation and areas of problems. More simply stated, the management and control system provides a structure against which to audit. Moreover, the management and control system is dynamic. While the audit is like a snapshot of compliance status at a given time, the management and control system is continually generating data and providing reports on the plant's and company's environmental performance. The more the audit can help strengthen this system, the better the environmental manager is able to meet management's need for reassurance.

Similarly, when a company chooses to audit the management and control system (phase 3) rather than a checklist of regulatory and corporate standards (phase 2), the environmental manager is better able to offer management assurance of enhanced environmental protection.

Training Employees

Some companies audit, at least in part, to train employees to follow environmentally acceptable procedures. In addition, a training component in the auditing program can help employees understand the environmental consequences of their actions. This could apply to the assembly-line worker who takes shortcuts in inspections or fails to wear protective clothing, as well as to the plant manager who fails to report exceptions to the proper regulatory agency.

Several companies, in fact, point to training as one of the most important objectives in their environmental audit programs. One such company has, in addition, implemented the audit program in a way that provides intensive training to middle managers who do not necessarily have technical or engineering training. Audit teams are drawn from a rotating pool of managers, who are trained to conduct audits in divisions other than their own. The exposure to other environmental management approaches gives them a better picture of how directly environmental considerations affect corporate operations, and the rotation exposes a greater number of managers to this experience.

When training is an auditing objective, management has an opportunity to improve environmental management practices throughout the corporation, reduce human error in routine procedures, and communicate to employees that management is concerned with sound environmental practices.

Detecting Risks

Finally, companies audit to provide information which can be used in the risk-management process as a means of detecting future risks. Stated another way, auditing is one component of the risk-management process by which a company identifies, assesses, and finally acts to control risks.

Here again, the distinction between auditing and risk management is important. The major focus of the former is current, known risks, while the latter seeks, in addition, to identify future, unknown risks.

One way of discussing the distinction is to categorize hazards (risks) by type. Category A in Figure 1 represents hazards for which there are

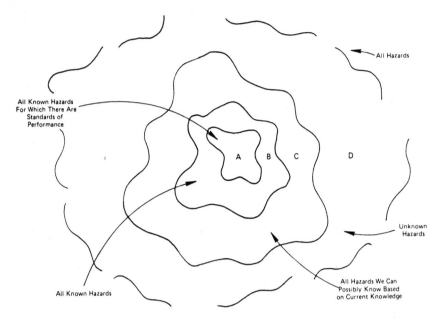

FIG. 1   Conceptual range of environmental hazards

standards—regulatory or company. The audit program can directly address these known, regulated hazards. Category B represents hazards that are known but as yet unregulated, and category C indicates hazards that could be known today if the right resources and expertise were applied. The suspected carcinogen falls into the B category; the toxic properties of a new chemical discovered by a competitor or an independent scientist are initially in category C. In these two cases, auditing can be used to verify the process by which the company manages or seeks to identify unregulated or soon-to-be-discovered risks. Although many companies use auditing as a vehicle to identify risks, this usually is not the major reason for establishing an audit program. Rather, risk identification and control is handled elsewhere in the environmental, health, and safety department.

Nevertheless, auditing can play an important if somewhat indirect role in controlling potential risks. The knowledge that the management and control system is working properly provides assurance that risks will be identified and acted on. The knowledge that the risk-management process is working properly is equally critical for anticipating risks and avoiding surprises. Companies wishing to stay on top of the environmental hazards associated with their operations are implementing such systems.

One such company indicated in the audit survey that it has a two-part environmental assurance system. One component is the auditing program, which is designed to verify compliance with corporate policies and applicable rules and regulations. The second component is a hazard- or risk-management program designed to control the risks generated by corporate activities. While these two components are synergistic, they operate independently.

Whatever the purpose of the environmental auditing program, it is important to keep in mind that auditing is only one component of an overall management system. Such a system includes planning, implementing, controlling, information flow and reporting, financial issues, legal concerns, training, and many other functions. Auditing is one means of checking that these functions are designed and implemented in a manner that is consistent with corporate policies and intent.

FUTURE DIRECTIONS OF ENVIRONMENTAL AUDITING

As the profession of environmental auditing grows and matures, a number of things are likely to happen. Boards of directors will demand audit reports from both the internal audit department and external environmental auditors. In order to protect their integrity and provide rules of conduct, environmental auditors will develop professional standards, and an auditing standards board will be created. Many companies will add statements of environmental performance to their annual reports and thereby assure stockholders that the corporation is managed according to good environmental practice.

1. Other respondents indicated that the chief executive officer, an environmental task force or committee, or the corporate environmental affairs group was the key driving force.

Detailing Your Environmental Risks

Introduction

Stuart E. Eizenstat
David C. Garrett III
Powell, Goldstein, Frazer & Murphy

The primary purpose of this chapter and of the succeeding chapters in this part is to evaluate the risks created by law which an environmental audit must be able to identify and to discuss the advantages of such an audit as an inexpensive means of protecting against more costly defensive measures which might be required should the government find noncompliance with environmental laws. To this end, an understanding of the information discussed below is important in designing and then assessing the effectiveness of an environmental audit. The approach suggested should be taken whether the environmental audit is sought in the context of a regulatory compliance check, the acquisition of an ongoing business, or an energy cost-efficiency check. If the audit is not thorough, minor aggravations which could be easily resolved now may become expensive problems in the future.

Under a plan being discussed by the Reagan administration, environmental audits may be incorporated into consent decrees which establish a time frame for achieving compliance with environmental laws. Such environmental audits would replace the usual penalties for noncompliance with the consent decree schedule, and the required components of a mandated audit would be prescribed in detail.

Environmental regulation is a matter of federal, state, and local concern. Consequently there are environmental statutes, rules, regulations, and ordinances, and agencies responsible for administering these laws, at all levels of government. Rather than reviewing the entire spectrum of environmental law, it is more effective to analyze the risks present at the federal level, since federal environmental laws affect all businesses, their managers, and their employees.

Nevertheless, it is important to be aware that there is extensive state and local environmental legislation which may make an environmental audit even more desirable. For example, in many cases where responsibility for administering a federal pollution-control program within a state has been delegated by the Environmental Protection Agency (EPA) to the responsible state environmental agency, the state's requirements on pollution sources and its enforcement procedures may be stricter than the corresponding federal requirements. This is particularly true with regard to the National Pollutant Discharge Elimination System (NPDES) permit program developed by the EPA and delegated to most of the states under section 402 of the federal Clean Water Act (CWA).[1]

NATIONAL ENVIRONMENTAL POLICY ACT

In 1969, Congress passed the National Environmental Policy Act (NEPA)[2] for the purpose of establishing a national policy with regard to maintaining and restoring environmental quality. Included in section 102 of NEPA[3] is the requirement that an environmental impact statement (EIS) be prepared in connection with "major federal actions significantly affecting the quality of the human environment." A major federal action in many instances may include the issuing of environmental permits. However, where a state has taken over a federal environmental permit program, an EIS under NEPA should not be required in connection with the state-issued permit.[4] Nevertheless, many states have also adopted laws requiring an equivalent study involving a comprehensive written report on the potential adverse effects related to the state-issued environmental permits.

It is not the intent to review here NEPA or similar state statutes. But these laws are important, particularly in the context of new construction, and an environmental audit with regard to a new permit may involve a review of many issues and factors normally associated with an EIS.

In order to maximize the effectiveness of an environmental audit, documentation maintained by federal, state, and local environmental agencies regarding a pollution source should be thoroughly reviewed by the company, as well as the company's own files. Most of this agency documentation is part of the public record and is, for the most part, immediately accessible, although certain information may be obtained only through a Freedom of Information Act request under federal law or similar state law.

THEORY OF NUISANCE

While the risks associated with lawsuits against businesses and individuals on the basis of a common-law theory of nuisance are not reviewed here, this theory must be kept in mind. These lawsuits, which typically allege that a particular location or source of pollution constitutes a private or public nuisance, usually request that the court enjoin the offending activity and award monetary compensation to the parties harmed. The United States Supreme Court, in *City of Milwaukee v. Illinois*,[5] held that the CWA preempts the federal common law of nuisance with regard to water pollution. It appears, however, that citizens may still have a right to seek relief under a federal common-law theory of nuisance for violations of other federal environmental statutes. Citizens clearly may seek relief under state common law to abate nuisances.

Lawsuits alleging nuisance are normally instituted by individual citizens or groups of citizens rather than by government agencies and are often pursued despite the fact that a business is in technical compliance with applicable environmental laws. It is axiomatic, however, that the potential for lawsuits alleging nuisance can be reduced by a thorough and effective environmental audit designed to detect problems that could form the basis for such actions.

CRIMINAL PROSECUTION IN GENERAL

In addition to the civil and criminal enforcement procedures and options contained in the federal environmental legislation discussed in the following sections regarding air, hazardous waste, toxic substances, and water, businesses and individuals may also find themselves subject to criminal prosecution under a variety of nonenvironmental federal statutes. These statutes include:

1. Aiding or abetting a crime (18 U.S.C. § 2)
2. Accessory after the fact (18 U.S.C. § 3)
3. Misprision (concealment) of a felony (18 U.S.C. § 4)
4. Conspiracy to defraud or commit an offense against the United States (18 U.S.C. § 371)
5. Submitting false statements to government agencies (18 U.S.C. § 1001)
6. Mail fraud (18 U.S.C. § 1341)

7. Obstruction of government agency proceedings (18 U.S.C. § 1505)
8. Failure to comply with Securities and Exchange Commission (SEC) reporting requirements under NEPA (15 U.S.C. §§ 77a to aa and 78a to jj)

Predictably, many lawsuits brought against businesses and individuals for violating federal environmental legislation include counts based on these general criminal statutes as well as the civil and criminal enforcement provisions found in an environmental statute. State and local enforcement actions may also include counts alleging violations of state or local general criminal statutes and violations of environmental statutes.

Factors which are reviewed by the EPA and the Department of Justice in determining whether a given case should be handled as civil or criminal under these general criminal statutes and federal environmental laws may include:

1. The severity and extent of any actual or potential health or environmental impacts resulting from the conduct in question, as determined, for example, by the type and quantity of pollutant released, the sensitivity of the area or of persons in the area where the pollutant is released, and whether the release is continuing
2. The nature, timeliness, and degree of disclosure made to the regulatory authorities
3. The nature, timeliness, and degree of effort made to control the problem or to mitigate its effect
4. Any history of recurrent or consistent violations by the source of pollution or any profile of bad faith or recidivism
5. Evidence of willful, negligent, knowing, or intentional noncompliance as a result of an informed policy decision or a corporate policy resisting compliance
6. The likelihood of meeting the burden of proof required for criminal convictions ("beyond a reasonable doubt" as opposed to the civil action standard of "preponderance of the evidence")
7. The likelihood of prompt judicial resolution of the matter
8. The necessity for extended discovery

Even where a matter has progressed to the point where criminal prosecution is being seriously considered, negotiations regarding settlement remain potentially fruitful. The EPA and the Department of Justice generally prefer to resolve violations of environmental statutes administratively rather than through judicial proceedings.

CONCLUSION

Again, an environmental audit can mitigate the risk of criminal sanctions against the employees and officers of a business. The following sections will review the major environmental statutes, enforcement actions pursuant to these laws, and the components of an environmental audit necessary to assist compliance with and minimize risks under these laws.

1. 33 U.S.C. § 1342 (1976). The CWA is codified at 33 U.S.C. §§ 1251–1376 (1976).

2. 42 U.S.C. §§ 4321–4361 (1976); Pub. L. 91–190, Jan. 1, 1970.

3. 42 U.S.C. § 4332 (1976).

4. For example, an EIS will not be required in connection with a state-issued NPDES permit. *Chesapeake Bay Foundation, Inc. v. United States*, 445 F. Supp. 1349, *dismissal vacated* in part 453 F. Supp. 122 (E.D. Va. 1978).

5. 451 U.S. 304, 101 S. Ct. 1784, 68 L. Ed. 2d 114 (1981).

Clean Air Act

Stuart E. Eizenstat
David C. Garrett III
Powell, Goldstein, Frazer & Murphy

Congress has enacted extensive legislation during the past 12 years for achieving improved air quality throughout the United States. The legislation is currently codified as the federal Clean Air Act (CAA).[1] Although the CAA has comprehensive provisions regarding ozone protection[2] and emission standards for moving sources[3] such as motor vehicles and aircraft, the primary emphasis is on the control of emissions from stationary sources such as industrial plants and power stations. This discussion will focus on stationary sources and the law and regulations affecting them.

Many portions of the CAA are currently the subject of review by Congress, and it is expected that significant changes may be made which could affect both stationary and mobile sources of air pollution. It would be fruitless to speculate on these potential changes, and this discussion of the CAA is directed to the current statute. In addition, no attempt has been made to analyze and resolve the growing controversy regarding acid rain, which also is likely to be addressed by the Ninety-eighth Congress.

HOW THE CAA WORKS

The heart of the CAA is section 109,[4] the national ambient air quality standards (NAAQS). These numerical standards are congressionally mandated maximum levels of certain criteria pollutants which, if exceeded, lead to unacceptable air quality. Primary NAAQS are those standards designed to protect the public health, while secondary

NAAQS are those deemed necessary to protect the public welfare. Welfare effects which secondary NAAQS are designed to limit include impairment of visibility and damage to buildings and plant or animal life. The Environmental Protection Agency (EPA) has adopted elaborate regulations regarding NAAQS for sulfur oxides, particulate matter, ozone, hydrocarbons, nitrogen dioxide, and lead.[5]

Congress also determined that national emission standards should be developed for new stationary sources as a long-term weapon against future air pollution [new source performance standards (NSPS)][6] and for certain hazardous air pollutants which may cause or contribute to increased mortality or an increase in serious irreversible or incapacitating reversible illness [national emission standards for hazardous air pollutants (NESHAP)].[7] The EPA has developed regulations regarding NSPS,[8] and an NESHAP has been developed for asbestos, mercury, beryllium, and vinyl chloride.[9]

It is the responsibility of each state to develop a state implementation plan (SIP), pursuant to section 110 of the CAA,[10] for the implementation, maintenance, and enforcement of NAAQS and, where the CAA program is delegated to the state, for NSPS and NESHAP. However, the EPA must review and approve each such SIP and revisions to an SIP. The EPA further monitors each SIP while retaining independent authority to monitor sources and enforce provisions of an SIP and of the CAA. For example, under section 114(a) of the CAA,[11] state and federal officials both have independent authority to enter and inspect an emission source and review all records regarding its operation and monitoring to determine if that source is violating any portion of an SIP or any national emission standards under the CAA. An enforcement action may be brought by the EPA under section 113(b) of the CAA[12] for failure to comply with the inspection, monitoring, and entry requirements of section 114 of the CAA.

Areas within a state which have air quality better than NAAQS are designated "attainment areas." New major emitting facilities[13] or modifications of existing major emitting facilities in these areas are subject to the EPA's prevention of significant deterioration (PSD) permit program under sections 160 to 169 of the CAA.[14] The PSD program requires regulated sources, i.e., those major emitting facilities whose potential to emit pollutants following the application of emission controls[15] exceeds 100 tons per year for NAAQS pollutants or 250 tons per year for other pollutants, to follow a detailed preconstruction review and permit procedure[16] described in section 165 of the CAA.[17]

Before a PSD permit application may be filed, a detailed source impact assessment must be developed which includes 1 year's prior air quality monitoring data regarding pollutants for which NAAQS have been developed.[18] These background data are intended to assist the EPA and the source's owner or operator in determining whether proposed emissions will exceed allowable increments in pollutant levels for sulfur oxides and particulates in any PSD area. In addition, new or modified sources subject to the PSD program must install the best available control technology (BACT) to reduce those pollutants whose potential emission rate exceeds 100 tons per year.[19] Failure to comply with the PSD permitting procedure described above may subject the source and its responsible owners, managers, or corporate officers to enforcement actions by the EPA and the Department of Justice under section 113 of the CAA[20] or by a state which has been delegated PSD permit authority by the EPA. Delegation of responsibility for administering the PSD permit program to the states is a top priority of the EPA.

Areas of a state having air quality below NAAQS for a given air contaminant are referred to as "nonattainment areas" for such contaminants and are subject to regulation under sections 171 to 178 of the CAA.[21] States are required by section 172(b)(6) of the CAA[22] to include a permit program for controlling major stationary sources in nonattainment areas as a part of their SIPs. The principal conditions for issuance of a permit in a nonattainment area include:

1. A net reduction in total emissions of the relevant pollutant either by regulation on a source-specific basis or by areawide regulation which creates a margin for growth[23]

2. The application of technology obtaining the lowest available emission rate (LAER)[24]

3. The compliance of all sources owned or operated by the permit applicant in the state with the applicable SIP or an approved compliance order[25]

4. A determination that the SIP is being carried out in the nonattainment area[26]

The central rationale of the nonattainment-area permit program is to offset the additional volume of a pollutant generated by the *new or modified* major stationary source through a legally enforceable reduction in the quantity of that same pollutant emitted by *existing* sources elsewhere in the nonattainment area by an amount that *exceeds* the new volume of the pollutant. In other words, the quantity of the offset must exceed the emissions from the new source and must represent emission reductions not otherwise required.[27] To the extent that a source reduces emissions of a pollutant beyond that required, these additional offsets may be "banked" for future expansion or sale to other companies. An environmental audit would allow a company to quantitatively identify emission reductions available for offsets, so that precise records of all surplus emission reductions may be kept. The administering agency should be informed of all the company's cleanup measures in order to establish the emission reduction as an offset.

More stringent controls apply to nonattainment areas than to attainment areas; however, because nonattainment and PSD area designations are pollutant-specific, it is possible for a given area to fall into both the attainment (PSD) and nonattainment categories for different pollutants. Moreover, an area may be in the nonattainment category for more than one pollutant, so that offsets may have to be obtained from a variety of sources in the area. Obtaining such emission reductions may be difficult and expensive, particularly where sources which are banking offsets intend to use such offsets for their own future expansion.

As a practical matter, achieving the goals and requirements of the CAA is handled through a permit procedure under each state's SIP.[28] A permit issued by a state environmental agency specifies the particular emission limitations that must be achieved by the source in order to comply with the state's SIP and the CAA. In addition, the permit typically describes the monitoring frequency and other restrictions and requirements to be followed by the source.

EPA has encouraged states to implement innovative methods of controlling air pollution through their SIP permit programs, including the use of an alternative emission reduction approach commonly called the "bubble concept." Under this bubble concept, various individual air pollution sources at a facility are evaluated together, in such a way that an increase in emissions from one source can be balanced by a reduction in similar emissions from another source without affecting the overall compliance of the facility. Thus the bubble concept allows a plant with multiple internal sources of air pollution to reduce emissions in those places where pollution-control costs are low and to relax emissions from areas of the plant where pollution-control costs are high. The bubble concept, however, has been held inapplicable by the United States Court of Appeals for the District of Columbia Circuit with respect to nonattainment areas.[29] An appeal is pending before the United States Supreme Court.

It is important, therefore, for responsible corporate officers to be aware of the pollutants emitted by their facilities and of the existence and contents of permits issued by EPA or state environmental agencies authorizing, where applicable, construction of a source of air pollution and operation of that source. This information, in addition to the foregoing review of the CAA, provides the necessary background for preparing and then evaluating an environmental audit regarding air pollution. Below is an overview of enforcement options under the CAA which an effective environmental audit should prevent. Many, if not most, of these enforcement actions represent the manifestation of problems which environmental audits are designed to identify and which business can then solve.

FEDERAL ENFORCEMENT UNDER THE CAA

Section 113 of the CAA[30] provides several methods for enforcing provisions of this statute, the regulations promulgated thereunder, and provisions of individual SIPs. These methods include administrative compliance orders, delayed compliance orders, delayed compliance (noncompliance) penalties, and actions in United States district court seeking civil penalties, injunctions, and in some cases criminal fines and imprisonment. These alternatives are not mutually exclusive or replacements for administrative remedies, and administrative options need not be exhausted by the EPA before a judicial remedy is sought.

An additional tool in the EPA's arsenal is the CAA's provision under section 306[31] for blacklisting a source or corporation convicted of violating section 113(c)(1) of the CAA,[32] thereby preventing the awarding of federal government contracts to that entity.

Compliance Orders

Administrative compliance orders and delayed compliance orders are similar in that they allow an emissions source which has failed to achieve compliance by the attainment deadlines specified in the CAA for meeting NAAQS,[33] NSPS,[34] NESHAP,[35] or other requirements to achieve compliance under a revised schedule. Although the EPA is no longer issuing administrative compliance orders under section 113(a),[36] it is still enforcing previously issued administrative compliance orders. Delayed compliance orders issued under section 113(d)[37] required compliance by July 1, 1979 but no later than 3 years after the date for achieving compliance specified in a new or revised SIP. Plants using innovative technology to reduce pollution may obtain an extension for compliance under a delayed compliance order of 5 years beyond that specified in an SIP.[38]

An April 13, 1981, consent decree entered into by ASARCO, Inc. with the EPA, involving compliance by ASARCO's copper smelter in Hayden, Arizona, with the NAAQS for sulfur dioxide and particulates, illustrates this principle.[39] Because Arizona's SIP did not yet have emission limits for these pollutants, the EPA allowed ASARCO 3 years from the anticipated date of adoption of such limits to achieve compliance with emission standards for sulfur dioxide and particulates.

A delayed compliance order offers significant additional benefits to a company in that it generally protects the company during its term from civil and criminal penalties for technical noncompliance and from citizens' suits. Thus, if a company has made a good-faith, but unsuccessful, attempt to comply with applicable deadlines and is issued a delayed compliance order, so long as that company's source complies with the terms of the order, no action based upon technical noncompliance and no citizen's suit or federal enforcement action may be pursued.[40] However, a delayed compliance order issued by the EPA (rather than a state) presumably does not prevent a more stringent state enforcement action under section 116 of the CAA.[41]

Noncompliance Penalties

Noncompliance penalties are intended to be a method by which the EPA may recover from a violator any economic benefits obtained during the period of noncompliance, thereby removing any incentive for noncompliance.[42] A recipient of a noncompliance penalty notice issued by the EPA, or by a state in which delegation of authority regarding these penalties has occurred, must calculate the penalty amount within 45 days of the notice or after denial of an exemption petition.[43] These self-assessed penalties are calculated under a formula found in section 120(d)(2) of the CAA[44] and regulations promulgated by the EPA for the assessment and collection of noncompliance penalties.[45] The penalty amount is calculated in two steps. First, the sum of three factors is obtained: (1) the quarterly equivalent of the capital costs of compliance and debt service over a normal amortization period (not to exceed 10 years) avoided by delay, (2) the operating and maintenance costs avoided by delay, and (3) any other economic value (such as competitive advantage) gained by delaying compliance beyond July 1, 1979. Second, from this amount are deducted any expenditures incurred during the noncompliance period but prior to receipt of the notice of noncompliance that will help achieve eventual compliance.

Major stationary sources which are not in compliance with SIP limits and stationary sources which are not in compliance with any NSPS or NESHAP are subject to noncompliance penalties.[46] A facility may be exempted from liability for technical noncompliance by the EPA (or a state) if the noncompliance is due solely to a mandatory switch from gas or oil to coal, to the use of innovative technology, to reasons entirely beyond the control of the owner or operator and sanctioned by a delayed compliance order, or to emergency energy or employment conditions.[47] Failure to achieve compliance by the date specified in a delayed compliance order will also result in assessment of noncompliance penalties.[48] The EPA can, however, determine that the noncompliance is *de minimis* in nature and duration and elect not to seek a penalty.[49]

Civil Penalties and Injunctions

Actions in United States district court seeking civil penalties and injunctions may be used where administrative remedies have not worked; however, it is not necessary for the EPA to have used its administrative enforcement options[50] prior to bringing a civil action. A defense based on EPA's failure to exhaust administrative remedies is not viable. According to section 113(b) of the CAA,[51] the EPA shall, in the case of any person who is the owner or operator of a major stationary source, and may, in the case of any other person, commence a civil action in United States district court in order to obtain a permanent or temporary injunction or to assess and recover a civil penalty of not more than $25,000 per day of violation, or both, whenever such person:

1. Violates an administrative compliance order or delayed compliance order issued under section 113(d)
2. Violates any requirement of an applicable SIP
3. Violates an NSPS or NESHAP or other specific provisions relating to ozone, vapor recovery, and smelter orders
4. Fails to comply with federal inspection requirements
5. Attempts to construct or modify a major stationary source in any nonattainment area for which a revised SIP has not been approved by the EPA
6. Fails to pay a noncompliance penalty due under section 120

Any action seeking civil penalties or an injunction may be brought in the district court of the United States for the district in which the violation occurred or in which the defendant resides or has its principal place of business. In determining the amount of any civil penalty to be assessed, the court shall take into consideration, in addition to other factors, the size of the business, the economic impact of the penalty on the business, and the seriousness of the violation.[52] The court may also award the cost of litigation (including reasonable attorney and expert witness fees) where appropriate.

Section 303 of the CAA[53] also provides that the EPA may bring suit to enjoin immediately any person causing or contributing to alleged air pollution presenting an imminent and substantial endangerment to the health of persons, where appropriate state or local authorities have not acted to abate such pollution. Prior to taking such action, the EPA administrator has the option of issuing an emergency short-term order to achieve the same end, which order may be extended if an injunction is sought. Any person who willfully violates such an order may be fined not more than $5000 for each day during which such violation occurs.[54]

Criminal Penalties

Criminal fines and imprisonment are authorized by section 113(c)(1) of the CAA,[55] in addition to the above civil actions, for any person, including specifically any responsible corporate officer,[56] who *knowingly*:

1. Violates any requirement of an applicable SIP
2. Violates an administrative compliance order issued under section 113(a) or delayed compliance order issued under section 113(d) or a primary nonferrous smelter order issued under section 119[57]
3. Violates any NSPS or NESHAP or other specific provisions relating to ozone and smelter orders
4. Fails to pay a noncompliance penalty due under section 120

Persons who are convicted shall be punished by a fine of not more than $25,000 per day of violation or imprisonment for not more than 1 year or both. If the conviction is for a violation committed after the first conviction of such person, punishment shall be by a fine of not more than $50,000 per day of violation or imprisonment for not more than 2 years or both.[58]

In addition, a person who *knowingly* makes a false statement, representation, or certification in any application, record, report, plan, or other document filed or required to be maintained under the CAA or who falsifies, tampers with, or *knowingly* renders inaccurate any monitoring device or method required to be maintained under the CAA, shall, upon conviction, be punished by a fine of not more than $10,000 or imprisonment for not more than 6 months or both.[59]

In contrast, there is no requirement for a *knowing* violation in a *civil* action initiated by the EPA or the Department of Justice. The requirement that a violation be a knowing one—that is, that defendants had a degree of knowledge that makes them legally responsible for the violation—suggests that, in order to prevail in any criminal prosecution under the CAA, the government must prove a bad or evil motive. This standard is more difficult to achieve than the degree-of-knowledge requirements under section 309(c)(1) of the CWA:[60] "willful or negligent violation."

A thorough environmental audit will provide the data necessary for responsible persons to make an accurate statement or representation or to take appropriate action in the event of a CAA violation and to reduce the possibility of an uninformed decision, followed by improper action, being interpreted as a knowing violation of the CAA.

In addition to the potential exposure of the corporation and responsible corporate officers to criminal fines and imprisonment under the CAA, the violation of pollution control laws in general, including the CAA, can often be a crime under the more general provisions of the United States Criminal Code, described previously.[61]

CITIZENS' SUITS

While the citizen suit provision of the CAA, section 304,[62] does not specifically preserve federal common-law rights of action, at least one court has held that since there was no intent to abolish such rights of action, the CAA has not preempted a federal common-law right of action based on nuisance against air polluters.[63] As a result, citizens may be able to seek relief against air pollution sources under both section 304 and federal common law, despite the United States Supreme Court decision in *City of Milwaukee v. Illinois,* discussed elsewhere.[64] Moreover, section 304(f)[65] contains a definition of emission standard or limitation that is broader than the definition of emission standard or limitation for the rest of the CAA.[66] It appears that Congress intended to provide considerable flexibility in determining the appropriate scope of a citizen suit under the CAA.

According to section 304(a),[67] a citizen or a group of citizens may commence a civil action on their own behalf against:

1. Any corporation or other person (including, under limited circumstances, the United States and other governmental instrumentalities and agencies) who is alleged to be in violation of an emissions standard or limitation mandated under the CAA, or any order issued by EPA or a state with respect to such standard or limitation

2. The EPA administrator (or state agencies) for failure to perform nondiscretionary duties under the CAA

3. Any person who proposes to construct or constructs a new or modified emitting facility without a permit

A citizen who is a proper party to bring a suit need not allege an "injury in fact" but must demonstrate a sufficient interest in a specific controversy to meet traditional concepts of standing.[68]

Two recent decisions have clarified the rights of citizens to participate in ongoing enforcement actions. In *United States v. U.S. Steel Corp.*,[69] the court held that a citizen's group had a right under section 304(b)(1)(B) of the CAA[70] to be involved in consent decree proceedings, including commenting on proposed modifications to the consent decree, but that this right did not extend to being a party to actual negotiations.

Citizens may also file suit against a corporation which is the subject of an EPA or state enforcement action if the agency is not prosecuting diligently.[71] For example, in *Gardeski v. Colonial Sand & Stone*,[72] the court held that if a state fails to diligently prosecute an enforcement action against a polluter, a citizen suit for an injunction and money damages may be maintained against the polluter. The New York Department of Environmental Conservation had previously obtained a voluntary consent agreement with the defendant, but the company almost immediately began violating the agreement. The state agency failed to meet any reasonable test of diligent prosecution in enforcing the consent agreement; the agency had several enforcement avenues open to it, yet it continued futilely to seek voluntary compliance.

While it is clear that citizen suits may be brought against corporations, two recent decisions[73] indicate that citizen suits under section 304 of the CAA may not be initiated against individuals such as "responsible corporate officers," because Congress did not expand the definition of person to include such individuals for purposes of section 304, as it had done in section 113(c) of the CAA.[74] Nevertheless, individual corporate officers may be subject to liability under state citizen suit provisions if state law so provides.

LIABILITY OF THE CORPORATION

A corporation which violates provisions of the CAA or an applicable SIP may be subject to civil penalties, injunctions, and criminal fines.

The majority of enforcement actions under the CAA and general criminal statutes relating to air pollution violations are resolved prior to trial through settlement agreements and consent decrees. Because the primary purpose of an enforcement action is to force an air pollution source to comply with applicable rules and regulations, settlements arising from enforcement litigation normally require installation of new or additional air pollution control equipment and the use of cleaner processes or lower-contaminant fuel.

Recently, during such settlement negotiations, EPA allowed firms to use the bubble concept to meet standards, although this is no longer permitted in nonattainment areas. Other enforcement actions that are settled often require the payment of civil penalties or criminal fines.

Most enforcement actions under section 113 of the CAA[75] seek civil penalties and equitable remedies rather than criminal fines and jail sentences. In some cases no civil penalties are assessed, particularly where significant capital expenditures are necessary to achieve compliance. For example, the EPA and Phelps Dodge Corporation entered into a consent agreement on March 26, 1981, to bring two large copper smelters into compliance with the CAA through innovative techniques and capital expenditures totaling approximately $150 million.[76]

While the focus of the EPA's enforcement actions has been major industries such as electric utilities and steel and chemical manufacturers, other minor industrial sources may become the subject of an enforcement action, particularly where there has been a history of consistent failure to meet applicable regulations. For example, on April 7, 1981, the United States District Court for the District of New Jersey entered an order against Hills Brothers Coffee, Inc., requiring it to pay a $4000 civil penalty for alleged repeated violations of CAA opacity standards by emissions from vacuum pumps at the company's facility in Edgewater, New Jersey.[77]

Small penalties often have been assessed for violations of section 203 of the CAA[78] (e.g., tampering with pollution control devices on automobiles) and section 211 of the CAA[79] (regarding regulation of fuel), which is applicable to mobile sources of pollution. A particularly interesting recent case in this regard involved a $3000 civil penalty that was assessed against Hudson Stations, Inc., a corporate gasoline station owner, which had equipped leaded gasoline pumps with a nozzle designed for use on an unleaded pump. This assessment was affirmed as reasonable by the United States Court of Appeals for the Eighth Circuit[80] because of the admitted violations of fuel-use rules under section 211 of the CAA, the interlocking system of corporate entities that owned 294 gasoline stations, and the appropriateness of the penalty when measured against the gross income for the total corporate structure.

At the other end of the spectrum is an agreement entered into by Dow Chemical Company and approved on July 21, 1981, to pay $240,000 in civil penalties to the EPA and a like amount to the state of Michigan. In addition, Dow agreed to reduce sulfur dioxide emissions by 60 percent by September 1, 1981, and particulate emissions by 80 percent by the end of 1982 at its Midland, Michigan, plant. This agreement arose out of an enforcement action brought by the United States District Attorney's office on behalf of the EPA against Dow on January 25, 1980, alleging violations of Michigan's SIP since August 1977.[81] Civil penalties sought in this action were in excess of $20 million.

Another example is the agreement of April 10, 1980, between the Department of Justice and N. L. Industries, Inc., providing for the payment of $1 million in civil penalties for past violations at N. L. Industries' titanium dioxide manufacturing plant in Sayreville, New Jersey, the installation of new air pollution control equipment, and the use of cleaner processes in the production of titanium dioxide.[82]

Perhaps the most significant enforcement litigation under the CAA involved the Tennessee Valley Authority (TVA). A final out-of-court settlement was approved on December 22, 1980, calling for approximately $703 million in capital expenditures at many of TVA's power plants.[83] This new settlement replaced the original settlement negotiated in December 1978, which carried a cleanup settlement tag of $1.02 billion. At this time, TVA has completed much of the construction work required by the settlement but still must meet several deadlines specified in the agreement. A failure to meet such deadlines could result in TVA's meeting a fate similar to that of United States Steel Corporation, which on December 23, 1980, paid a $345,000 penalty for failure to comply with a schedule requiring installation of air pollution control equipment at two of its coke-making facilities near Pittsburgh, Pennsylvania, under a consent decree it signed in May 1979.[84]

Although far less numerous than civil enforcement actions, criminal enforcement actions have been brought against corporations under section 113 of the CAA. On November 1, 1976, an order was entered by the United States District Court for the Eastern District of Kentucky assessing a fine of $125,000 against Allied Chemical Corporation for a knowing violation of a February 12, 1975, consent order regarding reduction of particulate emissions from two coke factories at Allied's Ashland, Kentucky, facility.[85] In addition to this fine for failing to meet the consent order's schedule of compliance, Allied was placed on 5 years' probation, with the provision that if it did not comply with the original consent order, additional fines of up to $800,000 would be assessed. It was subsequently determined, on the basis of monitoring of particulate emissions by the EPA, that Allied was not in substantial compliance for one 2-month period, and an additional fine of $100,000 was assessed by order of April 15, 1977. On November 10, 1981, Allied was discharged from its probationary status.

In *United States v. Occidental Chemical Co.*,[86] Occidental was fined for knowingly submitting false figures in information required by section 114 of the CAA.[87] In response to an EPA request for information, Occidental submitted an air pollutant emission report on March 17, 1977, which stated that fluoride emissions from the Z train at Occidental's diammonium phosphate plant in Lake City, Florida, had an average discharge rate of 0.82 pounds per hour. In actuality, Occidental was emitting fluorides at a rate of between 3 and 116 pounds per hour.

In March 1978, the management of Occidental became aware of this violation and, following further testing, ordered that the plant be shut down and the violation reported to the EPA and state officials. Following a meeting with the EPA, Occidental submitted a letter stipulating that it had operated the plant out of compliance with the knowledge of employees and had reported emissions as being in compliance to both the EPA and the Florida Department of Environmental Regulation. At a hearing on September 1, 1978, Occidental pleaded nolo contendere to one count of knowingly making a false statement, representation, or certification in violation of section 113(c)(2) of the CAA. The plea was accepted and Occidental was fined $10,000. The EPA's attorneys stated for the record that they would not pursue further enforcement action (i.e., civil actions) against Occidental or individual officers because of the voluntary nature of the disclosure.

LIABILITY OF RESPONSIBLE CORPORATE OFFICERS

The CAA specifically includes "responsible corporate officers" in the definition of persons who are subject to criminal fines and imprisonment for certain violations of the CAA or of an SIP. State law may provide that certain corporate officials may also be individually liable for penalties under that law. A "responsible" person was defined in *United States v. Dotterweich*[88] and *United States v. Park*[89] as one who has a responsible share in the furtherance of the transaction or occurrence which the statute forbids. Although this definition was developed in the context of a criminal proceeding under the federal Food, Drug and Cosmetic Act,[90] which does not contain a degree-of-knowledge requirement, the same basic rationale would probably apply to a responsible corporate officer under the CAA.

In other words, an officer who has the responsibility and the powers commensurate with that responsibility to devise whatever measures are necessary to ensure compliance with the statute and regulations is, by definition, a responsible corporate officer. An officer who has the power to prevent or correct a violation and fails to exercise that power could be subject to a criminal fine and imprisonment.

To a great extent, the EPA's enforcement efforts under the CAA have been guided by internal memoranda such as *Criminal Proceedings Guidelines*[91] and other similar documents. An excerpt from those guidelines provides insight into factors that the EPA considers important in determining whether to seek criminal sanctions against individuals:

> In considering whether it is appropriate to seek criminal sanctions
> against an individual, the regional office should identify that person in

the corporate hierarchy who was authorized to make the type of decision or take the type of action that resulted in or could have prevented
the alleged violation(s). . . .[92] [I]t would appear appropriate in criminal
cases to name the responsible corporate officers (including the president) as codefendants with the responsible corporate employee and the
corporation, since the individuals clearly have the authority to bring a
source into compliance with applicable regulations and/or EPA orders.
The basis for a criminal action against a corporate official will be based
on demonstrating that he had actual knowledge of the regulations and
the violations, and that the corporation and/or the corporation's agent
had continued to violate knowingly an applicable regulation and/or EPA
order, with the corporation, as directed by the president (or other
officer(s)), failing to correct or to prevent further violations of the applicable regulations and/or EPA order.[93]

The EPA's current enforcement policy under the Reagan administration probably has not changed in this regard. However, additional factors may be evaluated, and the degree of culpability necessary to trigger
an enforcement action against an individual may also change. Similarly,
responsible corporate officers of corporations within certain industrial
categories may be more susceptible than other individuals.

Civil enforcement actions against individuals are likely to occur
primarily within the context of enforcing a consent decree which officers
and directors have entered into on behalf of a corporation but have
failed to carry out, or where an individual has been intimately involved
in a course of conduct leading to delayed compliance. Civil enforcement
actions against individuals are, however, the exception rather than the
rule.

Criminal enforcement activities against responsible corporate officers
and employees for their corporation's violation of air pollution laws have
not reached the levels of those for CWA violations. This may be due in
part to the United States Supreme Court decision in *Adamo Wrecking Co.
v. United States*,[94] which limited the EPA's ability to maintain a criminal
enforcement action against a corporation and individuals for violating
air pollution regulations. The Supreme Court found that the NESHAP
for asbestos, which the EPA claimed Adamo had violated, was not an
emissions standard after all but was a work practice, and therefore criminal enforcement action was improper. However, this decision was reversed legislatively when Congress modified the CAA November 9,
1978, so that a work practice may now be specified and enforced as an
emission standard.[95]

Prior to the Adamo case, the EPA's air enforcement program had
occasionally resulted in individual indictments, especially in the area of
asbestos emissions control. For example, in 1976 a Florida wrecking firm

was fined $25,000 for violating regulations which required wetting of asbestos building materials during demolition, one of the wrecking company foremen was fined $1000, and both were placed on 5 years' probation.[96] Nevertheless, as the EPA and the Department of Justice gain sophistication in criminal prosecution of individuals under the CAA, additional indictments of responsible corporate officers and employees who have actual knowledge of air pollution violations or are in a position to correct or prevent such violations become more likely.

COMPONENTS OF AN ENVIRONMENTAL AUDIT FOR CAA COMPLIANCE

A thorough environmental audit will reveal past and present enforcement actions under section 113 of the CAA (and under state and local air pollution legislation) which will indicate whether there has been, and continues to be, a pattern of inability, reluctance, or recalcitrance in complying with applicable air pollution laws. Such a pattern, if it exists, may affect the severity of subsequent enforcement actions. Similarly, complaints of citizens found in the company's own files and those of federal, state, and local agencies could reveal the existence of significant past, present, and future problems.

Information from governmental files can normally be obtained by submitting a written request pursuant to the federal Freedom of Information Act[97] or equivalent state law. However, some governmental agencies may resist such requests, particularly requests for information regarding citizens' complaints, and the information may be available only pursuant to subpoena in the context of an administrative or judicial proceeding.

An audit will also reveal current permits, schedules of compliance, monitoring and testing programs, and other regulatory requirements that must be complied with in order to avoid enforcement actions by the EPA, the Department of Justice, or state agencies. In the context of the CAA the regulatory scheme is particularly confusing, because several permit programs exist. Sources must look to the current programs adopted by individual states to achieve compliance with the SIP at the outset. Permit programs developed by the EPA for modifications of existing sources or construction of new sources in PSD and nonattainment areas, which may be delegated to states, also may be applicable.

Finally, an audit should assist in anticipating what new regulatory requirements may be developed on the basis of the presence of air pollutants in emissions of a source that are not currently regulated but that may be regulated in the future. With this information in hand, persons responsible for operating and managing air pollution sources or persons considering the acquisition of a company with air pollution sources will be in a better position to assess the risks under applicable laws involved in operating and maintaining those sources.

1. 42 U.S.C. §§ 7401–7642, as amended (1976); *see* Pub. L. 91-604, Dec. 31, 1970 and Pub. L. 95-95, Aug. 7, 1977.

2. CAA §§ 150–159; 42 U.S.C. §§ 7450–7459 (1976).

3. CAA §§ 202–234; 42 U.S.C. §§ 7521–7574 (1976).

4. 42 U.S.C. § 7409 (1976).

5. 40 C.F.R. pt. 50 (1981).

6. CAA § 111; 42 U.S.C. § 7411 (1976).

7. CAA § 112; 42 U.S.C. § 7412 (1976).

8. 40 C.F.R. pt. 60 (1981).

9. 40 C.F.R. pt. 61 (1981).

10. 42 U.S.C. § 7410 (1976).

11. 42 U.S.C. § 7414(a) (1976).

12. 42 U.S.C. § 7413(b) (1976).

13. CAA §169(1); 42 U.S.C. § 7479(1) (1976).

14. 42 U.S.C. §§ 7470–7479 (1976).

15. The decision in *Alabama Power Co. v. Costle* [606 F.2d 1068 (D.C. Cir. 1979)] established that the EPA had to calculate "potential to emit" *after* the application of pollution control equipment rather than before.

16. 40 C.F.R. pts. 122–124 (1981).

17. 42 U.S.C. § 7475 (1976).

18. CAA § 165(e)(2); 42 U.S.C. § 7475(e)(2) (1976).

19. CAA § 165(a)(4); 42 U.S.C. § 7475(a)(4) (1976).

20. 42 U.S.C. § 7413 (1976).

21. 42 U.S.C. §§ 7501–7508 (1976).

22. 42 U.S.C. § 7502(b)(6) (1976).

23. CAA § 173(1); 42 U.S.C. § 7503(1) (1976).

24. CAA § 173(2); 42 U.S.C. § 7503(2) (1976). LAER is defined in CAA § 171(3); 42 U.S.C. § 7501(3) (1976).

25. CAA § 173(3); 42 U.S.C. § 7503(3) (1976).

26. CAA § 173(4); 42 U.S.C. § 7503(4) (1976).

27. Appendix S to 40 C.F.R. pt. 51 (1981) discusses the EPA's interpretation of this offset requirement. Portions of these regulations were stayed until further notice by an order published May 13, 1980, at 45 *Fed. Reg.* 31307, and the EPA is currently drafting a relaxation of these offset rules.

28. CAA § 110(a)(2)(D); 42 U.S.C. § 7410(a)(2)(D) (1976).

29. *Natural Resources Defense Council, Inc. v. Gorsuch*, 685 F.2nd 718 (D.C. Cir. 1982).

30. 42 U.S.C. § 7413 (1976).

31. 42 U.S.C. § 7606 (1976).

32. 42 U.S.C. § 7413(c)(1) (1976).

33. CAA § 109; 42 U.S.C. § 7409 (1976).

34. 42 U.S.C. § 7411 (1976).

35. 42 U.S.C. § 7412 (1976).

36. 42 U.S.C. § 7413(a) (1976).

37. 42 U.S.C. § 7413(d) (1976).

38. CAA § 113(d)(4); 42 U.S.C. § 7413(d)(4) (1976).

39. *United States v. ASARCO, Inc.,* Civ. No. 81-110-GLO-RAMB (D. Ariz. June 22, 1981).

40. CAA § 113(d)(10); 42 U.S.C. § 7413(d)(10) (1976).

41. 42 U.S.C. § 7416 (1976).

42. CAA § 120; 42 U.S.C. § 7420 (1976).

43. CAA § 120(b); 42 U.S.C. § 7420(b) (1976).

44. 42 U.S.C. § 7420(d)(2) (1976).

45. 40 C.F.R. pt. 66 (1981).

46. CAA § 120(a)(2)(A); 42 U.S.C. § 7420(a)(2)(A) (1976).

47. CAA §120(a)(2)(B); 42 U.S.C. § 7420(a)(2)(B) (1976).

48. CAA § 120(a)(2)(A)(iii); 42 U.S.C. § 7420 (a)(2)(A)(iii) (1976).

49. CAA §120(a)(2)(C); 42 U.S.C. § 7420(a)(2)(C) (1976).

50. For example, the EPA has developed a civil penalty policy which it utilizes in calculating the appropriate civil penalty to be assessed for purposes of settlement negotiations. The amount of the penalty varies with the severity, or class, of the violation. The most recent version of this policy, dated July 8, 1980, is currently undergoing review by the Reagan administration.

51. 42 U.S.C. § 7413(b) (1976).

52. Ibid.

53. 42 U.S.C. § 7603 (1976).

54. CAA § 303(b); 42 U.S.C. § 7603(b) (1976).

55. 42 U.S.C. § 7413(c)(1) (1976).

56. CAA § 113(c)(3); 42 U.S.C. § 7413(c)(3) (1976).

57. 42 U.S.C. § 7419 (1976).

58. CAA § 113(c)(1); 42 U.S.C. § 7413(c)(1) (1976).

59. CAA § 113(c)(2); 42 U.S.C. § 7413(c)(2) (1976).

60. 33 U.S.C. § 1319(c)(1) (1976).

61. See text in preceding chapter of this handbook under Criminal Prosecution in General.

62. 42 U.S.C. § 7604 (1976).

63. *United States v. Atlantic Richfield Co.,* 478 F. Supp. 1215 (D. Mont. 1979).

64. 451 U.S. 304, 101 S. Ct. 1784, 68 L. Ed. 2d 114 (1981); see text in association with footnote 5 in the preceding chapter, "Introduction," and footnote 8 in the following chapter "Clean Water Act."

65. 42 U.S.C. § 7604(f) (1976).

66. CAA § 302(k); 42 U.S.C. § 7602(k) (1976).

67. 42 U.S.C. § 7604(a) (1976).

68. *Metropolitan Washington Coalition for Clean Air v. District of Columbia,* 373 F. Supp. 1089 (D.D.C. 1974), *remanded on other grounds,* 511 F.2d 809 (D.C. Cir. 1974).

69. 87 F.R.D. 709 (W.D. Pa. 1980).

70. 42 U.S.C. § 7604(b)(1)(B) (1976).

71. Ibid.

72. 501 F. Supp. 1159 (S.D.N.Y. 1980).

73. *People v. Celotex Corp.,* 516 F. Supp. 716 (C.D. Ill. 1981); *People v. Commonwealth Edison Co.,* 490 F. Supp. 1145 (N.D. Ill. 1980).

74. CAA § 113(c)(3); 42 U.S.C. § 7413(c)(3) (1976).

75. 42 U.S.C. § 7413 (1976).

76. *United States v. Phelps Dodge Corp.,* Case No. 81-088-TUC-MAR (D. Ariz. Oct. 15, 1981).

77. *United States v. Hills Brothers Coffee, Inc.,* Case No. 81-954 (D. N.J. Apr. 7, 1981).

78. 42 U.S.C. § 7522 (1976).

79. 42 U.S.C. § 7545 (1976).

80. *Hudson Stations, Inc. v. EPA,* 642 F.2d 261 (8th Cir. 1981).

81. *United States v. Dow Chemical Co.,* Case No. 80-10011 (E.D. Mich. Sept. 28, 1981).

82. *United States v. N. L. Industries, Inc.,* Case No. 80-1015 (D. N.J. July 22, 1980).

83. *Tennessee Thoracic Society,* Case Nos. 77-3282, 77-3388, 77-3389, 77-3390 and 77-3394 (M.D. Tenn. Dec. 22, 1980).

84. *United States v. U.S. Steel Corp.,* Case No. 79-709 (W.D. Pa., modified Dec. 31, 1980).

85. *United States v. Allied Chemical Corp.,* Case No. 76-14 (E.D. Ky. Nov. 10, 1981).

86. Case No. 78-152-CR-J-C (M.D. Fla. Sept. 1, 1978).

87. 42 U.S.C. § 7414 (1976).

88. 320 U.S. 277, 64 S. Ct. 134, 88 L. Ed. 48 (1943).

89. 421 U.S. 658, 95 S. Ct. 1903, 44 L. Ed. 2d 489 (1975).

90. 21 U.S.C. §§ 301–392 (1976).

91. EPA policy guide published June 16, 1976.

92. Ibid. at 27.

93. Ibid. at 28.

94. 434 U.S. 275, 98 S. Ct. 566, 54 L. Ed. 2d 538 (1978).

95. CAA § 112(e); 42 U.S.C. § 7412(e) (1976).

96. *United States v. Big Chief Inc.,* Case No. Cr. 75-4 (E.D. La. Apr. 20, 1976)

97. 5 U.S.C. § 552 (1976).

Clean Water Act

Stuart E. Eizenstat
David C. Garrett III
Powell, Goldstein, Frazer & Murphy

Т he Clean Water Act[1] (CWA) prohibits the discharge of pollutants (i.e., dredged spoil, solid wastes, sewage, radioactive wastes, heat, and industrial, municipal, and agricultural wastes) from any discernible, confined, and discrete conveyance (point source) into the waters of the United States, except in compliance with permits issued in accordance with the CWA. National Pollutant Discharge Elimination System (NPDES) permits are issued by the Environmental Protection Agency (EPA) or by an authorized state agency to municipal and industrial facilities for the discharge of wastewaters meeting specified standards for pollution control. Permits for the discharge of dirt, rocks, and other such fill materials into the waters of the United States (dredge and fill permits) are issued by the U.S. Army Corps of Engineers or an authorized state agency.

In order to better understand the scope of federal jurisdiction over discharges of wastewaters and the resulting permit requirements, a discussion of the term "waters of the United States" is necessary.

Orginally, federal regulation of water pollution was limited to waters used in navigation and thus associated with interstate commerce. The United States Supreme Court, in *United States v. Appalachian Electric Power Co.*,[2] however, expanded the jurisdiction to *potentially* navigable waters. The Federal Water Pollution Control Act amendments of 1972 and the CWA amendments, however, still utilized the term "navigable waters" in designating the limits of federal jurisdiction, but this term was defined to mean "waters of the United States, including the territorial seas."[3] The EPA interpreted this jurisdiction to include navigable waters, their tributaries, interstate waters, and intrastate waters involved in any way with interstate commerce.

The EPA's jurisdiction under the CWA was further expanded by court decisions to cover discharges of pollutants onto land which "although above the mean high water line was periodically inundated with the waters of [the United States]."[4] In *United States v. Phelps Dodge Corp.*, the court held that waters of the United States included even "normally dry arroyos through which water may flow, where such water will ultimately end up in public waters."[5]

Consequently, the term "navigable waters" is potentially misleading and may provide a false sense of security to the uninformed. The recent regulatory change to the use of the term "waters of the United States" more appropriately describes the limits of federal jurisdiction.

The CWA jurisdiction appears not to extend to the situation in which a discharge never reaches the waters of the United States, as where a stream dissipates without being used by a downstream industry or without crossing a state line, or where a privately owned lake with no outfall is not a habitat of migratory waterfowl or is not involved in interstate commerce.[6]

The present regulatory definition of "waters of the United States" is as follows:

1. All waters which are currently used, were used in the past, or may be susceptible to use in interstate or foreign commerce, including all waters which are subject to the ebb and flow of the tide

2. All interstate waters, including interstate wetlands

3. All other waters such as intrastate lakes, rivers, streams (including intermittent streams), mud flats, sand flats, wetlands, sloughs, prairie potholes, wet meadows, playa lakes, or natural ponds, the use, degradation, or destruction of which would affect or could affect interstate or foreign commerce, including any such waters (*a*) which are or could be used by interstate or foreign travelers for recreational or other purposes, (*b*) from which fish or shellfish are or could be taken and sold in interstate or foreign commerce, or (*c*) which are used or could be used for industrial purposes by industries in interstate commerce

4. All impoundments of waters otherwise defined as waters of the United States under this definition

5. Tributaries of waters identified in paragraphs 1 to 4 of this definition

6. The territorial sea

7. Wetlands adjacent to waters (other than waters that are themselves wetlands) identified in paragraphs 1 to 6 of this definition

Waste treatment systems, including treatment ponds or lagoons designed to meet the requirements of the CWA [other than cooling ponds as defined in 40 C.F.R. § 423.11(m) which also meet the criteria of this definition] are not waters of the United States.[7]

Groundwater protection is not addressed by the CWA but is covered under the Safe Drinking Water Act, which is discussed elsewhere in this handbook.

NATIONAL POLLUTANT DISCHARGE ELIMINATION SYSTEM PERMITS

All discharges of wastes into the waters of the United States from point sources must be specifically allowed by an NPDES permit which provides pollutant limitations, reporting and monitoring requirements, and prohibitions. Courts cannot require more stringent standards under the federal common law of nuisance than those set by the EPA as administrator of the CWA.[8] The duration of NPDES permits is limited to 5 years. Permit holders must report all instances of noncompliance; incidents which endanger health or the environment must be reported within 24 hours.[9]

The EPA has established effluent limitations for various industrial categories on the basis of the available level of wastewater treatment and pollution-control technology. These industrial categories, including numerous subcategories, are found at 40 C.F.R. parts 405 *et seq.* The effluent limitations require different degrees of treatment depending on whether the source is an existing one or new and also on the type of pollutant. The designated use of the receiving stream (e.g., drinking water, propagation of fish and wildlife, recreational, agricultural, or industrial) may further limit the amount of pollutants permitted to be discharged by an industry if the standard set for the industrial category does not protect the level of water quality established for the receiving water body. Thus an individual NPDES permit may specify more stringent limitations than the categorical standard. In the absence of a "water quality situation," however, the CWA establishment of three classes of pollutants—toxic, conventional, and nonconventional—forms the basis for technology-based standards applicable to discharges.

Controlling Toxic Pollutants

Toxic pollutants were emphasized in the CWA amendments of 1977. The EPA is required by the CWA to develop effluent limitations for toxic pollutants applicable to the categories of industry that are the primary dischargers.[10] In order to apply for an NPDES permit, all industries listed in appendix A to 40 C.F.R. part 122 must test (or estimate, in the case of new sources) their effluent for the toxic pollutants indicated in appendix D to part 122. All industries which have reason to believe any hazardous substance[11] is discharged must indicate the substance on their application. Additional toxic pollutant regulations are established at 40 C.F.R. part 129 for manufacturers or formulators of products containing aldrin/dieldrin, DDT, endrin, toxaphene, benzidine, and polychlorinated biphenyls (PCBs).

The NPDES permits issued to control toxic pollutants require the utilization of the best available technology (BAT) economically achievable for the applicant's industrial category. At this time, BAT standards have been established for only a few industrial categories. The deadline for implementation of such technology for the control of toxic pollutant discharges from existing sources within the industrial categories is supposed to be specified when the applicable BAT regulations are developed. In any event, under the present law, BAT standards must be implemented no later than July 1, 1984. If effluent standards are not established for an industrial category by regulations promulgated at 40 C.F.R. parts 405 *et seq.*, the EPA will use its best engineering judgment in setting permit standards.

The CWA also regulates discharges of toxic and hazardous materials which might enter the waters of the United States through runoff from the plant site or disposal of wastes. The NPDES permit will include requirements for best management practices (BMP) as needed on a case-by-case basis to prevent such contamination. For example, BMP might require the installation of a catch basin or the covering of piles which might be sources of contamination.[12]

Controlling Conventional Pollutants

Conventional pollutants include biochemical oxygen demand (BOD), total suspended solids—nonfilterable (TSS), fecal coliform bacteria, pH (acidity or alkalinity), and oil and grease. The effluent standards for these pollutants are based on best conventional technology (BCT), which is typically less stringent than BAT. (The EPA is in the process of upgrading effluent standards for conventional pollutants from best practical technology, or BPT, to BCT, so existing permits and many industrial category standards at 40 C.F.R. parts 405 *et seq.* may presently require attainment of only the less stringent BPT standard.) BCT limitations must be met by July 1, 1984.

Controlling Nonconventional Pollutants

Nonconventional pollutants are those which are neither conventional nor toxic. These pollutants include chemical oxygen demand, phosphorus, aluminum, ammonia, chloride, color, iron, and nitrate. Nonconventional pollutants are subject to BPT until such time as the EPA develops more stringent BAT guidelines for their control. The CWA requires the EPA to develop BAT limitations for nonconventional pollutants, and compliance must be attained within 3 years after their establishment but in no event later than July 1, 1987.

New-Source Performance Standards

New sources must comply with more stringent standards than existing sources. Therefore, the determination of whether a source should be considered an existing one or new is an important aspect of the NPDES regulatory scheme.

New sources are facilities or equipment whose construction or installation was not begun before the proposal of new-source performance standards for their industrial category. With regard to modifications or expansions of existing plant facilities, if the new equipment totally replaces the process or production equipment which is subject to an existing NPDES permit or changes the nature or quantity of pollutants discharged, it would be considered a new source.

Any facility which may be a new source is required to submit information to the EPA prior to beginning construction, in order that a new-source determination can be made.[13]

Issuance of a permit for a new source by the EPA (rather than a state agency) may be considered a major federal action and therefore subject to the National Environmental Policy Act's requirement of an environmental impact statement.[14]

New sources whose discharges comply with permit limitations that are based on new-source standards promulgated for their category cannot be required to reduce their pollutant discharge level to meet any more stringent conventional or nonconventional pollutant standards promulgated during the ensuing 10 years or during the period of depreciation of the facility or equipment (whichever is shorter).

Traditionally, dams have not been considered pollutant discharge sources and have not been subject to NPDES permit provisions. However, on January 29, 1982, the United States District Court for the District of Columbia ruled that dams are also subject to this federal permit system and ordered the EPA to establish categorical standards for effluent from dams.[15] The court was convinced by arguments demonstrating that dams discharge accumulated sediments and more dissolved metals and higher heat than would be found in free-flowing rivers. This decision is likely to be appealed.

Pretreatment Standards

Industries which discharge wastewater to municipal sewage treatment works (typically referred to as "publicly owned treatment works," or POTWs) must comply with pretreatment standards which include both general regulations (40 C.F.R. part 403) and regulations specific to various industrial categories (40 C.F.R. parts 405 *et seq.*). These pretreatment standards are designed to prevent the discharge into POTWs of any pollutant which may interfere with, pass through, or otherwise be incompatible with the operation of such treatment works. A recent example of a violation of the pretreatment prohibitions occurred February 13, 1981, in Louisville, Kentucky, where hexane, an explosive and flammable solvent, was discharged from a soybean oil extraction plant into a sewer. In this highly publicized incident, several blocks of street were damaged when the hexane exploded in the sewer line. The company was indicted on four counts, which included not only two criminal violations of the CWA but also violations of the Rivers and Harbors Appropriation Act of 1899[16] and the Comprehensive Environmental Response, Compensation and Liability Act of 1980.[17] The company pleaded guilty and was assessed the maximum fine, $62,500.[18]

Permits for Discharges of Dredged or Fill Materials

Permits for discharges of dredged or fill materials (Dredge and Fill permits) are issued by the U.S. Army Corps of Engineers (COE) to govern the discharge of such materials into the waters of the United States.[19] Fill is material used primarily to replace water with dry land or raise the bottom elevation of a water body.[20] If such material is discharged for the purpose of waste disposal, an NPDES permit is necessary rather than a Dredge and Fill permit. A determination as to whether a given activity will be considered waste disposal will be made by the director of the COE in consultation with the NPDES permit authority (EPA or state agency).

The COE regulations governing the Dredge and Fill permit program of the CWA are found at 33 C.F.R. part 323 and are applicable to the building of any structure or impoundment in the waters of the United States, such as roads, dams, seawalls, and recreational, residential, commercial, or industrial developments.[21] Any land-disturbing activity in or around a water body may require a Dredge and Fill permit. In a recent court decision, the court held that land-clearing operations in wetlands are subject to the Dredge and Fill permit program, ruling that the definition of a point source in the CWA includes land-clearing equipment.[22] Maintenance of existing structures may be carried out without a permit if the activity falls within the ambit of the general permit program set forth at 33 C.F.R. § 323.4.

The COE evaluates permit applications on the basis of the probable impact of the proposed activity on the public interest, including such factors as conservation, economics, aesthetics, general environmental concerns, historical values, fish and wildlife values, flood-damage prevention, land use, navigation, recreation, water supply, water quality, energy needs, safety, and food production. Wetlands are considered vital areas that should be protected for their value as areas for spawning, erosion protection, and water purification.

ENFORCEMENT

The CWA gives the EPA the right to enter and inspect the premises of dischargers in order to enforce the act. At reasonable times, the EPA may review and copy records, inspect monitoring equipment and methods, and take samples. Information developed as a result of such inspections is open to the public, except when the EPA is convinced that confidentiality is necessary to protect trade secrets, and such evidence is admissible in court.[23] The CWA protects employees from being discharged or otherwise discriminated against because of their involvement in an enforcement proceeding. Upon petition, the Department of Labor investigates alleged discrimination and provides the opportunity for a public hearing. The Department of Labor has the authority to order any affirmative action deemed necessary to abate the violation.[24]

When the EPA determines that a discharger is in violation of limitations established by the CWA or an NPDES permit, the agency must issue a compliance order or institute a civil action. Orders must specify a deadline for compliance, considering the seriousness of the violation and any good-faith efforts to comply. If the violation is due to noncompliance with an interim compliance schedule or an operation and maintenance requirement, the deadline cannot normally exceed 30 days.[25]

Civil and Criminal Penalties

Stiff penalties are provided for violations of the CWA. Civil penalties can range up to $10,000 per day of violation, including violation of a permit limitation or condition.[26] The EPA has developed a penalty policy to calculate the amount of a civil penalty.[27] In brief, the penalty policy provides that the amount of the CWA civil penalty for failure to install or properly operate equipment required to meet wastewater treatment standards will be at least equivalent to any economic advantage gained by the discharger as a result of its failure to comply. The formula for computing the amount of the penalty also includes consideration of the harm done to public health or the environment, the degree of recalcitrance of the violator, and any unusual costs borne by the public because of the enforcement action. However, this policy is presently undergoing review by the Reagan administration and may be modified to encourage voluntary reporting and discourage litigation of the enforcement penalty amounts set by EPA.

Over 450 federal civil actions regarding the CWA have been settled, primarily by consent decrees. Civil penalties have ranged in the millions of dollars;[28] however, the two following examples are typical in the amounts and requirements of civil penalties.

In a consent decree, the Inversand Company agreed to comply with its NPDES permit by April 4, 1981, and to pay a penalty of $65,000.[29] In another civil case, American Cyanamid Company agreed in a consent decree to meet specific effluent limitations and to construct a wastewater treatment system at its Westwego, Louisiana, facility within a certain time frame.[30]

Willful or negligent violations of the CWA or of a permit are considered criminal and are punishable by fines of not less than $2500 or more than $25,000 *per day* of violation and/or by imprisonment for up to a year. The CWA's "willful or negligent" standard would appear to provide prosecutors with an easier burden of proof than that under other environmental statutes which require that the defendant *knowingly* violate the act. Also, the CWA states that knowingly making any false statement, representation, or certification in any application, report, or other document required under the CWA or tampering with a monitoring device is considered a criminal act and is punishable by a fine of up to $10,000 or by a lesser fine and/or 6 months imprisonment. The CWA specifically provides that any *responsible corporate officer* may be subject to these criminal penalties as well as corporations, government bodies, and other individuals.[31]

This criminal penalty is quite significant, since any report or permit application must be accompanied by the following statement:

> I certify under penalty of law that I have personally examined and am
> familiar with the information submitted in the attached document; and
> based on my inquiry of those individuals immediately responsible for

obtaining the information, I believe the submitted information is true, accurate and complete. I am aware that there are significant penalties for submitted false information including the possibility of fine and imprisonment.[32]

A company official at the level of vice president or above must verify the information submitted in a permit application. For reports, the authority to sign the above statement may be delegated by a written authorization to a person with responsibility for overall operation of a facility (e.g., plant manager).[33]

The EPA has considerable discretion in determining whether to prosecute violations as criminal or civil offenses and whether to seek indictments of individuals. The willfulness of pollution-control violations and whether they are repetitive in nature are considered when deciding the extent of prosecution. When actual or potential harm to health or the environment is involved, indictments against individuals are likely to be sought. Prosecutions of persons believed responsible for discharges of toxic substances are particularly harsh.

Often the CWA indictments also allege violations of other environmental statutes, such as the Rivers and Harbors Appropriations Act of 1899,[34] the Marine Protection, Research and Sanctuaries Act of 1972,[35] and the laws governing hazardous wastes.[36] In addition, many of these criminal cases also cite violations of federal criminal statutes regarding fraud, false statements, concealment of facts, and the like, that are discussed in the introductory section.

Case Histories

There are numerous cases of criminal prosecution of corporations and individuals for CWA violations. The following examples indicate their variety and magnitude.

In *United States v. Allied Chemical Co.*, Allied Chemical Company was fined $13.2 million after pleading nolo contendere to 940 counts of violating the CWA by polluting the James River in Virginia with the toxic pollutant Kepone and other chemical substances.[37] This fine was later reduced to $5 million when an $8 million fund was established by Allied to alleviate the environmental damage from the discharge. In an associated case, Life Science Products, which took over the production of Kepone from Allied after 1974, was fined $3.8 million. The two co-owners of Life Science Products were fined $25,000 each.

In *United States v. Potato Services, Inc.*, the company was fined $25,000 and its president $20,000 for polluting a river with untreated wastewater by bypassing aerators, reportedly in order to cut expenses.[38]

In *United States v. Ouellette*, the superintendent of a city sewage treatment plant was convicted on five counts of falsifying monthly NPDES monitoring reports.[39]

United States v. Tabb represents the first criminal prosecution brought under the CWA section regarding Dredge and Fill permits. Two corporations pleaded nolo contendere to five counts of polluting without a Dredge and Fill permit by discharging substantial quantities of fill into a river and altering its course. The defendants were fined $10,500 and required to perform extensive restoration work.[40]

In *United States v. Velsicol Chemical Corp.*, Velsicol was assessed a civil penalty of $30,000 for 300 violations of its NPDES permit by discharging larger than permitted amounts of two toxic pesticides, heptachlor and endrin, into the Memphis wastewater collection system, through which they entered the Mississippi River.[41] The court found that the company had falsified reports, had delayed construction of its wastewater treatment facility, and had an indifferent corporate attitude regarding the discharge of known toxins. Six present and former officers, employees, and attorneys were indicted on eleven counts of criminal statute violations: conspiracy to commit offense or to defraud the United States, false statements and concealing material facts, and mail fraud.

In *United States v. Distler*, the president of Kentucky Liquid Recycling, Inc. was convicted of criminally violating two CWA requirements for discharging highly toxic chemicals (which originated from Velsicol Chemical Corporation's refinery in Memphis) into the Louisville, Kentucky, sewer. Mr. Distler was fined $50,000 and sentenced to 2 years imprisonment.[42]

In *United States v. Frezzo Brothers*, Guido and James Frezzo were convicted on six counts, sentenced to 30 days in jail, and fined $25,000 each for willfully and negligently violating the CWA by allowing untreated runoff from manure composting (in connection with their mushroom farming operation) to enter a nearby creek. The corporation was fined $50,000. The defendants appealed this decision, arguing that they could not be charged with a criminal violation since EPA had not previously notified them of any CWA violation, but the court ruled that such notice is not required.[43] This ruling referred to a proceeding decision in *United States v. Phelps Dodge Corp.*[44] which had reached the same conclusion. On a second appeal, the conviction of the Frezzo brothers was reversed by the United States Court of Appeals for the Third Circuit and remanded for further proceedings to determine whether this source was an exempted agricultural operation under EPA regulations.[45]

Another mushroom compost operation, Hudson Farms, Incorporated, and its vice president pleaded guilty to criminal violations of the CWA, and the corporation was fined $50,000 while the officer was fined $5000 and given 2 years probation.[46] Two other composting operations received lesser fines.

The president of Oxford Royal Mushroom Products, Incorporated, was fined $100,000 and placed on 5 years probation after pleading guilty to five criminal counts of discharging pollutants without an NPDES permit. The company was also fined $100,000.[47]

In 1981, a paper recycling firm, Corning Fibers, Incorporated, of Well River, Vermont, was fined $50,000 for CWA violations, and its vice president and general manager was sentenced to 1 year in jail and fined $2500 after pleading guilty to ordering the discharge of untreated wastes into the river and falsifying reports to the EPA.[48]

Oil and Hazardous Substance Liability

The CWA establishes liability for a discharge or spill of any hazardous substance or oil into the waters of the United States in quantities which may be harmful.[49] For oil, the harmfulness of a quantity is determined by whether the spill creates a sheen on the surface of the water,[50] a result that may follow quite a small spill. Violations must be immediately reported to the National Response Center. The regulations at 40 C.F.R. part 117 designate hazardous substances by name and specify the amount of each which, if spilled, is considered potentially hazardous and must be reported. The person in charge of the vessel or facility must immediately notify the center or be subject to a fine of up to $10,000 and/or imprisonment for 1 year. The owner or operator of the vessel or facility is liable for the cost of cleanup and restoration within certain limitations.[51] If willful negligence or willful misconduct is shown, the full cost of removing the oil or substance is recoverable by the federal government.[52] Such spills are subject to a civil penalty of up to $5000 for each offense, imposed by the Coast Guard. Also, the EPA may commence a civil action to impose a penalty of up to $50,000. If willful negligence or willful misconduct is proved, the penalty can range up to $250,000 for each offense.[53] Plans for preventing and controlling spills of oil must be developed by certain facilities.[54]

The self-incriminating aspects of the requirement for reporting spills were reviewed in *United States v. Ward.* In reversing the decision of the United States Court of Appeals for the Tenth Circuit, the United States Supreme Court ruled that the penalty for oil and hazardous waste spills is civil rather than criminal. Therefore, compulsory self-reporting does not violate the Fifth Amendment privilege against self-incrimination.[55]

The oil and hazardous substance liability section of the CWA has been interpreted as requiring strict liability. The United States Court of Appeals for the Fifth Circuit held that a barge company which had contracted with a towing company to transport a barge was required to pay the cleanup costs due to a spill from the barge which occurred during towing. The United States Court of Appeals for the Fifth Circuit reasoned that if a third-party defense was allowed, the strict liability under this CWA section could be evaded. In a June 1, 1981, decision, the United States Supreme Court declined to review this ruling.[56] If a third party such as the operator of the tug boat is actually responsible for a spill, the CWA specifically provides that the cost of cleanup may be recovered from the third party by the company held initially liable.[57]

Liability for damages for discharge of oil and hazardous substances plus the penalty can amount to millions of dollars, as evidenced by the case of *Puerto Rico v. S.S. Zoe Colocotroni*.[58] As a result of this suit, Puerto Rico was awarded over $6 million for environmental damages and the United States was awarded over $670,000 plus interest in cleanup costs plus the maximum Coast Guard civil penalty of $5000 under the CWA and $2500 under the Rivers and Harbors Act. The amount of damages awarded to Puerto Rico was later remanded by the United States Court of Appeals for the First Circuit for further hearings by the district court.[59]

The United States Supreme Court allowed a ruling to stand which established that the statute of limitations for filing for cleanup costs under this CWA section runs for 3 years after the cleanup is completed, not from the date of the spill.[60] The oil and hazardous substance liability established by the CWA is the exclusive remedy that the government may use to recover its oil cleanup costs, according to numerous court decisions, as indicated in *United States v. Dixie Carriers, Inc.*[61]

Citizen Suits

The CWA provides that any citizen can initiate a civil action against an alleged violator of a discharge standard or against EPA for failure to perform a nondiscretionary duty under the act. "Any citizen" includes an environmental group. Notice of an alleged violation must be given to the violator, the state, and EPA 60 days prior to filing suit.[62]

On June 25, 1981, the United States Supreme Court reversed an appeals court decision and ruled that private parties cannot sue for money damages under the CWA or the Marine Protection, Research and Sanctuaries Act.[63] Nevertheless, corporations and individuals convicted for CWA violations would be subject to liability claims under common law. Both individuals and groups may seek restitution for alleged harm to them from the CWA violation. For example, in the Allied Chemical case of Kepone contamination, the company was sued by former emloyees, fishermen, seafood packers, seafood merchants, and owners of oyster beds in the contaminated James River and Chesapeake Bay area. The District Court for the Eastern District of Virginia ruled on September 15, 1981, that fishermen, marinas, boat retailers, and bait and tackle shops may recover damages for negligent contamination.[64] In the Velsicol case involving the discharge of toxic pollutants through the Memphis sewer system, a treatment plant employee, Joyce Mabray, sued the company and the city for the wrongful death of her fetus and for personal injuries. Tests showed high levels of the chemicals in her urine, and she underwent an abortion because of the health risk to her fetus.[65]

Blacklisting

The CWA, as well as the Clean Air Act (CAA), provides that federal agencies cannot contract for the procurement of goods, materials, and services with persons or facilities which have been found guilty for any criminal offense under the act. Grants and loans to such facilities are also forbidden. This contract prohibition extends to all facilities owned, leased, or supervised by such violators, and the blacklisting remains in effect until EPA certifies that the company is no longer in violation of the CWA (or CAA).[66]

Pursuant to this CWA provision, President Nixon issued Executive Order 11738, which required federal agencies to amend their procurement regulations to require compliance with the CAA and CWA as a condition to entering into, renewing, or extending any contract or awarding a grant or a loan.[67] Subsequently, regulations were promulgated which provide for a list of violating facilities, to include not only facilities convicted of criminal violations but also companies that the EPA determines to be in "continuing or recurring noncompliance with clean air or water standards." However, contracts or grants under $100,000 are affected by the listing only if a federal criminal conviction is involved.[68]

The blacklisting of a facility on the basis of continuing or recurring noncompliance, in addition to criminal conviction, was challenged in *ITT Rayonier v. United States.* However, the Court of Appeals for the Fifth Circuit, upholding the opinion of the district court, ruled that the issue was rendered moot by the settlement of EPA's enforcement action against ITT Rayonier and the subsequent removal of the company from the list prior to the case's coming to trial.[69] Therefore the legality of this regulation remains an issue to be decided by the courts in response to some future challenge.

Additional Considerations

In addition to the possibility of monetary penalties and imprisonment for CWA violations, companies should consider the disruption of their operation that could be caused by an administrative or court order requiring compliance with CWA standards within a short time frame, possibly immediately. Financing and installing the required wastewater treatment equipment within the time specified by such orders would be much more difficult than studying the CWA regulations and sampling effluent in advance of a possible enforcement action to make a judicious decision as to whether improved wastewater treatment is required. An environmental audit can aid this decision-making process.

Public relations is another important aspect of assuring compliance. The adverse publicity from an enforcement action is very likely to damage relations with the local community and customers.

AUDITING FOR COMPLIANCE WITH THE CWA

In order to determine whether a facility is in compliance with the CWA, all discharges should be checked to determine whether they could possibly be considered discharges of pollutants to the waters of the United States. *Each* point which would be considered a discharge source under the CWA must be covered by an NPDES permit (or a Dredge and Fill permit). Facilities which have permits should sample and test effluent from all sources of discharge to compare the pollutant levels with the effluent standard required in the permit. For toxic pollutants, compliance with the new categorical regulations specifying limitations must be attained within the time set by the regulations at the time of their promulgation, even if the permit has not yet been modified to incorporate the new requirement. Any discharge or potential discharge of toxic pollutants[70] must be reported according to the provisions at 40 C.F.R. § 122.61.

All monitoring and reporting should be checked for compliance with the permit requirements and the regulations, including the existence of a proper signature.[71] Review of the submission of noncompliance reports is particularly critical in assessing regulatory compliance and the possible need for additional wastewater treatment.

Facilities which discharge to POTWs should check compliance with the general pretreatment standards[72] and the pretreatment standards established for their industrial category.[73] Users of POTWs are also subject to all local ordinances and contract provisions governing such discharges. Monitoring compliance reports should be checked.[74]

If oil is stored at a facility, the regulations for spill prevention at 40 C.F.R. parts 110 to 117 may be applicable. A facility which stores any form of oil should review these regulations for their applicability and, if necessary, check compliance. Facilities which handle oil or hazardous substances should be aware of the regulations at 40 C.F.R. § 117 that specify the quantity of a spill which must be reported to the National Response Center and should train their personnel to follow appropriate procedures in the event of an accident. (The Superfund act, which is discussed elsewhere in this handbook, may also be applicable.)

1. 33 U.S.C. §§ 1251–1376 (1976). The Federal Water Pollution Control Act (Pub. L. 92-500) was amended in 1977 (Pub. L. 95-217) and its name was changed to the Clean Water Act. Minor amendments have been enacted subsequently.

2. 311 U.S. 377, 61 S. Ct. 291, 85 L. Ed. 243 (1940).

3. 33 U.S.C. § 1362(7).

4. *United States v. Holland,* 373 F. Supp. 665 (M.D. Fla. 1974).

5. 391 F. Supp. 1181 (D. Ariz. 1975).

6. *See United States Environmental Protection Agency General Counsel Opinions;* NPDES Permits, Opinion No. 30, Sept. 18, 1975, *In re* City of Ely, Nev.; Environmental Law Publishing Service, NILS Publishing Co. (1979).

7. 40 C.F.R. § 122.3 (1981). The exclusion of waste-treatment systems in the regulatory definition promulgated May 19, 1980 (45 Fed. Reg. 33424), was restricted to water bodies of human creation, but this restriction was suspended by a regulation published July 21, 1980 (45 Fed. Reg. 48620) because of petitions from various organizations.

8. *City of Milwaukee v. Illinois,* 451 H.S. 304, 101 S. Ct. 1784, 68 L. Ed. 2d 114 (1981).

9. 40 C.F.R. § 122.7 (1981).

10. 33 U.S.C. § 1317 (1976).

11. Hazardous substances are listed at 40 C.F.R. pt. 122, appendix D, table 5 (1981).

12. *See* 40 C.F.R. pt. 125, subpart K (1981), for the BMP criteria and standards.

13. 40 C.F.R. § 122.53(h) (1981).

14. 40 C.F.R. § 6.604 (1981). *See* discussion in the introductory chapter of this section of the handbook under the head, National Environmental Policy Act, and 42 U.S.C. § 4332 (1976).

15. *National Wildlife Federation v. Gorsuch,* 16 Env't Rep. Cas. (BNA) 2025 (D.D.C. 1982).

16. 33 U.S.C. §§ 401–466n (1976).

17. 42 U.S.C. §§ 9601–9657 (1976).

18. *United States v. Ralston Purina Co.,* Cr. No. 81-00126-01-L (W.D. Ky. Jan. 4, 1982); 12 Envtl. L. Rep. (Envtl. L. Inst.) 20257.

19. 33 U.S.C. § 1344 (1976).

20. 33 C.F.R. § 323.2(m) (1981).

21. Permits are also required for dredging under a program operated by the COE pursuant to § 10 of the Rivers and Harbors Appropriation Act of 1899, 33 U.S.C. § 403 (1976).

22. *Avoyelles Sportsmen's League v. Alexander,* 473 F. Supp. 525 (W.D. La. 1979); also *see* 511 F. Supp. 278 (W.D. La. 1981).

23. 33 U.S.C. § 1318 (1976).

24. 33 U.S.C. § 1367 (1976).

25. 33 U.S.C. § 1319(a) (1976).

26. 33 U.S.C. § 1319(d) (1976).

27. "Civil Penalty Policy," EPA Office of Enforcement, July 8, 1980.

28. *United States v. Crucible Steel,* Case No. 79-617C (W.D. Pa. June 25, 1979), *United States v. National Steel Corp.,* Civ. Act. No. 79-0002(W) (D.W. Va. Feb. 28, 1979), *United States v. U.S. Steel Corp.,* Case No. Civ. H-77-212 (N.D. Ind. Sept. 27, 1977), *United States v. IMC.,* Case No. Civ. 78-02500 (W.D. La. May 4, 1978).

29. *United States v. Inversand Co.,* Civ. Act. No. 80-3375 (D.N.J. Dec. 30, 1980).

30. *United States v. American Cyanamid Co.,* Case No. 80-4409A [5] (E.D. La. Dec. 19, 1980).

31. 33 U.S.C. § 1319(c) (1976).

32. 40 C.F.R. § 122.6(d) (1981).

33. 40 C.F.R. § 122.6(a) and (b) (1981).

34. 33 U.S.C. §§ 401–466(n) (1976).

35. 33 U.S.C. §§ 1401–1421, 16 U.S.C. §§ 1431–1434 (1976).

36. The Comprehensive Environmental Response, Compensation, and Liability Act of 1980 (Superfund act), 42 U.S.C. §§ 9601–9657 (1976), and the Resource Conservation and Recovery Act of 1976 (RCRA), 42 U.S.C. §§ 6901–6987 (1976).

37. Crim. A. No. 76-0129-R. (E.D. Va. Oct. 5, 1976). *See* 420 F. Supp. 122.

38. Cr. No. 76-18 (D. Me. July 21, 1976).

39. Case No. LR-CR 77-97 (E.D. Ark, July 20, 1977). *See* 11 Env't Rep. Cas. (BNA) 1350.

40. Cr. No. 78-0023 (W.D. Va., filed Feb. 14, 1978); *Pending Litigation* (Envtl. L. Inst.) 65553.

41. 12 Env't Rep. Cas (BNA) 1417 (W.D. Tenn. 1978).

42. No. CR 77-00108-01-L (W.D. Ky. 1979); 9 Envtl. L. Rep. (Envtl. L. Inst.) 20700; *aff'd,* 15 Env't Rep. Cas. (BNA) 1711 (6th Cir. 1981); *cert. denied sub nom. Distler v. United States,* 454 U.S. 827, 102 S. Ct. 118, 70 L. Ed. 2d 102 (1981).

43. 461 F. Supp. 266 (E.D. Pa. 1978); *aff'd,* 602 F.2d 1123 (3d Cir. 1979); *cert. denied,* 444 U.S. 1074 100 S. Ct. 1020, 62 L. Ed. 2d 756 (1980).

44. 391 F. Supp. 1181 (D. Ariz. 1975).

45. 642 F.2d 59 (3d Cir. 1981).

46. Cr. No. 78-222 (E.D. Pa. Nov. 2, 1978).

47. *United States v. Oxford Royal Mushroom Products, Inc.,* 487 F. Supp. 852 (E.D. Pa. 1980).

48. *United States v. Corning Fibers, Inc.,* Cr. No. 81-00055-01 and *United States v. Bushey,* Cr. No. 81-00055-02 (D. Vt. Nov. 24, 1981); 12 Envtl. L. Rep. (Envtl. L. Inst.) 20175.

49. 33 U.S.C. § 1321 (1976).

50. 40 C.F.R. § 110.3(b) 1981).

51. For vessels, liability is based on tonnage; for facilities the limit is $50 million, unless the limitations for small onshore storage facilities, found at 40 C.F.R. pt. 113 (1981), are applicable.

52. 33 U.S.C. § 1321(f) (1976).

53. 33 U.S.C. § 1321(b) (1976).

54. *See* 40 C.F.R. pts. 112 and 114 (1981) regarding spill prevention and penalties.

55. 448 U.S. 242, 100 S. Ct. 2636, 65 L. Ed. 2d 742 (1980); *reh'g denied*, 448 U.S. 916, 101 S. Ct. 37, 65 L. Ed. 2d 1179 (1980).

56. *United States v. LeBeouf Brothers Towing Co.*, 621 F.2d 787 (5th Cir. 1980), *cert. denied sub nom. LeBeouf Brothers Towing Co. v. United States*, 452 U.S. 906, 101 S. Ct. 3031, 69 L. Ed. 2d 406 (1981).

57. 33 U.S.C. § 1321(h)

58. 456 F. Supp. 1327 (D. P.R. 1978).

59. 628 F.2d 652 (1st Cir. 1980).

60. *United States v. Barge Shamrock*, 15 Env't Rep. Cas. (BNA) 1409 (4th Cir. 1980); *cert. denied sub nom. Shell Oil v. United States.*, 454 U.S. 830, 102 S. Ct. 125, 70 L. Ed. 2d 107 (1981).

61. 426 F. Supp. 1126 (E.D. La. 1978); *aff'd*, 627 F.2d 736 (5th Cir. 1980). Also *see In re Oswego Barge Corp.*, 16 Env't Rep. Cas. (BNA) 1777 (2d Cir. 1981).

62. 33 U.S.C. § 1365 (1976).

63. *National Sea Clammers Ass'n v. City of New York*, 616 F.2d 1222 (3d Cir. 1980), *rev'd sub nom. Middlesex County Sewerage Authority v. National Sea Clammers Ass'n,* 453 U.S. 1, 101 S. Ct. 2615, 69 L. Ed. 2d 435 (1981).

64. *Pruitt v. Allied Chemical Corp.*, 523 F. Supp. 975 (E.D. Va. 1981).

65. *See Mabray v. Velsicol*, 14 Env't Rep. Cas. (BNA) 1041 (W.D. Tenn. 1979), in which the district court remanded the case to the state court's jurisdiction.

66. CWA § 508, 33 U.S.C. § 1368 (1976); CAA § 306 42 U.S.C. § 7606 (1976).

67. 38 Fed. Reg. 25161 (Sept. 12, 1973).

68. 40 C.F.R. § 15.1(c) (1981).

69. *ITT Rayonier v. United States.*, 14 Env't Rep. Cas. (BNA) 1454 (M.D. Fla. 1979); *aff'd*, 16 Env't Rep. Cas (BNA) 1265 (5th Cir. 1981).

70. *See* Appendix D to 40 C.F.R. pt. 122 (1981).

71. *See* 40 C.F.R. § 122.60 (1981).

72. 40 C.F.R. § 403.5 (1981).

73. 40 C.F.R. §§ 405–460 (1981).

74. *See* 40 C.F.R. § 403.12 (1981).

Toxic Substances Control Act

Stuart E. Eizenstat
David C. Garrett III
Powell, Goldstein, Frazer & Murphy

The Toxic Substances Control Act (TSCA)[1] is fundamentally different from the environmental statutes discussed previously. Rather than governing pollutants as they enter the environment, TSCA regulates the manufacture, mixing, or importation of certain chemical substances prior to their distribution, where such regulation is deemed necessary for the protection of health and the environment from unreasonable risks. Incidents involving such substances as DDT, asbestos, lead, mercury, Kepone, Tris, and polychlorinated biphenyls (PCBs) resulted in considerable public attention and concern during the early 1970s, and Congress responded by enacting TSCA in 1976. TSCA has primarily affected chemical manufacturers, users of chemicals in the production of goods, and owners of equipment containing PCBs.

TSCA authorizes the Environmental Protection Agency (EPA) to take those actions necessary to protect health and the environment from chemical substances and mixtures posing an "unreasonable risk." Chemical substances are defined in the act in such a manner that naturally occurring substances are included. The EPA is given the power to determine whether an unreasonable risk exists with respect to the manufacture, processing,[2] distribution, or disposal of chemical substances and mixtures. In order to make that determination, the EPA is empowered to require manufacturers and processors to test the toxicity of chemicals; to monitor the effects of exposure to those chemicals; to provide monitoring records, employee health records, inventories of amounts produced, descriptions of by-products, and categories of use of those chemicals; to submit existing data concerning the environmental and health effects and the number of people exposed; to estimate the number of people who will be exposed, including the duration of exposure; and to describe the methods of disposal of the chemicals. When determining agency action in such matters, the EPA is required to consider the chemical's benefits, the economic and social consequences of restrictions, and the availability of substitutes. Immediate notification of EPA is required when a manufacturer, processor, or distributor of a chemical substance or mixture becomes aware that such substance or mixture may present a substantial risk of injury to health or the environment.

NOTIFICATION OF SUBSTANTIAL RISKS

EPA issued a policy statement in 1978 regarding notifications of substantial risks, providing its interpretation of the TSCA requirement.[3] EPA's policy stipulates that business entities as well as individuals are responsible for such notifications; and in the case of a business entity, the president, chief executive officer, and any other officers having authority and responsibility for the organization's compliance with this TSCA requirement must ensure that the company reports to EPA information on substantial risks. A company will be deemed to have obtained such information when "any officer or employee capable of appreciating the significance of that information" has knowledge of it.

Companies, therefore, have the responsibility for establishing and implementing internal procedures for transmittal of pertinent information, so that the company can comply at the prescribed time with the requirements of TSCA, found at 15 U.S.C. section 2607(e), regarding notification of substantial risks. The EPA, however, does not relieve the individual knowledgeable officer or employee from the responsibility to immediately report information which reasonably supports the conclusion that a chemical presents a significant risk.

"Immediate notification" consists of a written report to the EPA by certified mail within 15 days. For emergency incidents involving environmental contamination, the person (or company) must telephone the 24-hour emergency contact for the EPA regional office serving the affected area.

A risk is considered to be substantial if one of the following developments occurs:

1. An incident strongly indicates that a chemical (or a group of chemicals) causes cancer, birth defects, mutation, death, or serious or prolonged incapacitation.

2. A pattern of effects reasonably supports the conclusion that a chemical substance or mixture can produce such effects.

Substantial risks to the environment are considered by the EPA to be:

1. Widespread and previously undetected distribution of a chemical in the environment
2. Pronounced bioaccumulation not previously known to the EPA
3. Adverse effects of bioaccumulation not previously known to the EPA
4. Ecologically significant changes in species' interrelationships

An emergency incident of environmental contamination would be one in which any of the above effects occurs that seriously threatens humans with cancer, birth defects, mutations, death, or incapacitation or seriously threatens nonhuman organisms with large-scale or ecologically significant population reduction. Notification is not required if the EPA is known to have adequate information as a result of information published in EPA reports or because of previous reports to the EPA pursuant to TSCA or any other statute administered by the EPA.

Several hundred notifications of substantial risks have been received by the EPA. Most of the reported risks were not considered significant by the EPA, but some have resulted in the reported chemical's being added to the EPA's risk-assessment process.

TSCA requires that records of the adverse effects allegedly caused by chemical substances or mixtures on health or the environment which the EPA determines by rule to be significant must be retained by any manufacturer, processor, or distributor for at least 5 years. Consumer allegations of health injuries, reports of occupational health problems, and complaints or indications of environmental problems must be included in the records. Reports of employee health problems must be retained for 30 years.[4]

PREMANUFACTURING AND PROCESSING NOTICES

TSCA forbids the manufacture or importation of a new chemical substance *for distribution in commerce* or the manufacture or processing of an existing chemical substance for a new *commercial* use unless notice is given to the EPA at least 90 days prior to production.[5] New mixtures, however, are not subject to this notification. Such notices must identify the chemical and provide the information listed at 15 U.S.C. § 2607(a)(2) and test data prescribed by EPA as necessary to determine risks. The EPA published an interim policy governing premanufacture notifications in the *Federal Register* January 10, 1979, which was revised May 15, 1979, October 16, 1979, and November 7, 1980, and remains in effect.[6] The interim policy provides guidance regarding the submission of notices and describes the EPA's procedures for handling such notices, particularly confidentiality. A printed form to use for premanufacture notices is suggested but not required.[7]

For good cause, the EPA may extend the 90-day period allowed for the evaluation of a premanufacturing notification and delay commercial production up to 180 days after submission of a premanufacturing notice providing all the information required by TSCA.[8] After this evaluation period expires, the manufacturer or importer may begin production unless the EPA issues a proposed rule to prevent or control the production. Such proposed rules become effective upon publication, but the promulgation of a final, possibly modified, rule must follow formal rule-making procedures.[9] If the EPA determines that a chemical substance poses an unreasonable risk, its manufacture can be banned or restricted, special labeling can be required, or its disposal can be regulated.[10]

If the EPA is unable to decide whether a chemical substance should be restricted, a proposed order may be issued during the evaluation period to limit or prohibit production while further information is obtained and evaluated. The proposed order becomes effective at the end of the evaluation period unless the manufacturer protests; in such case, EPA must seek a court injunction.[11]

On April 25, 1980, the EPA for the first time ordered a delay in the manufacture of some new chemical substances under TSCA's premanufacturing notice system. This action concerned six new plasticizers similar to several others already in commercial use. The safety of the existing plasticizers had been a concern for the EPA because of a National Cancer Institute study which had indicated that they were carcinogenic, but regulatory restrictions on their use have not been promulgated to date. The EPA's order regarding the new plasticizers was based on the absence of data regarding health and environmental safety in the premanufacture notice submitted by the company and the likelihood of a hazard being posed by the new chemicals if manufactured. Further testing was required, but the company considered the cost of such testing to be excessive, and the expected adverse publicity which would arise from a court challenge to the order made that option seem ill-advised. The company, therefore, withdrew its premanufacture notice.

In 1981 the EPA proposed an order to prohibit production of two new dyes pending development of further information on their risk. Again the manufacturer withdrew its notice rather than proceed.

When the EPA concludes that a new chemical substance poses no unreasonable risk and, therefore, merits no restrictions, a statement of the reasons for not initiating any action must be published in the *Federal Register*.[12]

INVENTORY OF CHEMICAL SUBSTANCES

In order to determine what are "new chemical substances," the EPA was authorized by the act to compile an inventory of chemicals presently in commercial use.[13] In 1979 the EPA published such an inventory containing nearly 50,000 commercial chemical substances manufactured in or imported into the United States. In compiling the inventory, the EPA required manufacturers and importers to report production volume and manufacturing sites of each chemical,[14] but much of this information was provided on a confidential basis and is, therefore, not published as a part of the inventory. The inventory is available in printed form or on microfiche from the EPA Industry Assistance Office (800-424-9065), which was established pursuant to TSCA to assist the chemical industry with compliance. The computerized inventory is continually updated as premanufacture notices are evaluated and the production of new chemical substances is allowed.

The problem of determining what constitutes a significant new use of an existing chemical—necessitating the filing of a premanufacture notice—is not solved by the inventory. A prototype of a chemical use list was published by the EPA in the *Federal Register*[15] July 25, 1978, but never finalized. The EPA must determine by rule what constitutes a significant new use of any chemical listed in the inventory,[16] but to date the new uses of a chemical substance have not been regulated. Until regulations are published, the use of all existing chemicals listed in the inventory may proceed without notification of the EPA.

Coordination with Other Laws

TSCA is intended to apply only where action under other laws is deemed insufficient to protect health and the environment.[17] Often chemical substances are adequately controlled by the previously discussed environmental statutes or pursuant to the legislation enforced by the Consumer Products Safety Commission (CPSC), the Occupational Safety and Health Administration (OSHA), or the Food and Drug Administration (FDA). The following substances are specifically excluded from the ambit of TSCA:

1. Pesticides regulated by the Federal Insecticide, Fungicide, and Rodenticide Act

2. Tobacco

3. Materials regulated pursuant to the Atomic Energy Act

4. Foods, drugs, and cosmetics regulated by the Food, Drug and Cosmetic Act

5. Firearms and ammunition subject to tax under section 4181 of the Internal Revenue Code[18]

To coodinate control of chemical substances under these overlapping laws, an Interagency Regulatory Liaison Group composed of the concerned agencies was formed to avoid duplication of effort, develop consistent regulatory policy, and share information. This group no longer exists, however; as of September 26, 1981, the interagency agreement expired.

Existing Chemicals

Obviously, there is a tremendous backlog of existing chemicals which must be evaluated by the EPA to determine whether or not they pose an unreasonable risk. To help determine which potentially toxic chemicals should receive priority consideration for the promulgation of a rule, TSCA created the Interagency Testing Committee, composed of eight federal agencies concerned with industry, health, and environmental protection.[19] Priority consideration is based on the likelihood of unreasonable risks and the amount of exposure associated with a chemical substance or mixture. The priority list presently includes forty-four chemicals and is limited to fifty chemical substances at any one time. The EPA is required by TSCA to initiate rule-making proceedings within 12 months of the time when a chemical substance or mixture is added to the priority list or provide an explanation to the public as to why this was not done. The Interagency Testing Committee removes chemical substances from the list when satisfied with the EPA's action; but only five substances had been removed from the list as of October 30, 1981.[20]

Chemical Testing

As mentioned previously, if available data are inconclusive, the EPA may require submission of information regarding an existing chemical substance from the industries involved in its manufacture or processing. The EPA has required manufacturers, processors, and distributors of some chemical substances included on the priority list to submit available health and safety information regarding those chemicals but to date has only proposed testing requirements for three chemicals[21] and has completed assessment and action on none.

If insufficient information exists to determine the risks associated with a chemical substance, TSCA requires that the EPA obtain test data from the affected chemical industries.[22] The development of policies regarding testing of suspect chemicals has been controversial. The EPA has been unable to meet the 12-month deadline for action on chemicals added to the priority list and was sued for failure to meet this TSCA mandate.[23] The court ordered the EPA to establish a schedule for action, in response to which the EPA created a time frame for action on a total of thirty-seven chemicals and chemical groups. The EPA estimated that it could establish test rules for only fifteen to twenty chemicals per year and that the costs to legally support such rules would be $130,000 to $240,000 per chemical or chemical group.

If preliminary tests indicate that health risks warrant testing on mammals, the cost could be very high. The costs to industry to perform the testing required by EPA could be shared among the affected companies, but a method of allocation has not yet been established. Testing will be voluntarily performed, however, for several priority list chemicals by an association of chemical manufacturers using laboratory procedures approved by the EPA.[24]

EPA ACTIONS PURSUANT TO TSCA

Chemical substances undergo a risk assessment if they are included on the priority list or named in notifications of substantial risks or if assessment is recommended by other federal agencies. Although studies have been performed and reports and notices submitted on the risks of such substances, the EPA actions pursuant to TSCA have been limited.

Several actions to control risks have utilized the remedies available under other statutes. In March 1978, the EPA, in coordination with the FDA and the CPSC, issued final rules prohibiting the manufacture and processing of chlorofluorocarbons as propellants in nonessential aerosol applications.[25] Although subject to TSCA investigation, the uses of asbestos were restricted under the Clean Air Act; and tris(2,3-dibromopropyl)phosphate (Tris), the flame-retardant chemical used in children's nightwear, was controlled by action of the CPSC. Reporting requirements for Tris and polybrominated biphenyls (PBBs) have been established pursuant to TSCA[26] and have been proposed for asbestos.[27]

The major use of TSCA, so far, has been the ban on the manufacture, processing, distribution, *or use* of the group of chemical substances known as PCBs, which have been found to be toxic to humans and wildlife and to be persistent in the environment, where they accumulate in the food chain.

PCBs

TSCA specifically covered PCBs and instituted a ban on the manufacture, processing, distribution in commerce, or use of PCBs within a year after the act became effective. TSCA provided, however, for the possible exemption of PCBs used in a "totally enclosed manner."[28] The EPA's regulations instituting the ban on PCBs provided two major exemptions. PCBs were identified, for the purpose of the ban, as PCBs in concentrations greater than 50 parts per million, thus permitting manufacture, processing, distribution in commerce, and use of PCBs in concentrations below 50 ppm.[29] Also, the ban did not apply to PCBs used in a totally enclosed manner, which was considered by the regulations to include all intact, nonleaking, electrical capacitors, electromagnets, and transformers not used in railroad locomotives.[30] Transformers and capacitors containing PCBs are in wide use throughout the electric utility industry and in manufacturing plants; sudden cessation of their use would cause substantial problems. The EPA did propose regulations to prohibit the use or storage of large PCB capacitors, the PCB transformers, and electromagnets at agricultural chemical facilities, but these regulations were never enacted.[31]

The exemptions, however, were found by the United States Court of Appeals for the District of Columbia Circuit to be unsupported by the rule-making record. On October 30, 1980, the court remanded these parts of the regulations to EPA.[32]

The court's mandate would have had the effect of making the continued use of PCB capacitors, electromagnets, and transformers a violation of TSCA and subject to possible EPA enforcement action or citizen suits, but the portion of the mandate addressing the definition of "totally enclosed" was stayed by the court on February 21, 1981, in response to a joint petition of the parties involved.

During the stay, existing PCB regulations are to remain in effect, with the additional requirement that an "interim measures program" of inspection and maintenance be undertaken by PCB transformer owners and users.[33] This program went into effect May 11, 1981. The interim measures program provides that

1. Transformers containing levels of PCBs in excess of 50 ppm that pose an exposure risk to food and feed products (nonretail) must be inspected for leaks once every week.

2. Transformers in other locations containing levels of PCBs equal to or greater than 500 ppm must be inspected every 3 months.

3. Any "moderate leak" must be repaired and cleaned or the transformer replaced within 2 days of observance. Moderate leaks posing an exposure risk to food and feed products must be reported to the appropriate EPA regional office within 5 days from the date the leak is observed. (All leaks are violations of present regulations.)

4. A log must be maintained, as follows: each transformer location, date inspected, name of inspector, leaks observed, and description of all servicing performed.

For transformers near food and feed processing, the first inspection was to be performed before May 18, 1981, and other subject transformers were to be inspected by August 10, 1981. Capacitors, electromagnets, and PCB items containing less than a 50-ppm concentration of PCBs are not subject to the interim measures program during the court stay.

The EPA was required by the court to promulgate a new rule on the use of PCBs in totally enclosed electrical equipment by August 7, 1982. Proposed changes were published in the April 22, 1982, *Federal Register*, and comments were solicited.[34] Among other changes, the proposed regulations would phase out the use of large PCB capacitors over a 10-year period and expand the interim measures program to include inspections of such capacitors during the interim. The inspections of transformers would continue as described above, unless the transformers are contained in a diked area, in which case the inspection would be required annually instead of quarterly.

On April 13, 1981, the court issued an additional order which stayed for 18 months the remand of the regulation that exempted from the ban fluids containing PCBs in concentrations of less than 50 ppm. That order required EPA to conduct investigations relating to the need to control such concentrations and to report to the court within 11 months regarding plans for further action.[35] Additional regulations regarding PCBs in concentrations of less than 50 ppm have not been proposed to date.

Therefore, with the addition of a PCB interim measures program, the regulations at 40 CFR part 761 for PCBs presently remain in effect, and those regarding totally enclosed uses are proposed to continue in basically the same form. These rules not only prohibit the continued use of PCB fluids with concentrations of over 50 ppm except in a totally enclosed manner but also require marking of all PCB items and PCB storage areas to clearly identify the danger. Records must be kept on the disposition of PCB items. PCB items stored for disposal must be located in an impervious, diked area of sufficient volume to completely retain the PCB fluid if a leak occurs. Disposal of PCB fluid is prohibited except in an incinerator or boiler approved by the EPA for such liquids. Disposal of PCB transformers, large capacitors, or other PCB articles must be carried out in an incinerator or a landfill approved by EPA. Hydraulic machines containing PCBs must be drained of the liquid prior to normal disposal.

When these regulations concerning disposal were promulgated in 1979, no incinerators or landfills were approved for PCB disposal, thus necessitating long-term storage in diked areas. The first two commercial incinerators were approved by EPA on an interim basis in February 1981. Eight landfills have now been approved. Also, methods for chemical destruction of the PCB molecule have been developed by several companies, and limited interim approval has been granted by the EPA on a regional basis.

A manual for enforcement of the PCB rules, issued to the EPA regional offices in the spring of 1981, places the primary focus on inspection of railroads, the metals industry, the chemical industry, and utilities. Through a review of records and spot checks of transformers and capacitors, EPA inspectors will seek to detect violations of PCB regulations regarding labeling, storage, record keeping, and disposal. They will give the highest priority to disposal violations.

ENFORCEMENT

Entry and inspection pursuant to TSCA are similar to those under other environmental laws. TSCA authorizes the EPA to inspect at reasonable times any facility where chemical substances or mixtures are manufactured, processed, stored, or held prior to or subsequent to distribution in commerce, including transportation. Such inspections are limited to seeking information bearing on compliance with TSCA. The EPA may, by subpoena, require testimony and production of documents.[36]

The EPA may commence an action in United States district court to seize imminently hazardous chemicals, substances, or mixtures or articles containing them or to seek temporary or permanent relief as may be necessary to protect health or the environment from unreasonable risks. Such relief may include public notice and recall.[37] Any chemical substances or mixtures produced or distributed in violation of TSCA or of a rule or order promulgated pursuant thereto is also potentially subject to seizure.[38]

Civil and Criminal Penalties

The following violations are subject to civil and criminal penalties:

1. A violation of the EPA requirements to provide pertinent data or to test chemicals which may present an unreasonable risk
2. Failure to notify the EPA 90 days prior to manufacture or processing of a chemical substance or to obey a subsequent rule
3. The distribution in commerce or disposal of chemicals known to be produced in violation of TSCA rules or of an imminent-hazard order
4. Failure to establish or maintain records required by TSCA or a rule promulgated thereunder
5. Failure to submit any reports, notices, or other required information
6. Failure to permit entry and inspection[39]

EPA can assess civil penalties up to $25,000 per day of violation, with the amount depending on such factors as the gravity of the situation, the financial means of the violator, and the prior history of violations. Upon petition, an appeals court with jurisdiction may review such orders.[40]

Criminal convictions for knowingly or willfully violating TSCA may result in fines up to $25,000 per day and/or 1 year imprisonment in addition to or in lieu of any civil penalty.[41]

Enforcement Actions

As one would expect from the limited regulatory actions to date under TSCA, enforcement has focused primarily upon violations of the PCB ban and the related requirements regarding labeling, record keeping, storage, and disposal. Inspections conducted in 1979 indicated that over one-third of those subject to the PCB rules were in violation. The first civil penalty was imposed in 1978 against the General Electric Company of Waterford, New York, for illegally incinerating PCBs after the PCB regulations became effective. As of May 1, 1981, over $435,000 in civil penalties has been collected for violations of the PCB rules.

A criminal conviction under TSCA was obtained for the illegal dumping of thousands of gallons of transformer oil contaminated with PCBs along a North Carolina highway in the summer of 1978. Robert J. Burns and his sons, Timothy and Randall, owners and operators of a trucking firm, were involved in dumping the oil. The oil had been drained from transformers at the Ward Transformer Company, Inc., a North

Carolina company engaged in the business of buying, selling, and rebuilding used electrical transformers. The three Burns men pleaded guilty, and Robert Burns was sentenced to 18 months in prison and 5 years on probation, while his two sons received 5 years of probation. The president of Ward was convicted on eight charges of violating TSCA, sentenced to 2½ years in prison and 5 years on probation, and fined $200,000.[42] North Carolina is seeking $12.5 million for cleanup costs and punitive damages from the guilty persons.

These same persons are defendants in another suit involving PCB contamination. In this civil suit, oil contaminated with PCBs was allegedly shipped from the Ward Transformer Company by Robert J. Burns to Pennsylvania, where the oil was stored in a warehouse. The PCBs allegedly contaminated soil outside the warehouse and migrated into groundwater. The government included several statutes in its suit: injunctive relief was based on TSCA and on the Resource Conservation and Recovery Act (RCRA), and recovery of cleanup costs was sought under section 311 of the Clean Water Act (CWA) and under TSCA.

On April 14, 1981, the court ruled on several motions and established that RCRA could not be used to secure injunctive relief from PCB contamination, since the PCB rules promulgated under TSCA are comprehensive, and that the CWA was the government's exclusive means of recovering cleanup costs.[43]

Another issue, whether the Ward president and his son are subject to liability under the CWA as owners or operators of an onshore facility, remains as a factual issue to be settled at trial. The government claims that the Wards' involvement with Burns amounted to a joint venture.

Another enforcement action for PCB contamination relied only on the CWA and RCRA.[44] In settlement of this case, a consent decree established that the company responsible for disposing of PCBs in a municipal landfill (that contaminated a creek) would contribute to a fund for cleanup.

A case filed April 6, 1981 (just prior to the decision making TSCA the exclusive criterion in PCB enforcement), charged a company with an RCRA violation for improper and unsafe storage of PCBs at its storage and disposal facility.[45] PCBs were alleged to have leaked from transformers and capacitors onto the bank of a nearby river.

Other cases could be mentioned but would be repetitive of the TSCA problems of PCB contamination and the EPA's actions to force cleanup.

Citizen Suits and Petitions

Any person, including an environmental group, may commence a civil action to restrain TSCA violations or to compel the EPA to perform a nondiscretionary duty. Citizens also have the right to sue under common law to seek enforcement or any other relief.[46]

Also, any person may petition the EPA to initiate a proceeding for issuance, amendment, or repeal of a rule, setting forth the pertinent facts. The EPA must grant or deny such a petition within 90 days. If the petition is denied, the petitioner may commence a civil action to compel the initiation of rule-making proceedings. The court may award costs for the court action if deemed appropriate.[47]

Employees are protected against discriminatory actions taken by their companies because of their involvement in proceedings, enforcement actions, or suits.[48]

RELATIONSHIP TO STATE LAWS

If testing is prescribed by an EPA rule pursuant to TSCA, any duplicative testing required by a state or locality is preempted. TSCA's rules (other than disposal rules) also preempt state and local laws unless they are identical, are adopted under the authority of another federal law, or are prohibitions of additional uses.[49] In a recent suit, the court ruled that a city's ordinance regulating PCB disposal was not preempted, since it was promulgated pursuant to the CWA.[50]

States may not be delegated authority to administer TSCA in lieu of EPA but may be given grants to establish and operate complementary programs to prevent or eliminate unreasonable risks associated with chemical substances and mixtures.[51]

COMPONENTS OF AN ENVIRONMENTAL AUDIT FOR COMPLIANCE WITH TSCA

Although TSCA is aimed at controlling the chemical industry, many other industries, particularly the railroads and utilities, are affected by TSCA's regulations regarding PCBs. As mentioned above, PCB fluids are widely distributed as hydraulic oils and as part of transformers and capacitors, serving as coolants and electrical insulators.

An environmental audit should analyze samples of such fluids for the presence of these chemicals, and if found, compliance with the PCB regulations at 40 C.F.R. part 761 should be assured. For transformers containing PCBs (and large capacitors if the proposed regulations are promulgated), regular inspections must be performed as required by the interim measures program.

The chemical industry must be thoroughly familiar with the total

TSCA program: reporting substantial chemical risks to EPA, filing pre-manufacture (or import) notices, and testing and maintaining records. Any importer should be aware that a new chemical substance imported as part of an article is also subject to TSCA's premanufacture-notice procedures. For companies involved in the manufacture or importation of chemicals, evaluation for compliance with TSCA should become an integral part of routine operations.

1. 15 U.S.C. §§ 2601–2629 (1976); Pub. L. 94-469, Oct. 11, 1976, effective date Jan. 1, 1977.

2. "Processing" means the preparation of a chemical substance or mixture for distribution in commerce, including incorporation as part of an article. 15 U.S.C. § 2602(10).

3. 43 Fed. Reg. 11110 (Mar. 16, 1978).

4. 15 U.S.C. § 2607(c) (1976).

5. 15 U.S.C. § 2604 (1976).

6. 44 Fed. Reg. 2242 (Jan. 10, 1979), 44 Fed. Reg. 28564 (May 15, 1979), 44 Fed. Reg. 59764 (Oct. 16, 1979), 45 Fed. Reg. 74378 (Nov. 7, 1980).

7. *See* 44 Fed. Reg. 2283 (Jan. 10, 1979) and 44 Fed. Reg. 59764 (Oct. 16, 1979).

8. 15 U.S.C. § 2604(c) (1976).

9. 15 U.S.C. § 2605(c)(2) (1976). *See* 40 C.F.R. pt. 750 (1981) for rule-making procedures.

10. 15 U.S.C. § 2604(f) (1976).

11. 15 U.S.C. § 2604(e) (1976).

12. 15 U.S.C. § 2604(g) (1976).

13. 15 U.S.C. § 2607(b) (1976).

14. 40 C.F.R. pt. 710 (1981).

15. 43 Fed. Reg. 32222 (July 25, 1978).

16. 15 U.S.C. § 2604(a)(2) (1976).

17. 15 U.S.C. § 2608 (1976).

18. 15 U.S.C. § 2602(2) (1976).

19. 15 U.S.C. § 2603(e) (1976).

20. *See* 47 Fed. Reg. 5456 (Feb. 5, 1982).

21. 46 Fed. Reg. 30300 (June 5, 1981).

22. 15 U.S.C. § 2603(b)(3)(B) (1976).

23. *Natural Resources Defense Council v. EPA,* Case No. 79-2411 (S.D.N.Y. Jan. 9, 1981); 11 Envtl. L. Rep. (Envtl. L. Inst.) 20202.

24. 46 Fed. Reg. 53775 (Oct. 30, 1981); 46 Fed. Reg. 55004 (Nov. 5, 1981).

25. 40 C.F.R. pt. 762 (1981).

26. *See* 40 C.F.R. pt. 704 subpart E (1981).

27. 46 Fed. Reg. 8200 (Jan. 26, 1981).

28. 15 U.S.C. § 2605(e)(2) (1976).

29. 40 C.F.R. § 761.1(b) (1981).

30. 40 C.F.R. § 761.30 (1981). Also, eleven non-totally enclosed uses were allowed to continue under certain restrictions provided at 40 C.F.R. §761.31 (1981). On May 6, 1982, the *Federal Register* recodified these sections at 40 C.F.R. § 761.20 and § 761.30, respectively (*see* 47 Fed. Reg. 19526).

31. 45 Fed. Reg. 30989 (May 9, 1980).

32. *Environmental Defense Fund Inc. v. EPA*, 636 F.2d 1267 (D.C.Cir. 1980).

33. 46 Fed. Reg. 16090 (Mar. 10, 1981).

34. 47 Fed. Reg. 17426 (Apr. 22, 1982).

35. 46 Fed. Reg. 27614 (May 20, 1981).

36. 15 U.S.C. § 2610 (1976).

37. 15 U.S.C. § 2606 (1976).

38. 15 U.S.C. § 2616 (1976).

39. 15 U.S.C. § 2614 (1976).

40. 15 U.S.C. § 2615(a) (1976).

41. U.S.C. § 2615(b) (1976).

42. *United States v. Ward*, Case No. 79-4-CR-5 (E.D.N.C. May 22, 1981); *aff'd*, Case No. 81-5162 (4th Cir. Feb. 19, 1982).

43. *United States v. Burns*, 512 F. Supp. 916 (W.D. Pa. 1981).

44. *United States v. Duracell International, Inc.*, Case No. 80-1017 (M.D. Tn. Mar. 10, 1982).

45. *United States v. Lehigh Electric & Engineering Co.*, Case No. 81-0460 (M.D. Pa. filed Apr. 6, 1981.

46. 15 U.S.C. § 2619 (1976).

47. 15 U.S.C. § 2620 (1976).

48. 15 U.S.C. § 2622 (1976).

49. 15 U.S.C. § 2617 (1976).

50. *SED, Inc. v. City of Dayton*, 519 F. Supp. 979 (S.D. Ohio 1981).

51. 15 U.S.C. § 2627 (1976).

Resource Conservation and Recovery Act

James A. Rogers
Mitchell H. Bernstein
Skadden, Arps, Slate, Meagher & Flom

I n 1976, Congress "closed the loop" in environmental law by enacting the Resource Conservation and Recovery Act (RCRA);[1] under it the federal government was authorized to establish, for the first time, a comprehensive program for the cradle-to-grave management of hazardous waste. Prior federal laws had restricted discharges to the air and water; RCRA to a large extent was needed to address the disposition of wastes generated in complying with these earlier laws. Although the permit programs under the Clean Air Act may be close competitors, RCRA is probably the most complicated of the federal environmental regulatory programs.

Subtitle C of RCRA required the United States Environmental Protection Agency (EPA) to define "hazardous" wastes and called for standards applicable to generators[2] and transporters[3] of hazardous waste, as well as standards requiring owners or operators of facilities which treat, store, or dispose of hazardous waste to obtain permits for those activities.[4] Individual states with hazardous-waste programs that are equivalent to the federal program may be authorized to administer and enforce those programs (including the issuance and enforcement of hazardous-waste permits) in lieu of the federal program.[5]

This relatively new body of law has enormous teeth. RCRA grants broad enforcement powers to EPA, which may conduct on-site inspections of facilities where hazardous wastes are *or have been* generated, stored, treated, or disposed of (or from which they have been transported;[6] order sampling of wastes;[7] require the maintenance of records[8] and the furnishing of information relating to such wastes;[9] and issue compliance orders to remedy violations of Subtitle C.[10] Under provisions added by Congress in 1980, EPA may issue imminent-hazard orders to protect public health and the environment;[11] it may also issue orders which require the owner or operator of a hazardous-waste treatment, storage, or disposal facility to conduct such monitoring, testing, analysis, and reporting as may be necessary to ascertain the nature and extent of potential hazards.[12]

There are stiff civil penalties for violations of the requirements of Subtitle C,[13] as well as for violations of the compliance orders,[14] imminent-hazard orders,[15] and monitoring, analysis, and testing orders[16] which have been mentioned. There are also criminal penalties for knowing violations of permit, record-keeping, and other regulatory requirements,[17] and recent amendments to the statute create the felony offense of "knowing endangerment" of human life in connection with the transportation, treatment, storage, or disposal of hazardous waste.[18] Penalties include imprisonment for up to 5 years and fines as high as $250,000 for individuals and $1 million for organizations.

Perhaps more than any other federal environmental program, the RCRA hazardous-waste system is amenable to environmental auditing. Indeed, unless the corporate environmental and legal staff have the resources to stay on top of a rapidly changing field, it may be necessary to employ an experienced environmental auditing team if management is to determine legal exposure under the federal and state RCRA regulations. (An individual facility may be subject to both systems during the transition from federal to complete state authority.)

EPA'S REGULATIONS: OVERVIEW

The massive regulations carrying out RCRA Subtitle C are set out in 40 C.F.R. parts 260 through 265. The procedural system covering the RCRA permit program is found at 40 C.F.R. parts 124, 270, and 271.

Part 260 covers matters of general applicability, includes a comprehensive glossary of definitions, and establishes procedures for rulemaking petitions. Part 261, the basic building block of the regulatory program, establishes the criteria for identifying or listing hazardous wastes.

The first step in wending one's way through RCRA is to determine whether the material in question is a solid waste—that is, whether it is garbage, refuse, or sludge or other waste material which has essentially outlived its usefulness and which is, may be, or will be discarded.[19] Even determining what material is "in question" may not be easy, because some substances, such as excess solvents flushed down floor drains, may not be thought of as wastes by some people (although they *are* wastes within the meaning of RCRA).

There are, of course, certain specific exclusions from the definition of solid waste, including domestic sewage; any mixture of domestic sewage and other wastes that passes through a sewer system to a publicly owned treatment works for treatment; industrial wastewater discharges that are point source discharges subject to regulation under section 402 of the Clean Water Act; irrigation return flows; and source, special nuclear, or by-product material as defined by the Atomic Energy Act of 1954 as amended.[20]

Once it is established that a material is a solid waste, there are two ways in which it can be designated a hazardous waste: it can exhibit one of four characteristics[21] (ignitability,[22] corrosiveness,[23] reactivity,[24] or EP toxicity[25]) or it can be specifically listed in one of three lists[26] (hazardous wastes from nonspecific sources,[27] hazardous wastes from specific sources,[28] and *discarded* commercial products or manufacturing chemical intermediates and their off-specification species[29]). Again, there are certain broad exclusions from the definition of hazardous waste, including solid wastes associated with the exploration, development, or production of crude oil, natural gas, or geothermal energy and solid wastes from the extraction, beneficiation, and processing of ores and minerals.[30] The regulations (in part 260) also establish a mechanism for delisting a listed hazardous waste at a particular facility[31] because, although the waste may fall within a generic description, it may have properties or a composition substantially different from the wastes examined by the agency in creating the list.

Other provisions of part 261 expand the universe of materials which are considered to be hazardous waste. For example, the regulations provide that, with certain exceptions and limitations, any mixture of solid waste and a listed hazardous waste is also a hazardous waste.[32] They also provide that a hazardous waste will remain such until it is delisted or ceases to exhibit its hazardous-waste characteristic (as the case may be),[33] and that any solid waste generated from the treatment, storage, or disposal of a hazardous waste is also to be considered a hazardous waste.[34]

Even though a material may be deemed a hazardous waste, it may be subject to standards less rigorous than those that apply to other hazardous wastes. For example, the hazardous waste generated by a "small-quantity generator" essentially is not subject to regulation as long as the generator complies with substantially less burdensome management practices.[35] Similarly, if a hazardous waste is to be beneficially used or

reused or legitimately recycled, it is not currently subject to regulation—
unless it is a sludge or a listed hazardous waste (or contains a listed
hazardous waste), in which case it will be subject to regulation only
during transportation or storage *prior* to use, reuse, recycling, or reclamation.[36] (These summaries omit many exceptions and qualifications.
To further complicate matters, many key definitions and exclusions may
be significantly modified as the result of litigation.[36a] RCRA is a complex
world requiring extended study for complete understanding.)

Parts 262 and 263 set out the requirements applicable to generators
and transporters of hazardous waste. The principal feature of these
regulations is the requirement that a manifest—initiated by the generator and signed by the transporter—accompany the hazardous waste to
its destination at a permitted treatment, storage, or disposal facility
(TSDF).[37] The regulations also require the hazardous waste to be pack-
aged in accordance with applicable Department of Transportation regulations and to be properly marked prior to being transported off site.[38]

The generator regulations recognize that as a practical matter most
generators will store hazardous waste prior to shipment. Accordingly,
the regulations establish a 90-day grace period during which a generator
may, without a storage permit, accumulate waste on site prior to shipment to a permitted TSDF.[39] However, during this 90-day period the
generator must comply with certain management practices.

Under RCRA, any facility which treats, stores, or disposes of hazardous waste must obtain a permit from EPA or an authorized state
agency.[40] Part 264 establishes minimum national standards for acceptable management of hazardous waste, applicable to all TSDFs that obtain permits. The comprehensive regulatory scheme establishes general
facility standards (including requirements for identification numbers,
personnel training, facility security, and routine inspections);[41] standards governing preparedness and prevention (including requirements
for communication systems and fire-control equipment);[42] standards
governing contingency plans and emergency procedures;[43] standards
governing the use of the manifest system and establishing record-
keeping and reporting requirements;[44] standards governing the closure
of hazardous-waste-management facilities and postclosure care and
monitoring of hazardous-waste-disposal facilities;[45] and standards governing financial requirements for hazardous-waste-management facilities, including financial assurances concerning facility closure and postclosure and liability coverage for third-party property damage and
bodily injury.[46]

In addition, standards have been or will be established governing the
design, performance, and/or operation of specific categories of hazardous-waste-management facilities—including containers, tanks, incin-

erators, waste piles, surface impoundments, landfills, land treatment, and other treatment facilities.[47]

Eventually, every hazardous-waste-management facility, regardless of its age or operating history, must have a final RCRA permit issued under these part 264 "permitting" standards. Congress recognized, however, that the administrative task of issuing permits to every hazardous-waste-management facility would consume many years. Accordingly, the statute grants interim status to those facilities which (1) were in existence on November 19, 1980; (2) complied with certain notification requirements; and (3) applied for a final RCRA permit.[48] Until its application is finally granted or denied at the administrative level, an interim status facility is treated as if it had been issued a final permit.[49] These facilities are subject to interim status standards set out in 40 C.F.R. part 265. Although many of the requirements are the same as those set out in part 264, the two systems differ in one major respect—the interim status standards do not generally include *design* requirements. (For example, most interim status landfills and surface impoundments are not required to have liners or leachate detection, collection, and removal systems.) EPA has issued several important administrative rulings concerning eligibility for interim status;[50] operational changes during interim status are governed by EPA's permit regulations.[51]

STATE RCRA PROGRAMS

RCRA provides that individual states may be authorized to administer and enforce state hazardous-waste programs, consistent with the basic framework of other major federal environmental statutes, in lieu of the federal administration of RCRA Subtitle C.[52] States with authorized programs are responsible, among other things, for the issuance and enforcement of all final hazardous-waste permits.

To receive final authorization from the EPA administrator, a state program must be equivalent to the federal program, must be consistent with both the federal program and other applicable state programs, and must provide adequate enforcement of applicable requirements.[53] The administrator may withdraw authorization and reestablish the federal program if it is determined, following a public hearing, that the state is not administering or enforcing the program in accordance with these requirements.[54]

Congress recognized that the process of authorizing state programs would be a lengthy one. Accordingly, the statute establishes a transition period during which states with existing state hazardous-waste programs may obtain interim authorization to carry out such programs in lieu of the federal program.[55] (As will be seen, however, although the concept is laudable, it imposes on the regulated community and the states a confusing, shifting regulatory framework.) The standard for obtaining this temporary authorization is less stringent than the standard for final authorization; for the temporary authorization a state need only show that its existing state program is substantially equivalent to the federal program.[56]

Because EPA encountered great difficulty in promulgating final part 264 permitting standards for several categories of hazardous-waste facilities, it established complicated procedures to allow the states to obtain interim authorization in phases. Phase 1 interim authorization allows a state to run a program corresponding to that portion of the federal program which covers identification and listing of hazardous wastes (part 261), generators (part 262), transporters (part 263), and interim status standards (part 265).[57] Phase 2 interim authorization allows a state to administer a program for issuing final RCRA permits, corresponding to the federal program under part 264.[58] However, phase 2 interim authorization is further broken down into several components, each of which covers specific categories of hazardous-waste facilities; interim authorization for any component of phase 2 allows a state to issue final RCRA permits for the types of facilities included in that component.[59]

The last component of phase 2 of interim authorization is finally in place; *all* of the part 264 final permitting standards have been established; and states are now allowed to apply for final authorizations.[60] Moreover, all interim authorizations will lapse on January 26, 1985, after which EPA will again administer the federal program in any state that has not received final authorization.[61]

ENFORCEMENT PROVISIONS

Civil Penalties

Congress established several tough civil enforcement mechanisms in Subtitle C. It established civil penalties of up to $25,000 for *each* violation of the RCRA requirements;[62] it directed that *each day* of a violation shall be considered to constitute a separate offense for purposes of assessing a civil penalty.[63] Moreover, Congress expressly provided that federal enforcement authority is not extinguished when a state is granted interim or final authorization to carry out its own hazardous-waste program in lieu of the federal program: the EPA administrator need only give notice to the state in which the violation has occurred prior to initiating a federal enforcement action.[64] Thus, a state running the RCRA program may prosecute under both state and federal laws for the same act.

Congress also provided the administrator (as well as representatives of states with authorized hazardous-waste programs) with broad inspection authority in connection with both the enforcement of Subtitle C and the development of implementing regulations. Under the statute, any person who generates, stores, treats, transports, disposes of, or *otherwise handles or has handled hazardous waste* must, upon request, furnish information relating to such wastes and must permit duly designated enforcement personnel to have access to and to copy all records relating to such wastes.[65] Enforcement personnel are also authorized to enter and inspect, at reasonable times, any place where hazardous wastes are or have been generated, stored, treated, or disposed of or from which they have been transported and to obtain samples of such wastes and of any containers for such wastes.[66] EPA interprets the statute to allow the government to order a party managing hazardous waste to furnish information relating to the waste even if it is not contained in preexisting documents.

Upon the receipt of information that any person is in violation of any requirement of Subtitle C, the EPA administrator has two options: commencement of a civil action in federal district court seeking appropriate relief (which may include a temporary or permanent injunction in addition to a $25,000 civil penalty per day per violation) or issuance of a compliance order requiring corrective action.[67] The latter must state with reasonable specificity the nature of the violation and must specify a time for compliance; it may also assess a reasonable penalty, taking into account the seriousness of the violation and any good-faith efforts to comply, and may include a suspension or revocation of a hazardous-waste permit.[68] An order becomes final unless a hearing is requested within 30 days after its service,[69] and if corrective action is not taken within the time specified in the order, the violator is liable for an additional civil penalty of up to $25,000 for each day of continued noncompliance.[70] In addition, the administrator may suspend or revoke any hazardous-waste permit issued to the violator by the administrator *or* issued by an authorized state program.[71]

The administrator is also authorized to issue two other types of orders, violations of which may result in civil penalties or fines of up to $5000 per day. First, if the administrator determines that the presence or release of any hazardous waste at a site where it is or has been stored, treated, or disposed of may present a substantial hazard to human health or the environment, an order may be issued requiring the owner or operator of the site (or, in certain circumstances, the most recent previous owner or operator) to conduct such monitoring, testing, analysis, and reporting as the administrator deems reasonable to ascertain the nature and extent of such hazard.[72]

Second, in circumstances where the administrator determines that the handling, storage, treatment, transportation, or disposal of any solid waste or hazardous waste may present an imminent and substantial endangerment to health or the environment, EPA may issue such orders as may be necessary to protect public health and the environment.[73] In these circumstances the administrator may also bring suit on behalf of the United States in federal district court to immediately restrain any person contributing to such handling, storage, treatment, transportation, or disposal or to take such other action as may be necessary.[74]

Criminal Penalties

In addition to establishing civil penalties for noncompliance with Subtitle C requirements, Congress also enacted unprecedented (at least for environmental laws) criminal provisions in Subtitle C. In particular, Congress directed that a person will be subject to criminal penalties who knowingly transports hazardous waste to a facility which does not have a final RCRA permit (or interim status);[75] knowingly treats, stores, or disposes of any hazardous waste either without a final RCRA permit or in knowing violation of a material condition or requirement of the permit;[76] knowingly makes a false material statement or representation in any document or written material used for purposes of compliance with Subtitle C;[77] or knowingly generates, stores, treats, transports, disposes of, or otherwise handles any hazardous waste *and* knowingly destroys, alters, or conceals any record required *by regulation* to be maintained.[78]

Upon conviction of either of the first two crimes, a violator may be punished by a fine of $50,000 for each day of violation or imprisonment for 2 years or both;[79] upon conviction of either of the latter two crimes, a violator may be punished by a fine of $25,000 for each day of violation, or imprisonment for 1 year or both.[80] Repeated convictions of these latter two crimes, however, are punishable by fines of $50,000 per day for each day of violation or imprisonment for 2 years or both.[81]

In response to growing concern about the haphazard management of hazardous waste and the seeming lack of concern about its human health consequences, Congress in 1980 also created the crime of "knowing endangerment."[82] In short, a person who commits one of the first two crimes described above *or* knowingly manages a hazardous waste in violation of interim status standards *and* knows at that time "that he thereby places another person in imminent danger of death or serious bodily injury" *and* whose conduct in the circumstances manifests either "an unjustified and inexcusable disregard for human life," or "an extreme indifference for human life" will, upon conviction, be subject to a fine of $250,000 or imprisonment for 2 years or both. (In cases of "extreme indifference for human life," the maximum term of imprisonment is 5 years.) If the defendant is an organization, the maximum fine upon conviction is $1 million.

Because the crime of "knowing endangerment" is unique, Congress directed the courts to determine defenses according to the principles of common law and in light of the courts' reason and experience, especially with respect to the concepts of justification and excuse.[83] Congress also included special rules concerning determinations about "knowing" conduct[84] but made one point very clear—studied ignorance is not a defense, and circumstantial evidence, *including evidence that a defendant took affirmative steps to shield himself from relevant information,* may be used to prove possession of actual knowledge.[85] In short, Congress has sent out a simple but compelling message to the hazardous-waste community—management practices which jeopardize human life and limb will no longer be tolerated.

1. Strictly speaking, the Resource Conservation and Recovery Act of 1976, Pub. L. No. 94-580, 90 Stat. 2795 *et seq.*, amended the Solid Waste Disposal Act (which had been codified at 42 U.S.C. § 3251 *et seq.*). However, we here follow the common practice of referring to the Solid Waste Disposal Act, as amended (and now codified at 42 U.S.C. § 6901 *et seq.*) as the Resource Conservation and Recovery Act.

2. RCRA § 3002, 42 U.S.C. § 6922.

3. RCRA § 3003, 42 U.S.C. § 6923.

4. RCRA §§ 3004 and 3005, 42 U.S.C. §§ 6924 and 6925.

5. RCRA § 3006, 42 U.S.C. § 6926.

6. RCRA § 3007, 42 U.S.C. § 6927.

7. Ibid.

8. RCRA §§ 3002, 3003, and 3004, 42 U.S.C. §§ 6922, 6923, 6924.

9. RCRA § 3007, 42 U.S.C. § 6927.

10. RCRA § 3008, 42 U.S.C. § 6928.

11. RCRA § 7003, 42 U.S.C. § 6973.

12. RCRA § 3013, 42 U.S.C. § 6934.

13. RCRA § 3008, 42 U.S.C. § 6928.

14. Ibid.

15. RCRA § 7003, 42 U.S.C. § 6973.

16. RCRA § 3013, 42 U.S.C. § 6934.

17. RCRA § 3008, 42 U.S.C. § 6928.

18. Ibid.

19. 40 C.F.R. § 261.2 (1983).

20.   40 C.F.R. § 261.4(a) (1983).

21.   40 C.F.R. §§ 261.3 and 261.20 (1983).

22.   40 C.F.R. § 261.21 (1983).

23.   40 C.F.R. § 261.22 (1983).

24.   40 C.F.R. § 261.23 (1983).

25.   40 C.F.R. § 261.24 (1983).

26.   40 C.F.R. §§ 261.3 and 261.30 (1983).

27.   40 C.F.R. § 261.31 (1983).

28.   40 C.F.R. § 261.32 (1983).

29.   40 C.F.R. § 261.33 (1983).

30.   40 C.F.R. § 261.4(b) (1983).

31.   40 C.F.R. §§ 261.20 and 260.22 (1983).

32.   40 C.F.R. § 261.3(a) (1983).

33.   40 C.F.R. §§ 261.3(c) and 261.3(d) (1983).

34.   40 C.F.R. § 261.3(c) (1983).

35.   40 C.F.R. § 261.5 (1983).

36.   40 C.F.R. § 261.6 (1983).

37.   40 C.F.R. §§ 262.20 through 262.23 and §§ 263.20 through 263.22 (1983).

38.   40 C.F.R. §§ 262.30 through 262.33 (1983).

39.   40 C.F.R. § 262.34 (1983).

40.   RCRA § 3005, 42 U.S.C. § 6925.

41.   40 C.F.R. pt. 264, subpart B (1983).

42.   40 C.F.R. pt. 264, subpart C (1983).

43.   40 C.F.R. pt. 264, subpart D (1983).

44.   40 C.F.R. pt. 264, subpart E (1983).

45.   40 C.F.R. pt. 264, subpart G (1983).

46.   40 C.F.R. pt. 264, subpart H (1983).

47.   40 C.F.R. pt. 264, subparts I through Q (1983).

48.   RCRA § 3005(e), 42 U.S.C. § 6925(e).

49.   Ibid.

50.   45 *Fed. Reg.* 76630–76636 (Nov. 19, 1980); 46 *Fed. Reg.* 2344–2348 (Jan. 9, 1981); 46 *Fed. Reg.* 60446–60448 (Dec. 10, 1981).

51.   40 C.F.R. § 270.72 (1983).

52.   RCRA § 3006, 42 U.S.C. § 6926.

53.   RCRA § 3006(b), 42 U.S.C. § 6926(b).

54.   RCRA § 3006(e), 42 U.S.C. § 6926(e).

55.   RCRA § 3006(c), 42 U.S.C. § 6926(c).

56.   Ibid.

57.   40 C.F.R. § 271.121(b) (1983).

58.   Ibid.

59. 40 C.F.R. § 271.121(c) (1983).

60. See 47 *Fed. Reg.* 32378 *et seq.*, July 26, 1982.

61. Ibid.

62. RCRA § 3008(g), 42 U.S.C. § 6928(g).

63. Ibid.

64. RCRA § 3008(a)(2), 42 U.S.C. § 6928(a)(2).

65. RCRA § 3007(a), 42 U.S.C. § 6927(a).

66. Ibid.

67. RCRA § 3008(a)(1), 42 U.S.C. § 6928(a)(1).

68. RCRA § 3008(c), 42 U.S.C. § 6928(c).

69. RCRA § 3008(b), 42 U.S.C. § 6928(b).

70. RCRA § 3008(a)(3), 42 U.S.C. § 6928(a)(3).

71. Ibid.

72. RCRA § 3013, 42 U.S.C. § 6934.

73. RCRA § 7003, 42 U.S.C. § 6973.

74. Ibid.

75. RCRA § 3008(d)(1), 42 U.S.C. § 6928(d)(1).

76. RCRA § 3008(d)(2), 42 U.S.C. § 6928(d)(2).

77. RCRA § 3008(d)(3), 42 U.S.C. § 6928(d)(3).

78. RCRA § 3008(d)(4), 42 U.S.C. § 6928(d)(4).

79. RCRA § 3008(d), 42 U.S.C. § 6928(d).

80. Ibid.

81. Ibid.

82. RCRA § 3008(e), 42 U.S.C. § 6928(e).

83. RCRA § 3008(f)(4), 42 U.S.C. § 6928(f)(4).

84. RCRA § 3008(f)(1) and (2) 42 U.S.C. § 6928(f)(1) and (2).

85. Ibid.

Superfund

James A. Rogers
Mitchell H. Bernstein
Skadden, Arps, Slate, Meagher & Flom

The latest addition to the federal arsenal of weapons available to fight pollution is the Comprehensive Environmental Response, Compensation, and Liability Act of 1980,[1] widely known as Superfund. Although the popular name of the law implies that the focus of the statute is a reservoir of money, virtually all the provisions of the act that define legal risks are found in portions of the law other than those establishing the revolving fund.

Even though Superfund was signed into law on December 11, 1980, many of its most important provisions remain confusing to lawyers, insurance analysts, and other experts who have studied it extensively. Some of the act's provisions appear to be internally inconsistent; others seem to address problems (such as compensation for personal injuries) that Congress in eleventh-hour debates thought it was dropping from this legislation. Major issues—such as standards of liability for pollution releases, what groups of plaintiffs can avail themselves of the act's tough provisions, and the line between acceptable and unacceptable pollution—were left largely unresolved. The importance of these questions will clearly force the federal courts, and probably the Supreme Court, to answer them and to add some predictability to an enormous area of potential environmental liabilities that is now frighteningly uncharted.

Superfund has been widely characterized both as creating a source of money for cleaning up abandoned hazardous-waste sites and as imposing new liabilities on persons who in good faith entered into arrangements with waste handlers to take away hazardous substances that now are contributing to an environmental problem. This perception is correct as far as it goes. There is no question that orphaned disposal sites were a focus of the legislation, but the act covers far more territory, and the risks inherent in the less publicized sections are just as great.

There are three titles in the act. In terms of appreciating one's legal risks under Superfund, the last two titles—which establish the revolving fund for cleanup of hazardous-substance releases and the fund for waste-site postclosure care (as well as taxes to support these funds), and which set out other miscellaneous provisions—are far less important than the first. Title I is called "Hazardous Substances Releases, Liability, Compensation." It may be useful in attempting to decipher this portion of the statute to think of the legal exposure in terms of (1) requirements to *notify* the government with respect to releases of hazardous substances and locations of wastes and (2) liabilities associated with releases of hazardous substances. There are criminal sanctions for violations of the notification provisions and civil liabilities for releases—although the monetary damages can be so extensive that the distinction may not be meaningful.

Unlike other major federal environmental laws, Superfund does not direct the EPA or the states to issue comprehensive regulations against which conduct can be judged; a plant manager or corporate environmental director cannot simply compare day-to-day plant operations against specific regulatory commands. To determine whether one is subject to enforcement under Superfund, one must ask broader, more ambiguous questions: Have there been or are there now releases of certain substances? Does a situation rise to the level of an environmental problem warranting government intervention? Has one had commercial relationships with parties who are or may be the subject of investigations or proceedings brought under the act? Attempting to answer these questions and to determine exposure under Superfund often will require the assistance of outside experts of several disciplines, because the law is so confusing and because liability often hinges on subtle analyses of underground water and soil contamination.

REPORTING PROVISIONS

Before Superfund was enacted, the only federal law which proved effective in forcing disclosure of sudden releases of pollutants into the environment was section 311 of the Clean Water Act (CWA).[2] But that provision was limited to notification of spills into the "navigable waters of the United States." Congress borrowed the basic section 311 reporting scheme and in section 103 of Superfund expanded coverage to include a wide range of substances and releases from almost every conceivable source to surface water, groundwater, air, land, or subsurface strata.[3]

Like the CWA, Superfund calls for EPA to establish reportable quantities of designated substances; but unlike the former, Superfund's reporting obligations became effective immediately upon enactment and did not depend on the prior promulgation of reportable levels.

The key to understanding section 103(a) of the act is to focus on several carefully chosen words in that paragraph. Any person in charge of a facility (which can be a building, pipe, motor vehicle, landfill, or a site where hazardous substances have "come to be located," among a host of other things) who has knowledge of any release from the facility of a hazardous substance in quantities equal to or greater than certain specified levels must immediately report such release to the National Response Center. (In a proposed regulation, EPA has announced that the quantities should be measured over a 24-hour period, as under the CWA.[4]) A person who fails to report the release immediately may be fined not more than $10,000 or imprisoned for not more than 1 year, or both.

Perhaps in anticipation of the delays in promulgating implementing regulations, Congress provided in section 102 that until EPA issues standards for reportable levels of hazardous substances, the reportable level is 1 pound—except for substances listed under section 311 of the CWA, with respect to which the reportable levels previously established by EPA will be applicable. The agency has proposed reportable quantities for slightly more than half of the substances covered by this provision of the act (and has suggested revisions to the CWA section 311 reportable levels where necessary to make the two regulations consistent).[5]

Identifying a Hazardous Substance

A related problem is the threshold identification of a material as a hazardous substance. The term is defined[6] as broader than (but inclusive of) hazardous *wastes* as defined under the Resource Conservation and Recovery Act (RCRA) but narrower than the terms "pollutant" or "contaminant" used in other parts of the act. It includes 696 substances that are regulated under other federal laws, but explicitly excludes "petroleum, including crude oil or any fraction thereof which is not otherwise specifically listed or designated" under other environmental laws. Because petroleum products are so often involved in some respect in spill incidents or other releases, this appears to be a major exclusion. However, it can be argued that the mere presence of oil in a mixture of substances would not *insulate* a person from an obligation to report if one or more identifiable portions of the mixture (such as polychlorinated biphenyls, or PCBs) were released in greater than the reportable trigger levels applicable to that portion. Moreover, under one legal theory, even oil not containing listed hazardous substances in reportable quantities may trigger the reporting requirements: if oil contains enough contaminants, such as heavy metals, it may exhibit the characteristic of EP toxicity under RCRA and thus be deemed a hazardous substance because it is an RCRA hazardous waste.[7] The line between an exempted petroleum product and a nonexempted mixture of substances—some of which may be petroleum and some of which may be clearly designated as hazardous under other environmental laws—is not a clear one by any means. Because these issues often arise in connection with recurring discharges, it is the type of inquiry that is well suited for environmental auditors.

Identifying a Release

The act's definition of a "release" includes virtually all ways in which a material can enter the environment: spilling, leaking, discharging, escaping, and leaching, among others.[8]

"Federally permitted releases" (also defined in the act itself[9]) do not have to be reported. The apparent purpose of this statutory exemption is to avoid duplicative regulation; if the state or federal environmental agency has considered the relative risks of specific emissions and discharges in light of the detailed commands of federal and state law and has approved them, it makes little sense for them to be reported again as releases under Superfund. Thus Congress exempted from the act's disclosure requirements those emissions and discharges which are in compliance with, or at least subject to, permits issued under other environmental laws. Unfortunately, the act was drafted in such haste and the regulations issued under the other federal laws are often so complex that there is not a close fit in some cases. At the same time, a strict interpretation of the literal language of section 103(a) would require notification of many minor or routine releases of pollutants that, by all objective standards, are environmentally inoffensive. To fill in the interstices in these areas where literal application of Superfund would bring about absurd results, EPA has proposed, as part of its comprehensive Superfund reporting regulations, its intention to issue interpretations of the statute and declarations of enforcement discretion which will smooth the operation of section 103(a).[10]

Even with the EPA proposed interpretations, the application of the reportable release exemption provisions will be complex and uncertain in many situations. One has to assume that a "rule of reason" will prevail in the government's and court's reading of section 103(a) and (b). This is an area where environmental auditors may be helpful, particularly if they have dealt with EPA before with respect to commonsense construction of the Superfund reporting obligations.

Section 103 contains another reporting requirement that will lessen in importance as time passes but that will always deserve at least some acknowledgment by a company attempting to determine environmental compliance. In a nutshell, section 103(c) of Superfund requires notification by June 9, 1981, by any person who owns or operates a facility, or who at the time of disposal owned or operated a facility, or who accepted hazardous wastes for transport and selected a facility at which RCRA hazardous wastes are or have been disposed of, stored, or treated. EPA has published an interpretation of this requirement and a form to be used in notifying EPA.[11]

Section 103(c) thus provides a "snapshot" of the identity of hazardous-waste sites in the United States as of June 9, 1981. In commercial transactions in which the purchaser is acquiring assets, requiring the seller to provide copies of notifications under section 103(c) may be vital if one is not to inherit enormous environmental legal headaches. In that context, however, it is important to realize that there are some often-overlooked exceptions to this requirement. The class of substances covered under section 103(c) is for some reason only the RCRA hazardous wastes; because EPA has chosen to control handling of PCBs only under the Toxic Substances Control Act, those ubiquitous and long-lived pollutants are not covered by the section 103(c) notification requirements.[12] Also, EPA did not require notification with respect to inactive storage and treatment facilities at which there are no longer hazardous wastes or with respect to facilities which do not have interim status or final permits under RCRA because they were excluded from RCRA coverage (such as totally enclosed treatment facilities and generator storage facilities used for short-term accumulation).[13]

There are no civil sanctions for violation of section 103(c), and the criminal sanctions are triggered only if the person in charge of a facility *knowingly* fails to notify. Therefore it is unclear whether a legal obligation to notify arises if, after June 9, 1981, one discovers a site that should have been disclosed if one had been aware of it before that date.

LIABILITY FOR CLEANUP AND DAMAGES ASSOCIATED WITH RELEASES

In addition to the risks associated with failure to notify, Superfund establishes several forms of liability in connection with the release or threat of release of a hazardous substance from a facility or a vessel. Section 104 provides that the federal government may use the fund established by the act to abate environmental problems arising from releases of pollutants. It may then seek recoupment from private parties; section 107 of the act establishes classes of persons who are liable when the United States or a state seeks to recover these incurred cleanup costs. In addition to that avenue of relief, section 106 authorizes the federal government to file an action in federal district court to seek an order requiring parties to abate a danger arising from an actual or threatened release of a hazardous substance. Under this section the government may also issue administrative orders, presumably requiring a wide group of persons connected with a potential environmental problem to take appropriate actions. In the early Superfund cases the parties and courts have had difficulty attempting to parse these provisions, because Congress did not articulate the standards of liability that will apply and did not resolve such issues as whether one of several responsible parties can be held liable for the entire expense of cleanup. It is also unclear whether the extent of private liability is circumscribed by national definitions of cleanup cost-effectiveness that apply to government-financed efforts.

Determining Who Is Liable

Section 107 of the act is the centerpiece of the liability scheme. To appreciate the unprecedented sweep of that provision, one must remember that three of the key definitions—"facility," "release," and "hazardous substance"—have the same broad scope as described in the preceding discussion of the section 103 notification provisions. Section 107 specifies four groups of people who are liable for costs of removal or remedial action and for damages resulting from loss of natural resources incurred as a result of a release or a threatened release of a hazardous substance from a vessel or facility:

1. The owner and operator of the vessel or facility
2. Any person who at the time of disposal owned or operated the facility at which the hazardous substance was disposed of
3. Any person who arranged for disposal or treatment of the hazardous substance or arranged with a transporter for transport for disposal or treatment at the facility now containing the substance, where the facility is owned or operated by another party
4. Any person who accepts or accepted any hazardous substance for transport to the disposal or treatment facility, where the facility was selected by such person

These people have often been said to be "strictly liable" for the costs and damages incurred as a result of responding to the environmental releases. There is nothing in the statute itself, however, which states that strict liability—responsibility for payment if there is any connection to the activities that gave rise to the injury, even in the absence of negligence—is the rule of law under the act. Indeed, section 107(b) establishes a series of defenses to the liability scheme outlined above. However, because those defenses may be difficult to establish, and because Congress said that those are the *only* defenses available to potential defendants, commentators have assumed that the practical result is a form of strict liability.

Section 107(b) sets forth defenses in many respects parallel to the defenses available under section 311 of the CWA. For example, one can be excused from liability by showing that the release or threat of release and the damages resulting therefrom were caused solely by an act of God, an act of war, or an act or omission of a third party. However, Superfund's qualifications to the third-party defense probably render the defense of doubtful use to most persons involved in Superfund cases, especially those involving hazardous-waste sites: the third-party defense is not applicable when the third party is an employee or agent of the defendant or one whose act or omission occurs in connection with a contractual relationship, *direct or indirect,* with the defendant.[14] The government argues that generators of hazardous waste who engaged transportation firms to haul their wastes, or who dealt directly with hazardous-waste disposal site operators, established direct or indirect contractual relationships which make the third-party defense unavailable. Indeed, it is difficult to conceive of many relationships arising out of the handling of the wide range of hazardous substances under Superfund which could not be argued by the government to create, in some respects at least, an indirect relationship with the party who was in control of the facility from which the hazardous substance was released.

Even someone who is able to convince a court that there was no direct or indirect contractual relationship with the third party who is the sole cause of the release must in addition prove the exercise of due care with respect to the hazardous substance of concern and the use of precautions against foreseeable acts or omissions of any such third party and the consequences that could foreseeably result from that person's acts or omissions.[15]

Perhaps of more assistance to the defendant with respect to possible section 107 liability claims are two conditions apparently attached to section 107(a). First, with respect to cleanup costs, it appears that liability is limited to the costs of removal or remedial action actually *incurred.* Second, the removal and remedial costs incurred by the federal and state governments seem to be recoverable only if incurred in a manner not inconsistent with the National Contingency Plan (NCP)[16] established under section 105, which requires that dollars be spent in a cost-effective manner after evaluation of all possible alternatives.

The terms "removal" and "remedial" actions are important in determining potential Superfund liability; they are by no means synonymous. Indeed, these terms describe categories of activities that have different attendant legal consequences under section 104. "Removal" refers to measures that are taken quickly to address environmental hazards; it embraces many activities in the short-term cleanup of released hazardous substances.[17] "Remedial" actions are those "consistent with permanent remedy" and which are taken instead of, or in addition to, removal. Remedial measures may include the construction of confinement trenches and clay covers and the cost of permanent relocation of residents and businesses.[18] There appear to be small areas of overlap between the two terms; for example, both refer to providing alternative water supplies. However, the federal government may not undertake remedial action unless the site in question is on the National Priorities List and the state in which the release occurs has entered into a number of commitments with the federal government, including a cooperative agreement assuring that it will oversee all future removal and remedial actions for the expected life of such actions and pay at least 10 percent of the cost of the remedial action.[19]

Although clearly there are a number of major legal questions associated with the interpretation of section 107, for most observers a simple rule of thumb has developed: at least with respect to damages to natural resources and costs of cleanup work incurred as a result of a release or threat of release, if one generated, transported, or disposed of materials that are now posing an environmental problem at the site in question, one should assume that the government will assert liability.

The Power to Order Private-Party Abatement

The major federal environmental laws all provide that the federal government can take swift response action if there is a threat of imminent and serious danger to human health or the environment. Section 106 of Superfund is, in effect, another of these imminent-hazard response provisions insofar as it authorizes the federal government, as noted above, to proceed to court to secure such relief as may be necessary to abate environmental dangers resulting from hazardous substances. The statute also clearly authorizes the President to issue orders to protect public health and the environment. In addition to running the risk of incurring treble damages under section 107, as discussed below, any person who willfully violates, or fails or refuses to comply with, any order of the President issued under section 106 may be fined not more than $5000 for each day of violation. As acknowledgment that this provision is greatly similar to other imminent-hazard and emergency powers authorized by other federal environmental laws, Congress ordered EPA to publish guidelines for coordinating the use of the various response authorities available to the government.[20]

The cost recovery liability provisions of section 107 are not completely independent of the imminent endangerment powers set out in section 106. Section 107(c)(3) allows the federal government to recover as punitive damages an amount "at least equal to, and not more than" three times the amount of costs incurred by the federal government in a cleanup effort, if a person who is liable for a release or threat of release fails "without sufficient cause" to obey a federal cleanup demand. Lawyers for potentially responsible parties initially were concerned that the thousands of "notice" letters—which the federal government sends to parties to inform them of the government's allegation of ultimate liability for cleanup and to ask for voluntary remedial action—would be deemed to trigger exposure under the treble damage provisions. Recently the government has issued true administrative orders that unmistakably announce the intent to rely on section 107(c)(3) if the recipient does not comply; in light of the marked distinction between these orders and the "notice" letters, it is apparent that the latter do not have the same legal significance.

The intriguing element in the section 107(c)(3) *in terrorem* provision is that it refers to both sections 104 and 106 of Superfund as the basis upon which removal and remedial action orders can be issued by the President and therefore as the basis for later seeking treble damages. Unlike section 106, section 104 does not explicitly provide for the issuance of "orders" in connection with government-initiated cleanup activities. (In early cases the federal government has urged courts to infer from section 107(c)(3) a right to issue administrative orders under section 104, despite the difficulty in doing so in light of the purpose and context of section 104.) However, Section 106 is not clear as to the parties subject to these orders or, in any specific sense, what actions can be demanded of the parties. One court has held that nonnegligent off-site generators of waste can be sued under section 106,[21] but the only other court to rule on the issue has held that such generators are not covered.[22] One basis for the more expansive holding could be that section 107(c)(3), by focusing on persons who are "liable for a release or threat of a release of a hazardous substance," seems to say that the liability provisions of section 107(a) and (b) define the class of persons who run the risk of treble damages and therefore also implicitly defines the class of persons who can be subject to administrative orders and court actions under section 106. (Also, the argument goes, because section 107 does not include negligence as an element of liability, the government need not show negligence in proving a case under section 106.)

As noted above, instead of attempting to force "responsible" parties (again, as set out in section 107) to address an environmental hazard, section 104 authorizes the government itself to take action, consistent with the NCP, to abate the environmental threat. This section provides that the President may take action with respect to *any pollutant or contaminant* which may present an imminent and substantial danger to the public health or welfare. These provisions are among the few in Superfund not rigidly circumscribed by reference to hazardous substances, as defined in section 101(14). However, even though Congress expanded the universe of materials beyond those encompassed in the term "hazardous substance," it did not go so far as to invade the general Superfund exemption for releases of petroleum, including crude oil and any fraction thereof which is not otherwise specifically listed or designated under another statutory section referred to in the definition of hazardous substance.[23] The term "pollutant or contaminant" also does not include natural gas, liquefied natural gas, or synthetic gas of pipeline quality.

Allocating the Burden among Responsible Parties

The first Superfund proceedings brought by the federal government have involved large, abandoned hazardous-waste-disposal and purported "recycling" facilities, usually with scores of corporations having been customers of the now-defunct operations. In the usual case the federal and state governments are seeking total cleanup of surface and groundwater contamination from all the so-called generators, as well as from any transportation companies that may have been involved. In many cases it is impossible to determine the sources of particular substances that are now posing environmental threats. This problem of fingerprinting wastes is particularly acute in the case of common chemical intermediates and solvents, which may have been used by dozens of the customers of the same facility. In these situations the federal government has asserted that each generator is responsible for the entire cleanup cost, at least where the injuries to the environment are indivisible, under the theory of joint and several liability. The lively debate among practitioners as to whether joint and several liability applies in these cases is unlikely to provide reassurance to persons attempting to predict legal exposure, and until Congress or respected courts clear up the issue, the federal government will probably have an effective weapon in its efforts to force individual generators to the bargaining table. If there is joint and several liability, environmental lawyers should take heed of the lessons from the federal antitrust arena: if many defendants in a large case have settled for less than their full pro rata share, a "hardliner" may find itself facing an enormous and disproportionate judgment.

A related question troubling many lawyers representing parties in Superfund cases is whether there is a right of contribution among the defendants in cases brought under section 107. (Such a right would permit a defendant to be reimbursed for any damages paid over and above his judicially—or statutorily—apportioned share and would lessen the risk of being forced to pay enormous sums for cleanup costs that have escalated well beyond initial estimates.) Here again, the statute provides little elucidation, but remarks in the legislative history of Superfund may be read to suggest that courts will be willing to infer a right of contribution if they determine that there is joint and several liability.

Undoubtedly, as is true in any area of the law in which courts are asked to resolve difficult policy questions, the particular facts of the first cases may govern the resolution of the legal questions. For example, if the question of joint and several liability centers on a generator who contributed only small amounts of material to a poorly operated disposal facility, it will be difficult for the court equitably to impose complete liability for damages, including those resulting from releases of many other wastes. It is likely that eventually federal courts will arrive at various apportionment formulas in the litigated Superfund cases. The courts have shown an ability to fashion creative equitable rules in other areas of the law, and, particularly in light of Superfund's legislative history inviting reference to "evolving principles" of the common law, it seems likely that courts will allocate liabilities either on the basis of a simple division of overall costs and damages by the number of defendants, on the volume of waste sent by each party, or on the percent of the environmental problem contributed by each party (taking into account the different hazards posed by various substances).

If there is a right of contribution among defendants in Superfund cases, it may be of some solace to those defendants wishing to litigate; at the same time, it may make it difficult for defendants who settle to protect themselves from third-party actions brought by nonsettling defendants. Parties who desire to protect themselves from involvement in later litigation have taken a variety of creative measures to insulate themselves from contribution claims. For example, in early settlement agreements some generators were successful in obtaining the commitment of the federal government to represent in court that the settling parties had already provided funds to the government proportionate to their share of the overall liability and that the better public policy would be not to impose further liability on these parties. The federal government has taken the position that there is a right of contribution in Superfund cases, but on the basis of early settlement agreements it can be inferred that the United States at the same time prefers a policy which allows a party who in good faith settles with the federal government to immunize itself from actions brought by other defendants seeking to recover portions of judgments in excess of those defendants' proportional share of the overall liability. As with all Superfund issues, it will ultimately devolve upon the federal courts to adopt a federal liability scheme and contribution rule which effectuates this result.

In view of the many ways one can become liable for substantial sums under Superfund, it may be tempting to seek ways to shift the liability to other parties through contractual arrangements. Congress specifically declared that no indemnification, hold-harmless, or other agreements are effective to transfer from the owner or operator of a facility (or from any person who may be liable for a release or threat of a release) the ultimate liability imposed under section 107.[24] However, in the same breath, Congress explicitly approved the use of insurance, hold-harmless agreements, or indemnifications to effectively shift the ultimate monetary burden to a third party. In other words, no contract will insulate one from being named in a Superfund lawsuit (or will support one's dismissal), but one may enter into arrangements whereby a different party will pay the penalties or cost.

Because hazardous substances may remain beneath the earth's surface for many years or remain in other hidden places on a facility's property, it is essential to draft commercial purchase agreements with care. Purchasers are increasingly demanding extensive disclosure of past practices that may have created environmental problems, and environmental auditors are occasionally asked to physically inspect and "smoke out" potential risks. The purchaser of a site that contains hazardous substances clearly becomes an "owner of a . . . facility" under Superfund section 107, and may be buying legal and financial headaches that far outweigh the value of the property being purchased.

1. Pub. L. No. 96-510, 42 U.S.C. § 9601 *et. seq.*

2. 33 U.S.C. § 1321.

3. Superfund § 101(8) (definition of "environment"), 42 U.S.C. § 9601(8).

4. 48 *Fed. Reg.* 23552 (May 25, 1983) *proposing to add* 40 C.F.R. § 302.6.

5. 48 *Fed. Reg.* 23552 (May 25, 1983) *proposing to add* 40 C.F.R. § 302.4 and *modifying* 40 C.F.R. § 117.3.

6. Superfund § 101(14), 42 U.S.C. § 9601(14).

7. The difficulty with this theory is that many shipments of oil may exhibit another RCRA characteristic—ignitability—and thus would sweep within Superfund's coverage releases of these petroleum products. One presumes that Congress would have announced this intention with more clarity had this been the desired result; also

Congress would have chosen a phrase other than "*specifically* listed or designated" in § 101(14) if it had meant to allow these RCRA characteristics to dilute what the legislative history reveals was intended as a major exclusion.

8. Superfund § 101(22), 42 U.S.C. § 9601(22).

9. Superfund § 101(10), 42 U.S.C. § 9601(10).

10. 48 *Fed. Reg.* 23552, 23557–23560 (May 25, 1983).

11. 46 *Fed. Reg.* 22144 (Apr. 15, 1981).

12. *See* 46 *Fed. Reg.* 22145 (Apr. 15, 1981).

13. 46 *Fed. Reg.* 22149 (Apr. 15, 1981).

14. Superfund § 107(b)(3), 42 U.S.C. § 9607(b)(3).

15. Ibid.

16. 47 *Fed. Reg.* 31180 (July 16, 1982), *amending* 40 C.F.R. pt 300.

17. Superfund § 101(23), 42 U.S.C. § 9601(23).

18. Superfund § 101(24), 42 U.S.C. § 9601(24).

19. Superfund § 104(c), 42 U.S.C. § 9604(c).

20. Superfund § 106(c), 42 U.S.C. § 9606(c), 47 Fed. Reg. 20664 (May 13, 1982).

21. *United States v. Price* (D.N.J. No. 80-4104, slip op., July 28, 1983).

22. *United States v. Wade*, 546 F. Supp. 785 (E.D. Pa. 1982), *appeal dismissed on procedural grounds*, — F.2d — (Aug. 5, 1983).

23. Superfund § 104(a)(2), 42 U.S.C. § 9604(a)(2).

24. Superfund § 107(e)(1), 42 U.S.C. § 9607(e)(1).

Underground Injection Control Program

James A. Rogers
Mitchell H. Bernstein
Skadden, Arps, Slate, Meagher & Flom

Part C of the Safe Drinking Water Act (SDWA)[1] establishes a framework for the state and federal regulation of underground injection. While other sections of the SDWA focus on assurance of pure drinking water through regulation of *public* water systems of a certain size, part C imposes obligations directly on private parties injecting fluids beneath the earth's surface, in much the same ways that the Clean Water Act (CWA) and Clean Air Act (CAA) place limitations on industrial dischargers. Because there are many thousands of facilities that fall under the jurisdiction of this relatively new law and because the penalties for violation are substantial, an understanding of this part of the SDWA is essential in order to assess one's risks under the major federal environmental laws.

It is a relatively straightforward task to conduct an audit of facilities that fall within the purview of the state or federal underground injection regulatory programs. Many of the most important requirements will be established in permits, and one can compare actual operating practices with the permit mandates. For example, the owner or operator of a new well is under obligation to submit specific plans for testing, drilling, and construction as part of the permit application (and the permit will incorporate these plans by reference); allowable injection pressures and volumes will be clearly set forth in the permit document; and the owner or operator will need to have evidence of financial responsibility that has been approved by the permit-issuing authority. Many periodic monitoring reports must be maintained by the well operator. Finally, many of the design and operating requirements can be checked by relatively easy physical inspections of the facility.

Underground injection wells vary greatly, their design depending to a large extent on the type of materials being injected, the geological formations through which the well passes and into which the wastes are pumped, and the applicable regulatory requirements. In some cases wastes (which may be pretreated before injection) are pumped into subsurface cavities at rates up to 1000 gallons per minute; the great majority of wells operate at below 400 gallons per minute.[2] The more sophisticated injection wells are between 1000 and 6000 feet deep, with about three-quarters of them less than 4000 feet.[3]

The injection well for strong chemical wastes often consists of a metal pipe—sometimes within another metal pipe—surrounded by cement (at least in upper strata). The well opens in the disposal zone, which usually is below drinking-water aquifers and separated from them by impermeable materials. The well design is governed by the pressures to be employed, the corrosiveness of the wastes, the depth of the discharge zone, and the need to safeguard against accidental releases to aquifers through which the well passes (among many other factors).

REGULATING UNDERGROUND INJECTION

In the absence of an authorized state underground injection control (UIC) program the federal government does not automatically have authority to administer regulations in this area. Within 180 days after the date of enactment of the SDWA (December 16, 1974), the administrator of the Environmental Protection Agency (EPA) was to have listed each state for which a state UIC program was necessary to ensure that injection activities would not endanger drinking-water sources.[4] EPA has since listed all states and the District of Columbia.[5] Each state so designated was then provided by statute with roughly 9 months to submit to the administrator an application which, as with submissions under the other major environmental laws, showed that the state had adequate resources and legal authority to carry out a UIC program.

As described in more detail below, there are five categories of underground injection activities, one of which relates to the recovery of oil or natural gas (class II wells). In 1980 Congress amended the SDWA to allow states to assume primary jurisdiction over only this portion of the overall underground injection program.[5a] In 1982 states began applying to EPA for UIC authority, although in some cases only with respect to class II wells. As one might expect, most of the early applications came from states with established regulatory programs.

Once an application is received by EPA, the administrator must act within a specified time period. If a state's program is disapproved or if a state fails to submit an application, the administrator must—through the federal administrative rule-making process—prescribe a program for the control of underground injection in that state.[6] Although January 15, 1982, was the deadline for submission of state programs (the administrator had granted one 270-day extension), the state and federal governments have been tardy in complying with this statutory mandate. Because only a few states had approved programs as late as the middle of 1983, two environmental groups brought suit to compel EPA to initiate the process of promulgating UIC programs in those states that have failed to meet their obligations under the act.[6a] At this writing EPA is preparing proposed regulations to impose and enforce UIC programs in these states.

CIVIL AND CRIMINAL PENALTIES

There are both civil and criminal penalties for violation of a UIC program, and the federal government can initiate enforcement actions in the United States district courts even when a state has received primary enforcement responsibility. Congress generally contemplated that after a state had received primary enforcement responsibility from the federal government, the rights and obligations of any person carrying on underground injection activities in that state would be subject solely to state law and disputes would be resolved in the state judicial system. However, if EPA learns of a failure to comply with the state requirement, it may bring such noncompliance to the attention of the appropriate state officials; if they fail to take appropriate enforcement actions within 60 days, the administrator may commence a civil action in federal court.[7] The statute allows imposition of a civil penalty not to exceed $5000 for each day of violation after the defendant receives notice from the federal EPA of noncompliance with the law.[8]

In those states in which the federal government is managing the UIC program (and again, this is the situation only when EPA has affirmatively promulgated a state program, not simply when a state has failed to do so), Congress has allowed EPA to seek both civil and criminal penalties in appropriate circumstances. As with enforcement in a state that has primary enforcement responsibility, the ceiling on civil penalties is $5000 for each day of violation, but there is no required 60-day notification period.[9] If the violation of the federally run program is willful, the defendant may be fined not more than $10,000 for each day of violation, in lieu of the civil penalty.[10] There are no provisions for jail sentences under the federal law. One must remember, however, that there may be state enforcement procedures and penalties which are more stringent than those established as minimum requirements under the SDWA and that nothing in the latter act preempts the state provisions.

PERMIT PROGRAMS

Once a UIC program is established in a state, the fundamental rule is that all underground injections are unlawful and subject to penalties unless authorized either by a specific permit for that source or by a general rule which encompasses that source. One must examine several parts of Title 40 of the Code of Federal Regulations to glean the procedural requirements governing authorizations by permit or rule and the substantive technical standards applicable to both types of authorizations. The technical standards are contained in 40 C.F.R. part 146. The basic definitions, permitting requirements for an EPA-administered UIC program, and overview of the law are contained in 40 C.F.R. part 144. The minimum requirements for EPA approval of a state UIC program are set forth in part 145. Finally, the specific procedures for EPA issuance of UIC permits are contained in part 124. Recently there have been major changes in all the above parts, in large part settlements of several challenges to the original regulations brought by a number of industrial trade associations and the state of Texas.[11]

CATEGORIES OF WELLS

To many persons, underground injection brings to mind the type of pumping system described at the beginning of this chapter. The breadth of part C's coverage is far greater than this, however, and to appreciate the scope of the UIC program one must be conversant with a few key definitions. "Well injection" means the "subsurface implacement of 'fluids' through a bored, drilled, or driven 'well;' or through a dug well, where the depth of the dug well is greater than the largest surface dimension."[12] In other words, a well can be simply a hole in the ground that is deeper than it is wide, and this definition clearly embraces many types of penetration of the earth of human origin. The term "fluid" means "any material or substance which flows or moves whether in semisolid, liquid, sludge, gas, or any other form or state."[13]

Once having concluded that the facility in question is an underground injection well, one must then determine into which of five categories of wells the particular facility falls; the efforts required to comply with the SDWA can vary greatly from one category to another. One must know into what formations the fluid is being injected and, in a general way, what materials are in the fluid, in order to navigate in this five-well classification scheme.

Class I injection wells are those used by generators of hazardous waste or operators of hazardous-waste-management facilities to inject hazardous wastes[14] beneath the lowermost formation containing, within ¼ mile of the well bore, an underground source of drinking water, or USDW.[15] This category also includes injection into those areas of fluids (which include hazardous wastes) through industrial and municipal disposal wells.[16] A USDW is that part of an aquifer which is supplying drinking water, or could if needed.[17] In 1982 EPA amended the definition of a USDW to make it easier to demonstrate that even if an aquifer contains only 3000 to 10,000 milligrams per liter total dissolved solids (TDS), it should not be considered a USDW.[18] (Traditionally, scientists have assumed that an aquifer containing less than 10,000 milligrams of TDS per liter might become a USDW.)

Class IV wells are those in which hazardous or radioactive wastes are injected by generators of hazardous waste or operators of either hazardous-waste-management facilities or radioactive-waste sites, into or above a formation which contains a USDW within ¼ mile of the well.[19] The regulations prohibit construction of new class IV wells which will inject directly into a USDW,[20] and existing wells of this type must cease operations within 6 months following approval or promulgation of a UIC program.[21] In an effort to mesh the requirements of SDWA and RCRA, which both provide jurisdiction over injection of hazardous wastes, EPA has stated that anyone will be considered to have an RCRA permit who has a UIC permit and meets selected portions of the RCRA standards.[22] Until the UIC programs are implemented, however, the situation is more complicated. The RCRA hazardous-waste regulations apply to the aboveground treatment and storage of hazardous waste before underground injection[23] and to existing class I and class IV wells as well as new class I wells.[24]

Congress recognized that injection wells are important in the development of many fossil fuels. It restricted the ability of EPA to "interfere with or impede" the injection of brine or other fluids which are brought to the surface in connection with oil or natural gas production *unless* the requirements are essential to protect USDWs.[25] The agency's definition of, and restrictions on, class II, class III, and class V wells reflect this legislative concern. Class II, as noted above, includes wells which inject fluids that are brought to the surface in connection with oil and gas production or which inject fluids for enhanced recovery or for storage of liquid hydrocarbons.[26] Class III includes wells which inject for the extraction of other forms of energy or minerals.[27] Class V comprises the remainder of wells that are not included under the first four categories; it is a motley collection, ranging from cesspools (which are largely excluded by the UIC regulations) to wells used for in situ recovery of coal or oil shale (for which minimal requirements are established.)[28]

The technical requirements for four of the five classes are found in 40 C.F.R. part 146, which contains construction, operating, monitoring, and reporting standards. (Requirements for class IV are reserved—no doubt so that the regulations will be consistent with EPA's standards under RCRA for land-disposal facilities.) These requirements also include rather intimidating terms, such as "observed original hydrostatic head of injection zone," "modified Theis equations," and "lithology of confining zones"—clear signals that anyone forced into substantive evaluations under a UIC program must also have expert assistance.

As noted, there is overlap in the statutory coverage of injection wells under RCRA and SDWA, at least with respect to injection of hazardous wastes. There also is potential overlap with the CWA, although by no means as clearly as with RCRA. Congress included in section 402 of the CWA a requirement that state programs submitted for approval under the NPDES program include provisions that "control the disposal of pollutants into wells."[29] Congress did not include underground waters in the CWA definition of "navigable waters" and did not explicitly provide EPA authority to regulate underground injection under the CWA. EPA has asserted jurisdiction under the CWA for injection wells when they are associated with surface water discharges, and there has been scholarly suggestion that the penumbra of the CWA's overall purpose and other federal laws, such as NEPA, might provide the needed support for EPA.[30] This issue, however, is likely to become even more academic as the states begin to implement the UIC and RCRA programs.

1. 42 U.S.C. 300f *et seq.* Most lawyers refer to it as the Safe Drinking Water Act; it is actually Title XIV of the Public Health Service Act, which title was added by the Safe Drinking Water Act of 1974, Pub. L. 93-523, 88 Stat. 1660 (Dec. 16, 1974). It was amended in 1977, Pub. L. 95-190, 91 Stat. 1393 (Nov. 16, 1977), and again in 1980, Pub. L. 96-502, 94 Stat. 2737 (Dec. 5, 1980).

2. Winar, "The Disposal of Wastewater Underground," *Ind. Water Engineering*, March 1967.

3. Ibid.

4. § 1422(a), 42 U.S.C. 300h-1(a).

5. 40 C.F.R. § 144.1(c). The designations came in five stages; 43 Fed. Reg. 43420 (Sept. 25, 1978); 44 Fed. Reg. 21707 (April 11, 1979); 44 Fed. Reg. 35288 (June 19, 1979); 44 Fed. Reg. 56985 (Oct. 3, 1979); 45 Fed. Reg. 17632 (March 19, 1980).

5a. Pub. L. 96-502, 94 Stat. 2737 (Dec. 5, 1980), *adding* 42 U.S.C. 300 h-4.

6.   § 1422(c), 42 U.S.C. 300h-1(c).

6a. *National Wildlife Federation v. Ruckelshaus* [D. Colo. No. 83-JM-1333 (July 28, 1983)].

7.   § 1423(a)(1), 42 U.S.C. 300h-2(a)(1).

8.   § 1423(b)(1), 42 U.S.C. 300h-2(b)(1).

9.   § 1423(b)(2), 42 U.S.C. 300h-2(b)(2).

10. Ibid.

11. 47 Fed. Reg. 4992 (Feb. 3, 1982). *Natural Resources Defense Council v. E.P.A.* (D.C. Cir. No. 80-1607) (consolidated permit regulations) and *American Petroleum Institute v. E.P.A.* (D.C. Cir. No. 80-1875) (substantive UIC standards).

12. 40 C.F.R. § 144.3.

13. Ibid.

14. The definition of hazardous wastes is the same as that used in EPA regulations implementing the Resource Conservation and Recovery Act. 40 C.F.R. §§ 144.3 and 261.3.

15. 40 C.F.R. § 144.6(a)(1).

16. 40 C.F.R. § 144.6(a)(2).

17. 40 C.F.R. § 144.3.

18. 40 C.F.R. § 146.04(c).

19. 40 C.F.R. § 144.6(d).

20. 40 C.F.R. § 144.13(a)(1).

21. 40 C.F.R. § 144.13(a)(4).

22. 40 C.F.R. §§ 122.26(b) and 144.14.

23. Comment at 40 C.F.R. § 265.1(c)(2).

24. 40 C.F.R. §§ 265.430(b) and 267.1(b).

25. Section 1421(b)(2), 42 U.S.C. 300h(b)(2).

26. 40 C.F.R. § 144.6(b).

27. 40 C.F.R. § 144.6(c).

28. 40 C.F.R. § 146.05(e).

29. § 402(b)(1)(D), 33 U.S.C. 1342(b)(1)(D). The Federal Water Pollution Control Act amendments of 1972, Pub. L. 92-500, 86 Stat. 816 (Oct. 18, 1972).

30. *See* Eckert, "EPA Jurisdiction over Well Injection under the Federal Water Pollution Control Act," *Natl. Res. L.* vol. IX, no. 3, p. 455.

Occupational Safety and Health Act

Nancy S. Bryson
Environmental Defense Section
U.S. Department of Justice

The Occupational Safety and Health Act,[1] passed in 1970, is a broadly drafted remedial statute covering all types of workplaces in the United States and administered by the Occupational Safety and Health Administration (OSHA). The self-described purpose of the act is "to assure so far as possible every working man and woman in the nation safe and healthful working conditions and to preserve our human resources."[2] The act was designed to address a "drastic" national problem—14,500 people were dying from industrial accidents and 2.2 million more were being disabled on the job each year.[3]

The statute focuses on the employer's responsibility to provide safe working conditions and to maintain a safe workplace. One section[4] creates two new duties which employers are required to fulfill. The first is what is called a "general duty": to provide a workplace "free from recognized hazards that are causing or are likely to cause death or serious physical harm to his employees."[5] This duty, as may be inferred from the general language in which it is described, can encompass a very broad range of unsafe working conditions. It has been upheld, however, over challenges of unconstitutional vagueness, on the premise that the term "recognized hazard" used in the statement of the duty gives industrial employers fair notice of conduct which must be avoided.[6] It does not create a strict-liability responsibility; that is, employers will not automatically be held responsible for every unsafe condition at their workplaces. It does require that a good-faith effort be made to seek out and correct all "feasibly preventable forms and instances of hazardous conduct."[7] An employer may have actual knowledge of the facts creating the hazard. The existence of a duty to take corrective action in such a situation will depend on whether a reasonably conscientious safety expert familiar with the industry would have done so in the same situation.[8]

A second duty created by section 5(a)(2) requires employers to "comply with occupational safety and health standards promulgated under this act." These standards will be more familiar to managers accustomed to regulations issued under other environmental statutes. Unlike the general-duty clause, they pertain to specific chemical substances or specific working conditions and generally specify the means of compliance.[9] The secretary of labor is authorized by section 6 of the act to issue these standards or regulations.[10] They cover a wide variety of health and safety hazards.[11]

ENFORCEMENT PROVISIONS OF THE STATUTE

The secretary of labor is authorized to enforce the performance of these duties by employers, although to a great extent the efficacy of the statute depends upon voluntary compliance. The secretary has general inspection authority under the act[12] but currently employs only some 1100 full-time inspectors, compared with approximately 1300 in January 1981. Relatively few of the covered workplaces in the country can be reached by that small a staff, and inspection priorities are therefore required. For fiscal 1982, for instance, OSHA announced that it would identify, from figures compiled by the Bureau of Labor Statistics, the workplaces where the most serious hazards exist and would inspect those sites. In addition, section 8(f)(1) contains a provision whereby employees can notify the secretary of a suspected violation or imminent danger. The secretary is required to make a special inspection "as soon as practicable" upon determination that there are "reasonable grounds to believe that such violation or danger exists."

The inspection authority codified in section 8 authorizes the secretary of labor or the secretary's representatives to "enter without delay and at reasonable times" any type of workplace to examine working conditions, pieces of equipment, etc., and to examine records required to be maintained by the act or by applicable standards.[13] (These records are discussed later in the chapter under Health Standards.)

The act requires two basic types of records. The first is a log and summary of occupational injuries and illnesses.[14] This log must include all injuries and illnesses which result in fatalities and lost workdays, transfer to another job or termination of employment, or loss of consciousness or restriction of work or motion.[15] The second is an annual summary of the injury and illness log, which must be posted in the workplace.[16] These records must be maintaind for a 5-year period[17] and must be made available to the secretary of labor or employer representatives upon request. Individual standards, particularly those for toxic substances and hazardous materials such as cotton dust and lead may impose additional record-keeping requirements, discussed later in the chapter.

Representatives of the employer and employees may accompany the OSHA inspector during the examination of plant records and during the walkaround inspection of the plant. If the secretary of labor has reason to believe, as a result of the walkaround inspection or examination of records, that the employer is in violation of the general-duty clause or one of the section 6 standards, a citation will be issued.[18] The citation must describe "with particularity" the nature of the violation and the standard or provision of the act alleged to be violated, and it requires the employer to correct the violation within a reasonable time. The secretary may, in addition to requiring abatement, propose the assessment of a penalty for the violation.[19] The employer has an opportunity to contest both the citation and the penalty before an independent adjudicatory agency, the Occupational Safety and Health Review Commission.[20] Judicial review of the commission's decision is available to "any person adversely affected or aggrieved" in the court of appeals if a petition is filed within 60 days.[21] The secretary may also petition the appropriate court of appeals for enforcement of any final order of the commission.[22]

Civil and Criminal Penalties

The act sets a series of graduated civil penalties for violations. A penalty of up to $1000 may be assessed for each serious violation of the act.[23] A serious violation is defined as existing where "there is a substantial probability that death or serious physical harm could result from a condition which exists, or from one or more practices, means, methods, operations, or processes which have been adopted or are in use unless the employer did not and could not with the exercise of reasonable diligence, know of the presence of the violation."[24] A penalty of up to $10,000 may be assessed for each willful or repeated violation.[25] As with other regulatory statutes, "bad purpose" is not a predicate to a willful violation; the secretary of labor need only prove voluntary action, taken with either an intentional disregard of or plain indifference to the statutory requirements.[26]

A willful violation of the general-duty clause, as well as of a specific standard, has been upheld by at least one circuit court.[27] Repeated violations have been affirmed where a second or third citation involved the recurrence of a similar safety hazard at the same facility.[28] The most stringent civil penalty, $1000 per *day*, is reserved for those situations in which an employer fails to correct or abate a violation within the time period specified in the abatement order.[29]

Section 17 also authorizes the imposition of criminal sanctions for certain violations of the act. An employer who willfully violates any standard which results in the death of an employee shall, upon conviction, be punished by a fine of up to $10,000 and/or imprisonment for a term of up to 6 months. If the conviction is for a second offense, the permissible fine is $20,000 and jail time increases to 1 year.[30] Criminal prosecution is also authorized for "knowingly mak[ing] any false statement, representation, or certification in any application, record, report, plan or other document filed or required to be maintained pursuant to [the] act."[31] The penalty is, again, a fine of up to $10,000 and up to 6 months in jail.

The statute contains two other relevant enforcement provisions. The first of these is the imminent-danger provision of the act.[32] It authorizes the secretary of labor to file suit in district court "to restrain any conditions or practices in any place of employment which are such that a danger exists which could reasonably be expected to cause death or serious physical harm immediately or before the imminence of such danger can be eliminated through the enforcement procedures otherwise provided by this act." The district courts are authorized to issue any order necessary to correct or remove the imminent danger, including a shutdown of the work site.

The secretary of labor is also authorized to bring suit in district court against any employer who, upon investigation, is determined to have discharged or otherwise discriminated against an employee who exercised a right afforded by the act.[33] The district courts are authorized to enjoin such activity and to order all appropriate relief, including rehiring or reinstating the employee in the same job with back pay.[34] For an employer to be liable under this section, the secretary need only prove the discharged employee's reasonable and good-faith belief that conditions leading to the employee's refusal to perform certain job-related duties were dangerous and that the discharge was based on that refusal.[35]

HEALTH STANDARDS: WHAT HAZARDS CAN BE REGULATED AND WHAT CAN BE REQUIRED

The major costs for industry created by OSHA are the costs of complying with health standards issued by the secretary of labor under section 6(b)(5) of the act.[36] Of course, complying with the abatement orders discussed above, where compliance is required as a result of an enforcement action, can also be expensive. A number of these standards have been issued over the past 10 years for substances such as asbestos, vinyl chloride, benzene, lead, cotton dust, coke oven emissions, and various carcinogens. In addition to these specific toxic-substance standards, OSHA has initiated and in some cases completed more general regulations, such as those establishing a cancer policy to be relied upon in setting standards for materials discovered to be carcinogenic; the right of access by the government, workers, and unions to records relating to occupational safety and health; and general labeling requirements for containers of all hazardous materials present in the workplace.

In general, the specific standards set permissible exposure levels (PEL) for the regulated substance, such as cotton dust or lead. The PEL is customarily based on a time-weighted average; that is, total exposure is measured by an 8-hour workday or 40-hour workweek. The average is limited, however, by a maximum exposure level, the exceeding of which is itself a violation. The PELs established are, in almost every instance, much lower than the levels currently being achieved, with the result that engineering controls of various types—primarily dust- or particle-reduction systems—must be installed by a date specified in the particular standards. In some instances the engineering control may involve a switch to an entirely new production process. (See discussion of lead standard below.)

The standards set initial and periodic air-monitoring requirements to ensure that the PEL is being reached and maintained. The results of the monitoring tests are required to be maintained by the employer and will be examined by OSHA inspectors at the beginning of an inspection. These records can and should be internally audited to monitor the compliance of various work operations with the PEL.[37] The standards also may require biological monitoring of employees and extensive medical examinations and surveillance in certain situations, with similar record-keeping requirements and similar potential for in-house audits. In some cases medical removal protection is required; that is, workers who, for medical reasons, must be removed for a certain period from the exposures present in their jobs are entitled to maintenance of pay and seniority. The worker must be returned to the job when return is safe. The standards also, as a general matter, may require labels and warning signs for the regulated substances and the use of personal protective equipment such as respirators or other protective clothing.

The secretary of labor is authorized to set a health standard whenever it is determined that one should be created to serve the objectives of the act.[38] This can happen either at the secretary's own initiative or at the request of some interested party.[39] The secretary is required to give notice to the public of the proposed rule and to provide an opportunity for comment and a hearing if requested.[40] Hearings on these standards are usually held and are customarily very lengthy, creating a record of thousands of pages of testimony and exhibits and involving internationally known experts in the fields of health, economics, and technology.

In establishing a standard for toxic materials or harmful physical agents, the secretary of labor is directed by section 6(b)(5) of the act[41] to "set the standard which most adequately assures, to the extent feasible, on the basis of the best available evidence, that no employee will suffer material impairment of health or functional capacity, even if such employee has regular exposure to the hazard dealt with by such standard for the period of his working life."

An earlier section of the act[42] also provides that such a standard is one "which requires conditions, or the adoption or use of one or more practices, means, methods, operations, or processes, reasonably necessary or appropriate to provide safe or healthful employment or places of employment." These definitions have provided fertile ground for litigation over the past 10 years, as OSHA has issued increasingly sophisticated standards designed to protect workers from various workplace health hazards.[43]

The Benzene Decision

As a result of the litigation over standards, a number of general principles have emerged. First, in the area of regulable health effects, the secretary of labor, before promulgating any permanent health standard, must make a threshold finding that the place of employment is unsafe because it presents a significant risk of harm which can be eliminated or lessened by a change in practice. In the AFL-CIO case,[44] the Supreme Court was reviewing OSHA's new standard for benzene. That standard reduced the PEL for benzene from 10 ppm (parts per million) to 1 ppm. It was not based on evidence showing that risks from exposure at 10 ppm were absent at 1 ppm. Rather, the PEL was based on general evidence that benzene caused leukemia in persons exposed to high concentrations of it in the workplace, that there was no evidence of a safe level of exposure for humans, and that 1 ppm was the lowest exposure level which could be achieved by the regulated industry. The decision by the secretary to reduce exposures to the lowest feasible level was consistent with those made by OSHA in setting previous health standards for carcinogens such as vinyl chloride, asbestos, and coke oven emissions. It was also consistent with a general carcinogen policy then in the regulatory mill, which, among other things, stated that OSHA would as a matter of policy set the lowest feasible level of exposure where a carcinogen was involved.

The Supreme Court disagreed with OSHA's regulatory decision on benzene, however, and in so doing caused a restructuring of the cancer policy which is still under consideration by the agency. The court held that a safe workplace is not the equivalent of a risk-free workplace, and that the workplace could not be unsafe unless it threatened workers with a significant risk of harm.[45] Since OSHA had made no finding concerning the risk for benzene at exposures of 10 ppm compared to exposures of 1 ppm, the court invalidated the standard. In so doing, the court left open the question of whether OSHA was required to justify its standards on a cost-benefit basis.

The Cotton-Dust Standard

Shortly after its benzene decision, the Supreme Court reviewed another OSHA health standard, the standard for cotton dust.[46] Cotton dust, an airbone-particle by-product of the preparation and manufacture of cotton products, induces byssinosis, or "brown lung disease." Byssinosis is a disease which can occur in several forms, ranging from chest tightness and shortness of breath to chronic and irreversible obstructive pulmonary disease.

The new standard reduced the PEL for cotton dust in various cotton-industry operations. It was based upon a record showing that one out of twelve cotton-mill workers suffers from the most disabling form of this disease, while many others suffer from less disabling versions. The standard required that within 4 years the PEL should be met by the installation of engineering controls such as ventilation systems, in combination with work-practice controls such as special floor-sweeping procedures. OSHA estimated the cost of compliance at $656.5 million.

The Supreme Court reviewed and affirmed this standard. It found that the evidence of the various grades of byssinosis in the record established a substantial risk which OSHA had correctly regulated. It also found that cost-benefit analysis was not required by the statute or subsumed within the substantial-risk showing required by the benzene decision as a predicate to reducing the PEL. The court held that Congress had balanced costs and benefits in its directive to OSHA to adopt the most protective feasible standard, which included protection against the less serious forms of byssinosis.

The Lead Standard

In litigation over OSHA's lead standard, the controversy over what health effects constituted "material impairment of health" was refined further. Lead exposure occurs in many industries and causes a wide variety of harmful effects in the human body, ranging from lead poisoning to subclinical changes in the reproductive, renal, blood-forming, and neurological systems. OSHA designed its standard to protect workers against these latter changes, which occur at very low levels of lead exposure. That decision was challenged as being outside the agency's authority, since these effects did not constitute actual disease. The Court of Appeals for the District of Columbia Circuit rejected these arguments and upheld the standard, finding that OSHA was empowered to set a PEL that would prevent the subclinical effects of lead which are or may be precursors of commonly recognized diseases caused by lead exposure.[47]

The only constraints upon OSHA's authority to set health-protective regulations where sound scientific evidence of adverse effects exists are that the standards be economically and technologically feasible.[48] The Supreme Court discussed the meaning of economic feasibility at length in its cotton-dust decision, finding that the standard was economically feasible because it was within the financial capability of the cotton industry. The court held that OSHA had to assess whether the industry could maintain its long-term profitability and competitiveness while complying with the standard and had correctly found that it could do so in this case. In its discussion, the court noted that studies in the cotton-dust record showed that installation of new cleaner equipment would be less costly than retrofitting old equipment with dust-control devices. It also noted that the cost of compliance might increase long-term profitability if new equipment were installed, since "by going to newer equipment with controls there is a likelihood that increased production rates will result in recovery of some or all of the capital cost of control."[49]

The second requirement of the feasibility standard is technological feasibility. OSHA has traditionally been considered a technology-forcing statute.[50] The courts have upheld standards which only the most technologically advanced plants in an industry have been able to achieve, even if only in some of their operations some of the time.[51] The courts have also upheld standards requiring the development and diffusion of new control technologies to meet PELs never attained anywhere, where (1) the agency gives the industry a reasonable time to develop the new technology and (2) it presents substantial evidence that the industry, acting vigorously and in good faith, can develop the technology.[52]

The most striking examples of what can be required in terms of technology-forcing innovations are to be found in the lead standard.[53] The standard leaves the choice of particular engineering controls or work practices to the employer and simply specifies the goal—the PEL to be achieved. However, both the secretary of labor and the court, in upholding the standard, recognized that compliance, for primary and secondary smelters at least, might require fundamental changes in the methods of production. For primary smelters, which have 10 years to meet the PEL, compliance may require a shift from pyrometallurgy to a completely new hydrometallurgy process. For secondary smelters, which were given 5 years to comply, another complete change of production methods and equipment was found by the court to meet the technological-feasibility requirement of the act. As these developments indicate, continuing long-term profitability requires close attention to existing and planned OSHA requirements. An auditing program which identifies problem areas and operations in a plant or facility and keeps records of progress made toward compliance can obviously be of immeasurable value.

VARIANCES AND ALTERNATE METHODS OF COMPLIANCE

The statute authorizes the secretary of labor to grant variances from OSHA standards under certain circumstances. Temporary variances under section 6(b)(6)(A) can be granted to employers who establish that (1) they are unable to comply with a standard by its effective date because personnel or materials and equipment or necessary construction cannot be secured or completed by the effective date; (2) they are taking all available steps to protect employees against the hazards covered by the standard; and (3) they have programs for coming into compliance with the standard as quickly as practicable. In this area as well, records of problem areas and ameliorative steps taken as a result of environmental auditing can provide invaluable documentation. Employers are also required to certify that their employees have been informed of the request for the extension. The variance application is then subject to notice and hearing. If granted, it may not be effective for longer than 1 year, although it may be renewed twice. The secretary is also authorized to grant permanent variances under limited circumstances.[54] The proponent must show "by a preponderance of the evidence that the conditions, practices, means, methods, operations, or processes used or proposed to be used by an employer will provide employment and places of employment to his employees which are as safe and healthful as those which would prevail if he complied with the standard." Well-designed auditing records can provide exactly such information. As with the temporary variance applications, employees must be notified, and the application is subject to notice and hearing requirements. A list of pending variance applications, including the standard and company involved, appears on a quarterly basis in volume 3 of the CCH publication *Occupational Safety and Health Report*.[55] Variance applications which are granted are published in the *Federal Register*.[56]

Finally, OSHA has adopted a system of voluntary labor and management protection plans to supplement enforcement.[57] These plans essentially institutionalize the concepts of environmental auditing for OSHA compliance. They are designed to emphasize employee and management initiative programs to improve workplace safety and health "in ways simply not available to OSHA"—i.e., programs based upon the thorough knowledge of processes, materials, and hazards on the work site which comes from the day-to-day recorded experience on the work site supplied by auditing procedures.[58] In order to qualify, a business must first convince OSHA on paper that it meets a number of threshold criteria, including a good safety record, an accurate assessment of workplace hazards, and a program for dealing with them. Assistance of OSHA personnel in hazard recognition and abatement planning may be provided in any problem areas. Companies or industries participating in such programs will be removed from the general inspection schedules once the programs are in place and operating.

1. Pub. L. No. 91-596, 84 Stat. 1590, codified at 29 U.S.C. § 651 *et seq.*

2. 29 U.S.C. 651(b).

3. *Atlas Roofing Co. v. Occupational Safety Health Review Comm'n*, 430 U.S. 442, 444, n.1 (1977).

4. § 5(a), 29 U.S.C. 654(a).

5. 29 U.S.C. 654(a)(1).

6. *Bethlehem Steel Corp. v. Occupational Safety & Health Review Comm'n*, 607 F.2d 871 (3d Cir. 1979).

7. *Anning Johnson Co. v. Occupational Safety & Health Review Comm'n*, 516 F.2d 1081 (7th Cir. 1975); *Getty Oil Co. v. Occupational Safety & Health Review Comm'n*, 530 F.2d 1143 (5th Cir. 1976).

8. *Magma Copper Co. v. Marshall*, 608 F.2d 373 (9th Cir. 1979); *General Dynamics Corp. Quincy Shipbuilding Div. v. Occupational Safety & Health Review Comm'n*, 599 F.2d 453 (1st Cir. 1979).

9. This chapter discusses only the OSHA health standards for toxic substances in detail.

For a fuller description of the standard-setting process and the types of requirements imposed by the major health standards issued over the past 10 years, see discussion under Health Standards later in this chapter.

10. 29 U.S.C. 655.

11. Codified at 29 C.F.R. 1910 through 29 C.F.R. 1926.

12. § 8(a), 29 U.S.C. 657(a).

13. The Supreme Court has held that a warrant is required for such inspections under the Fourth Amendment where the employer does not consent to the inspection [*Marshall v. Barlows, Inc.*, 436 U.S. 307 (1978)]. Inspection warrants can be issued to OSHA by a district judge or U.S. magistrate [*Babcock & Wilcox Co. v. Marshall*, 610 F.2d 1128 (3d Cir. 1979)]; and injury statistics showing, in the secretary of labor's opinion, a high incidence of injuries in a particular industry may constitute probable cause for issuance of the warrant [*In re Establishment Inspection of Gilbert & Bennett Mfg. Co.*, 589 F.2d 1335 (7th Cir. 1979), *cert. denied*, 444 U.S. 884 (1979)].

14. § 8(c), 29 U.S.C. 657(c) and 29 C.F.R. 1904.

15. 29 C.F.R. 1904.2, 1904.12(c).

16. 29 C.F.R. 1904.5.

17. 29 C.F.R. 1904.6.

18. § 9, 29 U.S.C. 658(a).

19. § 10(a), 29 U.S.C. 659(a).

20. §§ 10 and 12, 29 U.S.C. 659, 661. The employer is required to submit what is known as a "notice of contest" within 15 working days of issuance of the citation [§ 10(c), 29 U.S.C. 659(c)].

21. § 11, 29 U.S.C. 660.

22. § 11(b), 29 U.S.C. 660(b).

23. § 17(b), 29 U.S.C. 666(b).

24. § 17(k), 29 U.S.C. 666(k). A penalty of up to $1000 per violation is also authorized for nonserious violations.

25. § 17(a), 29 U.S.C. 666(a).

26. *Georgia Electric Co. v. Marshall*, 595 F.2d 309 (5th Cir. 1979); *Western Waterproofing Co. v. Marshall*, 576 F.2d 139 (8th Cir. 1978), *cert. denied*, 439 U.S. 965 (1978); *Intercounty Constr. Co. v. Occupational Safety & Health Review Comm'n*, 522 F.2d 777 (4th Cir. 1975), *cert. denied*, 423 U.S. 1072 (1976).

27. *Empire-Detroit Steel Div. Detroit Steel Corp. v. Occupational Safety & Health Review Comm'n*, 579 F.2d 378 (6th Cir. 1978).

28. *Todd Shipyards Corp. v. Secretary of Labor*, 586 F.2d 638 (9th Cir. 1978).

29. § 17(d), 29 U.S.C. 666(d). The Occupational Safety and Health Review Commission has authority to determine the final penalty assessment, although the secretary of labor proposes what that penalty should be. The commission is required to consider "the size of the business of the employer being charged, the gravity of the violation, the good faith of the employer and the history of previous violations" [§ 17(j), 29 U.S.C. 666(j)].

30. § 17(e), 29 U.S.C. 666(e). *United States v. Dye Constr. Co.*, 510 F.2d 78 (10th Cir. 1975).

31. 29 U.S.C. 666(g).

32. § 13(a), 29 U.S.C. 662(a).

33. § 11(c), 29 U.S.C. 660(c).

34. Ibid.

35. *Marshall v. N.L. Industries, Inc.*, 618 F.2d 1220 (7th Cir. 1980).

36. 29 U.S.C. 655(b)(5).

37. As previously indicated, these standards require record keeping in addition to the injury and illness log and annual summary. For example, the lead standard requires an employer to maintain accurate records of all air monitoring, including samples and sampling techniques; the names, social security numbers, job classification, and exposure levels of all employees; and the type of protective devices worn, if any. Extensive medical records are also required to be maintained on all exposed employees. These records must be maintained for a period of at least 20 years. They must also be made available to employees and to the secretary of labor upon request [29 C.F.R. 1910, 10, 25(n)]. Similar record-keeping requirements are contained in the cotton-dust standard [29 C.F.R. 1910, 1043(k)] and others.

38. § 6(b)(2), 29 U.S.C. 655(b)(2).

39. Ibid.

40. § 6(b)(3), 29 U.S.C. 655(b)(3). OSHA is currently publishing a regulatory calendar which gives notice of final rules and proposals, advance notice of rule making, and rules in the preproposal stage. This calendar is published in accordance with E.O. 12291 and appears in volume 3 of the Commerce Clearing House *Occupational Safety and Health Report*.

41. 29 U.S.C. 655(b)(5).

42. § 3(8), 29 U.S.C. 652(8).

43. *Industrial Union Dep't AFL-CIO v. American Petroleum Inst.*, 448 U.S. 607 (1980); *American Textile Mfrs' Inst. v. Donovan*, 452 U.S. 490 (1981); *United Steelworkers v. Marshall*, 647 F.2d 1189 (D.C. Cir. 1980), *cert. denied sub nom. Lead Industries Assn. v. Donovan*, 453 U.S. 913 (1981); *Industrial Union Dep't AFL-CIO v. Hodgson*, 499 F.2d 467 (D.C. Cir. 1974); *American Iron & Steel Inst. v. OSHA*, 577 F.2d 825 (3d Cir. 1978), *petition for cert. dismissed*, 101 S. Ct. 38; *AFL-CIO v. Brennan*, 530 F. 2d 109 (3d Cir. 1975); *Society of Plastics Indus. v. OSHA*, 509 F.2d 1301 (2d Cir. 1974), *cert. denied sub nom. Firestone Plastics Co. v. United States Dep't of Labor*, 421 U.S. 992 (1975).

44. *Industrial Union Dep't AFL-CIO v. American Petroleum Inst.*, 448 U.S. 607 (1980).

45. 448 U.S. at 639–46.

46. *American Textile Mfrs' Inst. v. Donovan*, 452 U.S. 490 (1981).

47. *United Steelworkers v. Marshall*, 647 F.2d 1189, 1252 (1980), *cert. denied sub nom. Lead Industries Ass'n v. Donovan*, 453 U.S. 913 (1981).

48. § 6(b)(5), 29 U.S.C. 655(b)(5); *American Textile Mfrs' Inst. v. Donovan, supra*, 452 U.S. at 508–22, *United Steelworkers v. Marshall, supra*, 647 F.2d at 1264–65.

49. *American Textile Mfrs' Inst. v. Donovan, supra*, 452 U.S. at 526, n.47.

50. *AFL-CIO v. Brennan*, 530 F.2d 109, 121 (3d Cir. 1975).

51. *American Iron & Steel Inst. v. OSHA*, 577 F.2d 825, 832 (3d Cir. 1978).

52. *Society of Plastics Indus. v. OSHA*, 509 F.2d 1301, 1309 (2d Cir. 1974), *cert. denied sub nom. Firestone Plastics Co. v. United States Dep't of Labor*, 421 U.S. 992 (1975); *United Steelworkers v. Marshall, supra*, 647 F.2d at 1263–65.

53. 29 C.F.R. 1910, 1025 (1979).

54. § 6(b), 29 U.S.C. 655(d).

55. See, e.g., ¶12, 441 (1-26-82).

56. The statute also authorizes the secretary of labor to grant variances where necessary "to permit an employer to participate in an experiment approved by the Secretary . . . designed to demonstrate or validate new and improved techniques to safeguard the health or safety of workers" [§ 6(d)(6)(C)].

57. 47 *Fed. Reg.* 29025 (July 2, 1982).

58. 3 CCH OCC. Safety & Hlth Rep. ¶12, 439 (1-26-82).

Environmental Disclosure Requirements of the Securities and Exchange Commission

Stephen W. Hamilton

Skadden, Arps, Slate, Meagher & Flom

T he rules and regulations of the Securities and Exchange Commission (SEC) require all publicly held companies[1] to make certain disclosures regarding the effects of compliance with, and legal proceedings arising under, federal, state, and local environmental laws. These disclosures must be included in various public filings, such as the annual report on Form 10-K and the quarterly report on Form 10-Q, which publicly held companies must prepare and file with the SEC. It is important that disclosures regarding environmental matters be complete and accurate, since significant misstatements or omissions could result in criminal or civil liability under the federal securities laws.[2]

BACKGROUND

The SEC has been quite active in the environmental area over the past 10 years, with much of its time and effort directed at attempting to establish an appropriate threshold for disclosure of environmental information. Initially, the SEC's environmental-disclosure requirements were in accord with most of its other rules and regulations, which mandate the disclosure of economically "material" information relating to the business and financial operations of publicly held companies. A materiality standard functions to limit the amount of disclosure which is required, since information is considered material only if a reasonable investor would consider it important in making a decision on whether to buy, hold, or sell a security or on how to cast a vote.[3] Thus companies were required to furnish information about material legal proceedings arising under environmental regulations and any material effects compliance with such regulations might have on capital expenditures, earnings, or business operations.[4]

In 1973, however, the SEC reconsidered its position on environmental disclosure and adopted specific environmental-disclosure provisions.[5] These new rules required disclosure not only of economically material information but also of information which, while not particularly important from an economic point of view, was highly significant to certain constituencies interested in the social and ethical responsibilities of major corporations. In particular, the SEC's rules required disclosure of *all* environmental proceedings involving a governmental authority (sometimes referred to herein as a "governmental proceeding"), regardless of whether the proceeding was material to a company's business. As a result, multibillion dollar companies which were not required to disclose nonenvironmental litigation involving hundreds of thousands of dollars were nevertheless required to disclose governmental proceedings involving only hundreds of dollars.

The SEC's departure from its traditional materiality threshold for environmental disclosure was prompted by a number of factors, including its desire to satisfy its responsibilities under the National Environmental Policy Act (NEPA)[6] and to address concerns which had been raised by the Natural Resources Defense Council (NRDC) and other public interest groups. Over the next several years the SEC, prompted by continuing litigation with the NRDC regarding its environmental provisions,[7] continued to evaluate its environmental rules and held two major public hearings which considered the disclosure of environmental and other "socially significant" information.[8]

After several years of experience in administering its environmental rules, the SEC began to question its decision to depart from a materiality disclosure threshold in the environmental area. Specifically, the SEC noted that its requirement to disclose all governmental proceedings often generated lengthy discussions of relatively inconsequential matters which obscured information regarding more significant environmental proceedings and which tended both to place unnecessary burdens on public companies and to lessen the quality and utility of environmental disclosure to investors.[9] Despite these concerns, the SEC was unwilling to return exclusively to a materiality standard for environmental disclosures. Instead, in 1982 it adopted a compromise threshold for disclosure of environmental proceedings as a part of its integrated disclosure system.[10]

CURRENT RULES

In addition to the SEC's general requirement that companies must make full and accurate disclosure of all material (including environmental) information relating to their affairs, the SEC today has two specific rules directly applicable to environmental matters. The first of these provisions, which has remained essentially unchanged since 1976, is set forth in item 101(c)(1)(xii) of Regulation S-K.[11] Item 101 requires the disclosure of the material effects that compliance with federal, state, and local provisions relating to the protection of the environment may have on a company's capital expenditures, earnings, and competitive position. This provision also mandates disclosure of any material estimated capital expenditures for environmental control facilities for the remainder of a company's current fiscal year, for its succeeding fiscal year, and for any additional periods the company deems material.

This provision generally is considered relatively noncontroversial, and companies typically include an estimate of their capital expenditures for the remainder of the current fiscal year and their next fiscal year as part of the narrative business description required in the annual report on Form 10-K. Companies should be aware, however, that this provision can have more far-reaching consequences. For example, as discussed below, the SEC believes that under certain circumstances a company may have an obligation to develop and disclose estimates of capital expenditures for additional years if these expenditures are expected to be materially higher than those which otherwise would be disclosed. Companies should also carefully consider whether the necessary environmental compliance will result in significant indirect costs which should be disclosed, such as reductions in a plant's output capacity or a company's ability to compete. Further, the costs incurred to remedy past violations, such as expenditures for plant cleanups, must be disclosed.

The possible effects of proposed regulations may also present a pitfall in compliance with item 101. Estimating capital expenditures and the effects of environmental compliance may become much more complex if new or modified environmental laws or regulations have been proposed but have not yet been enacted or adopted. Assuming that such a law or regulation would, if enacted or adopted, have a material effect on a company's environmental costs, a company may be required to discuss the probable consequences of the proposed law or regulation and indicate how the company's environmental expenditures will be affected. With respect to the possible consequences of proposed regulations generally, the SEC has stated that whether disclosure is required "depends upon a balancing of the likelihood of a proposed rule's enactment and the magnitude of the rule's impact on the corporation if enacted in its proposed form."[12] In other words, the greater the impact a proposed rule would have on a company and the greater the likelihood that the rule will be adopted, the more compelling is the case for disclosure of the proposed rule's consequences. In any event, if the estimated capital expenditures which a company discloses are based in part on the future adoption of a proposed rule, this factor should be mentioned.

In addition, a company should be sensitive to the fact that estimates of the potential costs of a proposed rule which are submitted to an environmental agency as part of the rule-making process could prove troublesome to a company at some later time. Often such cost estimates, which are made to show the potential burden of the proposed rule and may be quite high, are not reflected in a company's SEC disclosure. While these differing disclosures may be entirely appropriate in many instances, if questions subsequently arise regarding the accuracy of the SEC disclosure, seemingly inconsistent statements made to an environmental agency and to the SEC may be an issue.[13]

The second specific environmental disclosure provision, instruction 5 to item 103 of Regulation S-K,[14] requires companies to describe certain pending legal proceedings and proceedings known to be contemplated by governmental authorities which arise under environmental laws and of which they or their subsidiaries or property are the subject. (The language of this instruction was clarified in 1982 to indicate that the laws covered by the instruction are those which have been adopted *primarily* for the protection of the environment, as opposed to those which merely relate to the environment.) Instruction 5 to item 103 contains three clauses which constitute a three-prong threshold for determining whether disclosure of a proceeding is required. Information must be furnished if an environmental proceeding meets any one or more of these thresholds.

If disclosure is required by one of the clauses of instruction 5, complete information about a pending proceeding, including the court or agency in which the proceeding is pending, the date the proceeding was instituted, the principal parties involved, the factual basis of the allegations, and the relief sought, must be furnished. Similar information (to the extent available) must be given on contemplated governmental proceedings. Upon the termination of a disclosable proceeding, information about the ultimate outcome of the proceeding must be provided.

The first clause of instruction 5 sets forth a general materiality threshold and requires disclosure of any environmental proceeding which is material to the business or financial condition of the reporting company. This is a traditional SEC disclosure standard based on economic materiality.

The second clause contains a current-assets threshold and states that an environmental proceeding must be described if the amount involved, exclusive of interest and costs, exceeds 10 percent of a company's current assets on a consolidated basis. This threshold also reflects what is essentially an economic materiality test, albeit an objective one. The amount involved may consist of claims for damages, potential fines or other monetary sanctions, and any capital expenditures, deferred charges, or charges to income that may result (as a result of cleanup costs, for example) from the proceeding. It is important to note that all damage claims, fines, and other expenditures must be aggregated in determining whether the 10 percent threshold has been exceeded. Therefore a proceeding involving a potential fine equal to 5 percent of a company's current assets and remedial capital expenditures equal to 6 percent of a company's current assets would be disclosable under this threshold.

The general materiality threshold and the current-assets threshold apply both to governmental proceedings and proceedings involving only private parties. Under both of these clauses, proceedings involving in large degree the same legal and factual issues must be aggregated in determining whether the disclosure thresholds have been exceeded.

The third clause of instruction 5, the so-called $100,000 threshold, applies exclusively to governmental proceedings and permits the omission of information about certain less significant governmental proceedings. This new threshold is the SEC's response to the substantial criticism which its former environmental provision had generated.

Under this $100,000 threshold, a company need not disclose information about a governmental proceeding involving a potential fine or other monetary sanction if the company reasonably believes that the fine will not exceed $100,000. This test applies only to proceedings involving fines and similar sanctions; therefore other types of proceedings, such as permit proceedings and requests for waivers or variances, are not disclosable under this prong of the SEC's rule. Similar government proceedings need not be aggregated in determining whether the potential fine may exceed $100,000, and similar proceedings which are disclosable may be grouped and described generically, which may lessen a company's disclosure burden.

The "reasonable belief" standard requires companies to make certain judgments about the probable outcome of a governmental proceeding involving a fine and therefore is less certain than, for example, a disclosure requirement based on the fine actually assessed. The SEC, however, believes that after-the-fact disclosure of an environmental proceeding would be less useful to investors than information about pending proceedings and has noted that companies already make similar types of judgments in connection with the accounting treatment of financial contingencies.[15] Companies should be able to rely on, among other things, their prior dealings with governmental authorities and the outcomes of proceedings involving similar issues brought against other corporations in forming a reasonable belief regarding the magnitude of the potential fine.

While the current version of instruction 5 is less onerous than its predecessor, which required disclosure of all governmental proceedings, it still requires more disclosure than most other SEC rules, which elicit only economically material information. A governmental proceeding involving a $200,000 fine, for example, may be of little financial importance to a company with millions, or even billions, of dollars in assets. This provision in some respects appears to be directed more toward requiring a public disclosure of possible environmental "sins" than at providing information relevant to investment or voting decisions.[16] The SEC apparently believes that such a provision helps to satisfy its responsibilities under NEPA (and, perhaps, to avoid future litigation with public interest groups such as the NRDC). In any event, management should keep informed of all governmental proceedings which could result in a fine of over $100,000, since it will be required to make judgments about their probable outcomes.

One very sensitive issue regarding the timing of disclosure deserves mention. The SEC's environmental rules do not specifically require a company to "turn itself in" by making disclosure about an environmental violation which has not yet come to the attention of a governmental agency or a private litigant. General materiality principles could, however, require a company to furnish information about a violation before a legal proceeding is pending or known to be contemplated. The courts have indicated that the issue of whether disclosure of an unasserted claim is required may involve a balancing of the magnitude of the possible liability to the company and the likelihood that such liability will ultimately be established.[17] In addition, accountants will consider the probability that an unasserted claim will in fact be asserted and the reasonable possibility that the outcome will be unfavorable, in determining whether disclosure of the matter is required in connection with the issuance of a company's financial statements.[18] Because of the difficult legal issues raised by unasserted claims, it is desirable to seek the advice of legal counsel in determining whether disclosure is appropriate.

SEC ENFORCEMENT ACTIONS

The SEC has brought three enforcement cases (and has published an interpretive release) which are of significance in understanding its environmental-disclosure rules and the procedures publicly held companies may wish to follow to satisfy these requirements. While these enforcement actions predate the SEC's 1982 amendments to its environmental rules, they establish important principles which are applicable under the present disclosure system.

The first SEC enforcement action in the environmental area was an injunctive action brought against Allied Chemical Corporation in 1977[19] and involved the discharge by Allied of certain toxic chemicals, including Kepone, into the environment. The SEC complaint, which was based on general materiality concepts rather than specific environmental-disclosure rules, alleged that Allied had failed to disclose to its shareholders the potential material financial exposure that could result from such discharges. Allied settled the SEC's action by consenting, without admitting or denying the allegations of the SEC's complaint, to the entry of an injunction against violations of certain reporting and antifraud provisions of the federal securities laws.

The Allied case is particularly significant because of the remedial measures which Allied undertook to perform in connection with the settlement of the case. In particular, Allied was required to complete an investigation of the material environmental risk areas and material environmental uncertainties of its business and to maintain policies, practices, and procedures which would alert management to these risks and uncertainties. Allied also was required to review these practices, policies, and procedures on a continuous basis and to make any modifications that management deemed necessary. The Allied case thus indicates the SEC's belief that an internal environmental-control, or audit, system is important to ensure that adequate and timely environmental disclosure is made by publicly held companies.

The second, and perhaps most significant, SEC environmental action was a 1979 administrative proceeding instituted against United States Steel Corporation (USS) to determine whether USS's environmental disclosures in its filings with the SEC were deficient.[20] USS consented, without admitting or denying the SEC's findings, to the issuance of the SEC's findings and agreed to comply with the SEC's order. The USS case, and an interpretive release which was issued in connection with it,[21] established a number of significant principles.

First, the SEC found that USS had generated internal studies which indicated that over the ensuing five or six years USS would have to make capital expenditures of between $700 million and $1.1 billion to comply with environmental regulations. USS had, however, disclosed only those costs which it had expected to incur in the next two or three years. The SEC stated that if a company has developed estimates which suggest that it may have material capital expenditures beyond those required to be disclosed for its current and succeeding fiscal years, or if it is reasonably likely that the company will incur material fines or penalties for future noncompliance, it may be necessary to disclose this information to prevent the mandatory 2-year disclosure required by item 101 from being misleading. In addition, the SEC stated that if a company "reasonably expects" that its environmental compliance costs for future years will be materially higher than those which it is disclosing at present, the company may have an obligation to develop and disclose estimates of future costs, as well as the source of the estimates and the assumptions and methods used in arriving at the estimates. The SEC thus believes that a company may not adopt a "hear no evil, see no evil" approach toward the total costs of future environmental expenditures.

Second, the SEC reiterated its broad interpretation of the term "proceeding," which it views as including many pending and even contemplated environmental disputes, regardless of whether such matters constitute a proceeding in the technical legal sense. The SEC stated that USS should have disclosed, for example, administrative proceedings initiated by USS, administrative orders which were not contested or were negotiated by USS and therefore were not the subject of active litigation, and notices of violation and other less formal indications of contemplated action by governmental authorities. Companies should be aware that less formal actions, such as negotiations with a governmental authority about an environmental problem, may rise to the level of a proceeding for purposes of the SEC disclosure rules.

Third, the SEC found that USS had a policy of actively resisting environmental requirements which USS deemed unreasonable, and the SEC criticized as incomplete USS's statement that it "has pledged to confront and resolve its environmental problems as effectively and efficiently as technology, time and money permit." The SEC stated that, while companies generally have no obligation to disclose their environmental policy, any statements which a company voluntarily chooses to make must be accurate. In addition, the SEC noted that if a company pursues a policy toward environmental compliance which is likely to result in fines, penalties, or other significant effects on the company, it must disclose the likelihood and magnitude of such fines, penalties, or other effects.

Finally, USS agreed to appoint an independent consultant to estimate the expense necessary to bring USS's facilities into compliance with environmental requirements and to appoint a task force to review its environmental disclosures and prepare a report to the USS audit committee, setting forth procedures to provide for timely and accurate environmental disclosure.

The third SEC enforcement action involved an administrative proceeding against Occidental Petroleum Corporation (Oxy) in 1980.[22] This proceeding was initiated to determine, among other things, whether Oxy had made the required SEC disclosures relating to the discharge of chemical and toxic wastes, primarily by Oxy's subsidiary, Hooker Chemical Corporation. The SEC found, among other things, that Oxy did not disclose certain pending or contemplated environmental proceedings, did not adequately disclose the effect on its business of complying with environmental laws, and did not disclose the significant potential liabilities for damages resulting from Oxy's environmental activities. The SEC noted that the costs of environmental compliance include both the costs of bringing a facility into compliance *and* the costs associated with past noncompliance, such as fines and the costs of plant shutdowns or cleanups. In addition, the SEC implied that Oxy's general disclosure that there could be no assurance that it would not incur material liabilities was not sufficient, given the facts known to Oxy at the time.

The SEC also found that Oxy did not have adequate methods or procedures to help it meet its disclosure obligations. As with Allied and USS, Oxy agreed (without admitting or denying any of the SEC's allegations) to take certain actions to improve its internal environmental monitoring procedures. Among other things, Oxy agreed to have an environmental audit prepared by a director, an environmental officer, and an independent consulting firm which would recommend to the Oxy board certain procedures which could be followed to ensure proper disclosure in the future. This report also would reasonably determine certain potential compliance costs and the maximum civil penalties that might be imposed on Oxy and would describe various other claims against Oxy.

Perhaps the most significant lesson which can be derived from the SEC's enforcement actions is the need for publicly held companies to maintain adequate internal controls—i.e., environmental audit programs—to monitor environmental compliance. Unless management is continuously furnished with reliable information regarding environmental activities and problems, the quality of a company's environmental disclosure (and ultimately its business decisions) will suffer. Over the long run, the benefits of an environmental auditing system, in which responsibility is assigned for collecting and analyzing environmental data and reporting such information to top management and directors, will almost certainly outweigh its costs.

1. Under the federal securities laws, publicly held companies include companies which have securities listed on a national securities exchange, companies which have total assets exceeding $1 million and 500 or more shareholders, and companies which had a registration statement become effective under the Securities Act of 1933 and have 300 or more shareholders.

2. Liability could arise, for example, under § 18(a) or 10(b) of the Securities Exchange Act of 1934.

3. *See TSC Industries, Inc. v. Northway, Inc.*, 426 U.S. 438 (1976).

4. *See* SEC Release No. 33-5170 (July 19, 1971) [36 FR 13989].

5. SEC Release No. 33-5386 (Apr. 20, 1973) [38 FR 12100].

6. 42 U.S.C. § 4321 *et seq.* NEPA, effective Jan. 1, 1970, required the SEC and other executive agencies to interpret and administer their policies, regulations, and laws "to the fullest extent possible" in accordance with the environmental protection policies set forth in NEPA. Ibid. at § 4332(1).

7. *See Natural Resources Defense Council, Inc. v. SEC*, 606 F.2d 1031 (D.C. Cir. 1979), *rev'g* 432 F. Supp. 1190 (D.D.C. 1977); *Natural Resources Defense Council, Inc. v. SEC*, 389 F. Supp. 689 (D.D.C. 1974).

8. *See* SEC Release No. 33-5569 (Feb. 11, 1975) [40 FR 7013]; SEC Release No. 34-13901 (Aug. 29, 1977) [42 FR 44860].

9. *See* Division of Corporation Finance, SEC, *Staff Report on Corporate Accountability*, 96th Cong., 2d Sess. (Comm. Print 1980) (Senate Comm. on Banking, Housing and Urban Affairs); SEC Release No. 33-6315 (May 4, 1981) [46 FR 25638].

10. SEC Release No. 33-6383 (Mar. 3, 1982) [47 FR 11380].

11. 17 C.F.R. § 229.101(c)(1)(xii).

12. SEC Release No. 34-17390 (Dec. 18, 1980) [45 FR 86593].

13. The SEC has recognized that corporations make inconsistent disclosures to various governmental entities but has declined to adopt a public interest group's proposed rules to remedy this practice. The SEC has noted, however, that "[i]nconsistent disclosures may give rise to concerns about the adequacy of information contained in [SEC] filings," and that it can bring enforcement actions under its general materiality standards if it believes such action is appropriate. Ibid.

14. 17 C.F.R. § 229.103.

15. *See* SEC Release No. 33-6383 (Mar. 3, 1982) [47 FR 11380]. The SEC lists the *Statement of Financial Accounting Standards No. 5*, issued by the Financial Accounting Standards Board in 1975, as the standard requiring companies to make similar types of reasonable-belief judgments.

16. The stated SEC rationale for this provision is that proceedings involving potential fines may be more indicative of "possible illegality and conduct contrary to public policy" and that therefore a disclosure threshold based on economic materiality is not appropriate in this context. *See* SEC Release No. 33-6315 (May 4, 1981) [46 FR 25638]. It is questionable, however, whether a fine proceeding is significantly more indicative of "bad" conduct than a private damage action or an action mandating capital expenditures to remedy past noncompliance.

17. *See*, e.g., *SEC v. Mize*, 615 F.2d 1046 (5th Cir. 1980), *cert. denied*, 449 U.S. 901 (1980); *SEC v. Texas Gulf Sulphur Co.*, 401 F.2d 833 (2d Cir. 1968), *cert. denied*, 394 U.S. 976 (1969).

18. *See* Financial Accounting Standards Board, *Statement of Financial Accounting Standards No. 5*, ¶ 10 (1975).

19. *SEC v. Allied Chemical Corporation* (D.D.C. Civ. No. 77-0373, Mar. 4, 1977).

20. *In re U.S. Steel Corp.*, SEC Release No. 34-16223 (Sept. 27, 1979).

21. SEC Release No. 33-6130 (Sept. 27, 1979) [44 FR 56924].

22. *In re Occidental Petroleum Corp.*, SEC Release No. 34-16950 (July 2, 1980).

Product Liability: The Present Situation

Stuart E. Eizenstat
Jesse W. Hill
Powell, Goldstein, Frazer & Murphy

O on a busy Monday morning, you, chairman of the board and chief executive officer of a growing Fortune 500 conglomerate, receive a call from your legal department, announcing the arrival that morning, via a deputy sheriff, of a lawsuit. Your legal department informs you that, some twenty-five years ago, one of the companies your firm acquired last year made a product that was used, some fifteen years ago, by a Mr. Brown. Mr. Brown is now retired, you are told, having had a long career in the construction industry. Mr. Brown's doctor has now informed him that he has lung cancer that is inoperable.

As you listen to the sad news about Mr. Brown, you are thinking "That's too bad, but what does it have to do with me or our firm?" The answer becomes vividly clear when the general counsel informs you that you have been sued for $5 million by Mr. Brown's attorney, and that there is in fact some real possibility of an award approaching that sum, since Mr. Brown has also sued your company for punitive damages. Lastly, your general counsel completes the job of ruining your day by informing you that his preliminary conversations with your insurance carrier have revealed the carrier's view that your firm has no insurance coverage whatsoever for the claims asserted by Mr. Brown.

A nightmare induced by too many cognacs after dinner last night? Unfortunately, no. For many manufacturers in today's environment, this scenario is far from being impossible. There are literally thousands of lawsuits pending in the United States that have originated from facts just like our example.[1] Moreover, millions of dollars of awards have been paid in settlements and in judgments on claims arising from such sets of circumstances.[2]

The potential exposure of a manufacturer in today's legal climate to product-liability claims grounded in the use, whether knowingly or unknowingly, of a hazardous substance in the manufacturing process is astronomical. Many corporate executives, however, are unaware of the nature and extent of this risk until the fateful day when the deputy sheriff arrives at their door. This chapter will attempt to explain in layman's terms the risks that strongly suggest to every product manufacturer the reasons for an environmental audit—reasons that are unemotional, that go beyond a feeling of general corporate responsibility to be a good citizen or considerations of general welfare, and that extend beyond normal concern for a workplace sufficiently safe to meet Occupational Safety and Health Administration standards. These powerful reasons are the enormous costs that can be incurred when manufacturers produce products using hazardous substances, even if they are unaware of the extent of the hazard or perhaps of its very existence. The risks are the product-liability claims against a company, with the accompanying enormous defense costs[3] and the potentially vastly greater amounts of money that will be needed to settle the claims, whether before or after judgment.[4]

It is no defense to say that "we only do what the entire industry does." In fact, if that is the case, the manufacturer may be in an even more untenable position. Similarly, it is no defense to say, "I didn't know that we used a hazardous substance in our product." Courts have regularly ruled that the manufacturer is held to the standard of an expert, and that if an expert knew or should have known of the danger, then the manufacturer is charged with that knowledge.[5] Finally, it may be no defense to say, "Talk to my insurance company. They will settle this claim because we've got full coverage." The interpretation of insurance policies that were purchased to provide product-liability coverage for manufacturers is one of the great legal debates presently pending in the United States courts.[6]

PRODUCT LIABILITY—ITS SCOPE AND THEORIES OF RECOVERY

Manufacturers and sellers of products have been sued by dissatisfied customers since well before the establishment of courts in the English colonies that became the United States of America. The major English common-law theories of recovery are based on negligence or breach of contract by the manufacturer or seller and are readily understood and accepted, at least in their general terms, by most reasonable, literate citizens—special legal education and expertise are not required. Within the past 10 years, however, and especially within the past two or three years, very rapid changes have occurred in the development of what is termed "strict-liability law," and an understanding of this subject requires greater attention and study than the commonsense understanding of an intelligent layman's recognition of older forms of the common law.

Of special significance in the development of strict-liability law is its component dealing with liability for injuries caused by the *content* of a product. Today a product may be legally defective, thus subjecting its manufacturer to liability, if the product contains a potentially hazardous substance. This liability is most often based on the manufacturer's alleged failure to warn adequately of the existence of the dangerous ingredient and its potential to cause serious injury years after sale.

Two important reasons for and uses of any environmental audit are to identify any hazardous or potentially hazardous ingredients in a manufactured product and to prescribe steps to reduce the possibility of a successful product-liability claim against the manufacturer.

This chapter will review the history of the development of the law of product liability, the legal theories that can be used to pursue the manufacturers of a defective product (including the emerging law of industry-wide liability), some of the chemicals or substances that should act as a red flag in any audit, and the possibility of an award of punitive damages against the manufacturer of a defective product.

"Product liability" is a term used to refer to the several related areas of law governing the liability of a manufacturer or distributor to a person who is injured by some defect in the product made or sold. The areas of law referred to are warranty, negligence, and strict liability. Claims made by an injured person against a manufacturer or distributor are often based on all three of these areas of law.

Warranty

A warranty about the characteristics, safety, or suitability of a product may be the basis for a legal action if the warranty proves to be untrue and a party is injured as a result of reliance upon the warranty.[7] Warranties may be either express, as when made in writing (or in some instances orally) by the manufacturer or distributor, or implied, as when imposed by the Uniform Commercial Code.[8]

This theory of liability is perhaps the easiest to understand and to prove when the facts of a particular claim fit within the limitations of the law of sales. The primary limitation is that the protection of the warranty usually is limited to the individual to whom it was given—the person who purchased the product directly from the manufacturer or distributor, a direct purchaser. This concept of one-on-one dealing is called "privity" and essentially means that only the person who received the warranty, made the purchase based upon such a warranty, and was injured as a result of the breach of the warranty may recover for such a breach. For example, customer A wishes to buy a shampoo which can be used by persons who are allergic to alkali and asks seller B if he can recommend such a product. Seller B assures customer A that he has for sale just such a product, and, in reliance on seller B's expertise in this matter, the product is purchased by customer A. Customer A uses the product, loses much of his hair, and suffers a burned scalp and temporary loss of vision.

The product in fact was not safe for the customer to use. Customer A may sue seller B for breach of warranty of fitness for a particular purpose,[9] even if the shampoo is safe for use by most people who are not allergic to alkali. If the manufacturer had expressly warranted this shampoo to be safe for use by persons allergic to alkali, customer A might also have had a claim against the manufacturer for breach of that warranty.[10] When the products are purchased by customer A for use by immediate family members (assume that the customer's spouse was the person needing a special shampoo), traditional rules of lack of privity would have prohibited the injured family member from suing seller B, since there was no contract between the family member and seller B, only a contract of sale between A and B. Most states have concluded that this is an improper result, however, and now an injured family member or guest of the purchaser may sue for breach of express or implied warranty if injured by the breach of warranty.[11]

Lack of privity remains a strong defense to product-liability claims in situations where there is a subsequent resale of the product or use of the product by a person not a guest or a member of the immediate family of the purchaser. In addition, the damages an injured party may recover are usually somewhat limited in lawsuits based only on breach of warranty.[12] Accordingly, a person who sustains a serious personal injury will often pursue another theory of liability in an effort to recover additional damages, and possibly even punitive damages, which may be available in a product-liability claim based on negligence.

Negligence

A manufacturer is required by the law of negligence to use reasonable care in the design and manufacture of a product. If the manufacturer fails to exercise that care, and the resulting product poses an unreasonable risk of harm to a person using the product in its intended manner or in a manner that should have been anticipated by the manufacturer, the manufacturer may be liable for all damages that result from the negligent acts or omissions. The three areas in which a manufacturer is most often accused of negligence are the design process, the manufacturing process, and the labeling or instructions that do or should accompany the product, describing risks in using the product and providing directions and precautions. For example, the manufacturer of a lawn mower must use reasonable care in the design of the machine (taking care that the cut debris is not thrown into the face of the operator, for instance); in the manufacturing process (using quality-control standards, testing devices and procedures, etc.); and in the accompanying instructions if there are any unusual features to the machine, if any unusual maintenance is required, or if its safe operation requires that special steps be taken. Moreover, when a product is capable of causing substantial physical injury if improperly operated, the prudent manufacturer will take care to give routine directions for the safe use of the product, even if these routine directions are essentially identical to the directions used on similar products made by other manufacturers. The question of whether directions, precautions, and warnings given by manufacturers concerning their products and the content of their products are adequate is one of the most difficult in the area of product-liability law, and a prudent manufacturer will give this matter careful attention.

Whether a negligence claim arises against a distributor essentially depends upon the role of the distributor in transferring goods from the manufacturer to the purchaser. Distributors can be generally divided into two groups: those who regularly inspect the goods they sell and those who do not. Some categories of goods are shipped to a distributor who merely stores them and then sells them, without any regular or anticipated inspection by the distributor of the goods. In this circumstance, the sealed-container doctrine often applies (except as to food products in most states), and the distributor will not be found negligent if he fails to test and inspect a product before selling it. Retailers of canned motor oil, for example, are not required to inspect and test the contents of each can before selling such products. If there is an obvious defect, such as extensive corrosion on the can, however, it may be negligence for the distributor to fail to detect the damage and remove the defective goods from inventory before sale.

The second large class of distributors embraces those who routinely and necessarily inspect goods received from the manufacturer before sale. A good example is an automobile dealer who receives cars and then services and tests them before sale. Negligence law requires that such a distributor exercise reasonable care in performing these tests and services, and a failure by the distributor to do so would be the basis for a negligence claim. Whether a particular distributor is in the category of those who have a duty to test and inspect or in the category of those who may rely on the sealed-container doctrine will almost always be an issue of fact and therefore usually will be decided by the jury.

Strict Liability

The basis for the relatively new portion of tort law known as "strict liability" is the existence of a defect which makes the product unreasonably dangerous to the user or consumer at the time the product leaves the seller's control. Under this area of law, one who manufactures a product containing a defect may be held strictly liable for harm caused to the ultimate user or consumer by that defect, even when the manufacturer exercised reasonable care, that is, even if the manufacturer was not negligent.[13] Privity (or lack of privity) and negligence (or due care) on the part of the manufacturer need not be proved, because they are not material. The most often articulated theory behind this legal doctrine is that a manufacturer should bear the costs of injuries sustained by innocent consumers, because the manufacturer is better able to assume and spread the risk of such economic loss through insurance or through absorbing such losses as a cost of doing business.[14]

Even under strict-liability concepts, however, the fact that a person is injured by a product does not automatically impose liability on a manufacturer; a defect must exist in the product and that defect must be a cause of the injury. If the injury is caused by a consumer's misuse or abuse of the product or failure to follow adequate directions or precautions, there is no basis for recovery under any of these three theories of product liability. Similarly, if the product is altered after it is sold by the manufacturer, the alteration may be the cause of a subsequent injury and not any defect contained in the product when sold by the manufacturer. Nonetheless, because the theory behind strict liability is not predicated upon fault on the part of the manufacturer, manufacturers should not be surprised if strict-liability claims are asserted against them for any injury that a consumer can allege resulted from a defect.

Perhaps the most significant development in the expansion of product-liability law of the past 10 years has been the birth of new doctrines that substantially expand the theories available to a plaintiff in seeking recovery from a manufacturer. Many of these theories have been the direct result of a court's effort to find a method for establishing liability where plaintiffs have obviously suffered some injuries but, often through no fault of their own, are unable to identify the specific manufacturer whose product caused this harm. The lack of ability to identify a product may be due to the widespread use of generic devices or products, the passage of time, or other reasons.[15] However, some courts have shown a willingness to depart far from the traditional requirement that the plaintiff prove that a defendant's product caused the specific injury for which redress is sought.

These new advances in product-liability laws are variously referred to as "market-share liability" or "industrywide liability"; although the concepts are interrelated, they have different origins. Their common result, however, is to remove the burden from the plaintiff to show what specific manufacturer made the product that allegedly caused the harm. Then, under market-share liability theory, the measure of damages assessed against a particular manufacturer is calculated on the basis of its market share at some point in time.

The theory of alternative liability is at least as old as the leading case of *Summers v. Tice*.[16] In that case, a plaintiff was injured when two of his hunting colleagues both fired in his general direction. The pellets from one of their guns struck him, causing injury. The plaintiff had no way of knowing which of the two defendants actually fired the shot that caused his injuries, although he did know that they were the only two persons whose conduct might have resulted in his injury. In those circumstances, the court concluded that the fair result was to shift the burden of proof to the defendants to establish which of them, in fact, caused the plaintiff's injury. This is a traditional legal approach and causes most observers little consternation. However, when it is applied to the product-liability field, as it has been in several recent cases, complications arise.

The theory of alternative liability was first applied in a product-liability context in a case involving blasting caps.[17] In that case, the plaintiffs were children who were injured by the unexpected detonation of the caps, and they were unable to identify the specific manufacturer of the caps with which they were playing. Accordingly, they sued all the manufacturers of blasting caps (there were only six at that time) and alleged that each of them had knowledge of the dangers involved in improper handling of the caps and that defendants had failed to take reasonable safety measures which would have removed this risk of harm. Under these circumstances, the court allowed the claim to go forward, stating that if the allegations were proved true, all the defendants would bear the risk of joint liability to the plaintiffs. Thus the concept of industrywide liability was brought into product-liability law.

Of ironic significance, however, was the court's simultaneous decision in a companion case.[18] The only difference in the second case was that the plaintiffs were able to identify the manufacturer of the caps involved, although the remaining manufacturers were sued as well. Once the court considered that development, and notwithstanding its sweeping analysis in the first case, it concluded that the known manufacturer alone should bear the entire risk of loss for the injury sustained by the second plaintiffs and dismissed their claims against other manufacturers.

The next major shift occurred in the well-known *Sindell v. Abbott Laboratories*[19] case decided in 1980 by the California Supreme Court in a 4 to 3 split. It is significant for two reasons. First, under the old industry-wide liability concept, it was apparently necessary for the plaintiff to join as defendants all possible manufacturers (hence the industrywide appellation).[20] Under the *Sindell* market-share theory, however, plaintiffs need join only a substantial portion of the manufacturers whose products were manufactured at the time of the exposure of which the plaintiff complained.[21] Then, as to those joined defendants, the burden was shifted, and it was up to each of them to establish to a jury's satisfaction that their particular product could not have been the one that caused plaintiff's alleged injury.

What is the significance of these decisions to a manufacturer? Although several courts have rejected the expansion of these theories,[22] we may be at a point in the development of the American legal system where the idea of making a manufacturer a virtual insurer of the safety of his product is gaining additional support, allegedly for public policy reasons. Some writers hope that the *Sindell* and *Hall* types of cases will be limited to their facts, as more and more courts review in detail the consequences of imposing insurer status on all manufacturers (not the least of which will be the incredible increase in product liability insurance premiums for all manufacturers, even assuming for the sake of argument that any insurer would still be willing to provide such coverage; the fact that the cost of such increased insurance would inevitably be passed along to consumers in the form of higher product prices to the extent coverage is available; and, to the extent that coverage is not available, the fact that many manufacturing processes would simply be stopped by prudent management officials or the company would elect to "go bare"). However, for purposes of considering the need for an environmental audit, it is sufficient to note that manufacturers who believe that their company is doing no worse than anyone else in the industry and who, in fact, may have no actual knowledge of the hazards of the product that they are manufacturing may nonetheless be held liable for very substantial damages and possibly even for the imposition of punitive damages as well. The additional cost of an environmental audit, both to attempt to identify the nature and extent of the danger contained in products and to limit the human suffering or pain in one's workers or customers, seems a modest price to pay in return for at least a diminution in the risk of product-liability claims.

INSURANCE

Insurance coverage for product-liability claims against manufacturers is generally available. It is most important, however, to recognize that such protection is offered only for an additional premium and with a special endorsement; it typically is not provided even in the basic "comprehensive" liability policies sold to manufacturers. In earlier times, when there was no strict liability, the barriers of privity and the requirement that a plaintiff prove negligence on the part of a manufacturer limited the manufacturer's exposure and need for insurance coverage. "Premises and operations" coverage was all that was needed, and insurance policies were drafted with that limited need in mind.

As a result, two exclusions contained in most comprehensive liability policies left manufacturers exposed to substantial uninsured liability, given today's product-liability law. A prudent manufacturer will want to give serious thought to paying an additional premium and obtaining an endorsement to his policy, to avoid being exposed to the uninsured liability that can result from the "goods or products" exclusion or the "completed operations" exclusion. The goods or products exclusion operates to eliminate insurance coverage for injuries sustained after goods have been sold to a customer and removed from the insured's (manufacturer's) premises.[23] In other words, once the goods leave the manufacturer's control, the insurance company provides no coverage for liability based upon a defect in the goods—a most undesirable result from the manufacturer's point of view.

The second exclusion that unwary manufacturers might overlook to their later dismay is the completed operations exclusion. This exclusion was intended to allow insurance coverage for liability resulting from an insured's activities away from the insured's main plant but to eliminate that coverage once the insured's employees had completed their "outside" work.[24] For example, a manufacturer who sends a field crew to install a piece of machinery at a customer's plant would have liability insurance for protection while the installation was carried out. Once the installation was complete, however, and the crew returned home, the operations would be completed and the insurance coverage would cease. If an employee of the customer was later injured because the equipment was improperly installed, there would be no insurance to aid the unfortunate manufacturer who had not obtained completed operations coverage.

There have been many court decisions interpreting these two exclusions, and sometimes courts have ruled that in a particular circumstance the exclusions did not apply and that the insured did have coverage.[25] One cannot rely on such a result, however, because even though courts will construe the language of the policy in favor of the insured, the courts will ultimately enforce the terms of the insurance contract. Manufacturers cannot feel comfortable about their product-liability-insurance coverage unless they have obtained the additional goods and products and completed operations coverage. The standard policy language for product-liability coverage obligates the insurance company "to pay on behalf of the insured all sums which the insured become legally obligated to pay as damages because of bodily injury or property damage to which this insurance applies . . . , if the bodily injury or property damage is included within the completed operations hazard or the products hazard. . . ."

Most policies sold today provide coverage based upon an occurrence within the policy period, even if a claim is not filed until later years. The alternative form is called a "claims made" policy, but this is becoming a rarity because of the underwriting difficulties involved. Under an occurrence policy, if a product is manufactured and sold in the year of coverage, the manufacturer will have the benefit of that coverage for claims based on that product even if they arise in future years. Frequent exclusions include the "business risk" exclusion, under which the insurer is not liable for damages caused by the failure of the product to perform as expected. This broad statement is subject to limitations, however, particularly when bodily injury results from the failure to perform. Other general limitations deal with product-recall expenses and pollution damage.

The traditional definition of "occurrence" has mixed application, however, when a manufacturer is sued for damages caused by exposure to a dangerous chemical or substance when, as is often the case, the harm does not manifest itself until many years after the hazardous exposure. Is the insurer who had the coverage when the exposure took place liable, or is it the insurer who had the coverage when the disease had progressed enough to be detectable by the injured person's physician? The debate over exposure vs. manifestation interpretations of "occurrence" remains a heated one, with literally millions of dollars and the continued economic survival of many manufacturers at risk. The dispute seems inevitably headed toward a Supreme Court that appears to have no desire to untie this Gordian knot.[26] In the interim, even manufacturers who believe that they have taken steps to protect themselves from the consequences of using a hazardous material cannot truly feel protected; they may well end up in a life-or-death struggle with not only plaintiff's counsel but also counsel for their own insurance companies.

One other area of great confusion remains the issue of insurance coverage for punitive damages, discussed in greater detail later in this chapter. Punitive damages originated in the area of negligence law, or more specifically in the area of intentional wrongdoing. They are generally said to be awarded both as additional compensation to the injured party and to deter the wrongdoer from repeating the misconduct. Because punitive damages are intended to punish a deliberate wrongdoer, many courts have concluded that it would be against public policy to allow a defendant to have a third party (the insurance company) absorb the punishment. Accordingly, in many states insurance policies are held not to cover damages awarded as punitive damages. Other courts have reached a contrary result, and all damages the insured may have to pay (up to the policy limits of liability) can be covered by a sufficiently carefully selected policy of insurance.

SPECIFIC HAZARDOUS SUBSTANCES AND THE ENVIRONMENTAL AUDIT

Carcinogens

In July of 1980 the National Toxicology Program of the U.S. Public Health Service published its first annual report on carcinogens. At that time it identified twenty-six substances as known carcinogens.[27] When the second annual report on carcinogens was released in December 1981, the number had grown to eighty-eight.[28] By no means has the list of known or suspected carcinogens been expanded to its limit, in the view of most researchers.[29]

The debate over what is or may be a carcinogen has not been confined to the scientific community, as lawsuits have been filed across the country alleging that plaintiffs have sustained injury or even death due to cancers caused by their exposure to one or more alleged carcinogenic substances. The asbestos cases are the most widely known, but suits have also been filed against manufacturers of prescription drugs (the DES cases) and have involved "agent orange," "agent white," polyvinyl chloride, and other chemical compounds. A full review of the nature and action of these carcinogens, the site of the tumors most regularly associated with them, and a detailed history of the categories of workers who are most often exposed to such substances is beyond the scope of this chapter. However, it is clear that a wide range of manufacturing processes use many of these substances in manners that nontechnical personnel would not fully appreciate or even anticipate. For this reason, an environmental audit is often the only way in which management can become aware of the potential risks involved in the manufacturing process or the products that are ultimately produced.

In addition, prudent manufacturers will wish to remember a lesson learned in the asbestos litigation. The dose necessary to cause a disease response in the ultimate consumer of the product will be substantially downplayed by plaintiff's counsel when there is any history of injuries to plant workers in the manufacturing process. Thus, while the asbestos industry has known since the 1930s that workers in a mining or weaving operation in which large quantities of essentially pure asbestos dust were breathed were at risk of developing some health complications, the manufacturers believed (and the debate goes on as to whether that belief was either accurate or rational) that the much lower levels of asbestos that would be breathed by the ultimate users of the product would not present so great a risk of harm, if it presented any risk at all. The plaintiffs' counsel have sought, often with great effectiveness, to persuade jurors that "a lung is a lung" and that a dust that harms a plant worker should be anticipated to cause the same harm in ultimate users of the product, even with lower levels of exposure. Accordingly, in any industrial situation in which plant workers show any increased incidence of lung disorders or carcinomas, remedial steps must be taken to avoid having a "Monday-morning quarterback," perhaps even 20 years from now, conclude that the manufacturer was callous or consciously indifferent to the consequences to consumers of using a product that was known to the manufacturer to be hazardous.

A good environmental audit would therefore seek to establish parameters for monitoring the health of in-plant employees, and, depending upon the nature of the product used, set up annual physical examinations, x-ray reports, safe work rules (such as use of respirators where indicated, radiation detection badges, etc.), not only to protect the employees presently working for manufacturers but also to provide evidence, if needed in the future, of the manufacturer's good-faith efforts to determine whether a risk to the ultimate users might exist. Company medical officers would, of course, have major input into the formulation of the plan, after consulting with the persons conducting the environmental audit.

Other Harmful Substances

A wide range of substances can harm those exposed to them in addition to those substances thought to be carcinogens. Chief among these are such substances as carbon monoxide (or fumes that contain carbon monoxide or other poisonous gases that might be released when a product is burned), lead, organic and inorganic dusts, pesticides and their residue, and a wide range of organic chemical compounds, industrial gases, industrial vapors, or industrial dusts.

The bulk of the product-liability claims involving carbon monoxide fumes have been based upon alleged inadequate warnings of manufacturers concerning the fumes that are released when a product is burned, whether intentionally (as with charcoal briquettes) or unintentionally (leaky flues in furnaces, etc.).

Most children's toys, furnishings, etc., no longer contain lead paint, and lead poisoning is no longer so common as it once was. However, lead products have remained in use in certain cosmetic items; and several cases of lead poisoning were reported in the 1960s among workers who were involved in building and maintaining missile silos.

The hazards of pesticides and industrial chemicals, vapors, fumes, and dusts are generally well known in the industries in which these products are used. However, many of the substances are used on occasion in other manufacturing processes and the services of a skilled industrial hygienist, toxicologist, or other expert in the field of industrial exposure is necessary if a manufacturer is to be comfortable with the content of his products.

PUNITIVE DAMAGES IN PRODUCT-LIABILITY CASES

Punitive damages are awarded in cases involving conduct that is deemed to be so unacceptable that extra money must be assessed to punish the offender and to deter similar future action.[30] A variety of opprobrious phrases have been used to describe the sort of conduct warranting the award of punitive damages, such as acting "deliberately or through wanton or gross negligence";[31] "willful misconduct, malice, fraud, wantonness, or oppression, or that entire want of care which would raise the presumption of conscious indifference to consequences";[32] reckless indifference to the safety of others";[33] and the like. The language of the *Restatement of Torts* perhaps best summarizes the societal concerns underlying these phrases: "Punitive damages may be awarded for conduct that is outrageous, because of the defendant's evil motive or his reckless indifference to the rights of others."[34]

Historically, punitive damages have been awarded in the area of intentional torts.[35] In the past two decades, however, such damages have often been sought, and occasionally awarded, in product-liability cases. Generally, these cases involve a manufacturer's alleged failure to communicate warnings about risks associated with a product to those likely to encounter such risks. The number of fully reasoned reported cases on this point is small; nonetheless, upon review the cases suggest some of the factors which a court will consider in deciding whether punitive damages should be allowed. These factors—the degree of a manufacturer's perception and appreciation of the risk, the type of product involved, and the presence or absence of certain aggravating elements—are discussed below, with particular reference to their application in product-liability litigation.

Preliminarily, it may be noted that such damages may not be recoverable at all in some classes of cases. For example, in some states punitive damages cannot be recovered in wrongful death actions[36] or in actions under a no-fault automobile statute.[37] Moreover, it has occasionally been argued that punitive damages are wholly inapplicable in the product-liability context, but that view has only rarely received judicial acceptance.

A second preliminary matter is whose conduct may be imputed to a corporation for the purpose of assessing punitive damages. For this purpose some jurisdictions—Prosser calls them a minority[38]—will impute to a corporation only the conduct of senior officers and employees.[39] The *Restatement of Torts* has taken this position.[40] Others will charge a corporation with the conduct of any employee, so long as it falls within the scope of employment of that employee.[41]

Finally, although the allegedly wrongful conduct in each case is the primary focus of inquiry, the unique character of product-liability cases justifies brief consideration of the policies which are cited to support the concept of punitive damages. Two policies are most often named: deterrence and punishment. With respect to the first, it may be noted that, to the extent that any wrongful conduct occurred, it sometimes took place a generation or more before a plaintiff's injuries, and in a time when attitudes and knowledge about environmental or occupational diseases were far different. Thus, even if tortious conduct did take place, there is nothing to suggest that any additional deterrence is necessary today, in a world where manufacturers are exceedingly sensitive to the potential hazards of their products and where a multitude of government regulations now precludes precisely the conduct which is alleged to have occurred.[42]

As to punishment, the lapse of time since the alleged wrongful conduct is again relevant. To assess punitive damages may well punish wholly innocent persons (shareholders of today are not always the shareholders of the past; managers also retire; etc.), with no effect except to enrich certain plaintiffs.

Perception and Appreciation of the Risks

Before punitive damages can be awarded for failure to warn of a risk to users of a certain product, there obviously must be some evidence that the manufacturer knew of the risk. With some products, such as drugs or machines which, if they do not function properly, will subject the user to serious bodily harm, the risk is obvious. At times, however, the question may arise whether a manufacturer did indeed perceive any danger.

For example, in *Thomas v. American Cystoscope Makers, Inc.*,[43] a surgeon had his eye burned when an optical device malfunctioned, apparently because the device was being used with an uninsulated eyepiece. The evidence at trial established that the manufacturer knew that such eyepieces were being used and that some risk might arise from such use; and that there had been an obscure reference in the medical literature to the danger of an accident like the one sued upon. There was no evidence, however, that the manufacturer knew of the specific hazard. In these circumstances the court found punitive damages to be unwarranted.

Similarly, in *Roginsky v. Richardson-Merrill, Inc.*,[44] there was evidence to show that the drug manufacturer had been informed by another drug company of test results suggesting that the drug might have certain adverse side effects. Rather than notify either the Food and Drug Administration or the medical community of these results, the company chose to repeat the experiments. The court held that this decision, even when coupled with other evidence suggesting that the company later may have communicated false information to the FDA, was not sufficient to warrant an award of punitive damages. Implicit in this holding is the court's view that knowledge of a single set of adverse test results does not constitute actual knowledge of a risk.

A corollary of this is that a manufacturer may have some awareness of certain risks and yet may not fully appreciate them. For example, in the *American Cystoscope* case, there was evidence that the manufacturer was generally aware that some risk was created by use of the uninsulated eyepiece but had no knowledge of the specific hazard. In disallowing punitive damages the court held: "But the fact that the danger should have been foreseen does not . . . [establish] that the risk was fully realized, or at least, realized to the extent necessary to show that degree of knowledge which, when consciously disregarded, deserves the opprobration of 'recklessness'."[45]

The importance of this factor is illustrated by contrast with *Gillham v. Admiral Corp.*,[46] involving a fire in a television set. The evidence at trial showed that the set's designer anticipated the possibility of fires and indeed developed a structure (ineffective) to prevent serious ones. This demonstrated beyond doubt that the danger was fully appreciated, and the court upheld an award of punitive damages.

Usually the evidence is not so clear, and the question then becomes what quantum of information is necessary to charge a manufacturer with actual or constructive knowledge that use of its product entails a certain risk. In the *American Cystoscope* case, an obscure medical reference was not sufficient, while in *Hoffman v. Sterling Drug, Inc.*,[47] the court held sufficient testimony that an article based upon a few case reports "established a definite connection" between use of a drug and certain toxic effects, particularly when coupled with evidence of later, similar findings. This issue cannot be resolved by a general answer; rather, it needs to be raised and developed with the facts of each case.

Implicit in the preceding paragraph is the question of timing. As the court in *Roginsky v. Richardson-Merrill, supra*, noted, hindsight is always better than foresight, and it is thus important to judge conduct in light of what was known when it occurred. For example, in *Johnson v. Husky Industries, Inc.*,[48] the court held that a manufacturer's conduct after an injury, involving changes in its label, and a postaccident lawsuit alleging similar facts, were not sufficient to warrant punitive damages. Similarly, in the *American Cystoscope* case the court refused to consider plaintiff's evidence of postaccident conduct in ruling on punitive damages.

Nonetheless, the critical point for our purposes is that a court can conclude, and many courts in fact have concluded, that only minimal medical literature, known in fact only to medical researchers, can be sufficient data to impute knowledge of a hazard to a manufacturer and thereby make a product that contains a dangerous component so defective as to allow a jury to award both compensatory and punitive damages.

Type of Product

In arguing against punitive damages it may be useful to discuss the type of product involved. As discussed more fully below, this may be of particular use where it is alleged that the failure to test a product warrants imposition of punitive damages. More generally, the type of product is relevant to show the degree of culpability involved. For example, ethical drugs, the purpose of which is to affect bodily functions, might well be said to pose a per se risk, and the failure to appreciate, test for, and warn of that risk could be a basis for punitive damages. Similarly, machines which propel human beings at high speeds quite clearly pose a risk, and a failure to appreciate this could be held to be culpable.

Aggravating Factors

In addition to the degree to which a risk is appreciated and the type of product involved, there are certain factors whose presence or absence may influence the decision on whether to allow punitive damages. The most important factors are a manufacturer's efforts to conceal risks from those coming in contact with its products and failure to test products for possible risks. Also relevant, although less compelling, is the availability of a substitute product.

Failure to warn of known risks

The deliberate concealment of known risks is, of course, the classic case for imposition of punitive damages in the product-liability area. Concealment can take two forms. It may be active, entailing falsification of data or test reports, or it may be passive, involving a failure to warn of known risks. Perhaps the best known reported case of active concealment is *Toole v. Richardson-Merrill, Inc.*[49] In the *Toole* case there was evidence that the manufacturer of an ethical drug falsified test data submitted to the FDA, withheld information concerning side effects from the FDA and the medical profession, and continued to represent that the drug had relatively minor side effects in the face of test results to the contrary. These circumstances, together with evidence of failure to test (discussed below), were held to warrant assessment of punitive damages.

Similarly, in *Gillham v. Admiral Corp.*, *supra*, there was evidence of repeated efforts to reassure purchasers of certain television sets which tended to catch fire that no real danger existed, and that evidence was one of the bases for sustaining a punitive-damages award. Again, in *d'Hedouville v. Pioneer Hotel*[50] evidence that the manufacturer of a highly flammable carpet consciously misrepresented its safety was one factor relied on to support an award of punitive damages. Finally, in *Southern Pacific Transportation Co. v. Lueck*[51] a case arising in simple tort rather than product liability, the Arizona Supreme Court affirmed the award of punitive damages for a death at an unguarded railroad crossing. Central to the court's decision was evidence that the defendant railroad company had obtained a state regulatory authority's approval of the crossing's design without disclosing studies recommending gates at the crossing or presenting data indicating that such gates increase crossing safety 90 percent.

The cases cited above involved active conduct which had the effect of misleading the public about the safety of certain products. Awards of punitive damages have also been sustained where there is evidence only of a failure to warn of known risks. Thus, in *Moore v. Jewel Tea Co.*,[52] a can of Drano exploded, causing severe burns. There was evidence that the manufacturer was aware of prior such explosions, and indeed had issued instructions to its employees concerning procedures to avoid them. No instructions, however, were given to consumers. This failure to warn was one factor cited by the court in upholding the award of punitive damages. Similarly, in *Boehm v. Fox*,[53] the failure of a manufacturer of a cattle-feed additive to warn of risks from improper use was, of itself, sufficient to support imposition of punitive damages.

Failure to test for risks

It is clear that, in some circumstances at least, a manufacturing firm has a duty to test its products for safety, and a breach of that duty may give rise to an award of punitive damages. The scope of this duty for assessing punitive damages, however, is not easily defined. Clearly, where the intended use of a product is such that a malfunction or defect will threaten serious harm, there is a duty to ascertain whether any defect or potential malfunction exists. For example, ethical drugs are intended to affect bodily functions; the danger of unanticipated side effects is clear; and a breach of the corresponding duty to learn of such side effects may well support punitive damages. Similarly, where certain external conditions might render a product dangerous, there is a duty to ascertain whether they in fact will do so. For example, in *d'Hedouville v. Pioneer Hotel, supra*, evidence that a carpet manufacturer did not consider flammability testing of its products important and that it marketed a certain type of carpet without sufficient testing was a central factor in sustaining an award of punitive damages. Likewise, in the Drano case, *supra*, the manufacturer's failure to ascertain whether the can was designed to avoid explosion was one basis for allowing punitive damages.

Availability of a substitute product

The availability of a functionally equivalent, safer substitute for a product with certain risks has also been a factor in product-liability punitive damage cases. For example, in *d'Hedouville v. Pioneer Hotel, supra*, a carpet manufacturer's continued sale of a relatively flammable carpet after development of a safer fabric was one factor supporting punitive damages. Again, in *Gillham v. Admiral Corp., supra*, a manufacturer of television sets failed to effect a relatively simple design change to avoid fires; this was a factor cited by the court in affirming the assessment of punitive damages.

Many factors could be considered in arguing that a substitute product or component may be used. Technology, market acceptance, cost, and production capacity are all legitimate factors for a manufacturer to consider when deciding whether a substitute is commercially feasible. For purposes of lawsuits by injured plaintiffs, however, courts may not take into account all these factors, and the availability of a substitute might well be determined by a jury that does not fully take into account all the problems of a manufacturer. If that thought distresses you, the authors' purpose is merely to warn of such a result, not to advocate it.

CONCLUSION

Product-liability law is rapidly changing in terms of the theories of liability that may be advanced, the standard of care that will protect a manufacturer from punitive damages (to say nothing of compensatory damages), and the types of insurance available to meet the truly phenomenal costs that can occur when a decision goes against a manufacturer. Competing societal needs and goals serve only to aggravate the tensions created in this time of flux. The only conclusion that can be stated with authority is that manufacturers who fail to concern themselves with the risk of claims based upon the potential toxic, carcinogenic, or other harmful content of their products do so at their absolute peril.

One step that may reduce this risk is having a detailed environmental audit performed by competent personnel. While it is impossible to outline all the steps that can or should be taken in such an audit, these are some of the measures that should be considered:

1. Review of workmen's compensation claims by plant workers
2. Review of customer complaints
3. Review of claims against the company by consumers
4. Review of chemical components used in the manufacturing process
5. Review of medical literature concerning possible risks associated with any chemical used in the manufacturing process
6. Review of chances for exposure of consumers to dangerous components
7. Review of possible use of substitutes for any dangerous components
8. Review of company's history and correspondence concerning efforts to find substitutes, awareness of the danger involved, and reaction to claims
9. Review of warning or caution labels and instructions concerning any dangerous components of the product line

With these steps, and such others as may be dictated by the particular circumstances of a given manufacturer, the risk of successful product-liability claims against a manufacturer can be minimized. When considering the need for and expense of an environmental audit, a prudent manufacturer will do well to remember that "an ounce of prevention is worth a pound of cure."

1. In its petition for relief under chap. XI of the Bankruptcy Code, Manville Corporation estimated that on Aug. 26, 1982, over 16,500 cases were pending against it alleging injury from exposure to asbestos-containing products manufactured by the company. The *Wall Street Journal* estimated in August of 1982 that some 30,000 claims had been filed against asbestos concerns collectively, *Wall Street Journal*, Aug. 27, 1982, p. 1. The asbestos cases are by far the most numerous, but hundreds of cases are pending involving formaldehyde and benzene exposure as well as many "agent orange" claims.

2. The Manville Corporation petition reported that the company had settled some 3500 asbestos-related claims at an average cost of $16,600 in the past but that its current cost was up to $40,000 per claimant. These figures did not include punitive damages awarded in five of the cases that were tried, which averaged over $600,000 per case. Settlements or verdicts involving millions of dollars have also been rendered in benzene, DES, and formaldehyde cases. The developments have become a part of the popular press. See, e.g., "Product Safety: A New Hot Potato for Congress," *U.S. News & World Report*, June 14, 1982, pp. 62–63 (reporting on toxic chemical damages); "Toxic Time Bombs," *Newsweek*, Sept. 6, 1982, p. 57.

3. Data from insurers about defense costs are difficult to obtain, but the Manville Corporation's petition in its chap. XI proceedings suggests that defense costs had reached the astonishing total of $2 million per month nationwide at the time of filing.

4. This analysis was the key reason for the filings for relief under chap. XI by Manville Corporation and by UNR Industries, formerly known as Unarco Industries and, earlier, as Union Asbestos and Rubber Company. UNR filed in Chicago in late July of 1982. Note that UNR had not made any asbestos-containing products since 1962.

5. Some courts have taken the language of the *Restatement of the Law, Second, Torts* 402A to what many defense counsel would argue to be extreme, if not absurd, lengths, typified by the following excerpt from the recent decision of the New Jersey Supreme Court in *Beshada v. Johns-Manville Products Corp.*, 51 U.S.L.W. 2038 (N.J. Sup. Ct., July 7, 1982):

> The important claim, for purposes of this appeal, is for strict liability for failure to warn. . . . The manufacturers respond by asserting the state-of-the-art defense—that the danger of which they failed to warn was undiscoverable at the time the product was marketed and that it was undiscoverable given the state of scientific knowledge at that time. . . . But in strict liability cases, culpability is irrelevant. The product was unsafe. That it was unsafe because of the state of technology does not change the fact that it was unsafe. . . . One of the most important arguments generally advanced for imposing strict liability is that the manufacturers and distributors of defective products can but allocate the costs of the injuries resulting from it. This can but be accomplished by imposing liability on the manufacturers and distributors. Those persons can insure against liability and incorporate the cost of insurance in the price of the product.

The court fails to provide guidance, however, as to how the manufacturer is to determine the nature or extent of the hazard created by its product or to warn of that hazard when, by definition, the nature and extent of that hazard are both unknown and undiscoverable at the time the product is made. Similarly, the insurance industry's underwriters are left to tea leaves or other techniques of clairvoyance in setting coverage limits and premiums.

6. A full review of this debate is beyond the scope of this chapter, and the debate will undoubtedly remain confused absent a ruling by the United States Supreme Court. The coverage issue is very complex, in large measure because of the conflicting results decreed by the courts that have reached decisions. The opinions of the Court of Appeals for the District of Columbia Circuit, in *Keene Corporation v. Insurance Co. of North America* [667 F.2d 1034 (D.C. Cir. 1981), *cert. denied*, 50 USLA 3716 (Mar. 9, 1982), *reh'g denied*, 50 USLW 3859 (Apr. 26, 1982)], remains absolutely irreconcilable with the opinions of the Courts of Appeal in the sixth and fifth Circuits in *Insurance Company of North America v. Forty-Eight Insulations, Inc.* [633 F.2d 1212 (6th Cir. 1980)] and *Porter v. American Optical Corp.* [641 F.2d 1128 (5th Cir. 1981)], all three of which are irreconcilable with the decision of the First Circuit in *Eagle-Picher Industries v. Liberty Mutual Insurance Co.* [682 F.2d 12 (1st Cir. 1982)]. When the Supreme Court denied certiorari in the *Keene* case, a landslide of coverage suits in the District of Columbia Circuit became inevitable, since that opinion was most favorable to insureds. Less than a month after certiorari was denied, over eleven such suits had been filed by manufacturers of asbestos, DES, and "agent orange." *See* " 'Keene' Spurs Delayed-Manifestation Disease Suits," *Legal Times*, May 24, 1982, p. 17.

7. Section 2-313 of the Uniform Commercial Code, adopted in virtually every state except Louisiana, provides that

(1) Express warranties by the seller are created as follows:

(a) Any affirmation of fact or promise made by the seller to the buyer which relates to the goods and becomes part of the basis of the bargain creates an express warranty that the goods shall conform to the affirmation or promise.

(b) Any description of the goods which is made part of the basis of the bargain creates an express warranty that the goods shall conform to the description.

(c) Any sample or model which is made part of the basis of the bargain creates an express warranty that the goods shall conform to the sample or model.

(2) It is not necessary to the creation of an express warranty that the seller use formal words such as "warrant" or "guarantee" or that the seller have a specific intention to make a warranty; but a mere affirmation of the value of the goods or a statement purporting to be only the seller's opinion or commendation of the goods does not create a warranty.

Subsection (2) therefore usually excludes from express warranty status the salesperson's opinion such as "This is a great buy" or similar remarks, often referred to as "puffery."

8. UCC § 2-314 finds in all sales (unless the contract specifically excludes it) an implied warranty that the goods sold are, in general, of "fair average quality" and are "fit for the ordinary purposes for which such goods are used."

9. UCC § 2-315 provides: "Where the seller at the time of contracting has reason to know any particular purpose for which the goods are required and that the buyer is relying on the seller's skill or judgment to select or furnish suitable goods, there is unless excluded or modified under the next section an implied warranty that the goods shall be fit for such purpose."

10. UCC § 2-313, set forth in footnote 7, above.

11. Typical of such amendments, which give persons other than the purchaser the status of third-party beneficiary of the seller's warranties, is the Georgia statute, Ga. Code 109A-2-318 (Acts 1962 at 156, 191): "A seller's warranty whether express or implied extends to any natural person who is in the family or household of his buyer or who is a guest in his home if it is reasonable to expect that such person may use, consume or be affected by the goods and who is injured in person by breach of the warranty. A seller may not exclude or limit the operation of this section."

12. UCC § 2-316 allows sellers to limit the nature and extent of many warranties, thereby limiting the scope of the warranties for which they may be sued. In addition, sections 2-718 and 2-719 generally allow a seller to limit the remedies and damages available to a purchaser in the event a warranty is breached. Most important is section 2-719(3): "Consequential damages may be limited or excluded unless the limitation or exclusion is unconscionable. Limitation of consequential damages for injury to the person in the case of consumer goods is prima facie unconscionable but limitation of damages where the loss is commercial is not."

13. Section 402A of the *Restatement of the Law, Second, Torts* provides as follows:

(1) One who sells any product in a defective condition unreasonably dangerous to the user or consumer or to his property is subject to liability for physical harm thereby caused to the ultimate user or consumer, or to his property, if

(*a*) the seller is engaged in the business of selling such a product, and

(*b*) it is expected to and does reach the user or consumer without substantial change in the condition in which it is sold.

(2) The rule stated in subsection (1) applies although

(*a*) the seller has exercised all possible care in the preparation and sale of his product and

(*b*) the user or consumer has not bought the product from or entered into any contractual relationship with the seller.

14. See, e.g., *Beshada v. Johns-Manville Products Corp.*, footnote 5 above.

15. An example from the asbestos litigation: many companies manufactured products that were very similar in appearance, such as asbestos cloth. Unless one actually saw the shipping tag affixed to a roll when it was first used, it was virtually impossible to tell one manufacturer's product from another's. Similarly, in cases involving diethylstilbestrol (DES), physicians often wrote a generic prescription for the drug, and a pharmacist would fill the prescription from whatever stock was on hand, without regard to the manufacturer. Moreover, in the DES cases the injured plaintiffs were the children of mothers who had taken the drug. Obviously, a plaintiff who was still *in utero* could not be expected to have personal knowledge of the drug taken by the mother. Passage of time means loss of inventory, production, and shipping records for all manufacturers, making identification of the specific product used, by manufacturer, often difficult if not impossible. This leads to a situation in which some injured persons may be forced to choose between committing perjury and facing the risk of no recovery.

16. 33 Cal. 2d 80, 199 P.2d 1 (1948). This result is now embodied in § 433 B(3) of the *Restatement of the Law, Second, Torts*: "Where the conduct of two or more actors is

tortious, and it is proved that harm has been caused to the plaintiff by only one of them, but there is uncertainty as to which one has caused it, the burden is upon each actor to prove that he has not caused the harm."

17. *Hall v. E. I. DuPont De Nemours & Co.*, 345 F. Supp. 353 (E.D.N.Y. 1972). Actually, the reported decision deals with two different complaints, those of Phillip Hall and others and those of Randy Chance and others. It is somewhat ironic that Hall is the name by which the decision is referred to by legal commentators, since the concept of industrywide liability was recognized only for the Chance plaintiffs. The amended Hall complaint set forth the name of the manufacturer whose product allegedly caused the injury, and the trial court therefore rejected for the Hall plaintiffs the concept of industrywide liability adopted in the same opinion for the Chance plaintiffs.

18. See footnote 17 above.

19. 26 Cal. 3d 588, 607 P.2d 924, 163 Cal. Rptr. 132 (1980), *cert. denied,* 449 U.S. 912, 101 S. Ct. 285, 66 L. Ed. 2d 140 (1980).

20. This is at least a reasonable construction of the Hall decision, since the trial court's opinion stressed that all possible tortfeasors (i.e., manufacturers) had been joined in the Chance complaint. This difference was also emphasized in Justice Richardson's dissent in the Sindell case.

21. Justice Richardson, writing for the three dissenters, noted one obvious problem created by the court's decision: "Notably lacking from the majority's expression of its new rule, unfortunately, is any definition or guidance as to what should constitute a 'substantial' share of the relevant market. The issue is entirely open-ended and the answer, presumably, is anyone's guess," 607 P.2d at 939.

22. See *Hardy v. Johns-Manville Sales Corp.*, 681 F.2d 334 (5th Cir. 1982). The trial court's use of collateral estoppel and judicial notice principles to preclude certain asbestos manufacturers from contesting the issue of whether their products were defective, based upon the Borel decision [493 F.2d 1076 (5th Cir. 1973), *cert. denied,* 419 U.S. 869, 95 S.Ct. 127, 42 L. Ed. 2d 107 (1974)], was reversed. This decision substantially erodes the impact of the Borel case, or at least the interpretations given by some trial courts and commentators to the language in the Borel opinion. The Hardy decision also seems to breathe new life into the state-of-the-art defense rejected by some courts: "[A] determination that asbestos generally is hazardous threatens to undermine a defendant's possibly legitimate defense that its product was not scientifically known to be hazardous, now or at relevant times in the past," 681 F.2d at 347.

23. Various texts were used before the 1966 revision to the standard comprehensive general liability policy, but the basic content was to exclude coverage for liability arising from an accident "caused directly or indirectly by the possession, consumption, handling or use of" or the existence of any condition or warranty of, any goods or products "manufactured, sold, handled or distributed" by the named insured *if* the accident occurred after the insured had "relinquished possession" thereof to others *and* away from the premises of the insured.

24. Again, the terms of the exclusion varied slightly from policy to policy, but the thrust was that coverage did not extend to accidents that were the result of operations if the accident occurred after such operations had been completed or abandoned at the place of the occurrence and away from the premises of the insured.

25. See, e.g., *Peerless Insurance Co. v. Clough*, 105 N.H. 76, 83, 193 A.2d 444, 449 (1963): "The plaintiff insurer gave the defendant coverage in a single, simple sentence easily understood by the common man in the marketplace. It attempted to take away a

portion of this same coverage in paragraphs and language which even a lawyer, be he from Philadelphia or Bungy, would find it difficult to comprehend."

26. See footnote 6 above and materials cited therein.

27. Among those substances most commonly recognizable to nonscientists are asbestos, benzene, benzidine, cadmium, chromium, diethylstilbestrol (DES), iron oxide, mustard gas, nickel, and vinyl chloride. Monographs on these and the other carcinogens are available from the U.S. Public Health Service, Department of Health and Human Services.

28. New substances likely to be known to nonscientists include beryllium, chloroform, formaldehyde, Kepone, acetate, lead phosphate, mirex, polychlorinated biphenyls (PCBs), and saccharin.

29. Other well-known products, generally thought by lay persons to be perfectly safe, have been associated by the National Cancer Institute with certain occupational cancers. Among the most striking examples are wood, associated with cancer of the nasal passages and sinuses in woodworkers, and leather, associated with the same cancers and cancer of the bladder in leather workers and shoe workers. See Galiher, "Defending Lung Cases Before Federal and State Boards," *Ins. Counsel J.*, January 1981 at 41. See, generally, Comment, "Tort Actions for Cancer: Deterrence, Compensation, and Environmental Carcinogens," 90 *Yale L.J.* 840 (March 1981). For a detailed review of cancer and legal issues geared to the attorney, see "Cancer and the Law," 5B *Lawyers' Medical Cyclopedia* (Allen Smith Co., 1972).

30. See, generally, W. Prosser, *Handbook of the Law of Torts* 9-14 (4th ed. 1971); *Restatement of the Law, Second, Torts* 908(1).

31. See, e.g., *Southern Pacific Transportation Co. v. Lueck*, 111 Az. 560, 535 P.2d 599, 609 (1975), *cert. denied*, 425 U.S. 913 (1976).

32. *Gilman Paper Company v. James*, 235 Ga. 348, 351, 219 S.E.2d 447, 450 (1975).

33. *d'Hedouville v. Pioneer Hotel Co.*, 552 F.2d 886, 894 (9th Cir. 1977) (applying Arizona law).

34. *Restatement of the Law, Second, Torts* 908(2).

35. See *Prosser*, footnote 30, above, at 10–11.

36. *Pease v. Beech Aircraft Corp.*, 38 Cal. App. 3d 450, 113 Cal. Rptr. 416, 423–24 (1971).

37. See *Teasley v. Mathis*, 243 Ga. 561, 255 S.E.2d 57 (1979).

38. See *Prosser*, footnote 30 above, at 12.

39. For example, *Lake Shore and Michigan Southern Ry. Co. v. Prentice*, 147 U.S. 101 (1893); *Roginsky v. Richardson-Merrill, Inc.*, 378 F.2d 832, 842 (2d Cir. 1967) (applying New York law).

40. *Restatement of the Law, Second, Torts* 909 provides: "Punitive Damages Against a Principal. Punitive damages can properly be awarded against a master or other principal because of an act by an agent if, but only if: (*a*) the principal or a managerial agent authorized the doing and the manner of the act, or (*b*) the agent was unfit and the principal or a managerial agent was reckless in employing or retaining him, or (*c*) the agent was employed in a managerial capacity and was acting in the scope of employment, or (*d*) the principal or a managerial agent of the principal ratified or approved the act."

41. See, generally, *Prosser*, footnote 30 above, at 12, and cases cited therein.

42. See, e.g., *Zahn v. International Paper Co.*, 469 F.2d 1033, 1033 n.1 (2d Cir. 1972), *aff'd on other grounds*, 414 U.S. 291 (1973).

43. 414 F. Supp. 255 (E.D. Pa. 1976).

44. 378 F.2d (2d Cir. 1967); but *see Toole v. Richardson-Merrill, Inc.*, discussed in text at footnote 49, reaching a contrary conclusion on essentially the same facts.

45. 414 F. Supp. at 267.

46. 523 F.2d 102 (6th Cir. 1975), *cert. denied*, 424 U.S. 913 (1976).

47. 485 F.2d 132 (3d Cir. 1973).

48. 536 F.2d 645 (6th Cir. 1976).

49. 251 Cal. App. 2d 689, 60 Cal. Rptr. 398 (Ct. App. 1967).

50. 552 F.2d 886 (9th Cir. 1977).

51. 111 A2.560, 535 P.2d 599 (1975), *cert. denied*, 425 U.S. 913 (1976).

52. 253 N.E.2d 636 (Ill. App. 1969), *aff'd*, 46 Ill. 2d 288, 263 N.E.2d 103 (1970).

53. 473 F.2d 445 (10th Cir. 1973).

Product Liability: Historical Perspective

Mark P. Denbeaux

Seton Hall Law School

The 900 years of common-law history contain countless numbers of cases. Each of these cases attempts to fit its facts to a general theory or principle which will be the basis of the decision. The reliance upon established principles to decide various factual situations is what is meant by *stare decisis* (literally, to follow decisions). The principles are designed to achieve two not-always-consistent goals: certainty and individual justice. The certainty requirement calls for like facts to be treated alike and means that honoring the principle may require an unfortunate or unjust result in an individual case.

Although *stare decisis* would seem to require that the guiding principles remain constant, this has never been completely true. Even in the days most strongly committed to certainty and mechanical application of *stare decisis* principles,[1] the rules and principles evolved. In fact, it is only partly recognized how often rules and principles have changed. Although it is well recognized that the nine centuries of common-law history have produced incomprehensible quantities of fact patterns, it is less well recognized that they also include a similarly bewildering collection of principles and rules. From such a rich data base different ages are able to draw different conclusions.

As each new cycle of the law looks to the past in part to solve the problems of the present and to guide the future, it discerns different patterns. With such a rich and ambiguous data base, different individuals inevitably draw different conclusions as well. Anyone can also discover "new" and "original" principles which he or she believes organize the relevant information. The situation is somewhat like a kaleidoscope, in which all the pieces are present at all times, but with each new turn they form a different image.[2] In the law, each era sees different principles which organize the relevant pieces, and thus legal history goes through different cycles in which the creative principles present a different image.

One question in our era is to what extent, if any, is product liability a new principle or concept? It is possible to view the concept of product liability as a new theme based upon new situations never before confronting the law or as a new response to previously existing circumstances. It is also possible to view it as an old theme reapplied to new and different circumstances. Product liability is usually seen as a dramatic creation of modern law, but it is also possible to see it as a modest refinement of an old legal principle.

However product liability is viewed, it is recognized to be a special refinement of the principle of strict liability. Strict liability is the antithesis of the current theory of liability based upon fault. The fault principle, although it is currently under great attack, dominates the law today. The dominant legal and social theory today is that people should not be liable for injuries they have caused except when they were at fault. Causation, the most slippery of all concepts, is also under attack but not nearly as much so as the concept of fault. Perhaps the greatest exponent of fault as a device to limit liability was Oliver Wendel Holmes.[3] Holmes viewed the law of negligence as the application of fault to the resolution of all actions for unintentional injuries. With proof of fault the plaintiff could be liable, without such proof he or she could not. That view remains the dominant one today.

Product liability is viewed as the major exception to that standard and as such is frequently seen as a new development in the law and a signpost to the direction of the law. The opposite view is that it is a perversion of the established order. It may be a refinement in the current doctrine and it may be a sign of the future direction of the law, but it is not at all clear that it is a new development. The concept of fault is so embedded in the law today that it is hard for us to comprehend any other system, perhaps because the principle pervades the rest of society as well. In fact, the concept of fault has a modest ancestry. Before the middle of the nineteenth century there was no body of law which systematically considered the subject of unintentional injuries, and certainly there was no doctrine that predicated the plaintiff's recovery upon proof of fault.[4]

The comprehensive system so strongly identified by Holmes in *The Common Law* in 1881 may have had its origin as recently as 1850, in an opinion of the Massachusetts Supreme Court, *Brown v. Kendall.*[5] The significance of *Brown v. Kendall* was that the absence of fault was used as a defense to otherwise certain liability, thereby creating a mammoth breach in the foundation of the law of that era and the centuries preceding. The prior law could be roughly summarized as "each person acts at his peril."[6] In that context, any actions which caused injury, regardless of fault, were actionable. Fault, then, and negligence as we know it today, arose from an effort to *limit* the liability of people who acted. There is some irony in the fact that men of action of today claim to be overburdened by law which limits their liability solely to injuries caused by their own fault.

Despite their objections to the negligence system as too burdensome, the same people extol its virtues when confronting the strict-liability aspects of product liability. Historians may disagree as to whether the change to negligence was or was not the result of an effort to aid, encourage, and protect the fledgling industries of the early industrial revolution,[7] but no one can dispute that the doctrine had that result. Thus the negligence system, based on fault as it is, served industry, especially the manufacturing industries, well.

The fledgling concept of product liability (its early history is in some dispute, but its first bloom did not occur until the post-World War II era) is viewed as novel because it relies upon strict liability rather than fault. That means that whether one is at fault or not, one may still be liable if it is shown that one's actions caused the injury complained of.

It is possible to argue that not only is the strict-liability dimension of product liability not new, but the departure from strict liability is a relatively junior heresy. That is, if negligence were to become effectively extinct in this particular cycle of legal history, by virtue of its brief duration it would not represent an important aspect of legal history, merely an interesting episode. By this analysis, strict liability is not new: at most, it is an old wave returning, and at least, it is a wave that never fully receded.

Clearly, such a view can be challenged. Interpretation of past legal epochs does not produce unassailable clarity. Thus while the English legal scholar F. W. Maitland viewed strict liability as the core of earlier law, others, including Holmes, have seen evidence of fault principles in the more distant past.

Nonetheless, fault as we know it today was not a requirement for liability before the nineteenth century. For instance, in 1616, in *Ward v. Weaver*,[8] a soldier was held liable for wounding another soldier while engaged in a duly authorized military exercise. No evidence was presented that the soldier was careless in any way, yet he was found liable. From the reported case the defendant seems to have received no benefit from the fact that he was carrying out his duties as part of the required drill. He caused the injury, hence he was liable. The case is interesting not merely because it seems so contrary to today's theory but also because it is often cited as a harbinger of fault liability in the law. This is because the language of the opinion seems to make distinctions about proof of causation which parallel, although in a different frame of reference, the current strict liability vs. negligence dichotomy. The *Ward v. Weaver* court discussed, as examples of no liability despite evidence of causation, circumstances in which no free will can be found in the causal act, e.g., "as if a man by force take my hand and strike you. . . ." Perhaps the most interesting aspect of this case is that it demonstrates the difficulty anyone faces in looking to the past to defend or attack current dogma.

The negligence doctrine never had full force and effect even during the heyday of the laissez faire, free-market, free-enterprise system. A case which today is viewed as one of the precursors of strict liability but which equally could be viewed as one of the vestiges of strict liability was *Rylands v. Fletcher,*[9] decided in 1868. Just as the principles of negligence were bursting forth in full bloom, *Rylands v. Fletcher* was decided upon a basis which imposed liability despite the absence of fault. The case today may stand for more than a careful reading of the facts would justify, but that is hardly a novel occurrence. In brief, a dam was built in an area which had been investigated by various engineers and determined to be safe. There was no possible basis for the dam owner to believe otherwise, nor could he have checked more carefully. However, it happened that the lake formed by the dam was located over ancient mine workings from a long-abandoned mine. The unforeseen result was the flooding of another mine. The court held the creator of the dam to be liable. "The question in general is not whether the defendant has acted with due care and caution, but whether his acts have occasioned the damage. . . . For when one person, in managing his own affairs, causes, however innocently, damage to another, it is obviously only just that he should be the party to suffer."

Not surprisingly, this doctrine was not well received by Oliver Wendell Holmes and others who advocated limiting liability to those instances in which the defendant is proved to have been at fault. Great efforts were made to limit the case when the case was recognized at all. Even the efforts to honor and apply the case have led to amusing contortions. For instance, the case of *Rylands v. Fletcher* is often said to stand for the proposition that ultrahazardous or unnatural activity may be treated strictly. Yet the "unnatural" activity involved was collecting water!

Other sources of strict liability predated the birth of negligence and continued long after, but most of them had a special quality which kept them from being viewed as a threat to the comprehensiveness of the fault principle. For example, innkeepers and common carriers had always been strictly liable for their charges. This line of cases continued throughout the nineteenth century and until the present. It was upon this precedent that the railroad industry was held to a strict-liability standard, or a closely analogous one, throughout the nineteenth century.[10] Thus application of strict liability as a precursor of product liability could be said to have occurred simultaneously with the birth of negligence.

Today, strict liability is most often applied to manufacturing. The standard statement of the law in this area is section 402A of the *Restatement (Second) of Torts* (1965):

§ 402A. Special Liability of Seller of Product for Physical Harm to User or Consumer

1. One who sells any product in a defective condition unreasonably dangerous to the user or consumer or to his property is subject to liability for physical harm thereby caused to the ultimate user or consumer, or to his property, if (*a*) the seller is engaged in the business of selling such a product, and (*b*) it is expected to and does reach the user or consumer without substantial change in the condition in which it is sold.

2. The rule stated in Subsection (1) applies although (*a*) the seller has exercised all possible care in the preparation and sale of his product, and (*b*) the user or consumer has not bought the product from or entered into any contractual relation with the seller.

Today, strict liability can arise from a manufacturing defect or a design defect. Obviously, if a product is manufactured in a way which is a breach of the assembly process—e.g., brakes are left out of a specific car—the manufacturer is liable. The more common and the more threatening aspect of liability occurs when manufacturers have defectively designed their products. Such defects apply to a wider range of possible injuries and thus increase the risk to the manufacturer.

Manufacturers of products who complain about their liability—especially in the absence of any proof of fault—frequently believe that their liability is the direct result of a modern gimmick used to compensate the injured at the expense of the producer. Whether such compensation is or is not fair is quite apart from the question of whether that new gimmick is being unfairly applied. Legal history does not justify a definitive answer, but it is fair to say that there is as much evidence (if not more) that negligence was the gimmick and that, as such, negligence was used to deny victims compensation in order to protect the fragile industries at the beginning of our industrial age. If that is true, it hardly seems outrageous to remove that protection at the current level of industrialization, and if that is done it is hard to attack the result as a violation of fundamental legal principles.

1. Of course, no period mechanically applied rules in order to decide cases.

> We are used to speaking of the criteria bearing on a judge's decision as
> "rules," but the concept of a rule is a difficult one and can lead to great
> confusion when we see decisions made in ways that do not seem to be ac-
> cording to "rules." If a decision is not "controlled" by a "rule," then it is said
> to be within the judge's "discretion."
>
> Actually, to say a decision must be "controlled" by a rule is the narrowest
> possible idea of a rule, what we may call a mechanical or perfect rule. A
> perfect rule may conveniently be thought of as a command which controls a
> decision without the necessity of any kind of discretion. It ideally consists of
> an "if" part and a "then" part. The former tells when the rule applies, and
> the latter tells the result of the rule's application. To qualify as a "perfect"
> rule both clauses must be exact and unambiguous. Consider this example:
> "If a man comes into the garden of Zeus, his right hand shall be cut off, no
> more, no less." To make this a perfect rule, we must provide exact and em-
> pirically unmistakable definitions of "a man," "the garden of Zeus," "coming
> into," "right hand," "his," "cut off," and where the hand stops and the wrist
> begins. Of course, language is inherently inexact at the edges, and it is de-
> batable whether a "perfect" rule is even possible in the real world. (Den-
> beaux and Risinger, 33 *Ark. L. Rev.*, 441–442, footnotes omitted.)

2. Obviously, with law, new "pieces" are being created, so that each new turn also includes at least the possibility of additional pieces.

3. Holmes, Oliver Wendell Jr., *The Common Law*, Boston, Little Brown, 1881.

4. Rabin, *Perspectives on Tort Law*, p. 1 (Little, Brown, 1976).

5. 6 Cush. (60 Mass. 1850) 292.

6. Professor Gregory in his law review article; "Trespass to Negligence to Absolute Liability," 32 *Va. L. Rev.* 359, at 362 describes the standard as "any contact achieved as the consequence of one's conduct against the interest of another, no matter under what circumstances it occurred, as long as the defendant's causative conduct was his voluntary act." Professor Gregory goes on to say, at 363, that "even an unintended trespassory contact was regarded as tantamount to a trespass; and a trespass of any kind was accepted as a wrong in itself, without inquiry into the circumstances leading up to it."

7. American judges in the early nineteenth century "disliked the imposition of liability without fault and reacted against any manifestation of this notion. . . . [M]any of our judges believed that the development of this young country under a system of private enterprise would be hindered and delayed as long as the element of chance exposed enterprisers to liability for the consequences of pure accident, without fault." Gregory, *op. cit.*, at 365.

8. King's Bench (1616), Hobart 134; Eng. Rep. 289.

9. L.R. 3 H.L. 330 (1868).

10. *Mobile, J. & K.C.R. Co. v. Turnipseed*, 219 U.S. 35, 46 (1980); *Fuller v. Illinois Cent. R.R. Co.*, 100 Miss. 705, 56 So. 783 (1911).

Environmental Audits in Acquisition and Divestiture

George S. Dominguez
Springborn Regulatory Services

I ndustry is no stranger to acquisition and divestiture analysis. In fact, in many companies it seems to occur with a sometimes surprising but necessary regularity, given our complex growth-oriented and problematical economy. Closely associated with such analysis is the interrelated question of risk assumption or aversion as companies examine not only the marketing or commercial elements of acquisition or divestiture decisions but the various levels and elements of business risk associated with them.

In this context, then, business has become extremely proficient and sophisticated in the evaluation procedures. It has learned to efficiently and effectively examine past, present, and, to the extent possible, future aspects of a number of factors which are essential to the acquisition or divestiture decision: markets and marketing factors; products and processes; facilities and equipment; licensing activities and potentials; franchising activities and potentials; patents (existing and pending) and opportunities; technology; personnel; and legal status, including product and other liabilities.

Inherent in most, if not all, of these areas, is the attendant question of risk: Just how much liability might the company be assuming in the product area? How valid is the financial analysis? What hidden costs or obligations might exist? How will market or products fare? These and myriad other questions are closely and carefully analyzed.

However, as one objectively reviews this impressive and comprehensive process, there is—or at least in all too many companies there has been—a striking and critical omission: the inclusion of a specific health, safety, and environmental audit. This omission is particularly ironic in view of the seemingly endless emphasis not only by government, the public, and the Congress on health, safety, and environmental issues but by most companies themselves as they recognize the importance of this area in the overall development and conduct of their business. In fact, this vital area represents a set of concerns which permeates company actions and decisions, from research and development through to the eventual disposal of the ultimate consumer product. Given the reality of these concerns, it becomes increasingly apparent that they must be factored into the overall acquisition and divestiture evaluation process. Just how important this is has been demonstrated in a number of specific and well-publicized situations in which companies have made acquisitions only to find afterward the serious and sometimes overwhelming liabilities and costs they have acquired.

In considering the implications of health, safety, and environmental matters in this vital evaluative and decision-making process, it is also important to place these concerns in the proper perspective. Each of these areas—health, safety, and environment—can and does involve potential obligations that range from immediate compliance costs to the longer-term but potentially financially ruinous implications of company liability associated with adverse health or environmental effects. In this connection, one has only to examine recent court awards in product-liability cases based on adverse health or environmental effects. Moreover, such obligations can occur in unsuspected areas or through indirect involvements, such as the liability associated with hazardous-waste disposal established under the Resource Conservation and Recovery Act and Superfund, to cite only two examples in the environmental field alone.

From all this, we can readily conclude that there is considerable need for companies to seriously and objectively include health, safety, and environmental factors in the overall acquisition and divestiture analysis process. However, before we proceed to a more detailed examination of just how this may be accomplished in practice, it is important to revert to the earlier mentioned concern with risk assumption or aversion. In the traditional business analysis situation, certain risk factors are carefully and critically assessed. These, however, tend to fall into those areas that business has traditionally faced: financial, marketing, conventional product liability, etc. These have been and unquestionably remain important; however, the critical point at this time is to recognize that safety, health, and environmental issues have given rise to an entirely new set of risks. These risks, involving the financial marketing consequences of safety, health, and environmental problems, also give rise to new company exposure as companies are confronted with highly negative media visibility over violations or incidents in any of these areas. Here again, one has only to examine the notoriety companies have faced over products of such diversity as Dow's "agent orange" and Procter & Gamble's Rely tampons. While the direct consequences of such concerns obviously affect the product and the company, there is also the less well documented and ascertainable but nonetheless real spillover effect on the company and its overall products, sales, market, and—very importantly—financial position. It is not unknown for stock value to be affected by such incidents; and SEC's advocacy of full environmental and related citations, litigation, and investment data reflects concerns (which the reporting obligation itself might intensify) over equity values and prices.

In assessing the totality of health, safety, and environmental analysis in the acquisition or divestiture situation, there needs to be thoroughgoing consideration of not only those immediate and long-term risks that business is familiar and comfortable with but also this new area of business risks—an area that is far less familiar, certainly far less comfortable to deal with, and unfortunately one which in many cases can be far more difficult to quantify. Difficult as it may be, however, the need has been more than amply validated in recent years. Given the current environmental legal obligations; existing safety, health, and environmental laws, rules, and regulations, public concerns and attitudes, and court decisions; and growing emphasis on expanded product and company liability, these concerns must be factored into any acquisition or divestiture decisions. Moreover, there is every reason to believe that despite current economic problems, these concerns will become even more prominent and important in the future.

OBJECTIVES IN SAFETY, HEALTH, AND ENVIRONMENTAL AUDITING FOR ACQUISITION OR DIVESTITURE ANALYSIS

Before undertaking any analysis or evaluation, it is always desirable to state clearly the reasons and objectives involved in undertaking it in the first place. Fortunately, in the case of health, safety, and environmental auditing in the acquisition and divestiture situation, this is completely feasible. Most, if not all, of these objectives will be, to a greater or lesser degree, self-evident from our previous analysis of the basic problem, but they can be explicitly identified as follows. The objectives of the audit are fivefold:

1. Determination of potential costs associated with all aspects of safety, health, and environmental matters, including any potential for costs associated with facilities upgrading, compliance, etc.
2. Determination of business risk and exposure
3. Determination of existing and potential product or other liability, short- and long-term (the latter, while particularly difficult, is particularly necessary)
4. Identification of areas requiring remedial action, immediate and long-term
5. Opportunities for risk and cost reduction or containment

All these specific objectives are important, but they have to be visualized within the overall context of the basic acquisition or divestiture analysis itself, which is fundamentally conducted to determine whether the company should or should not proceed with a specific acquisition candidate or consider divesting itself of certain products or segments of its business. It is for this reason that, important as safety, health, and environmental consideration are, they be assessed within this framework; and this is also the reason why the health, safety, and environmental auditing component should be formally included in the analysis process and why such evaluations should come about early in the acquisition or divestiture process.

COMPONENTS OF THE AUDIT

While many of the specific elements that should be examined in a health, safety, and environmental audit parallel those that have been reviewed elsewhere in this book, it is important to understand that in this instance they are being examined from a somewhat different perspective and certainly with a different ultimate objective in mind. Therefore the emphasis is less specifically compliance-oriented and more directed to identification of actual or potential problem areas and the costs that might be associated with them. With this significant difference in mind, it is still necessary to examine all the areas that would be reviewed in the more conventional auditing process, and this still requires the use of skilled experts in various relevant disciplines to make the assessment. In considering the elements of the audit, bear in mind that the level of detail and the emphasis placed on these elements will depend upon the specific circumstances and the nature of the business being audited. The major components that should be examined, reviewed, or evaluated in any audit are as follows:

- Agency-mandated compliance requirements—e.g., Environmental Protection Agency, Occupational Safety and Health Administration, Department of Transportation, Food and Drug Administration (should include assessment of past, present, and future)
- Compliance performance (including evaluation of any past violations)
- Compliance schedules, if any
- Variances, if any, and their status
- Product liability—all aspects
- Complaints—employees, consumer, community
- Product and process reviews (especially careful evaluation of processes, since these are occasionally overlooked, or given inadequate attention)
- Technology employed and its implications
- Facilities and equipment
- Legal aspects—outstanding litigation, fines, penalties, restrictions, actions pending or probable
- Insurance—levels, costs, availability, assignment, renewability, requirements, potential increases
- Internal and external reports (particularly regulatory agency inspection reports)
- Medical and exposure records (to the degree available and legally accessible)
- Citations and remedial actions
- Workers' compensation status
- Accident and injury statistics and comparison with available norms
- Labeling practices
- Waste-disposal practices (particularly important in view of the long-term liability that could be involved)
- Recalls, mandatory or voluntary
- Relevant regulatory compliance documents, e.g., National Pollution Discharge Elimination System permits, registration under the emission banking credits, Federal Insecticide, Fungicide, and Rodenticide Act
- Pending notifications, petitions, or product or facilities registration
- Good laboratory practices and good management practices, if applicable
- All safety, health, and environmental documents, including company-developed manuals, policies, and guidance documents

- Employee education and training programs
- Records documenting regulatory compliance, e.g., Toxic Subtances Control Act inventory, facilities registration inspection reports
- Packaging and processing compliance, where applicable
- Emergency procedures—first aid, spills
- Waste treatment facilities and their compliance with regulatory requirements
- Utilization of publicly owned treatment works (especially user charges and continued user availability, the latter also to be evaluated in the light of potential additional loading factors)
- Opportunities or problems associated with product or process substitution should this become necessary

CONDUCTING THE AUDIT

The actual conduct of the audit is just as important as its content and scope. In this respect, therefore, adequate thought should be given to several practical factors, including timing, personnel, documentation, and relation to other acquisition or divestiture activities.

Timing

As previously mentioned, many companies today have developed and employ sophisticated acquisition and divestiture analysis procedures. Clearly defined and predetermined procedures not only establish the elements to be considered, such as marketing, legal, product, and financial, but specify the sequence of evaluation and those who will be involved in each phase. Often the overall analysis will be under the direction of a project or program manager who specializes in acquisition and divestiture analysis and relies on an analysis team of fixed or variable composition that includes not only internal but often external experts in particular areas. The reports and recommendations of this team will in turn be employed in various stages by management as it proceeds with its decisions, deliberations, and negotiations. To the extent that this process may be highly formalized in some companies, these procedures may be set forth in various policy statements or internal acquisition and divestiture analysis manuals. Even in a less formalized environment, some procedure will be used to set the operational ground rules and the elements for review and analysis and to assign appropriate responsibility.

If safety, health, and environmental considerations are to be included in the acquisition or divestiture analysis, the attainment of the basic objectives already reviewed requires that (1) the safety, health, and environmental audit be formally integrated into the analysis process (that is, be recognized as an important, discrete element, just as critical as, for instance, financial analysis); (2) appropriate time and resources be made available to complete a comprehensive and professional audit; and (3) the audit be undertaken very early in the acquisition or divestiture analysis. As a practical matter, it is desirable to structure the audit in various phases corresponding to incrementally greater degrees of specificity and more detailed evaluation. In the first, or screening, phase a relatively gross assessment can thus cull out the most likely or unlikely candidates on the basis of some broad health, safety, and environmental assessment criteria.

Personnel

Anyone familiar with health, safety, or environmental considerations knows just how complex and sensitive each of these areas is individually, let alone when they are considered in the aggregate. Furthermore, the number of specialties and subspecialties that are, or can be, involved can be—to put it very conservatively—intimidating. The complexity of the subject and the number of potential specialties involved are factors that must be dealt with in real-world situations, because they are often cited as reasons why such an analysis cannot be made in the acquisition or divestiture situation, and because they pose practical problems that have to be considered in the audit and planning process.

On the basis of the previous discussion of the justification and need for an audit, it is obvious that these problems, while presenting difficulties, are not insurmountable. The solution lies in the establishment of an audit team which includes experts in at least the major relevant disciplines. Where these experts are not available within the company, the team can be augmented by outside consultants in the areas of expertise required. In fact, there are firms which will not only supply expertise in individual disciplines but will undertake the entire audit or specific portions, e.g., the safety component. From the standpoint of company capabilities as well as objectivity and credibility, the use of external consulting firms should be seriously considered, since, aside from any technical advantages, there is the important factor of perceived impartiality. This factor could be especially critical if the overall acquisition involves external financing: the institution making any loans or loan guarantees may react far more favorably to independent analysis and evaluation. This can be important in obtaining insurance. In any case, whether the audit is conducted by a team composed totally of company personnel, by a combination of internal and external experts, or by a consulting organization, these experts must be provided the time and resources necessary to accomplish their critical task reliably and competently.

Documentation

As indicated in the list of major audit components, it is essential for the audit team to examine all the documents the company has accumulated over the years in health, safety, and environmental areas. The auditors should carefully document their reviews, identifying the specific documents, records, permits, etc., reviewed and indicating who reviewed them, when they were reviewed, and any findings or conclusions. Where appropriate, actual copies of key documents may well be included in the audit team's final report.

It is helpful to develop an overall inspection procedure which provides not only checklists for various elements of the audit but documentation review forms setting out the particular elements to be reviewed in each instance.

Relation to Other Acquisition and Divestiture Activities

As previously indicated, it is extremely important that the health, safety, and environmental components of the audit be fully and effectively integrated into the total acquisition or divestiture analysis and that it be considered an integral component of the analysis. All those involved in the overall analysis should be aware of this evaluation in order to gain all the benefits to be derived from it. Conversely, the health, environment, and safety audit team should be aware of the activities of others engaged in the total analysis, so that they, in turn, can gain additional insights from the actions, reports, and recommendations or conclusions of these others.

To accomplish this integration efficiently, the entire acquisition or divestiture analysis should be planned so that all its major aspects—e.g., marketing, technology, legal, finance, safety, health, and environment— are appropriately scheduled. All participants should receive copies of one another's reports as the evaluation progresses, so that each can obtain insights and isolate critical areas for initial or subsequent examination. For example, if the marketing evaluation reveals that one of the most important reasons for considering an acquisition is the company's marketing position for one or more critical products, any regulations that could affect those products (existing or future) take on added significance; the company is especially vulnerable to specific regulations that could affect them. Similarly, if the company's position is dependent upon some critical technology, which may not be highly regulated at present but may be subject to substantial restrictions in the future, the entire position of the company from the technological and cost viewpoints could be altered radically. Conversely, if the company has a broad product line or a well-diversified technological base (or a product or technology base that is not "threatened" or sensitive), the emphasis on these sensitivity or vulnerability aspects of the audit is correspondingly lessened.

Even these few examples illustrate the need not only for full consideration of the safety, health, and environmental factors early in the analysis but also for interaction among activities at every stage in the process. This can be especially true in a multiphased program, which may involve examinations and reexaminations, in all areas to ensure that problems are identified and overall results improved through close coordination of all involved.

Finally, in order to give the safety, health, and environmental component the stature and recognition that it both deserves and requires, the head of the audit team should be an active participant in the overall acquisition or divestiture team and should receive all relevant documents and be a party to the review, planning, administration, management, and decision-making aspects of the entire study. Only in this way will the company derive the full benefit of the audit.

USING THE AUDIT RESULTS

The health, environmental, and safety audit, if it is to be of any value, has to be used with judgment and understanding. As we have seen, many elements of the audit are quantifiable and involve existing circumstances and conditions, hence are readily definable. Yet many other elements involve subjective judgments and/or predictions of future events, and these are equally important, no matter how difficult it may be to make such determinations. Often the present circumstances are less of a problem than events that the future may bring. Nevertheless, as corporate officials attempt to use the results of an audit, there may be, not surprisingly, a tendency to rely on and give more credence to the more immediate, definable, and quantifiable elements. Even though the less precise and less readily determinable projections of future issues or problems may not be given the same emphasis in the audit evaluation, they are not less important. In balancing present sales and market share against future predictions, judgment must be exercised in interpreting and using the results of the health, safety, and environmental audit. It is in this connection that expert opinion and professional judgment, whether based on in-house capabilities or the use of outside consultants, becomes critical.

Having recognized this need for balance and judgment in evaluating the evaluation, the problem still remains: Just what should be done with the results? How important are they? How useful are they? What use can be made of them? These are important questions and deserve careful consideration. After all, not only are important decisions to be made on the basis of the audit, but the audit itself represents a not insubstantial investment in time and labor. What should be done with the results?

The first step after completing the health, safety, and environmental audit is to write a complete yet concise report of the audit team's findings and conclusions. In preparing this report, careful attention should be given to documenting all aspects of the evaluation and of the conclusions that the audit team reaches. In this regard, it is also important, especially when considering such matters as potential additional investments for upgrading—for example, to meet Occupational Safety and Health Administration requirements or additional waste-disposal costs—to provide reliable cost estimates. Similarly, when projecting further requirements—a more problematical situation—it is imperative to differentiate between probable and possible events and to attempt to estimate the probability and timing of such events. For instance, will additional state regulations on waste disposal prevail, and if so, what will be their probable outcome, timing, and financial and other impact on the company? In advocating this approach, it is recognized that one could play this type of "what if" game almost endlessly. However, this serves to emphasize the necessity for professional judgment on the part of the audit team. Prognostications are important, but an audit team must be able to identify the urgent, if not critical, areas of concern and to single out those issues and areas where additional safety, health, or environmental concerns are most likely to arise. Once such issues have been identified, the audit team should provide assessments of alternative company responses. All this information then enables the company to:

1. Determine the present status of the acquisition or divestiture candidate vis-à-vis existing legal, moral, or ethical standards as established by the government, the community, product-liability considerations, or legal or self-imposed company standards.

2. Determine what the costs of compliance may be—both capital and operating. A practical note here on cost determinations: these can

often be difficult to calculate, particularly on a product-by-product basis, because so few companies have attempted to actually isolate compliance costs, with the possible exception of effluent treatment. The audit team can only attempt to make its cost estimates as reliable, accurate, and comprehensive as possible consistent with the company's cost accounting system. The distinction between capital and operating costs is particularly important when it comes to projections of potential future investment requirements. While the capital costs may not be too formidable, for many reasons the operating costs are often underestimated. Therefore it is especially important when projecting future compliance outlays to critically examine both overall and product-specific potential operating costs.

3. Determine the risk or exposure that the company could incur.

4. Establish timetables for any required investments, equipment, monitoring, process changes, compliance updating, etc.

5. Establish bargaining positions as appropriate in the negotiation of the acquisition.

6. Reach divestiture decisions.

Obviously, the ultimate objective of the audit is to assist the acquisition or divestiture decision. But early in the audit process, and long before the time when the audit team's data are to be used and its recommendations acted upon, it is important for company officials to consider whether the team is simply to make objective evaluations and state conclusions or take the next step and make actual recommendations. This may appear to be a fine distinction, and in fact it may at first appear illogical that the audit team, after undertaking the assessment, should *not* make actual recommendations. However, considering the degree of importance often associated with these studies and the legal implications of any stated recommendations (actual statements of compliance findings and specific upgrading recommendations, for example), such recommendations could be problematical. Therefore it is important to state the precise responsibilities of the audit team and indicate whether or not it is to make specific written recommendations. This consideration is important in the eventual use of the audit. If specific recommendations are made, those involved in the final decision will have additional information on which to base their decision; that is, they will have the recommendations of the experts before them to evaluate and act upon. Conversely, if no specific written recommendations are provided, they will have to make assessments of their own, perhaps in areas in which they have little expertise, but the objective findings of the audit will provide a basis for such assessments.

3

UNDERTAKING AN ENVIRONMENTAL AUDIT

The Auditor's Perspective

Walter J. Huelsman
Environmental Services, Coopers & Lybrand

While financial auditing is nearly as old as the entire field of business itself, environmental auditing, as a discipline and profession, has emerged only recently. Noncompliance with environmental regulations developed over the last dozen years can leave a company exposed to massive damage claims, fines, or even jail terms for its executives, as recent news stories attest. This kind of legal exposure has led companies to search for a reliable method of evaluating their compliance with environmental regulations, and environmental auditing has developed as a result. As financial auditing can tell whether someone is pilfering from the corporate till, environmental auditing can provide management with assurances that its employees are not playing fast and loose with environmental laws.

Because environmental auditing is so new, a number of different methods of auditing have been developed. Many of these methods contain similar elements, with the major differences being the level of detail and management's emphasis and reason for the audit. All the approaches to environmental auditing are being developed during a period of transition—one in which environmental laws and regulations are being revised at the federal level, modified and administered at the state and local levels, and interpreted through numerous legal proceedings—and hence are themselves in a state of development. Because of this, our discussion is limited to providing a state-of-the-art perspective on environmental auditing.

AN EMERGING FIELD

All the present major environmental laws have been passed by Congress in the last 12 years: Clean Air Act (CAA), 1970; Clean Water Act (CWA), 1973; Resource Conservation and Recovery Act (RCRA), 1976; Toxic Substances Control Act, 1974; and Comprehensive Environmental Response, Compensation, and Liability Act (Superfund), 1980; and the regulations implementing these laws have been promulgated 1 to 4 years later. The body of environmental knowledge on which to base an auditing system is therefore relatively new and, in fact, still in formation. It is also important to point out that the impetus for environmental-compliance auditing did not come from the promulgation of the large body of environmental regulations. Rather, it came from a series of Securities and Exchange Commission (SEC) rulings over the last few years on disclosure of environmental liabilities, along with the expanded liability provisions of the RCRA. Now, with the Environmental Protection Agency (EPA) promising to take a tough enforcement line in dealing with violators, there is even more pressure on corporations to carry out environmental audits.

Because all this is so recent, industry has only just begun to demand environmental auditing services from staff and from outside auditing firms. But the response to industry's needs is under way. Universities are beginning to address these needs in their curricula. For instance, engineering and law schools are offering specialized courses, and in some cases certificates, in environmental auditing. And traditional financial auditors are becoming more aware of the significance of pollution expenditures and contingent liabilities as the related costs become significant bottom-line issues.

Emerging from all this is a cadre of environmental auditing personnel who possess a variety of functional skills (e.g., auditing, technical, legal, financial, and management), and their numbers are growing. As the required disciplines are better defined and the need more clearly understood and supported, many corporations are establishing or expanding environmental auditing functions.

APPLICABILITY OF TRADITIONAL AUDITING STANDARDS

The audit approach used in traditional financial audits is directly applicable to environmental auditing. The two basic audit strategies for each, which are equally applicable in both manual audits and those employing electronic data processing, are to rely principally on validation proce-

TABLE 1   Comparison of Financial and Environmental Audits

Financial audit	Environmental audit
• Obtain and document a preliminary understanding of the client's business and accounting systems and consider factors that may affect audit strategy.	• Identify and document all environmentally regulated elements and processes of the client.
• Plan the most effective and efficient audit strategy.	• Develop audit guides or questionnaires by facility, process, and element.
• Perform functional or validation tests. Functional tests are designed to provide evidence of the operation of those accounting controls on which the auditor would like to rely. Validation procedures constitute direct tests of account balances and other key information.	• Determine, e.g., that the hazardous-waste manifest reporting system complies with regulations and is functioning correctly (functional testing); and review the hazardous-waste and manifest records to test compliance with the 90-day temporary-storage requirements (validation testing).
• Communicate recommendations for improving internal controls and appropriate suggestions regarding the operations of the business.	• Prepare a management report summarizing the completed audit guides and (optional) identify potential reductions in waste-disposal costs.

dures ("validation mode") and to rely on the system of internal accounting control to reduce validation procedures ("control mode"). A comparison of the elements of these strategies for financial and for environmental audits in Table 1 demonstrates the similarity.

Regulated environmental processes and substances are similar to the line items included in corporate financial statements. The financial auditor's methods of testing the account totals are thus very similar to the methods environmental auditors use to test environmental compliance.

INDEPENDENT AND INTERNAL AUDITING

Who should perform the audit? This is one of the first questions which should be addressed by management, and the decision will depend on the specific situation. A brief checklist may help the corporate environmental executive evaluate the particular situation and choose the most effective approach to environmental auditing. If the answer to most of the following questions is as noted, a company should consider using an independent audit firm.

- Does the company have an adequate environmental auditing staff? (*No.*)
- Is the audit required by an outside agency or the result of litigation? (*Yes.*)
- Can the company provide personnel from the facilities being audited who will be objective, unbiased, and independent? (*No.*)
- Is the company knowledgeable about all federal, state, and local environmental regulations which affect each facility? (*No.*)
- Can the company perform the audit within the desired time? (*No.*)
- Has the company had a formal environmental office or department in place for at least 3 years (average time of mature program), which includes formal training of divisional personnel? (*No.*)
- In a decentralized organization, is headquarters satisfied with the division's environmental reporting? (*No.*)

The magnitude of pollution-control costs, both capital and operating, is a concern of management, as are the potential massive liabilities which can result from government and public lawsuits for noncompliance with regulations, personal injury, or property damage. The control and reliability of the entire environmental process must therefore be a major concern of management. The independent auditor can address that concern by

- Providing independence and objectivity
- Providing all the technical skills (auditing, technical, legal, etc.)
- Bringing a standard of performance and consistency to the audit
- Assessing the financial implications of alternative methods of compliance

However, management also must evaluate both the cost and benefits of using an independent auditing firm. Such an evaluation should consider:

- Auditing firms with personnel located throughout the country, to minimize travel costs
- Development of an auditing program, as a one-time expense, that can be used to train company personnel
- Specialists, who can often identify potential areas for reducing the costs of pollution control

Independent environmental auditing and internal environmental auditing may be quite similar, depending on the stage of development of the internal environmental staff. A distinction should be drawn, however, between internal environmental auditing and coordination. In today's early stage of development, the majority of companies are coordinating their environmental activities rather than auditing them. Some of the differences among the three processes are:

1. Development of audit program
    a. Independent: Performed with all professional skills required as an independent contractor
    b. Internal: Performed by company employees
    c. Coordinator: May not have responsibility for performing or evaluating the program

2. Scope of services
    a. Independent: Performed to determine reliability of compliance reporting and to fulfill requirements of third parties, e.g., federal and state governments
    b. Internal: Same as independent auditor except may be considered less objective by third parties
    c. Coordinator: Disseminates environmental information and responds to inquiries only

3. Reporting
    a. Independent: Provides environmental compliance report to management and independent statement in certain situations
    b. Internal: Same as independent except for independent statements
    c. Coordinator: May or may not prepare a report

4. Regulatory acceptance (voluntary program under development by EPA)
    a. Independent: Acceptable
    b. Internal: Acceptable
    c. Coordinator: Not acceptable

The answer to the question of who should develop and/or perform the environmental audit will probably be a combination of independent and internal audit groups. This appears to be the most economical alternative and the one which utilizes the independent auditor's skills early on, while training internal personnel to perform future audits.

SETTING UP THE AUDIT

There are several types of environmental audit. Depending on the needs of the company or sponsoring entity, an audit may be limited, as in assessing compliance with a single permit issued under a single federal law, or broad, as in assessing compliance with all applicable regulations and the company's organizational policies and internal procedures. The audit can incorporate a single approach or be a hybrid of two or more types. What follows is a description of the various kinds of environmental audits.

Environmental Compliance Audit

The objective of this type of audit is to provide a snapshot of a company's environmental management by determining the compliance of its activities, past and present, with all relevant laws and regulations. Specifically, for each activity or source of emissions, the audit would help to determine whether any permits or licenses are required. It would also help to determine whether, under the terms of any permits, orders, or agreements with governmental agencies or under the current general provisions of any environmental laws or regulations, any of the following are required:

1. Meeting any limits on or standards for discharges, emissions, or wastes
2. Operating and maintaining any equipment for the control, abatement, treatment, or disposal of any discharges, emissions, or wastes
3. Monitoring, testing, or inspecting of emissions, wastes, or pollution-control equipment
4. Maintaining records and relevant information
5. Submitting reports to government officials
6. Demonstrating financial responsibility in the case of activities that are subject to continuing oversight after their immediate purpose has expired
7. Providing certain actions (e.g., notification and cleanup) in the case of known accidental or unusual discharges of regulated substances

In addition, the audit can review relevant proposed regulations or other environmental requirements to assess the scope of potential corporate liability and obligations that may arise in the future.

Procedural Compliance Audit

The objective of this audit is to determine whether all procedural requirements are being met. For each activity or source of emissions, the audit determines whether any required permits have been applied for or received and whether the requirements for such permits, agreements, or orders are being met satisfactorily. This type of audit will generally build on and incorporate the compliance audit and include corporate oversight.

Substantive Environmental Compliance Audit

This audit builds on the two types of audit mentioned above. Like those two audits, it will result in a determination of whether the company currently is in violation of any environmental laws. But in addition to assessing procedural compliance, this audit provides technical inspection, sampling, and testing of all discharges or emissions regulated under all applicable federal, state, or local laws. Specifically, this type of audit includes (1) taking samples of discharges to determine whether they are subject to regulation, (2) testing or inspecting to determine whether emissions fall within legal limits, and (3) checking equipment that is used for pollution control, abatement, treatment, transport, disposal, monitoring, sampling, etc., to determine whether it is operating and being maintained correctly.

In addition to measuring compliance with technical regulations, this audit assesses a company's performance in two other areas: (1) the integrity and reliability of the company's system for compiling, retrieving, and reporting information concerning compliance with environmental regulations and (2) the management and organizational structure of the responsible office and other divisions or offices as they relate to environmental management.

With the compliance problems presented by thousands of environmental regulations, companies are finding that a systematic approach to managing environmental issues is vital. Such an approach can also serve to develop companywide recognition of the importance of environmental compliance and reporting, as well as providing management with an early-warning system for potential liabilities. Moreover, under certain laws, an affirmative duty is placed on corporate officers designated by the corporation to obtain knowledge of the facts contained in reports or permit applications submitted to the government. Failure to take the steps necessary to ensure the accuracy and truth of information can, in certain circumstances, lead to additional liability for the responsible officer. The utility of this stage of the audit may be greater for larger firms which have many facilities, substantial in-house legal and technical capability, and an expansive reporting network. This is not to say, however, that this stage of the audit should be overlooked or its value underestimated by small companies.

The activities involved in a substantive environmental audit—other than those involved with measuring compliance with technical regulations—can conveniently be summarized in five groups:

1. Collection of information
   a. Existence of corporate policies, procedures, and guidelines
   b. Establishment and adherence to routine information-collection procedures
   c. Importance attached to these duties relative to other assigned responsibilities
   d. Level of detail and accuracy
   e. Qualifications and training of personnel assigned responsibility to compile data and information

2. Storage of information
   a. Consistency of format
   b. Ability to retrieve (manually or electronically)
   c. Control of access

3. Evaluation of information
   a. Timeliness of analyses
   b. Planning for follow-up action
   c. Competence of analyses
   d. Relation of analyses to determinations of compliance
   e. Qualifications of persons conducting analyses

4. Internal reporting of information
   a. Number of persons in chain of reporting
   b. Existence of and adherence to company guidelines specifying flow of information and reporting procedures
   c. Activities of company's chief environmental officer
   d. Role of advisory committees or task forces

5. Differences between designed system and actual operation
   a. Breakdowns caused by system design

b. Breakdowns caused by manner in which assigned duties are being carried out

c. Procedures to evaluate and correct problems

APPROACH TO ENVIRONMENTAL AUDITING

An approach to developing, implementing, and documenting an environmental audit program may take a few months for small companies or may require 1 to 2 years for large, decentralized companies. While the level of effort may vary, the major activities are the same. The major stages of development suggested by Coopers & Lybrand are cited in the following list:

- *Development stage.* Environmental substances and processes to be audited are defined; company scope and objectives are finalized; organizational issues are resolved; propriety and confidentiality issues are resolved; and facility audit guides are developed.

- *Review stage.* Corporate and divisional environmental policies and procedures are reviewed; audit guides are completed for each facility; environmental substances and processes are inventoried; responsibilities are documented; and compliance status is reviewed.

- *Assessment stage.* Preparation of a program report which primarily documents by facility the inventory of substances and processes and their monitoring procedures; identification of inconsistencies, status of compliance and noncompliance; and a recommended plan of action for correcting compliance problems.

- *Remedial stage.* Corrective actions are performed by the company, such as obtaining permits, installing reporting mechanisms, initiating training programs. As these actions are completed, the audit guides are modified.

- *Audit stage.* Perform corporate and facility audits, confer with cognizant agencies (if audit report is to be issued to third parties) and prepare environmental audit report.

In late 1981, the Environmental Protection Agency was considering an environmental auditing program which would act as a voluntary regulatory program for enforcement of air and water regulations. EPA was considering a "hold harmless" condition during the company's first cycle. Therefore, audits which identified noncompliance situations would not be issued a notice of violation.

Development Stage

Who should be involved and how do you get started? A senior executive should direct the initial audit. Once the company has selected its auditor, the scope of the audit should be finalized. To finalize the scope, the senior executive should involve management from environmental engineering, manufacturing, legal, finance, and other departments as appropriate.

During this process a full understanding of all environmental laws, regulations, ordinances, etc. applicable to the company's facilities should be assembled. The major efforts during this stage of the audit process are to:

- Finalize the purpose, scope (report content and documentation), limitations, sensitivity, and confidentiality of the project
- Finalize corporate and divisional management roles in the project
- Develop specific requests for information from company facilities (permits, plant layout, etc.) and from other departments which will enable the audit team to identify the substances, wastes, and emissions regulated at each facility
- Review state and local environmental regulations which apply to company facilities (often obtainable from the auditor's files and public information)
- Select appropriate data-collection methods, according to the level of confidentiality required by the company
- Analyze the facility and departmental information and develop site-specific audit guides, which are then approved by appropriate personnel prior to finalization
- Plan and schedule the facility reviews

Review Stage

A company may wish to test the audit guides and procedures at one or more facilities before reviewing all facilities. The actual process depends on several questions:

- Will more than one audit team be utilized?
- Are facilities significantly different?
- In how many different EPA regions and states are the company's plants located?

- What training or other activities are planned at the conclusion of the audit?

The actual facility review is performed as specified in the audit guides, concentrating on the following activities *for each identified regulated substance or process:*

- Review existing compliance reporting and testing procedures
- Obtain monitoring characteristics (to determine adequacy)
- Determine organizational responsibilities for the process
- Review regulatory reporting status and correspondence
- Assess adequacy of reporting
- Review compliance with relevant laws as appropriate, from generation to final disposal, contingency plans, etc.

An additional activity *for each facility* would be to provide orientation and summary briefings to facility management within confidentiality limitations.

In addition to the completion of the audit guides and documentation, a facility inspection is made (utilizing direct observation and interviews with plant personnel) to identify any additional substance or process which may be subject to environmental regulations. The documentation or communication of these substances will depend on the agreement reached with company executives during the development stage regarding sensitivity and confidentiality.

Assessment Stage

A program report is prepared, setting forth review-stage findings, and appropriate briefings are held. The data gathered are also organized. At this point the company determines its priorities and future actions.

A sample table of contents of the program report might be as follows:

- Executive summary
- Purpose of plan development
- Summary assessment of compliance by facility by regulated substance or process
- Summary assessment of existing policies, procedures, and organization related to environmental compliance

- Plan of action to remedy or improve the current process
- Appendices: audit guides, cost reduction observations

One method of organizing the documentation is to use the material to initiate an environmental compliance policy and procedures handbook. Such a handbook might contain:

- Corporate policies and procedures
- Inventory of regulated substances and processes by facility
- Related federal, state, and local regulations
- Schedule of permit expiration
- Compliance schedule
- Facility procedures and responsibilities
- Audit guide and program
- Procedure for updating the handbook

Remedial Stage

The company may not require this stage of activity if its compliance program is relatively complete. However, if there are areas which require further investigation, this is the time to do it. For example, further analysis may identify the need for additional permits. Missing reporting or monitoring procedures would be established and responsibilities clearly defined where needed.

Audit Stage

This stage is similar to the review stage except that it is devoted primarily to verifying that the auditing procedures are being performed. It should be noted that one aspect of this effort is to verify that the audit guide is being properly maintained—that new materials, products, or wastes are being tested. Also, the company may wish to develop an audit program that reviews all facilities over several years rather than all at once, to minimize costs. Such an audit program should begin by auditing those plants which are representative of the company and include those facilities with known problems.

An environmental audit report is prepared at the conclusion of this stage. It should disclose the status of the audit program, current and pending violations, citations, correction programs, consent decrees, etc., as discussed later in this chapter under Audit Report and Recommendations. The report may also quantify the costs relating to these activities.

AUDITING PROCEDURES

Environmental audits should be flexible in scope, type, and procedure and tailored to meet the specific needs of the company. Well-established procedures are central to conducting a good audit. Properly developed procedures will constitute an effective technique for evaluating the acceptability of environmental data, identifying deficiencies, and achieving corrective action; a valuable screening technique through which serious environmental problems can be identified for follow-up action; and a cost-effective approach to ascertaining the status of compliance.

Coopers & Lybrand's environmental audit focuses on several procedures and conditions, but the most important condition, and one which requires early confirmation, is the commitment of senior management. Environmental-audit programs are successful only if they have the support of senior management. The authority to allocate resources and personnel to ensure the integrity of the audit must come from the chief executive officer.

The procedures the audit team should follow in conducting the audit are discussed below. Different statutes, of course, will require gathering different information, but the procedures for the various areas audited are generally the same. Throughout the audit, auditors should follow the company's internal document-control procedures.

Scope of the Audit

Before beginning the audit the commitment of senior management must be secured to achieve the maximum level of cooperation within the company. The scope of the audit must be carefully drafted to consider the company's objectives, financial limitations, time constraints, sensitive areas or areas of special attention, the environmental processes to be audited, the roles of the participating parties and their specific areas of responsibility, and the type of environmental audit desired by the company.

Background Review

All available background information is reviewed before the audit team goes on site. This review is essential for effectively planning the site visit. It provides information on such things as the permittee's operations, permit limitations in force, compliance schedules, monitoring requirements, and history of violations. Some sources of background information generally reviewed are the following:

- *National Pollution Discharge Elimination System (NPDES) permit application.* The application provides data on wastewater characterization, water-pollution-control practices, water use, wastewater flows, and number and types of discharges.

- *NPDES permit and NPDES monitoring report.* The effluent-limitations portion of the permit provides information on quantitative limitations—for example, average and maximum concentrations and average daily and maximum daily loads. The self-monitoring-requirements portion provides the frequency and type of sampling and the flow-monitoring, analytical, and data-reporting requirements. The compliance schedule is the schedule the permittee must meet for abating pollution and complying with the specified effluent limitations.

- *Discharge-monitoring-report data.* These provide a record of effluent quality and permittee compliance based on self-monitoring data. A review of the data for the past year generally provides a good background.

- *Previous inspection reports.* Inspection reports from EPA regional and state files, which may describe the process operations and pollution-control practices, provide the audit team with details on pollution problems. In addition, a review of available site maps and process and wastewater-treatment flow diagrams are beneficial in providing familiarity with permittee operations.

- *Regional and state files.* A review of state and EPA regional files can provide the compliance history of the permittee. Consultant reports prepared for the permittee on pollution-abatement facilities are generally good sources of information. Aerial photography, if available, is helpful in gaining familiarity with the pollution source.

- *Company policies and procedures.* The policies and procedures provide a description of the existing environmental management, as well as authorities and responsibilities for data collection, record keeping, reporting, etc. This also provides a basis upon which to evaluate the efficiency and appropriateness of company operating procedures.

- *Various hazardous-waste reports.* Several reports are required by the RCRA. They identify a range of information: the amount and type of waste generated, handling methods, location of facilities, cost estimates for facility closure, manifest, etc.

- *Consolidated applications and permits.* Like the NPDES permits, these provide information on the various requirements intended to ensure that the state permit programs satisfy minimum statutory and environmental objectives.

- *List of all applicable regulations, laws, and ordinances.* From this, the auditor gains an idea of what regulations affect the plant and what information is provided to the government.

It is important to ensure consistency of the reviews at all operating locations. At the same time, however, the different environmental elements must be addressed thoroughly in the review from the perspective of regulatory requirements and internal procedures and controls. To accomplish this, during this background review, site-specific guides are developed. It is these guides or manuals that provide the auditor with a checklist of the information to be gathered and the desired procedural controls by which to record all data pertinent to assessing compliance. The audit manual contains specific questions to be asked, instructions to the auditors (e.g., "Physical inspection of document should be conducted"), and the inspection protocol required. The field guides or manuals also help to train new auditors, should that be an objective of the company. Such a checklist might include:

1. Qualifications of laboratory personnel
2. Thoroughness of record keeping
3. Clarity of responsibility
4. Evidence of procedures for monitoring, sampling, reporting, and record keeping
5. Procedures for testing and monitoring equipment
6. Procedures for verifying accuracy of data that has been collected at the facility
7. Procedures for integrating audit findings into report

Facility Assessment

The audit team visits the site of each facility subject to the audit to conduct visual inspections of physical conditions and processes, examine pertinent records and record-keeping procedures, interview personnel, determine success in meeting compliance schedules, and, if required, sample or perform physical measurements. All observations and samples should be documented on checklists and in the field guides, and documentation should be appropriately controlled and accounted for to ensure confidentiality.

The facility audit should:

1. Determine whether file information on waste generation and air and water emission rates is current; whether existing information

on wastewater treatment and hazardous-waste and air-emission compliance practices is correct; and whether off-site disposal practices, including those no longer used, are identified along with all past practices that may cause environmental damage. In some instances background information on these areas may not exist or may be limited and has to be developed during the inspection.

2. Determine whether the number and location of on-site discharges, of treatment, storage, and disposal sites, and of point sources are identified and whether there are any unpermitted discharges. (Photographs are useful in documenting the latter type of information.)

3. Review existing compliance reporting and testing and maintenance procedures.

4. Determine whether compliance schedules in the permits are being met.

5. Determine whether all pertinent parameters are being monitored; for example, whether changes in the manufacturing processes or waste-treatment practices have occurred and have resulted in different discharge characteristics which may require changes in monitoring or appropriate notification to government.

6. Evaluate permittee sampling and analytical procedures in terms of representativeness, frequency, type of sample, type of containers used for specific parameters, and methods of collection.

7. Determine organizational responsibilities for internal reporting and training.

8. Assess adequacy of internal reporting and review regulatory reporting status. Review records the company uses to prepare monitoring reports and other reports submitted to government.

9. Review compliance with identified statutes, citations, or violations dealing with hazardous wastes, air emissions, water emissions, groundwater, etc., as agreed upon in the scope of the audit.

10. Estimate the capital, operating and maintenance costs, and supporting expenses of corrective action.

11. If appropriate, evaluate flow-monitoring equipment and procedures in terms of frequency of testing, acceptability of devices used, and maintenance procedures.

In initiating the facility assessment, the audit team meets with the facility manager to determine whether he or she has any particular questions or concerns that are sensitive or require careful review and then meets with the staff to address the audit procedures and answer questions. On the basis of the questions and information contained in the field and audit guides, the team then proceeds to review the regulatory activities of the facility. The following outline provides a brief example of the type of information, by category, which the audit guides direct the auditors to collect:

1. Hazardous waste
   a. Identify any solid wastes that will result from operation of the facility or pollution-control equipment, determine character and volume of such waste, and identify location and method of disposal of such wastes.
   b. Are the wastes generated classified as hazardous?
   c. If any of the wastes are hazardous, does the company operate any storage, handling, or disposal facilities at the plant, thereby requiring a permit?
   d. If hazardous wastes are to be disposed of off premises, how are they transported, and is the disposal facility approved for those wastes?
   e. Review applicable provisions of the CAA and CWA with regard to toxic pollutants originated at the plant.

2. Water pollution
   a. Water discharges:
      (1) Identify each pollutant to be discharged in significant quantities.
      (2) Estimate anticipated volume of discharges.
      (3) Identify receiving body, either publicly owned treatment works (POTW) or water body.
   b. Water pollution control: Determine what effluent guidelines or regulations—best practicable technology, best available technology economically achievable, NSPS—have been proposed or promulgated for the pertinent industrial category.
      (1) Direct discharge (NPDES limitations for new point source apply):
         (a) Are water quality standards in receiving bodies such as to impose more stringent standards on the proposed plant?
         (b) Is the plant subject to new-source performance standards (NSPS)?
         (c) Identify state or regional water-quality planning regula-

tions under sections 208, 209 and 303 of the CWA that may impact on operations.

   (2) Discharge to POTW (pretreatment and related requirements apply):

   (*a*) Identify pretreatment requirements.

   (*b*) Identify applicable effluent guidelines.

   (*c*) Identify applicable local and regional water pollution control ordinances.

   c. Water use:

   (1) Identify potential for groundwater contamination in violation of the Federal Safe Drinking Water Act.

   (2) Review permitting of wells, dams, and discharges from or into these structures.

3. Air pollution

   a. Air emissions:

   (1) Identify all pollutants to be emitted in the operation of the facility.

   (2) Review estimates of the quantity emitted for each, with estimates of both raw and final emissions.

   b. Air pollution control

   (1) Identify pertinent air quality control region.

   (2) What requirements in existing state implementation plans apply to the plants in the industrial category in question?

   (3) Is the plant covered by proposed or contemplated NSPS?

   (4) Will the plant generate emissions subjecting it to special standards regulating hazardous pollutants?

   (5) Will the plant, on the basis of location and raw emissions level, be subject to review for prevention of significant deterioration?

   (6) Is the plant located in an area where violations of ambient air quality standards exist? Do the plant's emissions exceed cutoff limits, subjecting it to special review under nonattainment provisions?

   (7) Identify the control equipment used.

   (8) Review regional and local air pollution control regulations and ordinances for unique requirements.

During the audit, the audit team should be in contact with several corporate departments. For example, hazardous-waste regulations require review of shipping and transportation, purchasing, and warehousing and storage activities; water, air, and waste emissions involve plant engineering and production departments. In addition to these, the audit team must work closely with the legal, safety, and finance and accounting departments and existing special committees or task forces to ensure accurate and objective conclusions.

Analysis of Inspection Data

After the site inspection, the auditors assimilate their findings and reassess the applicable environmental requirements. Then they analyze the body of information to determine the degree of compliance with respect to each requirement. One method of determining compliance is to be certain that the reports submitted to federal, state, and local governments are accurate. Certain portions of the data contained in the reports can be selected for testing and traced to the original source document for verification. If, for example, the source document is a laboratory technician's notebook, the auditors' review would include observation of the technician making the usual sample collections to ensure conformance with permit requirements or regulations. The tests made by the laboratory are checked against the test protocols required by EPA for verification of the correct analysis. The attendant assumptions used in converting the raw data to the particular report that is submitted are also verified. On the basis of the review of the inspection data and the staff's activities, the auditors make recommendations for any necessary remedial action.

Preparation of Report

The auditors now prepare a written draft, copies of which are provided to the facility manager, legal counsel, and others with responsibility in the operations. When all parties concur that the report is an accurate reflection of the facts and activities of the operation and its status, the report is released to senior management. This is addressed further in the section below entitled Audit Report and Recommendations.

CONCLUSION OF THE AUDIT

At the conclusion of all site inspections, the auditors generally have assembled an extensive body of information. This information must be reviewed and the applicable requirements reassessed to analyze the company's compliance status and to uncover potentially sensitive areas. To do this, a checklist can be used, as illustrated in Table 2, which is de-

TABLE 2 Audit Checklist

Brief description of site and activity conducted
Proximity of neighbors
History of disposal and discharge problems
Technical staff
Laboratory facilities
Life expectancy of facility
Security: fence, guards, visitor control
Permits (number and type):

  Air
  Water
  Solid waste

Storage facilities
Chemical compatibility precautions
Manifest forms
Wastewater permit and receiving body
Transportation (owned or subcontracted)
Land disposal:

  Geology of site
  Hydrology of site
  Plot and cell plans (landfills, pits)
  Leachate collection, monitoring, and treatment
  Site preparation
  Closure plans
  Groundwater monitoring
  Ponds, lagoons, and holding basins

Incineration:

  Permit
  Emission tests
  Description of equipment

Recovery methods:

  Process
  Disposal of waste
  Disposal of reclaimants

Administration and management
Organization: staff, responsibilities
Employee training
Employee protective equipment
Employee exposure monitoring
Facility contingency or emergency plan; spill control and countermeasures
Record keeping
Reporting procedures, internal and external
Housekeeping

Source: Carl A. Gosline, "New Dimensions in Corporate Environmental Compliance Governance," 1981.

signed to provide an overview of a site, its operations and facilities, and its pollution-control practices, recovery practices, employee training and protection, and spill-prevention measures. Depending on the situation, each checklist item can be further developed.

Evaluation

On a broader scale, the evaluation of the audit information and the subsequent formulation of recommendations for any remedial action will involve review and assessment of information in three general areas: administrative, policies and procedures, and technical.

Administrative review

The data are reviewed by the auditors to determine whether all administrative requirements have been met. This involves review of reporting requirements, testing and monitoring requirements, operating conditions requiring permits, operations not covered by permits or rules, record keeping and retention, litigation and administrative proceedings, program plans as required by regulations, and other administrative activities required for compliance.

Policies and procedures review

Corporate policies and procedures relating to environmental compliance, authority, and responsibility are reviewed by the auditors. In addition, site-specific procedures are reviewed to assess their proper observance. This involves review of mechanisms for communication of significant information within the company, procedures for emergency situations, response to inquiries from the press or complaints received from EPA or state or local governments, internal controls, training programs, and quality-control measures.

Technical review

The auditors must also review all technical, operating, and engineering aspects of the sites visited. This involves review of the nature, character, and size of the operation; the physical, geographic, and demographic features of the location; the adequacy of the testing and sampling methods; the efficiency of the company's equipment in meeting permit standards; and the effectiveness of spill-prevention or contingency plans.

Analysis

Analysis of the information requires an independent, objective, corporate-level group or independent party. This team receives the field reports, analyzes the information, delineates information needs and submission schedules, and ultimately consolidates and synthesizes the vast amount of information. Obviously, only experienced personnel should participate in this review. Only they can provide the technical, business, and regulatory knowledge, as well as legal counsel, so necessary to the successful completion of the audit review.

In conducting the analysis, the audit team focuses on the following aspects:

- Current practices correctly and incorrectly followed
- Past practices of noncompliance
- Potential problems
- Adequacy of information reporting
- Organizational efficiency
- Potential cost savings
- Other observations or areas of concern requiring further corporate attention

As with the financial audit, the final result is a statement of assets and liabilities that are reported to the company's senior management.

Audit Report and Recommendations

The audit findings and recommendations are documented in a written report. The precise format in which the audit report is presented to management will vary according to the company. The presentation should be consistent with normal company information-management practices; it should be descriptive, not judgmental; and it should incorporate the information shown under the following heads.

Description of location and major activities

State the major activities conducted and describe materials received, products manufactured, and quantities shipped. Also include the size of the facility, operating schedules, and a physical description of the site(s).

Permits

List the number of permits, including necessary details, obtained under federal, state, and local regulations; permits in preparation or pending (similarly treated); and state compliance schedules, monitoring requirements, and reporting requirements.

Citations and penalties

List all citations and notices of violation, including the basis for each allegation and its status: settled, corrected, unresolved, or challenged. The listing serves as part of the basis for estimating the maximum penalties that could be imposed. Also include the statute of limitations for the jurisdiction in which the site is located; and estimate the penalty rate in terms of dollars per event, dollars per day, or other relevant basis, depending on the violation and the relevant statutes and regulations.

On-site treatment facilities

Identify and list all discharge points, including those to POTWs, pits, ponds, and lagoons; landfills; underground injection wells; stacks and vents; and any surface-water runoff control, containment, or collection system. Because permits usually contain specific information on waste composition, that information is not included in this part. Potentially harmful discharges that might not require permits, however, are identified.

Off-site disposal practices

List the character and volume of all wastes and disposal points for all sites, including those no longer in use, and identify all transporters. Name all disposal contractors and treatment operators, briefly describing their operations and locations.

Compliance programs

Describe activities planned or under way to remedy conditions where improvements are needed, including plans and programs for new facilities and programs for operator training, transportation control, etc.

Estimated capital, operating, and maintenance costs and supporting expense for pollution control

These data should be developed in two ways. First, state the company's existing permanent investment in pollution-control facilities and add to that the planned or authorized capital expenditures for the next 3 years (or longer, if major amounts of capital are perceived as being needed beyond that time). List expenditures for major projects individually; group minor projects. Treat operating and maintenance costs similarly. Combine costs of internal support staff and external assistance.[1] Second, generate data solely on those facilities not complying with environmental regulations, for which remedial measures are needed now. The cost of these measures then becomes the incremental cost for complying. The advantage of having both sets of facts lies in knowing the ratio of incremental cost to total cost. While it may not be a perfect measure, a low ratio of incremental costs to total costs indicates a high degree of compliance and good management.

In all cases, uniform criteria are needed to segregate pollution-control measures from other expenditures, some of which, although undertaken for other basic purposes, will reduce waste discharges.[2]

Organization and control

Describe internal reporting relationships within each site, up to the major-operating-unit line and staff executive levels. Also describe internal procedures, reporting practices, and training programs.

Uncertainties

The current regulatory climate presents a host of potential and unresolved issues—technological, legislative, interpretative, institutional, and legal—that may have a substantial effect on the company. The specific outcome is not always predictable or measurable. It is therefore necessary to identify the factors that could have a significant effect on the corporation and to qualitatively describe each potential problem. Examples of such factors include:

- Circumstances that could pose an unreasonable risk to the public health or environment
- Situations that could result in unacceptable interruptions to operations
- Situations that would shorten the useful life of the facility or the production of particular products at that location
- Problems for which remedial or control technology is not available
- Problems for which technology exists but at a cost that would jeopardize the financial viability of the operation or product competitiveness
- Prevailing attitudes that pose a potential for punitive administrative penalties and actions
- Innovative technology that could provide beneficial breakthroughs, even if commercially unproven for specific applications
- Alternative manufacturing methods that could yield fewer or smaller quantities of objectionable wastes

The audit report must present clearly and concisely recommendations for remedial actions in the areas of apparent noncompliance and alternative actions to reduce potential exposure to liability or to reduce the impact of the environmental regulations. Coopers & Lybrand's audits, in addition, stress the potential economic savings involved in adopting certain recommendations.

EVOLUTION OF ENVIRONMENTAL AND RISK MANAGEMENT

A number of major factors have affected environmental regulation and compliance in the United States over the past several years. The convergence of these factors has fueled the demand for a tougher approach to industrial compliance with environmental laws as a whole.

First, the public has become increasingly aware of the threat to human health and the environment posed by certain types of environmental pollution. Protection of the environment is now a generally accepted social objective, even though there is currently considerable controversy about the application of some of the rules promulgated under more recent statutes and amendments. (Nine major laws and at least fourteen related laws require careful attention, as shown in Table 3.) Because of this, public and congressional pressure on EPA to take forceful action to protect health and the environment from hazardous substances has been felt by corporations such as Allied in the Kepone incident. What resulted from this event was a review of the company's entire environmental program. The Kepone case truly sensitized Allied and a host of other companies to the significance of environmental management.[3]

Second, because the largest portion of the costs of environmental regulations is borne initially by the private sector, the SEC has concerned itself with possible effects on corporate earnings, potential liabilities, and operating constraints. It requires publicly held corporations to disclose information about their affairs to provide an investor with timely, accurate information upon which to base a prudent investment decision. With this requirement the SEC has brought an entirely new dimension to environmental compliance assurances and reporting. The SEC recently proposed to amend its legal proceedings regulations to broaden the present requirements for disclosure of any environmental proceeding to which a governmental authority is a party. The proposal would require disclosure of (1) all environmental proceedings, including governmental proceedings, that are material to the business or financial condition of the registrant; (2) damage actions involving potential fines, capital expenditures, or other charges exceeding 10 percent of current assets; and (3) governmental proceedings, unless the registrant reasonably believes that such proceedings will result in fines of less than $100,000. In addition, the proposal would add a requirement that regis-

TABLE 3 Federal Environmental Statutes

Major significance

National Environmental Policy Act (1969) (amended twice since 1970)

Clean Air Act, as amended (amended six times since 1970)

Federal Water Pollution Control Act, as amended (commonly referred to as Clean Water Act) (amended eleven times since 1970)

Federal Insecticide, Fungicide and Rodenticide Act, as amended (amended three times since 1970)

Safe Drinking Water Act, as amended (1974) (amended twice since enactment)

Toxic Substances Control Act (1976)

Resource Conservation and Recovery Act of 1976, as amended by the Solid Waste Disposal Act amendments of 1980 (amended two other times since enactment)

Surface Mining Control and Reclamation Act of 1977, as amended (amended once since enactment)

Comprehensive Environmental Response, Compensation and Liability Act of 1980 (Superfund)

Related laws

Hazardous Materials Transportation Act, as amended

Occupational Safety and Health Act of 1970, as amended

Federal Mine Safety and Health Act of 1977, as amended

Coastal Zone Management Act of 1972, as amended

Marine Protection, Research and Sanctuaries Act of 1972, as amended

Federal Food, Drug and Cosmetic Act, as amended

Rivers and Harbors Act of 1899 (Refuse Act)

Outer Continental Shelf Lands Act, as amended

National Gas Pipeline Safety Act of 1968, as amended

Hazardous Liquid Pipeline Safety Act of 1979

Administrative Procedures Act, as amended

Noise Control Act of 1972, as amended

Endangered Species Act of 1973, as amended

Atomic Energy Act, as amended

Source: Adapted from *A Handbook of Key Regulations and Criteria for Multimedia Environmental Control,* EPA, August 1979.

trants disclose or make available the names and addresses of governmental authorities from which compliance-related reports concerning environmental proceedings can be obtained.[4]

It is important that the SEC's disclosure requirements be understood and followed. Should the SEC find that a registrant failed to disclose material environmental problems in its reports, the company's ability to raise funds through stock offerings or debt instruments would be jeopardized. At best, the company would be involved in expensive, damaging, and time-consuming proceedings that could lead to an administrative order, from which the only relief would be resort to the courts.

Another factor is that the environmental statutes and their attendant regulations, permits, registrations, and legal issues are increasingly mature and have withstood careful judicial review. Although this is less true for the RCRA of 1976 and for the Superfund legislation of 1980 than it is for the CAA and CWA, the maturation of environmental management as a result of these laws has been evident.

Criminal sanctions have also been important in the development of compliance attitudes. The environmental statutes contain criminal penalty provisions that apply to directors, officers, and employees, and the penalties are severe. Amendments to the Solid Waste Disposal Act of 1980 (PL 96-482) introduced the concepts of "knowing endangerment" and "extreme indifference to human life." Conviction means a $250,000 fine and up to 5 years in jail. The amendments provided defenses involving the definition of "knowing" but made plain that affirmative steps to prevent discovery of relevant information could be used as circumstantial evidence of actual knowledge. In addition, there are other penalties under the United States Criminal Code: one cannot make false statements, obstruct proceedings, conceal knowledge, conspire to defraud the United States, aid or abet those committing offenses, or comfort or assist them after the fact without risk of criminal sanctions.

It is noteworthy that virtually every environmental statute provides for the prosecution of "any person," including an "individual," and in some instances "any responsible corporate officer." Moreover, these provisions have been successfully invoked. What has in the past taken the sting out of the various environmental statutes that have criminal provisions and the government's efforts to use them has been the tendency to be lenient with the guilty individual. Penalties assessed against corporate officials have historically been far less severe than those imposed on ordinary violators. Fines were typically minimal and jail sentences extremely rare. This, however, is beginning to change, with the Department of Justice's new emphasis on vigorous criminal enforcement.

The prospects are for more indictments of company personnel and harsher penalties, including jail sentences, for those companies and individuals who are ultimately convicted. From all indications from the Justice Department, every attempt will be made to identify the top corporate officers responsible for corporate acts, so that the law may be truly enforced and its real deterrent effect mobilized.

ADVANTAGES OF AN AUDIT

An environmental audit can provide evidence of a company's responsibility and reliability. Implementing a system of periodic environmental audits can be a useful step in constructing a positive corporate image in the eyes of the public, the employees, and the industrial clients or customers of the company. Probably never before has a company's good citizenship been as likely to become a public issue as in the management of hazardous waste. Perhaps more importantly, never before has it been as important for hazardous-waste transporters and disposers to demonstrate reliability and responsibility to their customers. The legal concepts embodied in Superfund and RCRA, for example, make every company involved in the chain of waste generation, transportation, storage, treatment, and disposal potentially liable for the actions of others in the chain.

An environmental audit also provides evidence of insurability. A newly developing field of insurance involves insurance against liability for "nonsudden occurrences," e.g., pollution damage. Regulations requiring owners and operators of hazardous-waste facilities to provide liability coverage were recently instituted by EPA. Under the regulations, firms are required to buy insurance or demonstrate by a financial test that they can meet liability claims. Since there are few or no actuarial data on which an insurance company can base a decision to provide or deny insurance to such a facility or to establish its premium, it is likely that such decisions will be influenced by, or dependent on, periodic environmental audits demonstrating compliance with governmental regulations to lessen the risks attributable to current operations.

Additionally, acquisition of, or mergers with, other companies may be as sensitive to considerations of environmental integrity as they are to considerations of fiscal integrity. An environmental audit can assess that integrity by examining the significant potential liabilities of the acquired corporation for environmental violations or required capital expenditures for compliance.

In considering the risk of undisclosed potential liabilities in this context, the acquiring firm must understand that the costs required to address environmental problems are potentially great. In many situations, practices of the past pose a risk of "time bombs" which require remedial action at great expense. Probably the most vivid example of this is Occidental Petroleum Corporation's acquisition of Hooker Chemical Corporation. Hooker had used four sites in the Niagara Falls, New York, area since the early 1940s for disposal of hazardous chemical wastes, the best-known being the Love Canal area. Since its acquisition by Occidental in 1968, Hooker has been subjected to claims of hundreds of millions of dollars by the federal government and by the state of New York, local governments, and citizens' groups. With the increase of corporate acquisitions, a strong argument can be made for a company to determine the state of environmental health of an acquired corporation, regardless of the form of the corporate reorganization.[5]

Finally, some observers fear that environmental auditing by companies will be assigned a low priority because of the current administration's emphasis on "regulatory reform," or deregulation. They should not overlook, however, the need to comply with environmental requirements imposed by the states. In fact, in addition to the merits discussed above, an environmental auditing program from the auditor's point of view should also:

- Reduce the adversarial tension between government and industry by removing the burden of costly and intensive government inspection where such inspection is redundant, thus rewarding responsible companies and moving the focus of enforcement away from confrontation and toward cooperation and assistance
- Improve the overall level of compliance with regulation by giving companies an incentive to institutionalize comprehensive procedures to ensure compliance with regulations
- Improve the quality of debate and decision making on future regulatory issues by developing within firms a detailed knowledge of their plants' actual and potential regulatory and environmental impact

To the extent that firms with extensive or even modest existing programs expand their programs, environmental auditing improves the quality of compliance. It is critical that companies not only comprehend the potential effects of environmental management but also have a functioning system for analyzing and reporting according to the rules. Auditing programs provide an additional incentive for the private sector to put its regulatory house in order and provide a strong marketing tool for meeting the requirements in a cost-effective manner.

CORPORATE LIABILITY

One of the foremost purposes of an audit is to reduce the exposure of a company and its officers to potential liability for noncompliance. In addition to potential criminal liabilities, causing environmental harm may also give rise to civil liabilities. As a result, violating a regulation may well involve a corporation in litigation with a risk of significant potential liabilities, regardless of the government's policies of enforcement.

Most environmental statutes provide for significant civil and criminal penalties in the event of noncompliance. As discussed earlier, under the RCRA, failure to abate a violation within the time specified by an EPA compliance order can result in a civil penalty of up to $25,000 for each day of noncompliance. Criminal penalties of $50,000 and a prison term of up to 2 years (for the first offense) may be imposed on any owner or operator who knowingly engages in certain activities without a permit or who knowingly makes a false statement or representation on any RCRA document. In addition, the act includes an offense, "knowing endangerment" of human life, which provides for a criminal penalty of $250,000 or a prison term of up to 5 years or both.

In an effort to ensure corporate compliance, some statutes impute certain illegal actions of company employees to the corporate officer under whose responsibility the violations occur. The severity of these penalties and the measures devised for bringing their weight to bear directly and personally on company officials are stark reminders of Congress's intent that compliance with these regulations be achieved.

An audit can reduce the exposure of a corporation and its officers in several ways. First, the audit can identify situations of actual or potential noncompliance and thus reduce the risk of a lawsuit. In most cases the audit can recommend remedial action and the areas of noncompliance can be remedied before they are detected by government inspectors. Many instances of noncompliance stem from failure to establish or carry out adequate procedures for assuring environmental compliance. Such failures frequently arise from misplaced emphasis or an internal, biased perspective, as opposed to lack of competence or good faith. A compliance audit can identify such failures through methodical, knowledgeable examination and an independent perspective.

In addition, the fact that a company has an independent audit program, the results of which indicate a good-faith effort to comply, may cause governmental agencies, which usually try to target probable violators, to direct their inspections elsewhere. The audit can serve as evidence of good-faith attempts to comply and may justify the exercise of discretion by the government as to whether to prosecute in the event an anomalous violation is detected by government inspectors. And finally, even if prosecution for a violation occurs, the good-faith efforts evidenced by the audit can provide substantial justification for a federal or state prosecutor or judge not to seek or impose substantial civil or criminal penalties.

THE AUDITOR'S ROLE

The auditor's role in the environmental audit is strategic. The experience the auditor brings to this exercise is valuable. The training and experience of an auditor in procedural testing, verification of information and procedures, and sampling of data for accuracy, as well as an auditor's objectivity, are important reasons for enlisting an independent party to conduct an environmental audit.

Making the proper assessment of a corporation's environmental health and compliance requires recognition that technology is but one of many factors in the management of a corporation that are intimately related. As with any management function, oversight is the key to thoughtful planning, systematic control, disciplined execution, and continuing guidance for directing efforts and employing resources. While requiring general comprehension and knowledge of the environmental field, adequate oversight does not necessarily require in-depth expertise in pollution-control technology, recognition of hazardous-waste products, or the ultimate fate and effects of waste disposal in the air, water, land, or subsurface strata. Nor is a detailed understanding of the extensive body of legislative intent, statutory language, regulatory interpretations, complex legal language, scientific uncertainties, and jurisdictional conflicts a prerequisite to adequate oversight in identifying problems and working toward solutions.

The test is whether the system is working to produce the results expected from corporate policies. The audit is not an evaluation of alternatives that will optimize a course of action to solve operating, engineering, scientific, legal, technical, employee, or public relations problems. The objective of an environmental audit is to reveal whether the system is controlling in a way that will yield expected and understandable results. The audit will succeed if it reveals shortcomings as well as satisfactory conditions and identifies the necessary steps to cure the shortcomings and augment the satisfactory conditions.

The auditor has the job of evaluating the impact of noncompliance upon the company by pursuing a disciplined and objective approach to the environmental audit. This approach requires that the company have precise internal controls of the budget and procedures for information and document control and that the auditor have freedom to engage technical experts, as well as experience in interviewing, in document inspection, and in organizing a large volume of information. The auditor also must have the organization to undertake a large project and the ability to produce high-quality work in the allotted time and within the budget.

In addition, the external auditor can provide a certified audit in a third-party role, conducting an annual or semiannual audit to determine whether the company is following its prescribed procedures as self-imposed or suggested by government. Should the government develop a voluntary environmental-audit program, such a program could at some point have as one of its criteria the certification by an independent third party that the company's audit procedures are being followed.

Moreover, smaller firms may prefer to have their audits done by a third party rather than by internal auditors. If a third party not only reviews the firm's internal audit procedures but also conducts the inspection and monitoring of the firm's pollution controls, government could decide to accept third-party certification of compliance in lieu of certification by a senior corporate officer.

The role of the auditor, therefore, can be broadly or narrowly defined. Either way the auditor is in the unique position of building credibility through application of third-party experience, neutralizing operating prejudices or biases by being objective, and conducting the appropriate analysis.

1. Carl A. Gosline, "New Dimensions in Corporate Environmental Compliance Governance," 1981.
2. Ibid.
3. "Auditing for hazards on the rise," *Chicago Tribune*, July 8, 1981, p. 18.
4. Coopers & Lybrand, *SEC Manual*, 1981 (internal publication).
5. Bingham Kennedy, "The Growing Need for Environmental Auditing," 1981.

The Engineer's Perspective

James T. O'Rourke

Industrial Group
Camp Dresser & McKee, Inc.

There are several ways for a corporation to look at the environmental auditing process. By nature, the audit is not an in-depth, quantitative study including detailed sampling and analysis; but the extent of the review can vary. The audit can be a snapshot of the company's overall compliance, a planning tool, a review of a particular problem area, or the foundation of a broader auditing program.

An audit can be viewed as a photograph of a company's total environmental management and compliance system at a given time. This approach assumes a process that gathers information on company operations and applicable environmental regulations that affect operations. The auditor then reviews how the company is satisfying various permits, discharge guidelines, and regulatory constraints. This photographic, or "snapshot-in-time," approach makes use of simple auditing techniques. If compliance problems are uncovered, the corporation must then decide on a course of remedial action. This approach leaves out much of the technical evaluation and analysis.

An environmental audit can be used as a management early-warning system to verify compliance with existing statutes, to identify the impact of future regulatory requirements, and to develop a strategic response to these regulations. This goes beyond a snapshot of the current situation and incorporates a "what-if" approach. Analogous to the corporate strategic planning process, this approach allows the corporation to plan for any adjustments it may have to make. The corporation maintains control over its environmental compliance and takes action to avoid future problems. Information gathered in this approach can be used for the planning of new facilities, for changes in product lines, for engineering changes, or for making financial projections.

Some companies may want to conduct an audit as a first step in establishing an in-house review procedure. In this case, the audit *procedure* may be as important as the audit *findings,* because the firm will want to use it as a model for future audits. Such an audit might include a methodology for screening the company's plants to determine which ones should be audited. In this case, the auditor may offer instruction to in-house personnel and indicate sources of further information on applicable processes and regulatory requirements.

A primary reason to conduct an audit is to minimize business risks, protecting a company from unexpected surprises in the management of its environmental affairs. With hundreds and even thousands of environmental regulations at the federal, state, and local levels affecting the operation of most corporations, it is easy for an environmental compliance problem to arise. Many corporations spread responsibility for the regulatory compliance activity among many functions—such as legal, engineering, or plant operations—or have decentralized the responsibility to each unit or plant in the company. This makes it difficult to ascertain whether there are any problems. An illegal environmental action or nonaction by anyone in a decentralized or ill-defined reporting structure can lead to legal, financial, or public-image problems. Also, the delegation of this responsibility to persons who do not or cannot (by job description) keep up to date on the current status of the relevant regulations can lead to oversights or to an incomplete understanding of the regulations themselves.

Simply stated, a corporation should view the environmental audit as a process that leads to better information about current operations; develops recommendations to bring all company units into compliance; protects the company from legal, economic, and public-image problems; and gives management an additional tool in its strategic planning process.

THE ENGINEER'S AUDITING ROLE

Most environmental regulations are premised on engineering principles and compromises between cost and engineering feasibility. Whether a company has a complex wastewater treatment plant, unique solid and hazardous wastes requiring disposal, or air pollution control equipment with attendant effluent sidestreams, engineering theory and judgment underlie all solutions to the problems which may be uncovered. The professional engineer has a crucial role to play in an audit—to identify deficiencies and recommend remedial actions. At a minimum, a corporation's engineering staff should be involved with legal and plant personnel in conducting an audit and in setting up an environmental auditing program. It may be beneficial to have an outside engineering consultant participate in initial audits or to periodically perform audits as a means of checking on in-house procedures.

Staff or plant engineers may have an understanding of the processes or specific plant operations, but an outside consultant can also bring experience gained with regulations and with similar technical processes encountered elsewhere. An outside consultant also has the advantage of working with other persons of comparable knowledge in many different disciplines, thus providing a client with an excellent overall technical capability.

An outside engineering consultant, if a corporation uses one, should work closely with in-house technical staff on the audit, while still functioning as an unbiased third party. A consultant can review the pertinent regulations and applicable permits and measure compliance against these by reviewing plant functions and operating data and observing plant operations.

When areas of noncompliance are uncovered, the engineer should recommend possible solutions for the problem. These solutions most often involve engineering process or operations changes, the areas that an engineer is best equipped to handle. Working with plant staff and company engineers, the consultant makes recommendations that may lead to elimination of the problem. Sometimes minor modifications, such as the addition of a chemical at a different point in the plant process, may be sufficient to improve performance; at other times, more comprehensive and capital-intensive physical modifications may be needed.

An outside engineering consultant can recommend changes in operation and process design that will make a facility function more efficiently. A plant may be fully in compliance with all permits and regulations, but a critical review of operations by an engineering consultant can result in recommendations that lead to cost savings.

AN ENGINEER'S LEGAL RESPONSIBILITY

An outside engineering consultant hired by a corporation to conduct an environmental audit has legal responsibilities in two general directions: to the corporation and to third parties, including state and federal agencies and people specifically endangered or harmed by the action or inaction of the corporation and the engineer.

Legal responsibilities to the corporation are, in large part, dictated by the contract for the audit. The scope of work and time of performance represent key terms of the contract defining the engineer's reponsibility to the corporation. The contract, for example, may also specify a standard of performance for the engineer's work. If not, the standard of performance would be embodied in the common-law concept of negligence, which generally requires a level of performance consistent with normal skills of the profession. To address the sensitive nature of an environmental audit, the contract may also include provisions obligating the engineer to keep the audit process and results confidential and to review its findings with the corporation's legal counsel.

Much more difficult to define than the responsibility to the corporation is the engineer's legal responsibility to endangered and injured parties and to state and federal agencies. Depending upon the terms of the contract, there may be some conflict between the two responsibilities, particularly in the area of confidentiality. Federal and state law (both statutes and common law) must be examined carefully to identify such legal responsibilities to third parties. The engineer's responsibilities may vary from state to state and will depend greatly upon the particular circumstances.

In the case of a third party injured by corporate activities within the audit's scope, for example, the engineer's legal responsibility may depend upon whether the engineer obtained knowledge of the conditions causing the injury. If such knowledge is obtained during the environmental audit, the engineer's first responsibility is to report the conditions to the corporation. If the engineer is aware that the corporation is not correcting the problem, the question of the engineer's legal responsibility to report such conditions to other parties (such as governmental regulatory agencies and the parties potentially affected) is raised.

State common law generally does not require the engineer to take such affirmative steps as notifying third parties, and the contract for services may prohibit such reporting by its confidentiality provisions. Before a decision is made on whether to report such conditions, however, the applicable state law (both statutory and common law) should be thoroughly researched in the context of the specific facts. In the interest of engineer-client relations and to protect the engineer from third-party liability in this regard, this question should be addressed by legal counsel before the audit starts and specific provisions incorporated into the contract for services to allow a breach of confidentiality in appropriate circumstances.

If, on the other hand, the conditions causing injury were not discovered by the engineer but should have been discovered, the engineer may be responsible for third-party injuries under common-law negligence provisions. The engineer can obtain protection in this area by way of liability insurance and by including an indemnification provision in the contract for professional services.

Finally, federal and state environmental statutes generally include provisions imposing civil and criminal penalties for making false statements or for destroying records relating to the required information. Any conduct of the engineer in performing or reporting on the audit that runs afoul of such provisions would create exposure to the penalties specified.

DETERMINING THE SCOPE OF THE AUDIT

As in all engineering projects, the first step in conducting the environmental audit is to define its scope. This depends primarily on what the company management's objective is in conducting the audit. Typically, management wants the audit to identify potential problem areas that may lead to regulatory noncompliance or seriously harm the company's public image. In this case, the audit serves as a regulatory review and technical assessment of the firm's operations.

For companies who want to focus on a specific area of concern, the scope of the audit may be fairly narrow, reviewing only one practice or regulatory area. For example, a company may want to audit the waste handling and off-site disposal practices of a firm it contracts with in order to protect itself against future liability. This would involve a specific audit, including a review of the contractor's financial and managerial operations as well as its technical operations. Another company may want only to determine its compliance with a newly promulgated regulation, such as new land-disposal regulations. Here again, the audit's scope would be fairly narrow.

Another important consideration in establishing the scope of the audit is whether it will encompass a single site or several. A large company with over 100 manufacturing sites may decide to examine only a few plants it suspects as having problems or only those plants with many divergent waste effluents. A methodology can be structured by auditing a similar plant or plants and extrapolating the approach for use at other sites by in-plant personnel.

The type of industry will also influence the scope of the audit. In general, an audit of a process industry, such as a chemical manufacturer, will be more complicated and time-consuming than an audit of a mechanical assembly plant of similar size.

Management should take into consideration the relevant cost-benefit ratios and suit the scope of the audit to its managerial objectives as well as its budget. For example, an audit that includes verification of the filing of all necessary permits and documentation with the appropriate agencies would be relatively expensive but would provide management with a high degree of assurance that its facilities were in full compliance with the law.

Clearly, management must determine at the outset what its purpose is in conducting the audit. An unclear objective or a poorly defined audit scope will undermine the usefulness of the audit. Management must define and communicate clearly both the objectives and the limits of the audit. An engineer can help management define the scope by paying a walk-through visit to a typical plant to be audited. To ensure an effective audit, management and the auditor should discuss the audit scope in depth and come to a detailed agreement before the actual audit begins.

SELECTING THE AUDIT TEAM

Once the scope of the audit has been defined and agreed upon, the audit team is assembled. The members of the audit team can significantly affect the success of an audit and should be chosen on the basis of their technical ability, experience, and familiarity with the type of industry being audited. The audit is qualitative, based upon observations and engineering judgment. Management will be taking the auditor's word in an area in which the financial liabilities can run very high. For this reason, trust between management and the audit team is essential in the environmental audit, just as it is in a financial audit.

The outside auditor offers a corporation the advantage of objectivity, being without a vested interest in the company's production objectives. Company personnel may be too close to operations to notice all potential problems. To compensate for the outside auditor's lack of detailed knowledge of a plant's operations and history, it is important for a company using an outside auditor to appoint contact persons who are knowledgeable about the company and its operations and who have the necessary time to work with the auditor. Typically, plant engineering personnel who have worked at the plant for a long time are good candidates for this position, since they are usually aware of process changes (piping systems, etc.) which may not have been recorded. They can help the auditor to identify problems which may otherwise go undetected until they reach a crisis point.

The audit team should be limited to the minimum number of people necessary to achieve the objective. This will help reduce fear and tension when the audit team visits the plant. The auditor must have a thorough knowledge of the applicable regulations—federal, state, and local. The key to many regulations lies in their interpretation; for this reason, the auditor should have experience in working with the regulations, not just know how they read.

To conduct an effective audit, the auditor must also be familiar with the types of operations and processes involved. The auditor who does not understand a given manufacturing process may easily overlook potential problems or violations. An auditor should ask questions about how processes are operated, to be sure that all sources are identified, and should have a current understanding of the new technologies available for the particular industrial application. A knowledgeable auditor will not only be able to alert the company to problem areas but may also be able to suggest appropriate process modifications where applicable.

Finally, the auditor must be able to work with plant-level personnel. When the auditor enters the plant, it is important to keep tension and distrust to a minimum. Plant personnel can easily be intimidated by the prospect of having someone from outside criticize their operations. The more they understand the purpose of the audit and feel comfortable with the people conducting it, the less fearful and more cooperative they will be. Often the line staff in an area are the only ones who can provide the auditor with the information needed to make a valid judgment, since they are familiar with the process line and the various waste streams peculiar to it.

CONDUCTING THE AUDIT

Gathering Data

Before visiting the plant, the audit team's first task is to gather as much existing data on the plant as possible. All current permits should be examined. Often, many of a plant's permits are outdated; it is not unusual for a significant number of a plant's permits to have expired without renewal, and in some cases permits may have never been issued. Of particular concern in manufacturing industries are operations that have changed since a permit was first issued, requiring updated or additional permits. Any significant changes in operations could alter existing source constraints. In addition to the permits, all correspondence with regulatory agencies should be examined, as well as pending applications, inspection records, and compliance schedule reports.

It is advisable, in the interest of efficiency, to use in gathering information a survey form and checklist completed by plant personnel prior to the visit. The audit team should collect the following information on a plant's operations:

- *An inventory of chemicals used.* Some wastes may be generated by operations incidental to production processes. Knowledge of chemical usage helps the engineer to identify the presence of potentially troublesome wastes. Estimates of annual or monthly consumption and typical inventories should be included. Chemicals purchased under proprietary names should be identified.

- *Process flow diagrams.* Drawings of the manufacturing processes should show major raw-material usage, manufacturing steps, products, and wastes (vapors, solids, and liquids). A process schematic diagram for the waste-treatment area should also be provided.

- *Materials balance.* This includes estimation of the distribution of raw materials into four categories: (1) those incorporated into products; (2) those destroyed or modified in the production process; (3) those evaporated, discharged, or discarded; and (4) those incorporated into products which are rejected and discarded. These classifications should include any by-products formed during the operations.

- *A list of personnel* responsible for managing the facility's compliance with permits and regulatory obligations, as well as those knowledgeable about the manufacturing operations and practices.

- *Monitoring data.* Results of routine analytical tests and other results representative of seasonal or other production-schedule variations for each waste stream for which monitoring is required, as well as any other available information on the composition of waste streams.

- *Waste treatment, storage, and disposal information,* including a complete list of hazardous wastes treated, stored, or disposed of on site and off site; and information on how wastes are stored pending disposal, how waste is disposed of from the site (copy of state manifest forms), and the ultimate disposal location.

Reviewing the Regulations

The data gathered in the steps outlined above should provide the auditor with a comprehensive overview of the plant's operations and waste-handling activities. The team's next step is to conduct a thorough review of all federal, state, and local regulations that currently apply or will apply to the plant. It is important to have a good understanding of the plant and operations before doing this, in order to be able to focus on the regulatory concerns that most significantly affect the plant.

The significant regulations include those implementing the following laws:

- Clean Air Act and amendments
- Clean Water Act
- Resource Conservation and Recovery Act (RCRA)
- Toxic Substances Control Act
- State and county environmental laws

Visiting the Site

The purposes of the site inspection are manifold. First, the audit team needs to compare the actual (observed) conditions at the plant with the background data collected prior to the plant visit by the survey form and also with existing regulations. The audit team will also look for potential problem areas that may not have been evident from the background information or that may have escaped the notice of regulatory agencies thus far. During the site inspection, the audit team can assess the awareness of the plant staff in managing the facility's compliance with permits and regulatory obligations.

The site inspection can take from a few hours to several days, depending on the size of the plant, the scope of the audit, and the size of the audit team. The inspection consists of a walk through the plant, with investigation of the areas or processes in question. One person should conduct interviews with plant personnel in specific areas to verify operating practices. More than one team can work simultaneously in the plant.

The auditor should review recent monitoring data, note the age and condition of treatment equipment, and inquire about recent visits by regulatory authorities and any reported violations. In general, the audit team depends upon the frankness of the plant personnel to obtain information on operating procedures and typical plant operating conditions. As mentioned earlier, this is why it is imperative to have an auditor who can gain the cooperation of the plant staff.

Some of the considerations that should be included in the site investigation are the following:

- *Air emissions.* Fossil-fuel-burning boilers, on-site incinerators, manufacturing equipment, process units emitting volatile organic compounds or particulates, and all other sources of air emissions should be investigated with regard to source registration, permit requirements, source constraints, compliance schedules, monitoring frequencies, and emission quality. Sources having emission-control devices should be noted and compared with requirements. Design and performance of the emission-control equipment should also be reviewed. Emission sources that are susceptible to wide fluctuations due to load rate should be noted. On-the-spot checks should be made for opacity, off-site odors, and worker exposure to vapors.

- *Drinking water.* Sources of water supply and recirculated plant water systems should be examined. Any process-water or drinking-water cross connections should be investigated to ensure that proper backflow-prevention devices are installed and operating.

- *Wastewater.* Discharges to municipal systems or receiving streams (including process, sanitary, surface runoff, and roof drains) should be investigated for flow rates and chemical makeup. All applicable pretreatment requirements, local sewer ordinances, and National Pollution Discharge Elimination System (NPDES) limits should be reviewed. Of special concern are any wastes which may interfere with the municipal treatment system or create a fire or explosion hazard. Existing wastewater-treatment and sludge-disposal systems should be investigated. Plant performance should be compared with NPDES permit requirements.

- *Spill prevention.* Any existing oil or chemical spill-prevention control and contingency or similar plans should be reviewed. Surface runoff patterns should be observed principally as they affect spill-prevention control and contingency plans for chemical spills. Quantities of bulk and drummed chemicals used at the site should be estimated. The overall site drainage system and existing soil and groundwater conditions should be considered in light of the impact of a spill. For example, a spill in a chemical storage area with no containment dike might flow into a storm drain, and the auditor would recommend construction of a dike to prevent this. Written safety, operating, and maintenance procedures should be reviewed.

- *Hazardous waste.* Any generation, transport, storage treatment, and on- or off-site disposal of hazardous waste should be examined in light of both Environmental Protection Agency and state regulations. For any hazardous-waste generation, quantities, frequencies, containment and shipping methods, and record keeping should be examined. For any storage or treatment facility, safety and surveil-lance systems should be reviewed. If a facility disposes of hazard-ous wastes by surface impoundments, lagoons, land application, injection into wells, waste piles, landfills, incineration, or other on-site methods, the inspection should include types and quantities of wastes and design criteria, actual construction features, and opera-tional procedures for the systems; for example, is a surface im-poundment or lagoon which has been used for many years still sufficiently impermeable to prevent migration of contaminants into the groundwater? Is RCRA-mandated groundwater moni-toring being conducted?

- *Solid waste.* Quantities of all nonhazardous wastes generated at the plant should be determined, as well as disposal methods and costs.

- *Liquid wastes.* Any liquid wastes that are burned should also be investigated to ensure that the combustion system is approved to burn the wastes. If an off-site system is used, the methods used to store the liquids before combustion should be evaluated with re-spect to their regulatory adequacy.

- *Polychlorinated biphenyls* (PCBs). All electrical-power service equip-ment, whether in-service or not, should be reviewed. Any disposal practices for PCBs should be investigated.

- *Old disposal sites.* Quantities and characteristics of any liquid or solid wastes that may have been disposed of on the plant site should be determined. Groundwater quality monitoring may be required if it is suspected that a problem exists.

- *Radioactive materials.* All radioactive materials used or handled at the plant site should be identified. Methods of disposal of such material should be well documented and available for inspection.

Depending upon the scope of the audit, the engineer may also evalu-ate noise pollution and worker health and safety, although these are not typically included in an environmental audit.

The auditor should be sufficiently familiar with the manufacturing processes to know which areas in a plant require special attention. The experienced auditor may well be able to suggest process modifications during the course of the audit which can improve a plant's environmen-tal management programs.

If any gross violations or potential problem areas are uncovered dur-ing the site investigation, the auditor should discuss them freely and in depth with the responsible plant staff at the time. It is better for all parties involved in the audit for the auditor to warn the plant staff of problems when they are discovered, instead of surprising them with the audit report. Their cooperation will help the audit to fulfill management's objective—identifying and correcting areas of potential liability.

Review, Analysis, and Reporting

After the site inspection, the audit team reviews its findings and identifies any areas where it thinks it needs more information. This may involve obtaining more records from the plant, interviewing certain plant personnel, or going back to inspect certain areas of the plant.

The audit team must be sure to have all the information it needs to make judgments about the company's environmental operations and compliance. Again, it is important to have the cooperation of both management and plant staff for this reason.

The audit report should include both an executive summary giving an overview of the company's environmental-management practices and a detailed listing of the problem areas identified. Each audit report, like each audit, will be different. The report should reflect the scope of the audit as it was defined at the start: the audit scope defines what management wants from the audit, and the audit report should make certain that management gets it.

The Insurance Broker's Perspective

Myra Tobin

Marsh & McLennan, Inc.

The insurance industry is often perceived by those outside it as monumentally conservative. Yet the industry fights hard to overcome its frequently undeserved reputation of having limited imagination and of failing to develop new insurance products for either the corporate or personal consumer. As new technologies bring social and economic changes in life styles, the insurance industry is constantly challenged to keep pace with the increased amount of legislation containing financial-responsibility regulations. Further, the liberal interpretations of laws and contracts by current courts contribute to additional uncertainty within the insurance underwriting community. Is the insurance industry to be criticized or applauded for its risk taking in the 1980s? That question may not have an answer until the year 2000 or beyond. This chapter examines one area in which the insurance industry has responded to a changing society's need to share the financial burden for environmental pollution, as well as its endorsement of a new risk-management tool for corporations—environmental auditing.

Senior managements of corporations experienced repeated attacks by the media during the 1970s as the private sector encountered increasing exposure to loss resulting from environmental pollution and the liabilities attendant upon those judged responsible. Initially, the concern of business and environmentalists was directed toward the waterways and the atmosphere. Today these groups have widened their area of concern to include impairment of land sites.

GLOBAL SCOPE OF POLLUTION

The problems of pollution are not confined to national boundaries, and a global approach to resolving pollution problems is imperative. International cooperation is needed to focus on planetwide effects of air, water, and land pollution brought about by human activities.

Especially pressing is the need for a global approach to pollution regulations. In most industrial countries the patchwork of environmental regulations already in effect and continuing to evolve requires corporations to complete so much paperwork and disclose so much data that the regulations not only threaten to make the cost of pollution control prohibitive but also may endanger the confidentiality of valuable corporate trade secrets.

An example of the potential negative effect of this patchwork of international laws can be seen in the chemical industry, where it is suggested that new chemical capacity will be directed toward countries that have the least restrictive laws. Chemical companies also may be forced to integrate forward and backward, controlling the process of manufacture from the source of raw materials to the end product, in an effort to obtain maximum protection from potential liability arising from breach of environmental regulations.

Obstacles to achieving a global approach are money, labor, and priorities. In the United States, different areas of the country have differing pollution priorities. For example, the Environmental Protection Agency (EPA) estimates that 60 percent of the hazardous waste in the United States is concentrated in ten industrial states. Clearly, hazardous-waste disposal would have top priority in these areas. In some areas the main problem may be water pollution; in others, it may be air.

Worldwide, environmental pollution is a concern mainly in urban areas, with each area being different because of factors such as climate, geography, industrial development, utilization of fuels for transportation and energy, and refuse-disposal procedures. Overcoming the pollution ailments of urban environments requires recognition of the interrelationship among problems of the urban community and cooperation from every segment of society: industry, government, and individuals.

LEGISLATION AND REGULATORY ACTION

The United States is a good example of the patchwork approach to pollution regulation. The National Environmental Policy Act of 1969 established for the first time an overall federal government policy on the environment and created a Council on Environmental Quality in the

Executive Office of the President. Title I of the law set forth a policy of federal action in cooperation with the state and local governments and other concerned public and private organizations and provided that the federal government should be responsible for improving and coordinating federal regulations concerning the environment. Prior to this act, states were responsible for most pollution-control activity.

The event that promoted this more stringent approach was the Torrey Canyon disaster which occurred off the Scilly Isles in March of 1967. The tanker, carrying 119,000 tons of crude oil, ran aground on the Seven Stones reef off the southwest coast of England. In the days that followed, the entire cargo drained into the sea. Various amounts of oil were dispersed, sunk, bombed, burned, or collected from the sea. Even so, a tide of crude that was finally estimated by British officials to be between 13,000 and 20,000 tons invaded more than 100 miles of the coast of Cornwall. Even larger tonnage washed ashore along 60 miles of the French coast of Brittany. The British government spent more than $5 million to clean up the spill.

The Torrey Canyon accident prompted the United States Congress to enact the Water Quality Improvement Act of 1970, which prohibited the discharge of oil into or upon the navigable waters of the United States, the adjoining shoreline, or the contiguous zone which extends 9 miles beyond the 3-mile limit. Water pollution was only one area of government action. The Clean Air Act also passed in Congress, as did several other pieces of legislation affecting solid-waste disposal. The resulting regulations for control of water and air pollution created a tremendous amount of paperwork for corporations. Not only were corporations faced with common-law liability in the event of a claim, but also they now had to be prepared to respond to statutory liability claims as well.

INSURANCE SOLUTION

Until 1970, comprehensive general liability insurance policies did not exclude coverage for pollution, but a series of large losses triggered an insurance industry study that proposed changes in such policies to exclude pollution coverage. The pollution-exclusion endorsement progressed through several drafts until most insurance carriers adopted the provision. For a typical manufacturing firm, the wording for this standard exclusion read:

> It is agreed that the insurance does not apply to *bodily injury* or *property*
> *damage* arising out of the discharge, dispersal, release or escape of
> smoke, vapors, soot, fumes, acids, alkalis, toxic chemicals, liquids or

gases, waste materials or other irritants, contaminants or pollutants into or upon land, the atmosphere or any watercourse or body of water; but this exclusion does not apply if such discharge, dispersal, release or escape is sudden and accidental.

Over the years, the wording became known in the industry as the "sudden and accidental" provision.

A different exclusion was adopted for oil and gas operations, because the insurance industry decided it could not underwrite such exposures profitably. The exclusion placed on these policies read:

It is agreed that, if with respect to operations described in this endorsement there is a discharge, dispersal, release or escape of oil or other petroleum substance or derivative (including any oil refuse or oil mixed with wastes) into or upon any watercourse or body of water, the insurance does not apply to bodily injury or property damage arising out of such discharge, dispersal, release or escape whether or not sudden and accidental.

This was, and still is, referred to as the *absolute exclusion* for oil on water.

Both these exclusions became the basis for the pollution coverage that is available today. There may be a variation in the wording negotiated for a specific corporation. However, this language continues to be part of current insurance contracts.

The attitude of underwriters in the early 1970s toward pollution hazards can best be described by comments from two insurance companies, the first as follows:

Recognizing that industry and individuals must make amendments to existing facilities to correct this serious problem, we are introducing an Environmental Pollution Exclusion Endorsement on all liability coverages effective May 1, 1970. The purpose of this endorsement is so we do not mislead our insureds into a belief that the pollution hazard is covered under the present policy forms.

The second comment:

The current emphasis on pollution creates a new source of liability claims and presents new exposures for business. In order to respond to this changing situation, we must re-underwrite exposures, modify coverage and adjust rates to current conditions. As a matter of policy, we do not intend to provide coverage for the cost of damages from pollution which was expected or intended or which results from a violation of governmental regulations.

PUBLIC CONCERN

With air and water disposal of wastes clearly regulated and not covered completely by insurance, the disposal of industrial waste on land became a common alternative. Waste was stored in 55-gallon metal drums, which became time bombs. Although the EPA had files of hundreds of documented cases of damage to life and the environment resulting from improper management of hazardous wastes, two incidents in the United States called worldwide attention to the perils of improper waste disposal:

- Love Canal, located near Niagara Falls, New York, was used by the Hooker Chemical Company for the disposal of 21,000 tons of chemical wastes between 1942 and 1953. As years passed, the site was partially excavated and the drums holding the waste corroded. Their contents percolated through the local soil into the yards and basements of private homes. In 1978 and 1979, the situation forced the evacuation of over 200 families.
- The Valley of the Drums, located about 25 miles south of Louisville, Kentucky, contained about 17,000 drums littering a 7-acre site. Some 6000 canisters were full, many of them oozing their toxic contents. In addition, an undetermined quantity of hazardous waste was buried in other drums and subsurface pits.

These incidents heightened concern about abandoned waste sites as well as about methods of disposing of hazardous waste. The EPA estimated that 90 percent of the most hazardous waste generated in the United States was disposed of by unsound methods, such as unlined surface impoundments, land disposal, and uncontrolled incineration. The publicity about Love Canal in 1978 came at a time when the EPA was bogged down in preparing and enforcing the regulations for the Resource Conservation and Recovery Act (RCRA) of 1976. The law had been passed 2 years earlier, but the complexity of the subject, as well as the emotion attached to the entire issue, stirred extensive debate among all sectors of society.

THE RESOURCE CONSERVATION AND RECOVERY ACT

The RCRA represented a major change in the federal role relating to solid-waste management. Rather than provide federal funds as incentives for state and local waste plans, RCRA established a direct federal role in hazardous-waste management.

Subtitle C of RCRA established a complex scheme for identifying hazardous waste and imposed mandatory operating standards for generators and transporters of such waste and for disposal sites. A permit system for disposal was also established. In addition, the act set up a requirement under which waste must be tagged and closely followed from initial generation to disposal, a "cradle-to-grave" regulatory system. Concluding that nonfederal efforts should continue to be the backbone of controlling hazardous waste, Congress provided that approved state management programs would be the preferred method of administration and enforcement.

With corporations being inundated with environmental legislation from all levels of government, the staffing of environmental departments attracted engineers, planners, and legal professionals into highly visible positions. These departments not only focused on the impact of the environmental legislation on each corporation's business but also researched and studied preventive measures. The results pointed to tremendous capital expenditures, which many corporations authorized, and to the need for implementing improved methods of disposing of hazardous waste. The risks were too great for a corporation which was lax in its approach to controlling pollution to continue business as usual. Fear of the potential liabilities from a disaster became a strong motivator for corporate corrective action.

The events leading to Love Canal and the costs of cleanup of the site and compensation for the victims affected the regulatory process under way on RCRA. Who was to pay the bill for Love Canal? Neither the federal nor the state government was prepared to step forward and compensate those who had to relocate. Simultaneously with this reported disaster, EPA first proposed in December 1978 a financial-responsibility section as part of the regulations for RCRA. It was strongly felt within government circles that other environmental disasters must be prevented. Should that be impossible, certainly someone should be identified to pay the bill.

Most of the environmental activity in corporations had been concentrated within the environmental engineering, environmental affairs, or legal departments during the 1970s. With the introduction of the financial-responsibility section into the RCRA regulations, a new member of the environmental team gained visibility—the corporate-risk manager. This person is charged with having the mechanism in place to pay the bills should the corporation have to demonstrate its financial responsibility when a pollution incident results in liabilities.

CORPORATE-RISK MANAGERS EMERGE

The corporate-risk manager has won new recognition during the past decade. The transition from the insurance clerk to the insurance buyer to the risk manager has evolved with the changing risks and structures of corporations. Trading dollars with insurance companies has ceased to be a feasible alternative to corporations which need to effectively handle their working capital, particularly cash. Increased deductibles and self-insurance have brought about new corporate philosophies on risk and methods of planning for corporate liability. Instead of transferring these liabilities completely to the insurance industry, corporations have tended to self-insure or to reimburse an insurance company for amounts covering the area characterized by frequency of losses which are predictable and to transfer the catastrophic losses to the insurance industry in the form of premium payments.

Two terms often used in the insurance industry in discussing risks of loss to a corporation are "frequency of loss" and "severity of loss." For example, losses covered under a typical general liability contract are those from bodily injury and property damage claims. Many individual losses may be relatively small in dollar amount, but a large number of small losses generates a significant total dollar expenditure. If a corporation has 80 percent of its losses within the range of $0 to $250,000, this predictable portion of total losses represents an expected frequency of loss within a specified time frame, usually a year. The frequency of loss can be analyzed from historical data on individual claims over a period of years, so that the risk manager can effectively forecast a major portion of the total corporate budget.

On the other hand, severity of loss refers to those losses which happen infrequently and individually represent large dollar amounts. The lack of a broad statistical base often does not permit an individual corporation to predict the amount of dollars to budget. A severe loss or catastrophic loss is the risk that a corporation wants an insurance company to accept and to pay from the insurance industry's broader pool of funds.

Along with the responsibility to balance risk-financing plans available from insurance companies to cover the loss-frequency portion of the risk with self-insurance, the risk manager gained in status within the corporate ranks. The new breed of risk manager has much less job security than the person he or she replaced, the old-time insurance clerk who knew nothing of finance. With this increased responsibility for the expenditures of corporate funds for higher self-insurance amounts, or larger retained-loss programs, the risk manager is now often directly responsible for or closely involved in controlling these losses. The loss-control program, with emphasis on prevention, minimizing loss, and safety, is an important tool, enhancing the effectiveness of the risk manager in managing the budget required to pay for the protection of corporate assets.

Corporate-risk managers of necessity must work effectively with all operating divisions and many staff functions within the organization. Effective communication skills become a second essential tool for the risk manager in implementing a successful loss-control program, especially for operations with managers of equal or greater authority.

The third tool, key coordinating skills, is necessary to bring satisfactory compromise to situations of conflict among different departments which may be engaged in projects that subject the corporation to increased exposure to potential liabilities. For example, the haste to introduce a new product into the market without proper testing or research and development may result in product-liability claims which could have been prevented by better planning; losses due to improper processes or materials handling can often be prevented through implementation of recommended changes by internal or outside audit teams composed of those who bring a risk perspective to the alternatives. Management decisions must reflect a careful weighing of the trade-offs of investment to prevent losses against liabilities that might occur without the expenditures.

The Risk Manager's Role

The coordinating role of the risk manager in a corporation's control of its environmental liabilities is complex. The cooperation of individual departments is critical, as the risk manager must bring many disciplines together to address the sources of potential loss. In regard to pollution of the environment and its consequential damages, the risk manager's area of responsibility includes a specific focus on the following aspects of effective risk management:

- Protection of health
- Protection of environment
- Protection of assets
- Financial planning
- Potential legal liabilities
- Management information systems and data analysis

Risk managers must work closely with a department of environmental engineering or environmental affairs as part of their functional responsibilities to protect the environment, the corporate assets, and the health of human and other living organisms. To institute the proper controls and analysis of risk, information systems are needed to monitor accidents and losses. This makes possible better management planning, with the ability to focus on areas which require financial commitment to minimize or prevent the downstream effect of legal liabilities. The legal liabilities a corporation may incur often go beyond the direct financial costs which can be identified and quantified. The image of a corporation may suffer from the treatment of a pollution incident by the media. Losses suffered by enraged citizens are sometimes overdramatized to make a particular point. The emotional impact of issues pertaining to the environment is difficult to counter on a rational basis. The result can be an opportunity cost in employee time, which now must be directed to resolve an environmental problem that possibly could have been avoided. The interdependency of the risk-management process requires team management not only in times of crisis but also even in the planning stages of controlling potential pollutants.

Hazardous waste has become one of the most serious environmental issues corporations face today. Pollution is not a new risk to the risk manager, but the emphasis on hazardous waste requires new knowledge and attention to specific compliance requirements and enforcement. The EPA is geared toward regulating procedures and processes that are part of the hazardous-waste cycle, i.e. generating the waste, transporting the waste, and disposing of the waste. Thus the EPA's regulatory tentacles reach into virtually every aspect of a manufacturing operation in which hazardous waste may be involved—and that covers a broad spectrum of industry, as well as institutions affected by RCRA. In order to meet corporate objectives, as well as compliance requirements of RCRA, a risk manager may initiate and participate in the development of a hazardous-waste-management control plan.

HAZARDOUS-WASTE-MANAGEMENT CONTROL PLAN

An effective hazardous-waste-management control plan must be integrated into all management functions. It is necessary in a successful business process to set policy, establish procedure, assign responsibility, institute an accountability system, and measure performance. Exceptionally high levels of hazard control are achieved when it is perceived as an important and integral part of planning, organization, direction, and control decisions. Unfortunately, there is usually a difference between issued policy and procedure and what actually occurs. Seldom is an activity as effectively managed as those responsible for it say it is.

Evaluations of hazard-control programs serve as appraisals of management performance in relation to issued policy and procedure. They are qualitative analyses of existing management systems, made to determine whether performance is effective and acceptable. Above all, the goal of an evaluation is to assist in improving the effectiveness of hazard-control management systems. Although a survey of operations is significant in the evaluation process, unsafe physical conditions and practices are important principally as they may identify management systems which can be made more effective. Through an analysis of the many evaluations made by the staff at M & M Protection Consultants, one conclusion stood out: "Management obtains that accident experience which it establishes as acceptable—acceptable being the organization's perception of what management does."

Management is what management does. If what management does gives negative impressions, it is unlikely that a hazard-control program will be successful. Hazard-control programs fail when personnel perceive what management does as an indication that management really is not interested in the control of hazards or is not sufficiently interested to give active direction to hazard-control activities through involvement and participation.

If accident experience is considered unsatisfactory by management, difficult questions must be asked. Has that experience resulted from the attitude management has displayed toward hazard control—displayed by what it does? Is the accident experience that which has been programmed—by inference? In every corporation that has achieved an outstanding record, the organization knows that upper-level management is involved, is held accountable, and holds subordinates accountable for accident experience.

Management's involvement can be demonstrated and made visible in many ways—by regularly communicating on environmental-safety subjects, by chairing environmental committees, by leading discussions of accident experience or other environmental matters at staff meetings, but more importantly, by emphasizing accountability. The corporate-risk manager can assist senior corporate management in coordinating and organizing these activities with the appropriate corporate personnel. From a risk-management standpoint, a successful hazardous-waste-management control plan should be in force. The goal of risk management, to effectively manage risk at the least possible cost, cannot be achieved without reducing, through a total management commitment, the number of incidents which lead to losses.

The following evaluation guide is offered by the Marsh & McLennan staff to those managers who are charged with responsibility for developing such a hazardous-waste-control plan:

1. Top management should become aware of the company's hazardous-waste exposures and of noncompliance penalties. Senior executives should become as informed as possible.

2. Technically sound and knowledgeable individuals should be assigned at both corporate and plant levels to establish procedures to evaluate the potential for personal injury and/or damage, short-term and long-term, due to hazardous-waste generation, transportation, and disposal.

3. Steps should be taken to ensure that federal, state, and local codes and regulations which apply to hazardous waste are thoroughly understood and are used as minimum requirements in hazardous-waste management. Such regulations involve the Department of Transportation (DOT), Toxic Substances Control Act (TSCA), Occupational Safety and Health Act (OSHA), and the RCRA.

4. Plant and/or laboratory operations which generate waste as well as all material-handling and waste-flow systems should be reviewed by qualified personnel.

5. Through the purchasing department, material safety data sheets should be obtained from suppliers.

6. Chemical materials should be categorized from the standpoint of DOT classification for transportation, safety during storage, and disposal-site requirements for processes and permit restrictions.

7. State agency relations should be developed to solve problems and establish good rapport.

8. Procedures should be established whereby all changes in production methods and techniques and waste storage are reviewed from a hazardous-waste-management standpoint prior to implementation.

9. Audits of control procedures and record keeping should be arranged and their implementation monitored in relation to developing hazardous-waste-liability trends.

10. Audits should be made of all operating and maintenance manuals by legal and engineering personnel for adequacy and accuracy in relation to hazardous-waste management.

11. The responsible individual(s) should visit all generation and storage areas to carefully evaluate existing procedures, containers, material identification, labeling, storage methods, and material flow.

12. When dealing with a contract disposal firm, written contracts should be asked for, carefully reviewing all technical and legal aspects. A personal visit to the contractor's facility should be made to evaluate (*a*) current permits and facility history; (*b*) the facility's ability to comply with RCRA; (*c*) adequacy of technical knowledge, laboratory facilities, and professional assistance; (*d*) adherence to record-keeping requirements; (*e*) acceptable "housekeeping" practices; and (*f*) location of facility with respect to nearby communities.

13. A certificate of disposal should be obtained from the disposal treatment facility operator.

14. When existing programs are found in need of improvement, all concerned parties must be brought together and involved. These should include plant manager, traffic manager, purchasing agent, risk manager, safety engineer, and environmental engineer or their equivalents. If necessary, legal staff and the disposal contractor should be included to discuss and plan an improved hazardous-waste-management control plan.

15. Conduct training programs for *every* individual involved in waste management and provide guidelines to change attitudes and improve operations.

16. Provide for the use of clear, complete, conspicuous, and durable precautionary instructions and warning labels, including identification of each component in a waste container by chemical name and percentage (not chemical formula, abbreviations, or trade name). Labeling should identify each waste, designating contents, hazard, generator's name, department, and date plus DOT labels and EPA warning labels.

17. Develop good policy and procedures for the selection of a waste hauler that has the ability to service responsibly the company's needs.

18. Develop good policy and procedures for the selection of a waste-disposal firm. State permits for operating of a landfill, incinerator, or acid-neutralization facility, biotreatment facility, and recovery operation should be checked. In some cases, one permit for each operation may be required. Be sure the disposal contractor is financially sound.

19. Undertake a review of all hazardous materials to determine the

availability and practicality of less hazardous substitutes, the feasibility of reprocessing, or the sale of waste through a waste exchange.

Audits of the management of hazard-control plans often indicate a serious lack of organized effort and communication concerning policy and procedures important to effective implementation. Hazard-control programs are successful only when management has clearly signified their importance, by management involvement and by establishing accountability. The additional elements of the evaluation guide which follow are required for management to give direction and support and to provide the necessary organization and administration.

20. Issue, under the signature of the chief executive, a company policy pertaining to hazardous-waste management.

21. Designate an executive, representing top-level management, as having the authority for hazardous-waste-management activities.

22. Establish sound objectives and goals and communicate them to all affected.

23. Establish clear lines of communication so that the designated executive can successfully work with other functions and divisions within the organization.

24. Establish a hazardous-waste-management control group consisting of management representatives. In the selection of the group, consideration should be given to including personnel representing the research and design, engineering, production, purchasing, marketing, legal, insurance, and safety functions.

25. Have audits conducted at appropriate intervals by independent, qualified personnel to evaluate the effectiveness of the program and to provide the basis for improvements.

ENVIRONMENTAL AUDITING

In today's business world, financial and legal audits are well-established and accepted business practices. Another type of audit is rapidly emerging as an important tool for corporations—the environmental audit. A comprehensive environmental audit conducted by a professional consulting team can be invaluable in assessing a corporation's environmental status. It helps ensure the protection of worker and community health, protection from unwarranted lawsuits, and the proper management of environmental programs.

Independent Audits

Considering the large number of environmental problems uncovered in the last 20 years, it is no wonder that corporate officers and directors are becoming increasingly concerned about their firm's potential impact on the environment. It is often difficult for even a competent staff of in-house environmental engineers to be objective and see the overall picture. Many have requested a third-party assessment of the firm's pollution potential so that they might more readily develop or ensure a sound environmental program. In addition, an independent environmental audit is often required for certain types of environmental impairment liability insurance (against the effects of gradual pollution) or for SEC disclosures.

Independent auditors, such as Clayton Environmental Consultants, Inc., a Marsh & McLennan subsidiary, perform environmental audits when corporations require a total assessment of environmental pollution (air emissions, water pollution, and hazardous waste) and occupational health. A multidisciplinary consulting team conducting an audit can yield many advantages, including:

- Independent verification of a corporation's compliance with federal, state, and local statutory and regulatory requirements.
- Determination of the extent to which the facility's operations or products may bring complaints and/or lawsuits from nearby residents or users.
- Compliance with SEC rules, which require full disclosure of significant environmental liabilities by publicly held companies.
- Protection of the company against third-party liability through an audit of its formulators, suppliers, and distributors.
- Assessment of merger or acquisition candidates for potential environmental liabilities (including products, pollution damage, and workers' exposure to hazardous substances). Purchase of a company with severe environmental problems can have serious financial implications for the buyer, particularly in certain types of industries.
- Determination of eligibility for insurance coverage for operations that may be termed hazardous. A specific type of environmental audit, the environmental impairment liability survey, is nearly always necessary to assess the risk and thus determine adequate insurance coverage.
- Determination of the extent to which employee or community health is endangered, irrespective of compliance status.

- Determination of the extent to which employees are adhering to corporate policies regarding environmental protection, employee safety and health, handling of hazardous materials, disposal of hazardous waste, etc.

Scope of the Audit

The first step in conducting an environmental audit is a complete walk-through survey of the plants or operations in question. For a multiloca-tion corporation, the independent auditor may choose facilities at random from those considered to have a significant potential impact on the environment. All the processes at the facility are reviewed; interviews are conducted with the plant management, supervisors, and personnel and, if possible, with regulatory agencies. All operations are assessed for their potential (or actual) contribution to air pollution, water pollution, hazardous waste, occupational safety and health, and product safety.

For example, a typical environmental audit program conducted by an independent auditor involves, but is not limited to, consideration of the following:

- National air quality standards.
- New-source performance standards.
- National emission standards for hazardous air pollutants.
- Considerations for prevention of significant deterioration of air quality from plant expansion, relocation, or new facility construction.
- Application of bubble concept to plant facilities.
- National Pollutant Discharge Elimination System programs.
- Pretreatment programs for discharges into publicly owned treatment works.
- Non-point-source (water) pollution control.
- Identification of hazardous wastes.
- Inventory and premanufacture notifications under TSCA.
- TSCA reporting and record keeping.
- Compliance with OSHA standards.
- Programs to deal with exposure to toxic substances that do not have permissible exposure limits or threshold limit values.
- Industrial safety programs, including use of protective devices.
- Employee hearing-conservation programs and medical surveil-lance programs.

In order to assess properly the above items, the consulting team requires cooperation by management and plant employees. All applicable company records and operations must be made accessible, permission must be given to contact the regulatory agencies with which the corporation interacts, and questionnaires need to be filled out. The consulting team will also ask for a written notice from management that it has truthfully informed the consultants of all facts which might have a bearing on the audit.

Of course, inherent in any such investigation is the confidentiality of the investigation and even the existence or nature of the investigation.

Environmental audits which accompany a corporation's hazardous-waste-control plan have been made on a periodic basis by most corporations. In order to comply with the RCRA and its regulations, the burden was placed on corporations as well as individuals to identify themselves as generators, transporters, owners, or operators of hazardous-waste facilities. An identification number is now required for any corporation that generates, handles, or disposes of hazardous waste. In the future this waste will be tracked through the use of a manifest system. Environmental audits will become a routine check to determine whether the system is working. These regulations are enforced by the EPA, and offenders are subject to both civil and criminal penalties.

FINANCIAL-RESPONSIBILITY REQUIREMENTS UNDER RCRA

RCRA and its regulations did not change any liabilities which a corporation had under common law for damages to a third party. However, it did establish financial-responsibility requirements for those who treat, store, or dispose of hazardous waste. Compliance may be achieved by obtaining insurance or qualifying for self-insurance.

The EPA issued final financial-responsibility requirements in April 1982 for owners and operators of hazardous-waste facilities which dispose of, treat, or store hazardous waste. The requirements as to insurance, self-insurance, and data submission, which affect all 50 states and United States territories, are part of the regulations accompanying the RCRA and are briefly summarized in this section.

Insurance

An owner or operator of one or more facilities must demonstrate liability coverage of at least $1 million per occurrence, up to a limit of $2 million annually, for sudden and accidental occurrences. An owner or

1. [Name of Insurer] (the "Insurer"), of [address of Insurer], hereby certifies that it has issued liability insurance covering bodily injury and property damage to [name of insured] (the "insured"), of [address of insured], in connection with the insured's obligation to demonstrate financial responsibility under 40 CFR 264.147 or 265.147. The coverage applies at [list EPA Identification Number, name, and address for each facility] for [insert "sudden accidental occurrences," "nonsudden accidental occurrences," or "sudden and nonsudden accidental occurrences"; if coverage is for multiple facilities and the coverage is different for different facilities, indicate which facilities are insured for sudden accidental occurrences, which are insured for nonsudden accidental occurrences, and which are insured for both]. The limits of liability are [insert the dollar amount of the "each occurrence" and "annual aggregate" limits of the Insurer's liability], exclusive of legal defense costs. The coverage is provided under policy number _____, issued on [date]. The effective date of said policy is [date].

2. The Insurer further certifies the following with respect to the insurance described in Paragraph 1:

(a) Bankruptcy or insolvency of the insured shall not relieve the Insurer of its obligations under the policy.

(b) The Insurer is liable for the payment of amounts within any deductible applicable to the policy, with a right of reimbursement by the insured for any such payment made by the Insurer. This provision does not apply with respect to that amount of any deductible for which coverage is demonstrated as specified in 40 CFR 264.147(f) or 265.147(f).

(c) Whenever requested by a Regional Administrator of the U.S. Environmental Protection Agency (EPA), the Insurer agrees to furnish to the Regional Administrator a signed duplicate original of the policy and all endorsements.

(d) Cancellation of the insurance, whether by the Insurer or the insured, will be effective only upon written notice and only after the expiration of sixty (60) days after a copy of such written notice is received by the Regional Administrator(s) of the EPA Region(s) in which the facility(ies) is (are) located.

(e) Any other termination of the insurance will be effective only upon written notice and only after the expiration of thirty (30) days after a copy of such written notice is received by the Regional Administrator(s) of the EPA Region(s) in which the facility(ies) is (are) located.

I hereby certify that the wording of this instrument is identical to the wording specified in 40 CFR 264.151(j) as such regulation was constituted on the date first above written, and that the Insurer is licensed to transact the business of insurance, or eligible to provide insurance as an excess or surplus lines insurer, in one or more States.

FIG. 1 Hazardous-waste-facility certificate of liability insurance

1. This endorsement certifies that the policy to which the endorsement is attached provides liability insurance covering bodily injury and property damage in connection with the insured's obligation to demonstrate financial responsibility under 40 CFR 264.147 or 265.147. The coverage applies at [list EPA Identification Number, name, and address for each facility] for [insert "sudden accidental occurrences," "nonsudden accidental occurrences," or "sudden and nonsudden accidental occurrences"; if coverage is for multiple facilities and the coverage is different for different facilities, indicate which facilities are insured for sudden accidental occurrences, which are insured for nonsudden accidental occurrences, and which are insured for both]. The limits of liability are [insert the dollar amount of the "each occurrence" and "annual aggregate" limits of the Insurer's liability], exclusive of legal defense costs.

2. The insurance afforded with respect to such occurrences is subject to all of the terms and conditions of the policy; provided, however, that any provisions of the policy inconsistent with subsections (a) through (e) of this Paragraph 2 are hereby amended to conform with subsections (a) through (e):

(**a**) Bankruptcy or insolvency of the insured shall not relieve the Insurer of its obligations under the policy to which this endorsement is attached.

(**b**) The Insurer is liable for the payment of amounts within any deductible applicable to the policy, with a right of reimbursement by the insured for any such payment made by the Insurer. This provision does not apply with respect to that amount of any deductible for which coverage is demonstrated as specified in 40 CFR 264.147(f) or 265.147(f).

(**c**) Whenever requested by a Regional Administrator of the U.S. Environmental Protection Agency (EPA), the Insurer agrees to furnish to the Regional Administrator a signed duplicate original of the policy and all endorsements.

(**d**) Cancellation of this endorsement, whether by the Insurer or the insured, will be effective only upon written notice and only after the expiration of sixty (60) days after a copy of such written notice is received by the Regional Administrator(s) of the EPA region(s) in which the facility(ies) is (are) located.

(**e**) Any other termination of this endorsement will be effective only upon written notice and only after the expiration of thirty (30) days after a copy of such written notice is received by the Regional Administrator(s) of the EPA Region(s) in which the facility(ies) is (are) located.

Attached to and forming part of policy No. _____ issued by [name of Insurer], herein called the Insurer, of [address of Insurer], to [name of insured], of [address], this _____ day of _____, 19_____. The effective date of said policy is the _____ day of _____, 19_____.

I hereby certify that the wording of this endorsement is identical to the wording specified in 40 CFR 264.151(i) as such regulation was constituted on the date first above written, and that the Insurer is licensed to transact the business of insurance, or eligible to provide insurance as an excess or surplus lines insurer, in one or more States.

FIG. 2 Hazardous-waste-facility liability endorsement.

operator of one or more surface impoundments, landfills, or land treatment facilities must also demonstrate liability coverage of at least $3 million per occurrence, up to a limit of $6 million annually, for nonsudden accidental occurrences.

Requirements applicable to nonsudden accidental occurrences will be phased in over 3 years. Owners or operators doing $10 million or more in business annually were to submit evidence of such coverage by January 1983. Coverage was required by January 1984 for owners and operators with sales of $5 to $10 million a year and by January 1985 for others.

States that administer their own hazardous-waste-management programs must include financial-responsibility requirements at least equivalent to the federal requirements. Eventually, the EPA will monitor each state's hazardous-waste-management program, which may include the minimum financial-responsibility guidelines set forth by the EPA or establish a higher standard.

Self-Insurance

The financial-responsibility requirements may also be met by satisfying the EPA's financial tests detailed in the *Federal Register* dated April 16, 1982. The criteria for these tests follow.

Under alternative 1, the owner must have all the following:

1. Net working capital and tangible net worth each at least six times the amount of liability coverage to be demonstrated by the test
2. Tangible net worth of at least $10 million
3. Assets in the United States amounting to either at least 90 percent of the owner's total assets or at least six times the amount of liability coverage to be demonstrated by this test

Under alternative 2, the owner must have all the following:

1. A current rating for the owner's most recent bond issuance of AAA, AA, A, or BBB as issued by Standard and Poor's; or Aaa, Aa, A or Baa as issued by Moody's
2. Tangible net worth of at least $10 million
3. Tangible net worth at least six times the amount of liability coverage to be demonstrated by this test
4. Assets in the United States amounting to either at least 90 percent of the owner's total assets or at least six times the amount of liability coverage to be demonstrated by the test

Data Submission

Data submitted must include the following:

1. A letter to the regional administrator signed by the owner's chief financial officer that includes the required data from the firm's independently audited year-end financial statements and the cost estimates for closure and postclosure care
2. A copy of the independent certified public accountant's report on examination of the owner's financial statements for the latest completed fiscal year
3. A statement from the owner's independent certified public accountant to the owner stating that the accountant has compared the data which the letter from the chief financial officer specifies as having been derived from the independently audited year-end financial statements for the latest fiscal year with the amounts in such financial statements and, in connection with this procedure, no matters came to light which caused the auditor to believe that the specified data should be adjusted

If the auditor's opinion that is included in the statement on examination of the owner's financial statements is an adverse opinion or contains a disclaimer of opinion, the owner will be disallowed from using the financial test to satisfy the financial requirements. EPA's regional administrator may disallow use of the financial test on the basis of other qualifications expressed in the auditor's opinion of the firm's financial statements. If the opinion raises questions as to whether the firm will continue as a "going concern," the regional administrator will disallow use of the financial test. Other qualified opinions will be evaluated on a case-by-case basis. The owner must provide alternative financial assurance within 30 days after disallowance.

After the initial submission of the letter from the chief financial officer and the accountant's reports, a new letter and new reports for each subsequent fiscal year must be submitted to the regional administrator within 90 days after the end of the firm's fiscal year. Alternatively, the owner must deliver to the regional administrator, by the end of this 90-day period, a notice of intent to provide substitute financial assurance as specified in the regulations and, within 120 days after the end of the fiscal year, establish the substitute financial assurance.

Closure and Postclosure

As part of the standards for facilities, EPA requires that funds be available for proper closure of facilities that treat, store, or dispose of hazardous waste and monitoring and maintenance of disposal facilities after they have closed. The facility owner or operator must keep at the facility a written estimate of the cost of closing it, in accordance with the closure plan required by another part of the RCRA regulations. Compliance date for this section was July 6, 1982. Currently, hazardous-waste facilities are operating under an interim provision until a final permit is granted.

During interim and permitted status now, the mechanisms available for certifying financial responsibility include a trust fund, a surety bond guaranteeing payment into a trust fund, a letter of credit written so that drafts will be deposited by the issuing institution directly into a trust fund, an insurance policy, passing of a financial test, or a guarantee from a parent organization (which would be subject to a financial test). When certifying for any *single* facility, the owner may combine all the mechanisms *except* the financial test. When certifying for *multiple* facilities, the owner may combine *all* the mechanisms. *During permitted status only,* an additional but noncombinable mechanism will be added: a surety bond guaranteeing performance of closure and postclosure care.

Among the highlights of the RCRA regulations are the following:

- State and federal governments are exempt; local governments are not.
- Cost estimates are to be figured in *current* dollars. (Cost estimates on interim-status facilities were due as of May 19, 1981.)
- Cost estimates must be refigured each time the closure or postclosure plan is altered.
- Cost estimates must be refigured, in addition, each year on the anniversary of the first estimate, solely to account for inflation.
- The latest revised estimates prepared pursuant to the two preceding items must both be kept at the facility during its operational life.
- It is the owner's responsibility to *increase* the level of financial-responsibility filing to equal that of the current cost estimates within 60 days of any change in those estimates, except as regards the financial test. (The other mechanisms as designed will *not* automatically increase to make up any increase.) Should a cost estimate *decrease,* however, reduction in the level certified can be made only with the regional administrator's permission.
- The owner must file with the regional administrator by the appropriate effective date in order to be in compliance with these regulations. It is necessary to deliver, as applicable, the bonds themselves, the letters of credit themselves, originally signed duplicates of

the trust agreements, certificates of insurance, and the various financial test documents.

- Letters of credit must be accompanied by another letter from the owner which refers to the letter of credit by number, issuing institution, and date and provides in addition the EPA identification number, name, address, and amount of funds assured for each facility to be covered by the letter of credit.

- Substitution of one mechanism for another in midstream is acceptable in all cases; but the existing mechanism may not be canceled under any circumstances without the permission of the regional administrator.

- For permitted-status facilities, the pay-in period for the trust fund option will be the term of the initial permit or the remaining operating life of the facility as that operating life is estimated in the closure plan, whichever is shorter. This applies to both closure and postclosure costs.

- For interim-status facilities, the pay-in period for the trust fund option will be the 20 years beginning with July 6, 1982 or the remaining operating life of the facility as that operating life is estimated in the closure plan, whichever is shorter. This, again, applies to both closure and postclosure costs.

- Even though EPA may be administering its own financial requirements in a state, that state may also have issued requirements pertaining to closure and postclosure costs of facilities. In such a case, an owner may submit a request to the regional administrator asking for permission to substitute a state-required mechanism for the federal mechanisms applying to closure and postclosure. The regional administrator *may* allow such an exemption.

Trends in Financial-Responsibility Requirements

The pollution-insurance requirements listed under Insurance, above, have been controversial from the start, and their future is still uncertain. They were promulgated in January 1981, to become effective July 13, 1981. The effective date of the financial requirements was deferred twice; and the EPA at one point announced its intention to withdraw these requirements in their entirety.

Yet whatever the outcome of these or any other agency-mandated coverage requirements, corporations will still be held accountable for pollution resulting from their operations. And, since environmental-protection cases have become *causes célèbres*, the frequency of litigation and the size of settlements will continue to increase.

Risk managers, therefore, should expect pollution risk to remain in the media spotlight, thus generating a high level of awareness and concern by the general public. If a corporation has pollution liability, it should determine whether coverage is mandated by federal or state governments in sites where the firm operates and generates, transports, or treats hazardous wastes. Irrespective of a corporation's compliance with the financial-responsibility requirements and with the stated limits of liability, the common-law liability for which a corporation may be sued is unlimited.

BROADENING OF POLLUTION INSURANCE

During the 1980 to 1982 period, the insurance industry reassessed its position regarding the underwriting of pollution insurance. The EPA requirement for financial responsibility paved the way for an insurance product during a time when the insurance industry needed a new source of premiums. The casualty-insurance market itself has been very "soft" since 1978, when the cycle shifted to a period characterized by relatively lower premiums, a so-called buyer's market, and plenty of reinsurance available to assist insurance companies in further spreading the risk. Thus the timing was right from an insurance market perspective to broaden coverage for pollution to include gradual pollution or pollution other than sudden and accidental. Pollution liability is only one exposure in the casualty-insurance area, which, broadly defined, consists of insurance coverage for claims and third-party liability lawsuits against a corporation.

The markets for pollution coverage have been expanding dramatically. In 1980 only three underwriters offered gradual-pollution coverage; now at least a dozen do so. The gradual-pollution coverage originally available allowed the comprehensive general liability (CGL) policy to continue to respond to pollution incidents that were sudden and accidental in nature. After initial reluctance, more insurers are now willing to write pollution liability insurance as a total pollution cover. They are writing the sudden and the gradual coverages within the CGL form or writing one policy form, if insured separately, in a specialty insurance market.

The Gradual-Pollution Policy

When comparing the various policies, certain cautions need to be borne in mind.

Policy language should be carefully reviewed, as forms can differ markedly. For example, some forms may define pollution as "an emission, a discharge, release, or escape of any solid, liquid, gaseous, or thermal contaminants" which results in environmental damage. Other forms use language such as "the generation of smell, noises, vibrations, lights, electricity, radiation, change in temperature, or any other sensory phenomena" arising out of a firm's operations.

Defense costs may or may not be found in the policy language. The obligation to defend is not always clear in policies that use the language of indemnification as opposed to paying on behalf of their insured. All the earlier pollution forms written to meet the EPA's proposed regulations included the defense cost within the limit of liability. Now, however, a number of policies grant supplemental defense costs normally found in the CGL policy. Since there is little, if any, gradual-pollution liability loss history, it would be prudent to maintain appropriate limits to respond to defense costs.

Cleanup cost recovery is another area where policy forms differ. The primary purpose of pollution liability coverage is to respond to third-party injuries. All policies now provide cleanup coverage. However, only the newly written or revised policy forms provide reimbursement for cleanup of the insured's site, since many insurers feel that this is actually "first party" rather than liability coverage. Any such reimbursement is generally at the discretion of the insurer.

Certain forms contain a retroactive date, meaning that the coverage on a claims-made form will go back to, but not beyond, a particular date. This is, in effect, a narrowing of coverage, unlike those forms that contain no retroactive date for the commencement of coverage for pollution incidents discovered and first reported during the term of the particular claims-made policy.

The claims-made form should contain a discovery period to report losses in the event that an insured changes underwriters. Wording of policies should be examined for the length of time of such a period and the conditions under which the extension is granted.

Exclusions must be examined carefully. Pollution forms often eliminate coverage for situations covered under other contracts of insurance, e.g., employee-related injuries or nuclear incidents. Two exclusions that merit particular attention are punitive damages and genetic damages. Many forms either list punitive damages as an exclusion or exclude it through the definition of the word "loss." Other forms will reimburse only for compensatory damages, thus eliminating punitive damages from consideration. The genetic-damage exclusion is found in a few forms, but underwriters will frequently consider a "buy-back" of the exclusion for an additional charge.

The current soft insurance market has enabled brokers to negotiate coverage tailored to a corporation's exposures.

Role of the Insurance Broker

An insurance broker offers insurance services to a corporation, partnership, or individual client and represents the client in the planning and purchase of insurance. The process begins with the broker's understanding of the needs of the client for protection against risks. Analysis, inspections, and corporate management philosophy are important ingredients of a corporate risk-management program. The program ultimately provides the structure for the financing of the risk that will be retained by the corporation and the risk that will be transferred to the insurance industry by purchase of an insurance policy.

Marsh & McLennan, for instance, through its brokerage network of client executives and account managers, works with corporate risk managers and insurance buyers in the design of the risk-management program and in the planning of the purchase of insurance. The risk manager will require the input of many departments within the corporation to assemble the information necessary for an underwriter's evaluation of the risk. The more complex risks, such as pollution exposures, require detailed applications to be completed by the risk manager. The information gathering begins with the risk manager's identification of the corporation's pollution exposures. Supporting this are details of the raw materials used in the products, the manufacturing process, and the disposal of any waste by-products. The risk manager frequently requests the broker to assist him in the information-gathering phase and in meeting with key environmental personnel within the corporation.

Applying for Insurance

The application for pollution liability, including gradual pollution, includes:

- Identification of all exposures to potential pollution losses
- Description of operations
- Information describing any hazardous waste, type and amount disposed in each location, and method of disposal (duplicate of information provided the EPA in compliance with RCRA)
- Loss history of pollution accidents and pending litigation
- Description of loss control and contingency plans for pollution
- Environmental audits or risk assessments performed internally or by outside consultants

Initially, underwriters have accepted for review environmental audits that have been updated by corporate personnel. Most insurance companies will require that an outside consultant perform an environmental audit or risk assessment at some point, either before or during the underwriter's review. This may consist of audits at repesentative locations, at all locations, or at a single location. The objectives of the audit are to provide the underwriter with a better appreciation of the risk to be accepted, to assist in determining the underwriter's exposure to loss, and to add further input to the judgment as to the price to be charged and the terms of the contract to be offered.

Insurance brokers such as Marsh & McLennan spent considerable time developing interest on the part of the insurance industry in broadening the coverage of pollution liability to include gradual pollution. There is now an insurance market of several carriers with whom brokers can negotiate coverage on behalf of clients. Once the application and environmental audits have been reviewed by the underwriter, the negotiation between the broker and the underwriter on the coverage terms, the price, and the service requirements begins. Presentations may be made to one or more insurance companies, depending on the type of risk and the marketing plan agreed to by the risk manager.

The Underwriting Process

The underwriter's review may take anywhere from 1 to 3 months, depending on the number of applications being evaluated and the amount of additional information that may be required. The negotiations with underwriters may sometimes include the risk manager or other members of the corporation. As mentioned earlier, the receptiveness of an underwriter to a given risk may be influenced by external forces beyond the fundamental risk being reviewed. The overall position of the insurance industry within the market cycle, the availability of reinsurance, the profitability of the insurance industry, and interest rates are all external factors that may affect the underwriter's acceptance of the risk and the premium quoted for the pollution protection.

Once the negotiations are completed, an insurance broker will evaluate the various quotations and prepare a presentation for the risk manager. Typically, the presentation will include a discussion of the proposals, an analysis of the premiums and coverage terms offered, and a recommendation.

In general, the premium being quoted today for pollution coverage reflects the overall depressed rates of insurance throughout the industry. Underwriting losses suffered by many insurance companies since 1980 have been tolerated only because investment income has more than offset the losses to produce a positive net income. With declining interest rates, the insurance industry may be forced to take a tough look at the risks it is now accepting.

The future premiums for pollution liability exposures will be heavily influenced by the losses and awards to claimants in the coming years. There is typically a 5- to 10-year lag from the time a claim is made until it is resolved. This loss history will ultimately be factored into the prices corporations will pay for pollution liability.

The Management Decision

Evaluation of the quotations by the risk manager and the corporate management is based on the premium, the financial stability of the insurance company, the coverage terms and conditions, the expenditures needed to comply with coverage requirements, the amount of risk retained by the corporation, defense-of-claims provisions, environmental audits required, and amount of liability being purchased.

Brokers are often asked how much insurance a given corporation should buy. As a corporation may be sued at common law for an unlimited amount, the conservative risk manager is always safe in obtaining as much insurance as is available in the insurance market. Today the capacity in the insurance market for pollution coverage, including gradual pollution, ranges from $100 million to perhaps as high as $400 million. With the uncertainty of pollution claims and the impact of inflation, many corporate risk managers are capitalizing on the depressed insurance premiums to obtain high amounts of liability coverage.

It is presently not possible to predict the future of the insurance market in providing this coverage. Market stability will be determined by the flow of losses and the financial ability of the insurance industry to respond. The ability of corporations to respond to losses from pollution liability will depend on a well-designed risk-management program, monitored by environmental audits and supplemented by an insurance program for catastrophic loss.

BIBLIOGRAPHY

Ball, Robert Jr.: *Marsh & McLennan Professional Services Casualty Bulletin* (various, 1980–1982).

Manuele, Fred A: How Do You Know Your Hazard Control Program Is Effective? Address delivered before National Safety Congress, 1979.

Case Study:
Atlantic Richfield

William G. Kelly
Environmental Services
Atlantic Richfield Company

A tlantic Richfield Company's environmental review program had its beginnings in the late seventies when, as a result of decentralization, eight separate operating companies were formed. Each company set up its own environmental group, and a policymaking body—the Corporate Occupational and Environmental Protection Council (since renamed Health, Safety and Environmental Protection Council) was created. The council is made up of engineering or operating vice presidents from each of the various companies. As a result of the development of the Atlantic Richfield environmental protection policy, the council felt that it was necessary to establish a review program to ensure policy compliance throughout the company.

Originally patterned after the safety and health review program initiated in 1972, the environmental review program underwent changes in style and substance to encompass the expanding domain of Atlantic Richfield Company activities from oil and gas, minerals, and metal manufacturing to chemicals and solar products.

The review program, which is designed to help managers achieve fullest compliance with corporate policy, focuses on the management systems that a facility uses to protect the environment and takes into consideration engineering and ecological design, operating procedures, maintenance, training, and emergency preparation.

Atlantic Richfield has expressed its total commitment to the environmental standards it sets. William F. Kieschnick, chief executive officer, stated during an interview on environmental concerns that "the need to constantly be aware that our company is meeting the standards that we set for it is a need that must be met." The environmental review program is designed to accomplish this. The standards are set out in the Atlantic Richfield environmental protection policy, which serves as a guide for the operating companies.

ENVIRONMENTAL PROTECTION POLICY

Realizing that the world's natural resources of air, water, and land are vital to human global existence, progress, and continued development, we consider environmental protection to be a paramount concern in our total activities, domestic and international. Therefore it is our policy to:

- Manage our operations with diligence and with an awareness that our goal is to protect the environment by employing the best control mechanisms, procedures, and processes which are proved technically sound and economically feasible
- Entrust each line manager with responsibility for the environmental performance of his or her activity
- Comply with all environmental legislation, regulations, and standards and provide self-monitoring to ensure compliance
- Assist all levels of government in the promulgation of sound, cost-effective environmental laws, codes, rules, and regulations based on scientific facts
- Consider the expense of environmental protection as a legitimate cost of doing business in modern society, assuming that environmental regulations are uniformly applicable throughout an industry
- Encourage and support—with technical ability, time and money— environmental programs and research efforts sponsored by trade associations and other organizations seeking solutions to technological and ecological problems
- Train our employees in environmental matters, actions, and responsibilities relating to their particular assignments
- Secure ecological guidance in our long-range planning, using recognized consultants and employing the services of experts of various disciplines
- Enhance communication and understanding with our stockholders, civic groups, environmental and conservation organizations,

universities, and the general public through publications, speakers, exhibits, demonstrations, and the media
- Maintain a corporate environmental protection group to review, advise, coordinate, and implement environmental protection activities and programs

The policy is established by the Corporate Health, Safety and Environmental Protection Council. The review program is the council's method of ensuring that the policy is carried out at all Atlantic Richfield facilities. At Mr. Kieschnick's direction, the review program was designed to provide management with quantified assurance that we are constantly meeting standards.

The objective of the review program is to assess and improve the total environmental protection performance of Atlantic Richfield. It is the company's policy that line managers are responsible for the environmental performance of their activities and that achievement in protecting the environment is regularly measured. The review program supports this policy by outlining what managers and supervisors are accountable for and by providing a mechanism for measuring achievement. Atlantic Richfield is a systems-oriented company, and facility managers are expected to establish management systems to protect the environment. The environmental review program focuses on those systems at a facility and evaluates their adequacy. Generally, adequacy and effectiveness are demonstrated by compliance—compliance with environmental regulations and compliance with company environmental policy.

ENVIRONMENTAL REVIEW CRITERIA

The review program determines whether a facility has environmental protection systems in place and whether those systems are working effectively to protect the environment. The program is carried out by a small review team which evaluates these systems, using specific review criteria. These criteria define what is expected of managers in ten critical areas and provide the basis for recommendations for improvement. The review criteria are as follows:

1. Policy: Managers and supervisors know and apply Atlantic Richfield environmental protection policy

The criteria developed for evaluating effective management systems are based on the corporate environmental protection policy. Systems developed to implement the criteria must be predicated on knowledge, acceptance, and application of the policy. Operating companies and individual facilities may have complementary policies, but these must embrace the intent and spirit of the corporate policy.

2. Regulations: Facility personnel know and comply with regulations

One of the major policy statements requires compliance with environmental legislation. Compliance is mandatory for maintaining the credibility of the company. Up-to-date copies of environmental laws, regulations, and permits affecting the facility must be readily available. There should be a system to obtain them and disseminate the essential information to responsible management.

3. Operating procedures: Facility has written operating procedures which include emission and effluent limitations; provides for self-monitoring

Because of the technical nature of operations, most facilities utilize operating manuals delineating specific operating procedures. Inherent in many of the procedures are precautions to protect the environment. Whenever possible and appropriate, the procedures should incorporate emission and effluent limitations required by operating permits and other regulations. Rules common to all operations, including waste treatment and disposal, can be incorporated in a general environmental protection rules book. Compliance with applicable laws, regulations, and permits should be demonstrated through a documented self-monitoring system.

4. Training and motivation: Employees are trained to work in an environmentally acceptable manner; management motivates employees to be concerned about the environment

Each facility should have a program to provide environmental training for employees. It should facilitate participation and provide information as well as include specific instruction. New regulations, new employees, and new assignments promote the need for an ongoing training program. The system should be formally structured, and documentation is necessary for its effective management. Any program fails if the participants do not believe that it is necessary and vital to achieve acceptable performance. The form and character of the system used to provide motivation are neither specific nor universal. The system is dependent upon the style of management and the circumstances that prevail and may include award programs, posters, recognition events, contests, emission-reduction goals, performance appraisal, discipline, incident-reduction goals, positive management response to suggestions, letters of recognition or commendation, etc. Environmental performance will demonstrate whether the necessary motivation system has been provided.

5. Environmental emergencies: Proficient personnel are available during all operations to carry out written, up-to-date procedures

It is important that all emergency environmental-procedure plans be documented in a clear and concise manner. Examples of these include spill-prevention, containment, and countermeasure plans, contingency plans, emergency-episode plans, plans covering hazardous material spills, and plans which cover accidental discharges to the environment as a result of an operation upset and/or bypass or turnarounds. These plans should be updated to reflect changes in operational procedures and personnel. As important as having such written plans is having a system requiring periodic drills and training in order to ensure personnel familiarity with the plans.

6. Incidents and follow-up: Prompt and effective steps are taken to study and avoid recurrence of serious incidents

When environmental incidents such as oil spills, excess emissions, or unusual discharges occur, written reports should be prepared even if not required by law. Documentation should include any citations and/or legal actions which ensue. The reports should be maintained in such a manner as to allow easy access for review. A management system should provide review of these incidents by responsible facility personnel, with the objective of preventing future incidents.

7. Environmental protection information: Effective systems provide for gathering and distributing current environmental protection information and applying it to existing or new operations

A system for the distribution of environmental information should be maintained between the operating company's environmental staff and each of its facilities and internally within each facility. This information should include required technology, standard publications, and up-to-date environmental and technological information. In the design of new facilities and continued operation or modification of existing facilities, this information is critical and should be systematically reviewed.

8. Maintenance: Controlled maintenance systems provide prompt and effective correction of deficiencies or noncompliance

Controlled maintenance systems, both preventive and corrective, can minimize actual or possible environmental effects. Examples of these include maintenance of valves, fittings, emission controls, mobile equipment, etc. that will minimize fugitive emissions; maintenance of transfer facilities that will minimize spills; and, of course, good housekeeping.

9. Third-party actions: Third-party contractors perform in an environmentally sound manner under the supervision of a knowledgeable contract administrator

Activities of others working for, with, or on behalf of Atlantic Richfield are important; the actions of these third parties reflect upon Atlantic Richfield. The third party—whether it be a drilling contractor; a cleanup contractor handling construction, maintenance, or spills; a chartered tanker; a contract carrier; or a waste hauler—should be aware of Atlantic Richfield's environmental procedures and concerns and, to the extent necessary, be required to follow them. Third parties should be chosen and their activities monitored with environmental consequences in mind. Appropriate controls should be established as needed.

10. External communication: Established systems provide effective communication with the government and the public

The facility should have a system to assist all levels of government in promulgation of cost-effective and sound laws, codes, rules, and regulations. This can be accomplished by direct communication through environmental-staff personnel of the operating company and through the corporate response groups. A system for communicating with the public, including environmental and conservation groups, should provide for availability of speakers, exhibits, and other public relations methods of conveying to the public our concern for environmental protection.

THE REVIEW PROCESS

The environmental review program is conducted for the council by the environmental services group at corporate headquarters in Los Angeles. As discussed earlier, the Corporate Health, Safety and Environmental Protection Council is made up of operating or engineering vice presidents of each of our separate operating companies. The council is chaired by the corporate director of health, safety and environmental protection. The manager of environmental services acts as staff to the council, and it is under the aegis of the council that the review program is carried out.

Once a year, generally in the late fall, each operating-company vice president is asked to nominate a group of ten to fifteen middle-management, generally fast-track, employees to form an intercompany review panel. The panel has 125 members, selected to provide a mix of engineering, operating, and environmental backgrounds to ensure a balanced review of a facility. The panel members range from plant managers of smaller facilities up to vice presidents of some organizations; even ship captains have served successfully on the panel.

Each panel member serves for 2 years and in that time will probably conduct one environmental review and one health and safety review. Atlantic Richfield schedules approximately fifteen to twenty environmental reviews at major facilities each year and a like number of health and safety reviews.

At approximately the same time that the council is nominating the panel members, it also nominates facilities to be reviewed in the coming year. Reviews are scheduled so that each major operating facility is reviewed at least once every 4 years. The term "facility" must be defined. Refineries, chemical plants, smelters, etc., are generally completely contained at one site; thus, if a review is scheduled at the Philadelphia refinery, everybody knows exactly the limits of that facility. On the other hand, when a review is scheduled at an operating district within the ARCO Oil and Gas Company, the "facility" may encompass several states. Similarly, when scheduling a review at a pipeline district, the geographic coverage may be rather large.

Using a pipeline district as an example, a review team would view the district manager as the facility manager and would review the operations under the manager's jurisdiction. In the short time allotted for the review, it is frequently impossible to physically visit each and every widely scattered unit. In such a case, the review team would select several operations representative of the types of management systems within that facility. Recently a review was completed at Atlantic Richfield's marketing facilities in the northeastern United States. Obviously, it was impossible to visit every terminal and bulk plant in that area. However, the review team was able to measure the effectiveness of the environmental systems in place by visiting a representative sample of the many operations under the distribution manager's jurisdiction.

Once the council members have completed their facility nominations, the corporate manager of environmental services appoints small teams from the panel membership for specific review projects. The teams will typically have a leader and two or three additional team members from the panel, a corporate environmental advisor, and a corporate legal advisor. After much discussion among the operating companies and corporate offices, it was agreed that each team member's company should bear that member's expenses for participation on the team. The facility manager provides services as necessary for the team. This arrangement seems to be working quite well and equitably distributes the cost of the program among the operating companies.

Team members always review a facility outside their own operating company; a team member from a refinery would never visit another refinery but might visit a chemical plant, a smelter, or some other facility not related to the member's normal job assignment. This method of assignment provides that a team reviewing an ARCO Solar Industries facility might include a person from ARCO Chemical Company, another from ARCO Metals Company, and a third from ARCO Transportation Company, plus a corporate environmental advisor. In the course of conducting the review, the team members have ample opportunity to discuss one another's management methods and experiences. This cross-fertilization or cross-pollination among persons from different companies is a valuable ancillary benefit of the review program.

The scheduling of review team members may be beneficial to individuals in yet another way. For example, when plant A is being scheduled for review, we look at the panel membership, and if a person from plant A is on the panel, we will try to schedule that person as a member of a review team at plant B several months before plant A is to be reviewed. In that way, panel members become familiar with the processes and can go back to their own plants more adequately prepared for the upcoming review.

A frequently heard comment is, "But doesn't that mean that you are really trying to find everything in good shape?" Since most plants have at least 6 months notice that a review is about to take place, they have that time to really fine-tune their environmental management systems. But remember, again, that the purpose of the review program is to help managers achieve fullest compliance, and the scheduling and conducting of reviews tends to enhance their environmental awareness.

A comprehensive environmental review procedure manual has been prepared. This manual describes the review process in detail for the team members and the facility to be reviewed. The manual is designed to apply to any facility—mine, smelter, refinery, chemical plant, pipeline, ship, or exploration or production field. It was developed by corporate environmental services with considerable input and review by environmental groups from the operating companies. The manual discusses what the team should look for under each of the ten criteria and describes how to make those determinations. It also outlines benchmarks or standards to be met. A general checklist for each criterion enables the team and the facility to verify that the most important aspects have been considered. While the manual is designed to guide review teams, it has also been used by some facility managers as a model in setting up the types of management systems which should be in place to protect the environment.

Once the facility has been nominated and the team assigned, a copy of the review procedure manual is sent to the facility manager, the review team leader, and each member of the team. Thus the facility to be reviewed has a complete understanding of the process which the team will use to review that facility. Contained in the manual is a preview questionnaire which the facility is required to prepare. Approximately 6 weeks before the review takes place, the team leader and the environmental advisor visit the facility to discuss the completed preview questionnaire and to make appropriate arrangements for the review team. Following the initial meeting, the team leader sends to the other team members and to the legal advisor a copy of the questionnaire, plant layouts and brochures, and any other pertinent information which results from the preview conference. Thus the team members and advisors all receive a substantial written briefing prior to their arrival at the facility.

The Site Visit

Each review is scheduled to take approximately 10 days. Several different approaches have been tried with respect to timing. The general pattern now is that the reviews start on a Monday, with the team members traveling from their home base to a hotel or motel near the facility and arriving Monday afternoon or evening. The team assembles at its headquarters, where the team leader discusses the facility and the preview data which have been gathered. The environmental advisor discusses the review program and procedures in some detail and presents a general discussion of environmental regulations and requirements governing the facility. The legal advisor counsels the team on the review process, with discussions on conducting interviews, gathering and evaluating data, and preparing a preliminary report. The legal advisor is generally with the team only for the first day or two but remains available by telephone throughout the 10-day period. The environmental advisor stays with the team during the entire review and participates in the complete process, including the interviews. It is important to note here that the team leader is, in fact, in charge of the review process and directs the activities of the team; the environmental advisor specifically does not play this role but serves as environmental consultant to the team, answering members' questions and providing guidance on environmental matters.

Each team member comes to the review with a different operating background. Each looks at a specific situation at the facility being reviewed and views that situation from his or her own operating perspective. Thus many times, during the course of the review, team members will form different opinions about a specific management system or its effect. These discussions frequently last far into the night, but eventually the team must reach a consensus on each criterion in the review process. These discussions among the team members on the environmental aspects of an operation with which they are unfamiliar are an experience which tends to heighten their environmental awareness. It is a broadening experience for the participants, and they go back to their assignments with a better understanding of the diverse operations of the company.

On the second day of the review, the team arrives at the facility in the morning and is met by the management. A meeting is held with key management personnel to discuss the review program schedule and any other pertinent information. The team leader points out during this initial meeting the nature of the review process. The work product does not constitute a report card; it is not an adversary action. He emphasizes again that the purpose of the review is to help the facility manager. This viewpoint is well known within Atlantic Richfield, and the reviews are generally welcomed by the facility personnel. One facility even rented a large trailer, positioned it near the entrance gate, and put a large sign, "Environmental Review Team," on the trailer. Thus every person in that facility was aware of the fact that the review process was going on. Some facility managers have prepared badges or identification patches so that the team's presence is recognized within the facility; others have prepared special hats or jackets as suitable identification. One facility had the team's hotel sign read "Welcome Atlantic Richfield Company Environmental Review Team." These examples indicate the acceptance the program has within the operating companies.

At the termination of the initial meeting, the team is given a general facility tour, usually conducted by the facility's environmental coordinator. This is a brief familiarization tour of operations rather than a tour with more specific objectives.

One-on-one interviews

Enter now one of the most interesting aspects of the review process—the one-on-one interview. Following special outlines in the procedure manual, the team interviews a predetermined sample of approximately 10 percent of all the employees at the facility. These interviews are conducted with managers, supervisors, technical staff, and hourly employees. Each interview is one-on-one—one team member and one employee together in a private room. The team member establishes a candid, informal relationship during the interview and assures the interviewee of complete anonymity. Separate interview guides are prescribed in the manual for each category of employee. It was determined early in the review process that the same question must be phrased differently according to the level of work responsibility of the employee being interviewed. While the questions for managers and supervisors are directed more toward systems and results, the questions for hourly employees are directed more toward their perceived awareness of environmental activities at the facility.

As an example of the interview process, management representatives may be asked to describe the environmental training program in operation, while hourly employees may be asked whether they have received any environmental training: "Have you received any environmental training?" rather than "Is there an environmental program at this facility?" When employees say "No, there is no training program," what they may really be saying is that they do not remember the training sessions they may have attended. This does not mean that there is no such program; it may perhaps mean that there is a program but that it is not working, if the employees do not remember attending. The situation may be likened to observing an employee in a hard-hat area not wearing a hard hat. Does the fact that one employee is seen without a hard hat mean that the facility does not enforce the hard-hat rule, or does it mean that the employee does not remember the plant rules? An amazing amount of information is freely and candidly obtained from employees during the one-on-one interview. While each interview is scheduled for 1 hour, interviews with hourly employees usually take 20 to 30 minutes, while interviews with managers and supervisors usually take the better part of the hour. Generally the team members will conduct the interview as a normal conversation without taking copious notes; after the interviewee has left, notes on that interview are completed. Taking notes during the interview sometimes seems to inhibit the free and candid exchange of information.

Interviews generally continue for 2 days (the third and fourth days of the review) and frequently begin early in the morning and continue late into the evening so that all three shifts in a major facility are adequately sampled. Each evening, following the interviews, the team members meet at their motel for a debriefing and discuss the general findings brought out in their interviews. Again, the various backgrounds of the team members come into play as they judge the interviews from their individual perspectives. Frequently, lengthy discussions ensue as team members describe what they have heard and how they have interpreted their findings. Specific situations come to light in the interviews which are noted for further investigation as the review continues. We have determined that it is most desirable to complete the interviews early in the review process, since the team members gain from them a much more specific understanding of the operations at the facility.

The results of the interview process give the team an idea of what areas to focus on as the review progresses. Following the interviews, the team tours the facility in considerable detail to observe operations as they have been described in the interviews. The team leader generally hands out assignments so that individual members check out different areas of operations: one team member may be assigned the wastewater treatment plant, another checks records, a third may check sample gathering and testing, etc.

Checking records

The review process is not an audit in the literal sense of the word. The team looks at National Pollution Discharge Elimination System (NPDES) reports over the past year or so and then picks a representative statistic on that report for review. For example, suppose a facility has an NPDES permit with a limitation of 25 parts per million (ppm) biochemical oxygen demand (BOD). The team picks a report which shows a monthly evaluation of, say, 20 ppm. The team then reviews the management systems, asking such questions as "What check did the facility manager make before he signed the report?" "Who checks the reported variations against the permit limitation?" "What system is in effect to determine that 20 ppm actually represents the facility's performance that month?"

Laboratory notebooks are examined to locate the specific tests which determined the 20 ppm. Sample records are checked to determine that the treated-wastewater stream was sampled appropriately. Experience has shown this to be an effective method of determining that management systems are in place and are effective. Should the team members note, for instance, a reported BOD exceeding the limitation, they will again check to see what management system is directed toward determining the causes for this and what is being done to prevent or minimize recurrences.

The team specifically does not decide whether a facility is or is not in compliance with a specific regulation or parameter, since determining compliance is a legal issue. If the team encounters what appears to be a noncompliance situation, such as a reported 30 ppm as compared to the

25 ppm BOD limitation discussed above, that finding would be part of the report, and the plant manager would be expected to respond to it. Again, remember that the purpose of the review is to help plant managers improve management systems. The team would point out this finding in the final report, so that management might take appropriate action as necessary.

When the team checks records, specific items under each of the ten criteria are reviewed. The team will look to see that the facility has a complete copy of all environmental regulations pertaining to it and that these regulations are readily available to the management. There should be, for instance, an environmental training program and documentation indicating what training sessions have taken place and who has attended these sessions. Environmental records such as inspection reports, logs, permits, or other routine documentation such as hazardous-waste manifests are checked to make sure they are current and complete. The team will also check to see that the facility is making the required reports to regulatory agencies.

On this fifth day also, the team will require the facility to conduct an environmental emergency drill. This may be an oil-spill drill, or it could take the form of a hypothetical chemical spill into the waste treatment system or an emergency shutdown of a baghouse in a metals operation. The purpose of this exercise is to see that proficient personnel are readily available and fully capable of responding to an environmental emergency of the type which can occur at a specific facility.

Prior to the environmental emergency drill, the team reviews the required written emergency procedures as part of its regular review, including such items as oil-spill response plans, emergency air-episode plans, spill prevention control and countermeasure (SPCC) plans, or whatever the facility has prepared. In conducting reviews to date, a consistent finding is that facilities are anxious to demonstrate their capability to respond to environmental emergencies.

The facility report

The review process requires that the team prepare a written preliminary report prior to leaving the facility. Because the team members, following the review, return to their own work assignments, it is essential that they reach a consensus and document their findings in writing while they are still together and operating as a team.

On day six of the review, Saturday, the team members begin to assess the environmental performance of the facility and reach a consensus on their findings. It is important that they identify and document the facts which led them to their findings and recommendations. If consensus cannot be reached, the problem is noted and the team returns to the specific area involved to determine additional facts that may lead to resolution of the problem. Usually the team leader assigns one or two criteria to each of the team members, and they then begin drafting the written report.

The team is required to determine actual facts and not report "findings" based on mere conjecture or recall. One approach frequently used is to have each team member draft a portion of the report. The members then share these sections, and day seven, Sunday, is spent in integrating these individual sections into a team work product, the draft preliminary report. Again, as this process takes place, problem areas will arise, and in some areas it will be apparent that the team must revisit the facility to confirm facts or determine supporting data. Usually by Sunday evening the team has been able to prepare a complete written draft.

The draft preliminary report at this point consists of findings for each of the ten criteria and the team's recommendations. The findings represent facts established during the review process. The team is careful not only to zero in on adverse findings but also to document completely the positive findings where management systems are indeed in place and work well. A facility manager responds much more positively to the report when positive findings are documented as well as findings which represent opportunities for improvement in the facility's management systems and practices.

The recommendations which the team makes are generally directed toward encouraging the facility manager to develop or improve management systems without specific instructions on how to accomplish the change. If, for instance, the team notes that there is no environmental training program at the facility, that will be the finding, and the recommendation might be that a training program should be developed. If, while the team is drafting its report, a question of legal interpretation arises, the lawyer assigned to the team can provide legal counsel by telephone.

Day eight begins with the team returning to the facility with its preliminary draft. Generally, the facility makes available a secretary who prepares a typed rough draft. While the preliminary report is being typed, team members continue to collect information on any unresolved items. They also now begin discussing how they will present the report to facility management. The team leader advises the facility manager that the report is nearing completion and that the team will be prepared to present its findings and recommendations to the manager the next day. The manager is invited to have present whomever he or she wishes. Usually, the manager's immediate staff will be present and perhaps also the facility environmental manager and attorney. It is the facility manager's prerogative to decide who will be present and how many copies of the report will be prepared.

Once the team receives the typed rough draft, it is thoroughly reviewed to make sure that the report reflects the team's findings accurately and clearly. Here again, the background and experiences of the various team members come into play as they determine the best way to convey to the facility management their specific findings and recommendations.

Finally, on day nine, the facility manager meets with the team to review the preliminary report. The team leader appraises the facility criterion by criterion, explaining each finding and recommendation in the report, and team members join in if appropriate to clarify specific points. It is required that the facility manager fully understand each point and agree with the findings before the preliminary report is considered finished. If there are any areas of disagreement between the team and the facility manager, these areas must be resolved before the team leaves the facility. This process has been known to take several days while the team reassesses certain findings. Occasionally the plant manager and team visit a specific area in question to clarify facts. Sometimes the facility manager is able to bring to light facts that were not known to the team and that cause the team to change its findings. Much more frequently, however, the facility manager learns of management systems that are perhaps not accomplishing the objectives for which they were designed. The meeting is generally kept on a positive note, with the team carefully discussing the positive as well as the negative findings. Once the team leader and the facility manager have agreed on the findings and recommendations, the meeting is concluded. The team's assignment at the facility is then completed and the team members return to their own work assignments.

The next step is for the facility manager to report back to the team leader in writing within 45 days. The facility manager is expected to respond to the findings and recommendations on each of the criteria, including, where appropriate, a discussion of what actions have been taken or are planned in regard to each, with the anticipated timetable from inception to conclusion. The facility manager's response is directed to the team leader. The team leader integrates the response into the preliminary report, so that under each criterion the final report will show a finding, a recommendation, and a facility response. Occasionally, a team leader who feels that the facility manager's response is inappropriate or not acceptable may talk to the facility manager directly or may initiate a conference call among the team members and the facility manager. Once these issues are resolved, the final report can be completed. A facility manager who determines, for one reason or another, that something the team has recommended is not going to be accomplished must then explain the reasons why the recommended action will not be taken.

Follow-up

When the final report is completed, the team leader forwards it to the person to whom the facility manager reports for review. Each level of management above the facility manager is then required to review the report, up to and including the president of the operating company. Thus each level of management is made aware of the environmental protection situation at that facility. Once the president of the operating company completes the review of the report, it is forwarded to the Health, Safety and Environmental Protection Council for inclusion in its permanent records. Copies of the final report are also transmitted to the operating-company environmental manager and to the corporate legal department. The facility manager is required to send a progress report every 6 months to the council, outlining progress made and projects accomplished on individual items in the final report. The facility manager's report is made in conjunction with the operating-company environmental manager and legal department. The operating-company staff is responsible for following up with the facility manager to determine that the programs are being carried out.

The corporate environmental advisor does not follow up with the facility, since that is the responsibility of the operating company's environmental staff. The process used in the Atlantic Richfield environmental review program is copied closely from our health and safety review program, which has been in effect for over 10 years. The health and safety program uses the same anonymous-interview technique which has proved so effective over the years. An early concern was the validity of utilizing people from the panel who were not trained in environmental matters, and in two of the earliest reviews the teams were specifically organized to test this. Two of the largest, relatively newer, facilities were selected, in which the environmental situation was well known at corporate headquarters. In the first review, a review of an aluminum smelter, the team leader was a ship captain who had never seen any of the shore-based facilities. The other two team members likewise came from facilities not even remotely associated with smelting. It did not take the captain, who by necessity is highly systems-oriented, any time at all to mete out assignments to the team members. The team readily determined the environmental facts and correctly assessed the environmental performance of that facility.

Another early review was conducted at an oil refinery in Washington state. Here again, an intercompany team demonstrated that it was perfectly capable of assessing the environmental performance of a facility by following the review procedures manual. It was during these two reviews that the process indicated the need to break up the interview guide into separate sections, as indicated earlier, because the questions directed more at facility management were not understood or were misinterpreted by hourly employees.

After these two reviews demonstrated the basic effectiveness of the program, the operating companies were invited to send representatives to a workshop organized to develop the procedures manual into a universal document which could apply to any type of facility. Each year, an additional workshop is conducted on the procedures to ensure that the program is kept up to date.

PROGRAM BENEFITS

Many ancillary benefits accrue to Atlantic Richfield from the environmental review program. It has certainly helped to enhance the environmental awareness of all employees. It is encouraging to note during the reviews how the environmental awareness of executive management is conveyed throughout the operating facilities. Many of the people on the review panel are future facility managers and are thus learning early on about environmental considerations through practical experience. Since panel members are assigned to a team reviewing a facility outside their own company, they have an opportunity to compare other environmental management approaches to their own facility practices. As a result, they gain a keener understanding of how closely environmental considerations are interwoven with all Atlantic Richfield Company's operations.

The review process has also proved to be a workable method for reviewing prospective acquisitions. On several occasions, review teams have been sent to conduct an environmental review of a facility being considered as an addition to Atlantic Richfield Company. In these cases, however, the team members have been from the environmental staff of either the corporate or the operating-company groups.

Once the environmental review process was introduced within the company, specific efforts were made to publicize its existence. Atlantic Richfield's *mgr* magazine, which is published and distributed to all management employees throughout the company, carried a feature article on the review program that received a great deal of comment. The writers looked not only at the deliberations of the team but also at the reactions of the facility personnel involved. Without exception, responses have been positive.

At Atlantic Richfield, we feel that the environmental review program has demonstrated and will continue to demonstrate that our company is constantly meeting the standards that we set for it.

Case Study: General Motors Corporation

Joseph P. Barzotti

Environmental Auditing
General Motors Corporation

The late sixties and seventies may be considered the era of environmental regulations. During this period the Solid Waste Disposal Act, the Clean Air Act, the Resource Recovery Act, the Federal Water Pollution Control Act, the Noise Control Act, the Energy Policy and Conservation Act, the Resource Conservation and Recovery Act, and the Toxic Substances Control Act were enacted. This period also marked the creation of the Environmental Protection Agency (EPA) and the tightening of controls on the workplace by the Occupational Safety and Health Administration (OSHA). As a result, General Motors and many other corporations either established or expanded their environmental departments to ensure compliance with the laws and to increase employee awareness of regulatory requirements. This chapter traces the development and explains the operation of the plant audit activity within the General Motors Environmental Activities Staff.

PLANT AUDIT PROGRAM

Since 1970, each General Motors manufacturing facility has reported to the firm's plant environment division its compliance with air and water quality regulations and with company standards. This information, submitted by the plants, was compiled and summarized in a report for distribution to management. However, noncompliance situations continued to arise as new laws were enacted and new regulations promulgated. Corporate management, in order to be assured of sufficient information on environmental problems and correctional actions, requested on-site audits of actual plant operations similar to financial audits. In response to this concern, the in-plant performance review program, or plant audit, was initiated in November 1972. The initial review group consisted of five auditors and one supervisor plus a secretary. Auditors were selected from engineering personnel experienced in environmental matters.

As a primary objective, the plant audit provides corporate, divisional, and plant management with an accurate and periodic engineering evaluation of actual environmental conditions at each manufacturing facility. The audit results not only in identifying environmental deficiencies at the plants but also in educating plant personnel to establish or renew programs to achieve and maintain compliance with applicable standards and regulations. Deficiencies identified by the audit must be addressed in a program and a schedule for corrective action developed by the plant. Audit personnel are available to assist the plants in formulating corrective-action programs and to monitor these programs once they are in place. The ultimate goal of the plant audit is to assist all United States and Canadian manufacturing facilities in achieving and maintaining compliance with environmental laws and regulations and with company standards.

In scope, the audit function encompasses air and water quality, hazardous and waste-materials handling, energy conservation, and certain OSHA-related functions that are considered normal plant engineering responsibilities (noise abatement, maintenance records, etc.). The energy conservation and OSHA portions of the audit have been undertaken at the request of the company's manufacturing staff. Other OSHA-related functions such as safety and industrial hygiene are not audited, since they are the responsibility of the industrial relations staff.

The normal audit schedule is based upon auditing all manufacturing facilities within a 4-year cycle, using a staff of ten auditors plus a supervisor and a secretary. The frequency of audit at a specific facility is determined by that plant's potential for impact on the environment. At present, members of the plant audit group perform on-site reviews every other week. The intervening week constitutes the time necessary to prepare detailed final reports, review state, provincial, and/or local regulations, and consult with plant environment staff specialists. A facility audit is normally performed by a two-, three-, or four-person review team. Each auditor is a specialist in one or more of the environmental areas. Auditors are normally selected from among engineering personnel responsible for environmental functions at General Motors manufacturing facilities. Through cross-training and auditing experience, each member of the review group becomes capable of performing multiple functions.

THE AUDITING PROCESS

The general procedure used to determine the environmental status of each plant involves four steps: preliminary preparation, operation and records review at the plant, report of the results, and review of the subsequent compliance program.

Prior to the on-site visit, the manufacturing facility is contacted by telephone and informed of the audit procedure and of the documentation that must be available for review. During the week prior to the visit, the review team gathers preliminary information from several sources, including previous audit reports and the latest information supplied in plant-generated reports and interviews with plant environment staff specialists (air quality, water quality, and waste materials) whose function it is to assist General Motors facilities with environmental concerns within their specific disciplines. Federal, state or provincial, and local environmental regulations applicable to the facility are also reviewed during this week.

Upon arrival at the manufacturing facility, the review team meets with plant personnel responsible for each of the environmental areas. After discussing the objectives of the review, plant personnel and audit team members divide into groups to perform the review. Checklists for each area are used as guidelines to ensure that all pertinent information is examined. The number of plant personnel involved directly or indirectly in the audit process varies, but usually at least twenty participate. The actual auditing process involves reviewing plant records, procedures, and test data plus observing actual plant operating situations such as stack emissions, water-discharge conditions, and control-equipment operations. The review team determines whether each plant's information is in conformity with current and projected regulations and company standards. The audit also measures the plant management's awareness of applicable regulations and notes whether compliance programs have been established and maintained.

During this phase of the audit, the team members also provide accompanying plant personnel with ideas on how other plants are handling similar problems. This information is important, since it may provide the plant with some useful tips on alternate solutions.

Once the information-gathering portion of the on-site review is complete, the audit team identifies specific deficiencies. To avoid any surprises or disputes over the audit results, the review team discusses each finding in detail with responsible plant personnel prior to presentation to plant management. A preliminary report on the identified deficiencies is presented during a meeting with the plant management staff on the final day of the audit.

Following the on-site environmental review, the audit team prepares a formal report detailing deficiencies and often includes pertinent observations on the plant's environmental programs. The report directs plant management to develop a corrective-action response (compliance plan) to the deficiencies identified in the report.

COMPLIANCE PROGRAM

The formal corrective-action response to the audit findings must include specific engineering solutions and completion schedules for each deficiency. To assure management's commitment to the corrective-action program, the plant manager is requested to review the formal response. The corrective-action program is reviewed and critiqued by all applicable staffs and the plant audit group.

The ultimate objective of the plant audit is to assure that all General Motors facilities achieve and maintain compliance with current and projected environmental regulations. An adequate corrective-action program is the key to meeting this objective. During subsequent audits of each facility, auditors give special attention to the implementation of the plant's corrective-action program from the previous review. This process appears to have gained acceptance and support from management and plant engineering personnel.

In addition to conducting the compliance reviews, the plant auditors provide the following services:

- Perform special audits of a plant to address specific environmental concerns (such as community or agency complaints) or evaluate compliance status with regard to newly implemented regulations
- Conduct assistance visits at the plants to provide consulting services in the environmental areas
- Report the status of the corporation's pollution problems by issuing a self-audit questionnaire and compiling the data annually
- Perform air-quality compliance certifications, when required, for new plants or major installations
- Communicate new environmental-control methods and technologies to facilities being audited

• Project possible future corporate environmental concerns from trend analyses that have been performed on computerized audit results

UPDATING THE PLANT AUDIT PROGRAM

The plant audit activity itself is periodically reviewed with a view to improving efficiency and redirecting resources to focus on current regulatory concerns. In recent months the plant audit activity has been giving more attention to procedures related to water quality, toxic-waste disposal, and groundwater contamination. For example, the water-quality audit procedure has recently been revised to emphasize the maintenance of proper records and include the review of sampling and laboratory techniques. Additionally, new laboratory quality-control/quality-assurance (QC/QA) procedures have been issued to all plants. The audits will be directed at evaluating compliance with these corporate QC/QA requirements.

An example of regulations requiring increased attention are those implementing the Resource Conservation and Recovery Act and similar state laws dealing with the proper disposal of hazardous wastes. As these regulations become effective, local General Motors facilities, in conjunction with the Environmental Activities Staff, develop methods to comply with them. Special efforts are also being made to meet the requirements of the 1976 Toxic Substances Control Act, which regulates the manufacturing, processing, and use of chemicals. These two acts require industry to be aware of all chemical substances entering plants and to be able to trace these substances through the manufacturing process to final disposal. The new regulations have required additional audit attention and forced the plant audit group to rearrange its priorities and introduce new investigative techniques.

CONCLUSION

The environmental audit program's focus is on prevention of problems. Its goal is to ensure that all General Motors facilities achieve and maintain compliance with current and projected environmental laws and regulations and with company standards. Additionally, the plant environmental audit group acts as an instrument through which solutions to common problems are shared among General Motors facilities. This self-identification of potential problems has enhanced the corporation's reputation with government agencies at the local, state, and federal levels.

Case Study: Olin Corporation

Robert W. Cutler
Regulatory Audits
Olin Corporation

When Olin Corporation designed and implemented its environmental auditing program in 1978, we were unable to identify any other company that had one. Today there are over a dozen well-established programs, and we receive an inquiry a week from companies that are considering instituting such a program. Environmental auditing has been the subject of many seminars, industry workshops, and government forums during the past 2 years, in part because the Environmental Protection Agency (EPA) is considering a voluntary program under which regulatory surveillance, and possibly penalties, would be reduced for companies that have an environmental auditing program. If the current trend continues, the practice of environmental auditing may become as commonplace in companies with environmental concerns as financial auditing is now.

HOW THE PROGRAM WORKS

As in any new undertaking, there are more questions than answers. Many of the questions that members of industry and government have posed to Olin over the past few years have opened new perspectives and offered new approaches. Perhaps the one question asked most frequently is the most basic question: How is an environmental audit performed? My experience as Olin's regulatory audit manager and numerous discussions with individuals outside Olin involved with or responsible for developing such programs provide at least the rudiments of an answer.

The key to a successful environmental auditing program is top management's support and commitment. Without management support, an auditing program will probably be unsuccessful. Top management is ultimately responsible for the operations of the company and must report the success or failure of the company's activities to the stockholders, the public, and sometimes the government. It is in top management's best interest to provide adequate resources to establish an environmental compliance and management review system which ensures that each operating location is reviewed as frequently as necessary. As the system develops, certain procedural issues may require clarification. At that time, top management's support of the auditing effort is essential. In addition, management must be committed to taking action to correct any deficiencies uncovered by the auditor.

The regulatory auditing department's activities include identifying environmental and other regulatory concerns. We communicate these concerns to those individuals within the company who are in a position to formulate and initiate improvements. We try to ensure that decisions are made at the appropriate level of management. For example, at Olin, a plant manager does not have the authority to commit the company to expenditures exceeding $100,000. Accordingly, in addition to gaining the plant manager's support for our recommendations, we communicate our concerns to the individual responsible for the operation who is authorized to make such a commitment.

Although the auditing department at Olin makes recommendations for improved compliance procedures, we do not have responsibility for or authority over any of the activities reviewed. Accordingly, our reviews do not in any way relieve operating management of their assigned responsibilities. Our findings frequently result in differences of opinion. These differences, which are both inevitable and healthy, should surface first at the exit interview and then be resolved during the report clearance process, when it is either confirmed that we have interpreted the facts correctly or additional facts are provided to allay our concerns.

An environmental compliance and management review system should be organized to accomplish the company's compliance objectives. Responsibilities should be clearly assigned and procedures specifically delineated. Each company will, of course, have unique needs and methods. However, an environmental compliance and management review typically operates at several management levels. At the operating locations, coordinators are responsible for regulatory compliance in their areas of expertise. These coordinators are supported at the division level by a technical support staff that provides assistance by continuously monitoring the regulations and determining appropriate methods of compliance. A lawyer is generaly available to work with both the plant operating personnel and the technical support staff, to ensure that their knowledge of regulations is current and that the efforts taken to comply with those regulations are appropriate and legally sound. These three functions, working in harmony, create the basic compliance system.

However, as in all real-life situations, circumstances can arise that create difficulties for even the best-designed and best-implemented system. Personnel may be transferred or change jobs, and their replacements may be less well trained. If two or more divisions with separate technical support staffs or legal departments are involved, these staffs or departments may interpret regulations differently, resulting in disparity between compliance efforts. To satisfy management's need to be assured that the system is operating as intended, the independent internal auditor is responsible for reviewing the activities and reporting to management the results of the regulatory compliance system.

BASIC ASPECTS OF THE PROGRAM

A typical regulatory auditing program has four basic aspects: personnel training, preparation, fieldwork, and reporting.

Personnel Training

The personnel who conduct environmental audits must be trained in auditing techniques. Although outside consultants or outside personnel can be used, a decision was made at Olin to build a permanent in-house auditing staff. The individuals on this staff are drawn from many departments, including manufacturing, environmental affairs, research, and financial auditing. They are all experienced managers with engineering and technical backgrounds; they have worked in the plants and are thus familiar with operations and accepted by plant personnel. All the auditors understand and are able to apply their expertise to a variety of regulatory areas. This approach has worked well in practice, and it enables us to assemble an auditing team without undue constraints on scheduling.

The auditors are trained thoroughly in auditing methods, and they are well-versed in asking questions in ways that elicit cooperation and stimulate dialogue. Methods of analyzing systems and evaluating controls are also an integral part of an auditor's training.

Starting in 1978, we made a continuing effort to identify all Olin reports submitted to government agencies and Olin records maintained for inspection by those agencies. Over 4300 reports or records were identified, and specific employees were assigned responsibility for each. These reports and the responsible individuals are listed on an "authorized list." For example, reports related to air regulations include *Application for Certification to Operate Air Contamination Sources, Air Pollution Emissions Report,* and *Stack Monitoring Records.* Other typical reports include *NPDES Monitoring Report* and *RCRA Hazardous Waste Manifest.* The basic preparation for performing an audit centers on the authorized list. This list provides the auditor a good overview of what regulations affect the plant and what reports are submitted to the government.

It is important to ensure that the reviews are consistent at all operating locations. The entire regulatory subject, such as air pollution, must be covered thoroughly in the review, including both regulatory requirements and internal controls. To accomplish these objectives, we have developed audit programs on over thirty subjects. These programs guide the auditors by listing questions and procedural controls related to a regulated subject. They are also helpful in training new auditors.

Preparation

An audit program is prepared by first studying a regulation and determining how it relates to the company. One auditor will be assigned responsibility for practicing an audit of this regulation and preparing a draft of the audit program. This draft is then given to another auditor, who reviews it; together, the two auditors design the audit program to reflect anticipated conditions in the field. The resulting draft is then reviewed by the legal department, to ensure that the interpretations presented in the program reflect the regulatory requirements and to indicate which portions should be assigned highest priority. Olin has audit programs in many areas, including company policies, safety inspections, equal employment opportunity, plant emissions, transportation, hazardous-waste transportation, and labeling.

Fieldwork

The typical audit at Olin is not a surprise audit. Olin's auditors believe that the cooperation of plant personnel is essential to ensure that all information is received, and they feel that a surprise audit would be detrimental to that effort. However, an occasional surprise audit has some merit and may be performed.

Generally, we try to complete the fieldwork in 1 week, usually with an audit team of two or three members. Upon arrival at the location, the team meets with the plant manager to determine whether there are any particular concerns, questions, or areas that should be addressed or reviewed. The audit team then meets with the staff to answer any questions they may have concerning the audit and to determine each staff member's areas of responsibility or regulatory involvement. The team then reviews the plant's regulatory activities; for example, all stacks and vents are marked and all possible emissions are identified.

During an audit, the team interacts with several departments. The Occupational Safety and Health Administration (OSHA) review usually leads to the safety and medical departments. Equal employment is a personnel function. An audit of pesticides and other controlled products leads to manufacturing and quality assurance. The regulation of hazardous wastes and their transportation results in visits to shipping, purchasing, and warehousing. An audit of plant emissions (water, air, and solid waste) involves the engineering and production departments. Radioactive materials are usually taken care of by the maintenance department. In addition to all these departments, the auditors coordinate closely with division, corporate, and legal staffs to ensure that the team's observations are factual and their findings legally responsive.

In practice, we spend most of our time reviewing environmental issues. A review of water discharges may account for 25 percent of the time spent at a plant. Another 20 percent is spent studying air emissions, and a further 20 percent studying solid-waste disposal; 12 percent of the time is devoted to OSHA inspections, and the remaining time is spent reviewing affirmative action, pesticides, transportation, and other regulatory areas.

One method for determining whether a location is in compliance with regulations is to check the accuracy of reports submitted to federal, state, and local governments. Certain portions of the data included in the reports are selected for testing and then traced to the most basic source document to verify their accuracy. If the source document is a financial record, the review ends at that point and the financial auditors assume responsibility for ensuring that procedures and controls are adequate. However, when the source document is in an area such as a laboratory (e.g., a laboratory technician's notebook), the review proceeds.

The actual review begins in the field, with an observation of the technician making the usual sample-collection rounds, to ensure that the samples are being taken where and in the manner required by permits or regulations. The tests that the laboratory makes are checked against the EPA-required test methods to verify that the correct analysis is being performed. Conversions and assumptions used in transforming the base data to the data that are finally reported to the government are verified. In addition to determining that these tasks have been performed correctly, the auditors review the frequency and the method of collecting the samples to ensure that they are in accordance with the location's permit, for example, to determine whether samples are collected daily and are composite or grab samples. Instances of excursions are reviewed to determine whether they were reported as required by the agencies (e.g., 5-day excursion notice). While performing this review, the auditors conduct a physical tour of the location to observe the outfalls and to determine that what is actually seen corresponds to what is descibed in the permit. Finally, the auditors test the procedural controls in the system to ensure that they are operating as intended. For example, all smoke-monitoring tapes should be reviewed by plant personnel daily and notations made on the tape to indicate that this has been done.

In addition to typical plant audits, we also review the technical staff's support activities. Our purpose is to ascertain that their reviews are complete and documented and that staff members consistently follow up to ensure that staff recommendations have been implemented. We review their procedures and offer suggestions, if appropriate, for better communications or procedures.

Reporting

At the conclusion of the visit, we hold an exit interview with the plant manager and staff. The purpose of this interview is to ensure that observations are complete and consistent with all the facts and to provide plant personnel an opportunity to assist us in interpreting these facts correctly. We then prepare a draft report of the interview, which is reviewed with the plant manager, group legal counsel, and the person within each division who has been assigned responsibility for ensuring that our recommendations are thoroughly considered. When all parties agree that the report accurately reflects the facts and legal requirements or Olin procedures, the report is released.

A HYPOTHETICAL AUDIT

To illustrate how this general approach could be applied, let us perform a hypothetical audit during which we, as auditors, discover some hypothetical problems. As an example, we will perform an audit of a hypothetical facility's air-pollution compliance efforts.

Before beginning the audit, we determine, from the authorized list, that John Smith, a member of the plant engineering staff, is responsible for preparing an annual source emission inventory and a point-source emission report. The lawyer responsible for handling the plant's regulatory concerns provides us with a copy of the state regulations and discusses some paragraphs considered central to our review. During a visit to the division's environmental affairs department, we obtain maps, applications, and other background information.

Upon arrival at the plant, we discuss our proposed activities with Dave Adams, the plant manager. Visibly proud of his team's efforts, Dave describes a point-source inventory that the engineering staff completed last year. He mentions that the state inspector has reviewed the plant. Dave introduces us to Sam Jones, the engineering manager.

Shortly afterward, Sam and John take us on a tour of the plant. They point out a new addition to the plant and describe some of the process changes made during the past year. We note the ammonia tank farms and loading stations at the side of the plant.

Later, John and I compare the point-source inventory with the plot plan. We plot on the maps the twenty-eight vents listed on the inventory, and John soon finds himself climbing on roofs and up towers with me to locate any other vents. The final count is thirty-seven vents, including new vents, release vents from storage tanks, and exhaust fans. With this information, we return to the interior of the plant and determine where each vent or opening is and what substances could leave through it.

Back in John's office, we review the state regulations and tentatively conclude that, in addition to the twenty-eight points for which the plant has prepared applications for an operating certificate, five new applications could be required. These include one point in the new addition, a storage tank containing a listed air contaminant, a loading station, and two process-area exhaust fans. We recommend to John that he confer with his division technical specialist and lawyer to determine whether these points are, in fact, required to be registered.

We then review the twenty-eight applications for operating certificates and determine that the materials described are correct and the emission quantities are reasonable. No exceptions are noted. Two of the applications are for coal-fired boilers. The certificate states that smoke-monitoring devices must be in place and running and that the monitoring tapes must be retained for 3 years. We review, in detail, the monitoring tapes for four randomly selected months during the preceding 2 years. This review discloses that the monitors are occasionally inactive and sometimes indicate exceptionally high opacity readings. We discuss these observations with the operations staff, and it turns out that the monitor is sometimes off when the boilers are running and that there is no regular maintenance program to clean the monitors. We recommend that the operator initial the tapes daily and note downtimes and functional problems on the tapes. We also recommend that a periodic maintenance program to clean and calibrate the monitors be instituted and that these actions be documented.

One department uses methylene chloride as a solvent. Department usage records show that five times more solvent has been emitted than is stated on the application. The amount is greater than the maximum allowed by state regulations. However, during the exit interview, we are shown that the solvent was not actually emitted; instead, the department had collected the spent solvent and shipped it to a reclaimer. We suggest that confusion could be lessened and citations avoided by including disposition data on the department's usage report. Our suggestion is accepted.

While making a perimeter check, we note that the vegetation is healthy and the fence is in good repair.

We present our recommendations to Dave Adams at the exit interview. We discuss the authorized list and recommend that *Application for Operating Certificate, Smoke-Monitoring Tapes,* and *Methylene Chloride Usage Reports* be added to the authorized list and that responsibility for each form be assigned. He says that he appreciates the information and assures us that corrective action will be taken.

In about 2 weeks our report is issued, and for several months, Sam and John keep us advised of their progress. The following year, when we make our second visit, we are pleased to note that our concerns have been addressed and that Dave, Sam, and John have instituted monitoring and control systems that have prevented any recurrences of the problems previously found.

PROGRAM RESULTS

The Olin regulatory auditing department has been in existence for 4 years, and we have seen many benefits as a result of this program. Our reviews have helped ensure a common approach to policies and procedures throughout all company divisions and locations. Our findings have resulted in clarification of issues that had previously been interpreted differently at different locations. Above all, our efforts have reduced the company's exposure to regulatory compliance problems.

Case Study: Pennsylvania Power & Light

Michael F. Basta

Environmental Auditing
Pennsylvania Power & Light

All industry is faced with the dual, and often conflicting, goals of maintaining the delicate ecological balance while simultaneously pursuing industrial and technological development. To ensure that neither goal is subordinated to the other, a huge body of environmental law, expressed in thousands of compliance standards, has emerged over the past decade. The cost of this regulation to taxpayer and customer has spiraled as well. But the environment, especially as it affects health, remains a high priority in the minds of Americans. Over 80 percent of the people contacted in a recent poll felt that air-quality standards should remain as stringent as they are now, regardless of cost. However, the public seems to be receptive to alternatives to government regulation, so long as the innovation meets existing environmental objectives.

With the prospect of federal-agency budget cuts and the trend toward reduced regulation, a display of initiative on the part of private industry to both regulate itself and shoulder some additional responsibility for sensitive environmental management is being received favorably by government agencies and the public alike. For the first time in more than a decade, private industry has an opportunity to demonstrate its ability and sincerity in wanting to achieve the social objective of a clean, healthy environment.

At Pennsylvania Power & Light Company (PP&L) we have a strong commitment to achieving environmental compliance at our power plants and all our facilities. Our policy is to use the best practical abatement methods to meet local, state, and federal requirements. To assure ourselves that this is being accomplished, we set up an environmental auditing group to develop an effective review process. This is a formal and comprehensive system, much of it patterned on quality-assurance programs in the nuclear-power industry. The program was set up to notify line and corporate management of the status of a facility's environmental compliance, help line management attain compliance, and get line management in line with corporate philosophy and goals.

Since compliance with environmental regulations is a part of our overall business philosophy, environmental auditing at PP&L plays a crucial role in making sure we are managing to achieve specific results and not merely paying lip service to our objective of conducting our business in compliance with environmental standards. It is the role of the environmental audit to help the line manager achieve corporate objectives. Auditors are not viewed as performing a policing function; rather, their audit provides management assistance to the line organization so that the performance the company's action plans are designed to accomplish can be achieved. If no independent audit were undertaken, that might be an indication that the management was not really dedicated to achieving a high level of performance in that area. The audit is a planning tool which indicates areas where the company's procedures or policies could be improved.

If one of your company's facilities is not meeting environmental standards, auditing will find this out, and the company will be able to correct the problem before it becomes serious. If any questions are raised publicly, you will have audit findings which present an objective overview of problems and suggested (and implemented) solutions. Not only can you defuse exaggerated accounts of pollution and noncompliance, but by having precise, reliable information, you can prevent the company from underestimating a particular problem.

ORIGIN OF ENVIRONMENTAL AUDITING AT PP&L

PP&L's environmental quality assessment program is a result of a 1974 arm's-length efficiency review by an outside consultant. The purpose of the review was to help the company determine whether it was taking advantage of all significant opportunities to reduce costs without a degradation in the quality of service it provides to its customers. The review resulted in the recommendation that PP&L should develop improved quality-control procedures for environmental compliance. To implement this and other recommendations, PP&L established, in 1976, the environmental management division, of which the environmental auditing section is a part. The following is a summary of the environmental management division's mission:

- To manage the environmental affairs of the company so as to make it socially responsive and openly willing to balance community attitudes and values against its own interests and make its facilities comply with all environmental regulations
- To establish and maintain company awareness and understanding of the environmental community, its issues, its concerns, its legislation, and its technology; and to develop company positions on related issues and effectively present them to mold legislation
- To obtain all environmental permits; to ensure timely provision and proper use of equipment, methods, and procedures that will permit the company to meet and maintain compliance without the use of consent agreements; and to be constantly prepared to manage noncompliance incidents and their sequels, including spill cleanup, reporting to and negotiating with regulatory agencies, and initiating press releases
- To ensure compliance by routine surveillance and periodic formal audits

Specifically, the goals of the auditing section are to:

- Verify compliance with federal, state, and local regulations and to verify compliance with corporate policies and standards
- Determine the degree of company adherence to established environmental procedures, instructions, specifications, codes, and other applicable contractual and licensing requirements
- Determine the adequacy of methods of collecting and reporting environmental data
- Report discrepancies to responsible PP&L managers with responsibility in company planning, engineering, construction, and operational activities
- Recommend improvements in environmental procedures to the audited group and to upper management, so that findings can be utilized as a management tool
- Increase personnel awareness of environmental regulations

SCOPE OF THE ENVIRONMENTAL QUALITY ASSESSMENT PROGRAM

At PP&L, audit team members have a broad background in environmental science and technology, including water pollution, wastewater, air pollution (ambient and emission), radiochemistry, and quality assurance. However, to make audits more effective and to gain maximum efficiency from a limited staff, team members are required to become familiar with all the various areas of environmental auditing. By arranging audit teams so that each member has responsibility for a different area of an audit each time, everyone becomes familiar with all facets of the audit process by the time a complete audit sequence of all our facilities is accomplished.

At PP&L we conduct environmental assessments of our power-production facilities, which include coal, oil, hydro, and nuclear units, division operations, strip and deep coal mines and coal-loading facilities, and an oil pipeline. We also conduct environmental assessments of work done for the company by outside consultants.

The scope of individual audits may include all the areas listed below or a portion of them, depending on the facility audited:

- Verification that sampling and analysis are implemented and documented as required in the facility's National Pollutant Discharge Elimination System (NPDES) and industrial-waste permits
- Verification of implementation of a spill-prevention control and countermeasure plan (SPCC) (including applicable fire marshal regulations)
- Visible emissions test, using Environmental Protection Agency (EPA) method 9 and a comparison of visible emission vs. opacity-monitor readings
- Verification that any special requirements are being met: system agreements, letters of understanding, etc.
- Verification of implementation of calibration plans for in-stack monitors
- Verification that corrective measures provided for in previous audits have been or are being instituted
- Verification that the facility's ambient-air monitors are operating and that the telemetered data are accurately received at the plant
- Monitoring of volatile organic compounds (VOC)
- Verification that the facility is in compliance with EPA interim drinking-water regulations

- Verification that asbestos is removed and disposed of in accordance with EPA standards for air pollutants
- Verification that the pipeline is operated and maintained and that documentation is established and maintained as required by Department of Transportation rules governing the transportation of liquids by pipeline.
- Verification that the facility's environmental response manuals are complete and up to date
- Noise-level monitoring at fence line and, as appropriate, at property line of nearest inhabitant
- Verification of hazardous-waste-regulation compliance
- Verification that all permits are current
- Verification of compliance with Office of Surface Mining (OSM) regulations.
- Verification that the pipeline gravitometers meet the requirements of Nuclear Regulatory Commission regulations
- Monitoring of soil and erosion control
- General environmental inspection of the facility
- EPA regulations on polychlorinated biphenyls (PCBs) disposal and marking
- Preparedness, prevention, and contingency plans (PPC)
- Dams and encroachments

The specific environmental regulations that delimit the scope of the audits are:

- Environmental Protection Agency Regulations on National Emission Standards for Hazardous Air Pollutants, 40 CFR 61
- Interim Primary Drinking Water Regulations, 40 CFR 141
- Pennsylvania Water Resources Regulations, Pennsylvania Code, title 25, chapters 91–99
- Pennsylvania Solid Waste Regulations, Pennsylvania Code, title 25, part I, article I, chapter 75: subchapter C, Solid Waste Management; subchapter D, Hazardous Waste
- Office of Surface Mining Reclamation and Enforcement, 30 CFR, parts 700–717
- Pennsylvania Erosion Control Regulations, Pennsylvania Code, title 25, chapter 102, Erosion Control

- Pennsylvania Air Pollution Control Regulations, Pennsylvania Code, title 25, part I, chapters 121–141
- Environmental Protection Agency Regulations for Manufacturing, Processing, Distribution in Commerce, and Use Prohibitions for Polychlorinated Biphenyls under the Toxic Substances Control Act, 40 CFR 761
- Environmental Protection Agency Regulations on Oil Pollution Prevention, 40 CFR, Parts 110, Discharge of Oil, and 112, Oil Pollution Prevention
- Local ordinances, where applicable
- Company policy, where applicable

CONTROLLING DOCUMENTS

Guidance for and standardization of the planning, conduct, reporting, and follow-up of environmental audits is crucial to having a successful environmental auditing program. At PP&L, two documents supply guidance in this area. The first is a departmental procedure document which provides instructions for the preparation of all internal audit programs performed by the environmental audit section or other group, except where special procedures have been approved for major projects. The second document is the environmental quality assessment manual. This document states that it is the policy of PP&L to use the best-practicable pollution-abatement methods to comply with all federal, state, and local requirements relating to discharges into the air and water from PP&L and subsidiary facilities. This policy includes the review and reporting of the effectiveness of pollution-abatement efforts—a review done by personnel other than those responsible for the area being reviewed.

The environmental quality assessment manual applies to all company facilities: power production, bulk power and distribution, mines, pipelines, and service centers.

The following is a list of the procedures included in the environmental quality assessment manual (EQAM):

1. *Preparation and revision of environmental quality assessment procedures.* Describes the guidelines to be observed in the preparation and revision of environmental quality assessment (QA) procedures.
2. *Audit scheduling and planning.* Provides guidance and standardization for the scheduling and planning of audits.

3. *Auditor training and qualification.* Establishes the necessary requirements for qualifications and training of personnel performing activities within the environmental management division audit/ modeling section.

4. *Audit preparation.* Provides guidance and requirements which are to be met when preparing for an audit.

5. *Audit performance.* Provides guidelines which are to be observed in the performance of an environmental audit.

6. *Audit report preparation.* Provides guidance and standardization for preparation of environmental audit reports.

7. *Reporting of deficiencies.* Provides guidance and standardization for documenting and/or reporting deficiencies.

8. *Corrective action.* Establishes a method for correcting problems detected during an environmental audit, while ensuring that corrective measures not only will resolve the original problem but also will provide a basis for preventing its recurrence.

9. *Record retention.* Defines requirements and responsibilities for the classification, storage, maintenance, and disposition of the auditing section's environmental-quality-assessment records.

10. *Performance measurement.* An important part of any program to ensure that it remains effective and efficient and responds to the purpose for which it was designed; establishes and maintains a feedback mechanism with which to meet these objectives.

THE AUDIT PROCESS

Environmental assessment is a process for reviewing facility operations and practices to determine compliance with all relevant environmental laws, regulations, and company policies. The eleven-step process for performing environmental audits at PP&L is described in the following sections.

Preparation

The preparation portion of the process is the most time-consuming, entailing lengthy review of information pertinent to the facility being audited. However, the lead time for preparation is always much greater for the first audit and decreases as proficiency in the audited area is acquired.

As an example of the type of preparation work necessary for a typical power plant audit, the following information would be reviewed: federal regulations (such as the NPDES regulations and the oil pollution prevention regulations); state regulations (such as those pertaining to erosion control and air pollution); plant procedures (such as those for controlling and analyzing fugitive dust); and past audit reports.

After all this information is reviewed, checklists are prepared for each regulation and, in some cases, for each section of the regulation. The questions are specific and are for our own use. They ensure that we are both auditing all the necessary areas and using the correct regulatory requirements.

Audit Notification

The initial notification of upcoming audits is made at least 30 days in advance. This notification includes the audit dates, which we try to keep flexible and arrange ahead of time with the auditees; the controlling documents; the names of the auditors, indicating the lead auditor, who is responsible for setting up and coordinating the audit, writing the audit report, and following up on the reply; the audit scope, which is a very general description of what the audit team will be looking at; and finally, the time and place of a preaudit meeting.

Detailed Schedule

The detailed schedule is sent out 2 weeks prior to the audit. It also allows for flexibility. The times are so arranged that if changes are necessary, the audit can still be completed on schedule.

Audit

The actual audit generally takes 2 to 3 days. An audit consists of a preaudit meeting and exit interview along with the audit itself. The *preaudit meeting* is where the detailed schedule is reviewed with the appropriate personnel to determine whether any conflicts exist. The areas to be audited are explained, as well as the governing regulations and any special monitoring or sampling which will be performed, and questions are fielded. The *exit interview* is where the findings of the audit are discussed. This is the first chance for management at the audited facility to correct any misunderstandings and comment on the audit.

We rely on the use of a camera during the audit to document our work. Photographs are taken of most of the areas that are audited, particularly any questionable or controversial areas. We also use a noise meter and take samples of various ponds or discharges to run a check on sampling and analysis procedures.

During the audit, the checklists are completed for each area. At the completion of the audit, forms detailing all findings are completed. These indicate the regulatory requirements, audit findings, and replies, when received. The checklists classify the findings in three main categories:

- "Significant findings" are those in direct violation of federal, state, or local regulations and require that corrective action be taken. Also, a reply must be sent from plant management to the environmental auditing section, indicating the corrective actions.

- "Noncompliance findings" are also in direct violation of a regulation but can no longer be corrected (e.g., a discharge sample not taken when required). These generally do not require that an answer be sent from plant management to the environmental auditing section; however, at the discretion of the environmental auditing supervisor, one can be requested (for example, if the problem is a recurrent one).

- "Notable findings" are matters which we feel should be mentioned and which may at some time present a problem.

Our audits are set up to find deficient areas but not to suggest solutions. We do, however, answer questions or provide help whenever asked.

Draft Audit Report

A draft report is written from checklists and lists of findings. The audit reports take a standard form as follows:

I. Executive summary. This is a general overall statement about the audit, such as the history of the audited facility and which areas are improving. This is also where we summarize the findings.

II. General. This section includes a general, overview statement along with a listing of the areas audited, indicating both the auditing group and the facility being audited and naming the audit team leader; giving the date, location, and participants in the exit interview; and defining the types of findings.

   A. Conduct of audit

   B. Scope of audit

   C. Audit participants

III. Audit results. Part III is subdivided into the areas audited, and then each area is again subdivided by type of finding, with the significant findings first. Also, a general statement about each area is made and any analysis results are recorded.

A. Air
   1. Regulatory: corrective
      a. Requirements
      b. Findings
   2. Regulatory: noncorrective
      a. Requirements
      b. Findings
   3. Nonregulatory
      a. Requirements
      b. Findings
B. Water, etc.

The drafts are then reviewed by the audit team members to assure continuity and proper interpretation and are sent to the persons actually involved in the audit. They are not sent to upper management. We usually allow 1 to 2 weeks for comments.

Auditee's Draft Report Review

After comments on the draft report are received (either verbally or in writing), a meeting is scheduled to go over the report with all those involved. Although not all comments or suggestions by the auditees create changes in the report, we take their comments seriously and make changes where appropriate.

Final Audit Report

The comments are incorporated into the report, and it is typed in final form. Photographs are attached, along with a copy of lab analyses, where applicable. The final report is then reviewed and signed both by the supervisor of environmental auditing and the audit team leader, and it is sent to the same people who received the initial correspondence.

A cover letter is sent along with the report explaining the format of the report and describing the procedure for replying. A preliminary corrective-action report is required within 30 days and follow-up reports every 60 days until all deficiencies are corrected.

Audit Reply

Generally the audit reply is received within the allotted time. If it is not, a telephone call is made to remind the auditees. Very rarely is anything else necessary on our part to expedite the reply.

Audit Reply Review

The audit reply is reviewed by the audit team members first and then with the supervisor of the auditing section. The reply is compared with the report to ensure that all the significant findings are answered, and then the solutions are reviewed.

Generally the reply is in order and the solutions suggested are viable. However, when a conflict occurs, either because a finding was not answered or the answer is not acceptable, a telephone call is made to the appropriate field personnel. The matter is discussed to try to resolve the problem as easily as possible. If an agreement cannot be reached, the auditor must weigh how serious the unanswered finding is. If the finding is serious or very controversial, it can be brought to the attention of the appropriate vice presidents or department heads, stressing the need for immediate resolution. If the finding is not so serious, the audit can be closed out by including a statement in the closeout letter indicating that the auditees should "be aware that they are in violation of a certain regulation and that their answer was not satisfactory."

Audit Closeout

The audit closeout is sent to the same people who received the report. This confirms that the reply has been reviewed and accepted (with any exceptions noted). Should there have been an unresolvable conflict, it would be mentioned in this letter for upper management's information. The closeout letter also indicates the schedule of our next audit.

Performance Measurement Program

After the audit is completed and closed out, questionnaires are sent to the auditees to determine their opinion of the effectiveness of the program and of the competence and professionalism of the auditors. This allows us to make changes in our program if necessary to make it more effective. The evaluation, covering the areas of personnel, procedures, and general overview, is as follows:

1. Personnel
   a. In general, did audit personnel appear to be adequately prepared for their audit assignments? If no, specify.
   b. If audit personnel appeared to be adequately prepared in general, were there any specific areas where preparation was lacking? If yes, specify.
   c. Did you feel the auditor's evaluation of your facility's conditions was fair? If no, specify.

2. Procedures

    a. Would you suggest any changes in the procedures used by the auditors during the audit? If yes, specify.

    b. Do you feel the audit was performed in a responsible and professional manner? If no, specify.

    c. Do you feel any changes should be made in the scope of the audit? If yes, specify.

    d. Do you feel the audit report in its present form is easy to read and understand? If no, how can it be improved?

    e. Do you feel the audit report fairly represented the conditions noted during the audit? If no, specify.

3. General

    a. After the environmental audit, were you more aware of the requirements imposed by environmental permits and regulations? Comment.

    b. Do you feel you are better prepared for an EPA/DER environmental audit? If no, specify.

    c. Are there any additional environmental areas that you feel should be audited? If yes, specify.

    d. Now that several audits have been performed on your facility, has your attitude toward the environmental audit changed? If yes, how?

    e. Do you look upon the audit as a service performed for your department or division?

    f. Are there any additional services the audit or auditors could provide as part of an audit that would benefit your facility? If yes, specify.

    g. We currently perform audits on a 2-year frequency. Do you think this frequency is adequate? If no, what frequency would you suggest?

INVOLVEMENT OF COUNSEL

One of the main purposes of the environmental audit is the gathering of information and discovering of potential problems so that these problems can be corrected. This may require fairly broad dissemination of the results of the audit, particularly on a plant or other level, so that those responsible for the operation in question can remedy improper situations. In addition, a public utility is subject to much closer scrutiny by regulatory agencies than many companies in the general business sphere. We all have various requirements in terms of compliance and reports to our respective public utility commissions.

Pennsylvania Power & Light Company prides itself on maintaining a close and careful relationship with the Pennsylvania Public Utility Commission and with other agencies—local, state, and federal—which have some degree of control over the company. It certainly does not help those relationships to attempt to keep the results of an environmental assessment from appropriate government agencies or officers and perhaps even get involved in a court battle over release of these documents. Therefore, a Pennsylvania Power & Light Company audit is generally not of the restrictive type that would be necessary to claim attorney-client privilege.

CONCLUSION

Environmental audits help ensure our company's compliance with environmental-quality standards by routine surveillance and periodic formal checks of all PP&L facilities. Each audit provides an up-to-date view of where our facilities need to be improved and what measures we are taking to improve them. Environmental issues raised by self-audit findings as well as day-to-day operating reports from each facility allow the company's management to focus time and resources on areas that require attention. Furthermore, broad-based problems at many plants or problems which persist over a period of several audits help managers to identify personnel and training needs. They also help provide justification for large expenditures for pollution-control devices.

The environmental audit is one way industry can take a leadership role in improving the environmental regulatory process. Audits can provide regulatory agencies with organized accounts of each facility's environmental compliance record. While differences in the interpretation of compliance standards may still occur, audits enhance communication between industry and regulatory agencies. But regulatory agencies should critically examine these self-auditing efforts in order to be completely assured that each voluntary program is performing according to corporate or regulatory guidelines. At PP&L, we believe that auditing ourselves to assure environmental compliance is not only socially responsible, it is also the best way of doing business.

Reporting Environmental Audit Findings

Maryanne DiBerto

Center for Environmental Assurance
Arthur D. Little, Inc.

The reporting of environmental audit results has long been a concern and dilemma for those with audit programs. It often is a painstaking process to provide for clear and appropriate disclosure without incurring additional risks and liabilities. Audit reporting continues to be an evolutionary process, even among those firms with long-established environmental auditing programs. The reasons for this evolution range from a desire to report audit findings more explicitly to changes in the report's format made necessary by the emergence of new regulations.

In the summer of 1982, we surveyed and compared the various ways in which environmental audit teams report, disseminate, and follow up on audit findings. Our survey focused on environmental audit groups at the corporate level within an organization.

While all the companies surveyed produce a formal written environmental audit report, the primary purpose of that report varies considerably. There are clear linkages, however, between each company's program objective and the purpose of its audit report.

The role of the legal department in the audit reporting process has also evolved over time. In many of the companies surveyed, the legal department had been significantly involved in the initial development of both the company's audit program and the overall process for audit reporting. In just over half of those surveyed, the legal department's role in the audit reporting process is now primarily one of commenting on the audit team's accuracy in interpreting regulations.

The distribution of the audit report varies among the companies surveyed. Almost 70 percent submit the audit report to top corporate management. In 38 percent of the companies, top corporate management is the primary addressee of the audit report. Just over half the companies surveyed also provide the audit report to the legal department.

Finally, we identified differences from company to company in report format, report length, and the timing and updating of follow-up procedures.

BACKGROUND

We interviewed thirteen companies about their environmental audit reporting process. These companies were selected because we felt that their programs reflected a diversity in the audit approach as well as in the reporting process. The corporations in this survey represented automotive, chemical, electronic, iron and steel, petroleum and natural gas, utility, and multiindustry companies. Many have operations overseas as well as in the United States, and their annual sales range from $900 million to more than $60 billion.

In examining the environmental audit reporting process, we interpreted the word "environment" broadly to include not only pollution control but also occupational health and safety and product safety. However, where audits of pollution control were separate from health and safety auditing within a corporation, we focused on the auditing programs for pollution-control activities.

We should acknowledge the variety of names used to describe similar programs. "Audit" is the most common, although "surveillance," "survey," "review," and "assessment" are also used. Some companies have deliberately chosen not to use the word "audit," sometimes at the request of the legal or financial staff. Others use "audit" precisely to lend credibility to their programs.

Participants in our study included several of the older, more established audit programs and those with extensive efforts in terms of number of audits conducted per year. For example, almost half the corporations in our survey have had an audit program in effect for 4 years or more; more than half conducted thirty or more audits during 1982. The size of the audit team and the duration of the audit varied with the size of the facility being audited. The length of the audits typically ranged from 2 to 5 days, although at two of the companies audits may take as long as 10 days. The audit team typically had three to five members.

Some companies maintained a full-time auditing staff; at others environmental auditing was only part of an individual's or department's overall responsibility. Whatever similarities or differences were found among those audit programs surveyed, a written audit report was central to each program, and this written report is the focal point of our survey.

FINDINGS

In the course of our study, a number of key steps emerged in the audit reporting process. Figure 1 schematically depicts these steps and identifies the approximate time at which each occurs after the audit has been completed. Although these steps differed in the timing and personnel involved in each, we found them to be generic among all the companies surveyed. This chapter further expands on the activities within each of these steps.

Purpose of the Report

In order to determine how audit findings are reported, we first focused on the report's purpose. While all the companies surveyed prepare a formal written report, the purpose of the report varies considerably. Some aim primarily to provide top management with information on the facility's compliance status, while others are trying to help the facility manager and initiate corrective action.

We found a strong linkage between the report's purpose and the overall audit program's objective. For example, where the primary objective of the audit program was to provide assurance to management, the purpose of the audit report was to provide top management with information on the more significant findings. Where the primary purpose of the audit program was to provide plant management with information on the environmental status of the facility, the purpose of the audit report was primarily to help the facility managers.

In addition to the reports issued for individual audits, we found several other reporting activities at different times and at various levels within each corporation. These reporting activities serve primarily to provide an overall status report of the audit program. The reporting ranges from monthly to yearly, at levels ranging from the board of directors to department heads.

Report Preparation

In most instances a written draft of the report is prepared by the audit team within 2 to 3 weeks of the audit. This draft report is reviewed

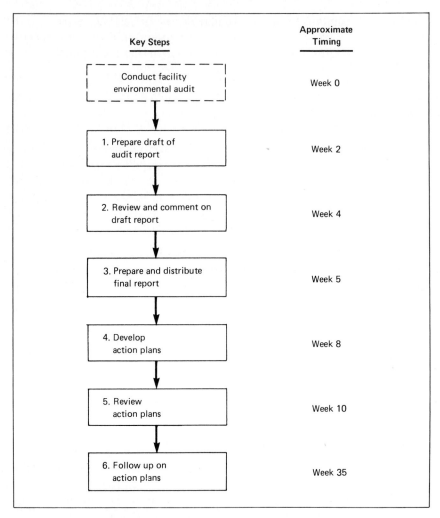

FIG. 1   Key steps in the environmental audit reporting process

before a final report is issued. Typically, the auditor maintains control over the content of the report during this review. The legal department is given an opportunity to comment on the draft report in just over half the companies surveyed. Comments by the legal department cover the report's accuracy in interpreting regulations and, in some instances, the wording of the audit findings. Two of the companies interviewed prepare their audit reports on site. In both these instances the legal department is involved as a member of the audit team.

Format and Content

We found a strong linkage between the format and content of the audit report and the report's primary addressee. In many programs whose primary purpose is to help the facility manager rather than provide assurances to upper management, the primary addressee of the audit report is, not surprisingly, the facility manager. In these situations, exceptions as well as recommendations and good practices are described in the report.

Given the audit program's overall purpose of helping the facility manager, these audits were almost always conducted by those directly involved in environmental management (e.g., corporate environmental staff, division environmental staff, environmental staff from other facilities). Thus the development of recommendations and/or action plans to correct identified deficiencies are not outside either the authority and responsibility of the auditors or the scope of the audit program.

On the other hand, where the primary purpose of the audit program is to provide assurance to upper management, some key differences were identified in the reporting process. Here, the report is often limited to a factual description of the findings and exceptions. Because of the focus on determining current environmental status and the frequent involvement of those independent of day-to-day environmental management (e.g., full-time auditors, environmental staff from other divisions or facilities, outside consultants, etc.), specific recommendations and action plans are often outside the scope of the audit report.

The reports of all those interviewed contain sections on compliance with regulations and compliance with corporate policies. In addition, some list the regulations applicable to the facility; some describe the facility and its compliance history; one includes questionnaires from the audit; and one identifies specific areas in which the facility can save money.

Table 1 presents four alternative report formats. These represent composite highlights of the reporting format of survey participants and are shown to illustrate the array of choices available.

The length of the audit report varies widely. Some reports ranged from six to ten pages, while others were twenty to thirty pages long. The lengthier reports contained an executive summary highlighting the major categories or findings of the report.

Our survey revealed a clear intention among those interviewed to make appropriate disclosure of the audit findings. In all instances the reporting describes specific findings rather than merely listing general topics. In many instances the findings include statements that qualify the facts reported. Examples of such qualifying statements include, "On the

TABLE 1 Alternative Audit Report Formats

Alternative 1	Alternative 2

I. Background
 	
  A. Purpose of audit
  B. Scope of audit
  C. Conduct of audit
  D. Audit participants
 	
II. Regulatory Compliance
 	
  A. Air
 	
    1. Findings
    2. Exceptions
    3. Recommendations
 	
  B. Water, etc.*
 	
III. Corporate Policy and Procedure Compliance
 	
  A. Air
 	
    1. Findings
    2. Exceptions
    3. Recommendations
 	
  B. Water, etc.*
 	
IV. General Observations
 	
  A. Items of potential concern
  B. Good practices of the facility
	I. Introduction
	
	  A. Purpose of audit
	  B. Scope of audit
	  C. Scope of report
	  D. History of plant
	
	II. Compliance Issues
	
	  A. Air
	
	    1. Regulatory compliance
	      a. Regulations applicable to facility
	      b. Findings
	      c. Exceptions
	
	    2. Corporate policy compliance
	      a. Policies applicable to facility
	      b. Findings
	      c. Exceptions
	
	  B. Water, etc.*
	
	III. Recommendations

Alternative 3	**Alternative 4**

I. Executive Summary
 	
II. General
 	
  A. Conduct of audit
  B. Scope of audit
  C. Audit participants
 	
III. Audit Results
 	
  A. Air
 	
    1. Regulatory: corrective
      a. Requirements
      b. Findings
 	
    2. Regulatory: noncorrective
      a. Requirements
      b. Findings
 	
    3. Nonregulatory
      a. Requirement
      b. Findings
 	
  B. Water, etc.*
	I. Background
	
	  A. Scope of audit
	  B. Conduct of audit
	  C. Audit participants
	
	II. Audit Questionnaires
	
	III. Audit Findings
	
	  A. Regulatory
	
	    1. Air
	    2. Water, etc.*
	
	  B. Corporate policies and procedures
	
	    1. Air
	    2. Water, etc.*
	
	IV. Action Items

*Additional sections, as appropriate, for solid waste, safety, health, and product safety, depending on the scope of the audit.

basis of our review we believe that . . ." or "We were unable to confirm that . . . ."

Report Distribution

Our survey revealed that the environmental audit report has relatively wide distribution in all but one company, in which only two copies of the report are distributed—to the facility manager and to the environmental director.

Almost 70 percent of the companies surveyed submit the audit report to top corporate management (e.g., president, executive vice president, or group vice president). Of the companies surveyed, 54 percent also distribute a copy of the final report to the legal department. However, none of the companies surveyed includes legal counsel as a primary addressee of the audit report. Thus the audit report appears to be prepared more as a management tool for enhancing environmental performance than as a legal device protected under attorney-client privilege.

Other recipients include the environmental functional area staff, plant engineering, manufacturing, and the audit team members. In all instances the facility manager receives the report, either as an addressee or as a copy recipient.

Report Response

We found a strong emphasis on formal audit report follow-up and, in general, a significant involvement by the audit director (or team leader) in the report response. Most of the companies surveyed have a formal procedure for responding to the audit report. The timing of the response varies from 15 to 60 days. All responses are prepared by the facility manager, and within most companies the audit director is the primary addressee of the audit response. In four of the five companies which do not require a formal response, action plans are either prepared on site by the audit team and facility manager or are incorporated as recommendations or specific action plans into the final audit report. In the four companies requiring no formal response, environmental affairs or line management—not the audit team—assumes responsibility for ensuring that corrective action is taken.

In all but three companies, the audit director routinely initiates a check on the status of the action plans. In some companies checks occur monthly, in others within 60 days, and in still others every 6 months. Three of the companies surveyed which have routine checks have a representative of the audit program return to the facility to follow up on action plans.

TABLE 2 Company Profiles

	Company A	Company B
Audit program objective	Verify practices are in compliance with regulations and corporate policies and systems are in place to ensure continued compliance; provide assurance to management.	Primarily to determine status of compliance with company policies and procedures and local, state, and federal environmental regulations.
Number of audits in 1982	Thirty-four.	Thirty.
Team size and audit duration	Four to six members; 2–5 days.	One to three members; 3 days.
Purpose of audit report	Provide information to top management on the more significant findings of the audit.	Notify line and corporate management of the status of facility's environmental compliance; help line management attain compliance; get line management in line with corporate philosophy and goals.
Report primary addressee	Division president.	Facility manager.
Report reviewer(s)	Legal, corporate environmental affairs, business area manager, facility manager, audit team.	Occasionally legal, primarily no reviewer.
Report preparation: Final report issued	One month after audit.	30 days after audit.
Length	Four to five pages.	Thirty pages.
Content	Purpose, scope, conduct of audit, exceptions.	Federal, state, and local requirements; exceptions; good practices; recommendations.
Report distribution	Division president, legal, corporate environmental affairs, business area manager, facility manager, audit team.	Group vice president, division head of audited group, section head of audited group, supervisor of audited group, department conducting audit, facility manager.
Report response	Written action plan within 2 months.	Required within 30 days; follow-up every 60 days until problems corrected.
Report retention	Formal policy: reports 10 years (or longer where subject to regulations).	Minimum of 3 years or longer as required by corporate policy.

Company C	Company D	Company E
Maintain compliance with federal, state, and local regulations.	Determine compliance with all governmental regulations, reporting requirements, and corporate policies and procedures.	Assure corporate management of facility's compliance with corporate policy.
Thirty-two.	Seventy.	Thirty-nine.
One to six members; 1–5 days.	Three members; 5 days.	Three members; 1–10 days.
Disseminate information about facility's compliance with regulations; document exceptions; report on facility's quality of management.	Report findings of audit; initiate corrective action; provide formal acceptance by operating management of the findings and start of corrective action.	Establish with corporate management that facility management and audit team have agreed on pollution control status of facility and the corrective actions to be taken.
Facility manager.	Vice president manufacturing, facility manager.	Manager, environmental engineering.
Environmental affairs, legal, audit director.	Chief internal auditor, legal, facility manager.	Facility management.
3 to 8 weeks after audit.	Within 1 month of audit.	On site.
Twelve to thirty pages.	Two to four pages.	Ten pages.
Exceptions, recommendations, summary of applicable regulations, detailed description of facility, good practices/violations/citations, cost-effective operations.	Findings of audit, recommendations, areas brought to management's attention, good practices.	Questionnaires from audit, listing of exceptions, action items (recommendations), good practices.
President, division management, legal, environmental affairs, facility manager.	Group president, division vice president, vice president manufacturing, legal, environmental affairs, facility manager.	Manager of environmental engineering; summary to group vice president.
Written response within 15 days; 6-month follow-up.	Written response within 60 days; repeat audits have statement in report concerning previous audit's recommendations.	Action plans prepared on site at the completion of audit; these plans checked monthly.
Reports kept until facility is reaudited (every 2 years).	10 years.	No established policy; everything pertaining to audit is retained.

TABLE 2 Company Profiles (*Continued*)

	Company F	Company G
Audit program objective	Provide corporate, division, and plant management the environmental status of each facility.	Obtain optimum performance of environmental control installations at facilities.
Number of audits in 1982	Seventy.	Twenty.
Typical team size and audit duration	Two to five members; 5 days.	Five members; 1–5 days.
Purpose of audit report	Advise management of the status of the facility.	Document the findings and recommendations of the audit team and have facility management correct deficiencies called to their attention.
Report primary addressee	Facility manager.	Facility manager.
Report reviewer(s)	Environmental affairs, legal, manufacturing, facility manager, audit director.	Vice president environment, legal, facility manager, audit team.
Report preparation: Final report issued	Within 2 months of audit.	Within 90 days of audit.
Typical length	Twenty pages.	Two to six pages.
Content	History of facility, exceptions, good practices.	Exceptions, recommendations, areas where facility can save money.
Report distribution	Legal, environmental affairs, manufacturing, facility manager, summary to division general manager.	Vice president operations, group vice president, legal, environmental affairs, facility manager, facility engineering, facility environmental engineering, audit team.
Report response	Written response within 30–60 days. 60-day follow-up to action plan on selected facilities.	Written response not required since agreement on corrective actions reached between audit team and facility manager before audit team leaves plant. Periodic checks with facility manager as well as yearly 1-day review at facility.
Retention policy	Reports retained until facility is reaudited; all reports kept on microfilm.	No policy; everything kept.

Company H	Company I	Company J
Make sure management systems are in place to ensure environmental compliance; help facility manager achieve fullest compliance.	Provide assistance to field people, substantiate compliance with regulations and policies, verify that adequate systems are in place, inform corporate management of status.	Provide facility management with environmental status of the facility.
Fifteen.	Approximately 175. (Corporate environmental staff participates in over half of the approximately 320 audits conducted by the operating divisions.)	Four.
Four members; 10 days.	Two to six members; 1–10 days.	Four members; 2–3 days.
Provide facility management with a snapshot of where plant is with regard to environmental regulations and policy.	Provide information to facility management on where they stand and what they should do; provide information to corporate management on status.	Help the facility manager—report is primarily for the benefit of the facility audited.
Facility manager.	Division president.	Facility manager.
Audit team, audit director, facility manager.	Legal, environmental affairs, facility manager, audit team.	No review.
On site.	Within 30 days of audit.	Within 4 weeks of audit.
Twenty-one pages.	Four to thirty pages.	Four to twelve pages.
Exceptions; good practices; recommendations on policy, regulations, operating procedures, training, emergencies, environmental protection information, maintenance, contractors, external communications.	Good practices, exceptions, recommendations.	Strengths of program, items needing immediate attention, items needing eventual attention, items needing further clarification/study.
Executive vice president, chairman environmental committee, division operating management, audit director, facility manager.	Division president, corporate environmental affairs, legal, facility manager, environmental file.	Two copies: director, environmental affairs and facility manager.
Written response within 45 days; 6-month follow-up on action plans.	Action plan requested within 30 days.	No formal response requested; corporate environmental affairs follows up within 6 months with written status report/visit.
Final reports retained indefinitely.	Seven years for report and action plan; "no conscious effort to destroy."	Until next audit; drafts and working papers destroyed when final report issued.

TABLE 2 Company Profiles (*Continued*)

	Company K	Company L
Audit program objective	Assure compliance and ensure that environmental risks are properly managed.	Assure compliance with federal, state, and local regulations and ensure that internal management systems are in place to assure compliance.
Number of audits in 1982	Five.	Four to five.
Typical team size and audit duration	Two to five members; 2–5 days.	Three to five members; 3–5 days.
Purpose of audit report	Inform appropriate levels of management of any problems the facility may have and to indicate what is being done to correct those problems.	Bring to facility's and management's attention areas of concern uncovered during audit.
Report primary addressee	Two audit reports: first addressed to facility manager, followed by second report addressed to president.	Division vice president.
Report reviewer(s)	Regional operations director, corporate environmental affairs.	Audit team, facility management.
Report preparation: Final report issued	Within 1 month of audit.	Within 6 weeks of audit.
Typical length	Two to three pages.	Six to ten pages.
Content	Statement of overall compliance status and management's ability to handle environmental risks; exceptions; action plans.	Purpose of the audit, exceptions, recommendations regarding environmental management and control systems.
Report distribution	Corporate environmental affairs, division operating management, legal, corporate environmental control manager, product standards director, audit director, facility manager.	Division vice president, vice president operations, general manager operations, line management, environmental manager, environmental affairs, facility manager, audit team.
Report response	No response required. Audit director follows up with a 6-month visit to facility and issues status report on findings and action plans.	Written report of plans in action prepared by facility within 3 months of audit report's issuance.
Retention policy	Retained for 2 years (until facility is reaudited).	No formal policy; all reports now retained.

Provide independent review of environmental programs and facilities and make recommendations for improvement.

Seventy-five.

One to five members; 1–3 days.

Provide an updated record of environmental program at facility and plan for future action.

Division general manager.

Facility management, audit team; legal.

Within 1–2 weeks of audit.

Three to twenty pages.

Facility background, team participants, permit status, analytic procedures and record keeping, problems identified, action plans.

Division general manager, corporate environmental affairs, facility management.

Action plans incorporated into audit report; periodic checks on these plans by division environmental staff.

Final reports maintained in divisional and corporate files consistent with corporate retention policies.

We found that in those companies where audits are repeated within a specified time, the auditor or audit director is directly involved in, and central to, action-plan follow-up; but where an audit team is unlikely to return to the facility for some time, operating management assumes responsibility for follow-up.

Report Retention

We found several retention policies for audit reports. Some companies have no formal policy and retain audit reports indefinitely. Others have a formal specific policy of retaining reports 7 to 10 years and even longer if required by federal regulations. Still others retain reports until the next audit at the facility (which in these cases ranged from 2 to 5 years). One company retains all audit reports and action plans on microfilm indefinitely.

Although the most common policy is to retain reports for a specified period, some survey participants expressed concern over destroying reports when the specified time came. For example, one company which retains reports until the facility is reaudited expressed concern over a possible lack of substantiating documentation if, for example, problems reappeared which had been thought to be corrected. Typically, retention policies were established to ensure that the reports were kept for a period consistent with their utility and to keep the records volume at a manageable level.

OUTLOOK

When asked about future changes in the reporting process, some of those interviewed indicated a desire to streamline their reports. Others stated a desire to standardize reports to ensure consistency in reporting and to facilitate report writing. Conversely, others were opposed to report standardization because it was too difficult to achieve and there were too many differences from facility to facility.

During this study we identified a variety of approaches to reporting audit findings. Whatever the approach used, however, the interviewees view the audit reporting process as still evolving. As the reporting process continues to evolve, the ultimate goal of clear and appropriate disclosure will continue to demand accurate communication of audit findings.

We anticipate that the reporting process will continue to improve and to be refined. We believe the audit report will become increasingly important to both facility and corporate management and therefore will become a more integral part of the corporation's environmental management and control system.

Table 2 provides profiles of those companies that participated in our survey. The companies we interviewed used a variety of terms to describe their programs—auditing, assessment, review, survey, surveillance. We use the generic term "auditing" to represent all of them, chiefly to protect the confidentiality of the respondents. Similarly, general terms have been used for organizational titles and departments within the companies. Collectively, they illustrate the variety of options in reporting audit results. Certainly there is no perfect method; each corporation has chosen its approach to reflect its own goals and objectives.

Alternative Approaches to Environmental Auditing

J. Ladd Greeno
Gilbert S. Hedstrom
Center for Environmental Assurance,
Arthur D. Little, Inc.

Anyone who has lived in Boston for any length of time knows that you can get on any street in downtown Boston, go in either direction, and end up at the Common. Surprising as this may sound to those unfamiliar with Boston geography, the downtown area is actually located on a peninsula, with the streets in a "hub-and-spoke" pattern. Many of the streets downtown follow the contour of Beacon Hill, thus beginning and ending at the Boston Common. So while the traveler may indeed be able to follow many different routes to the Common, some are long and circuitous while others are short and direct.

In much the same way, environmental managers looking for guidance as to how to design an environmental audit program are often somewhat overwhelmed by the many choices available and look for the most direct, logical route to follow. To provide a framework for examining these choices, we need first to examine the variety of forces that work to shape an environmental audit program and then explore some ways to sort out the many choices available.

FORCES THAT SHAPE AN ENVIRONMENTAL AUDIT PROGRAM

The ultimate shape of an individual audit program is determined by a wide variety of forces, which can be described in three broad categories. The first category, program objectives, refers to the goals or motivations behind the development of an environmental audit program. The second category, program characteristics, relates to how the overall program is designed, given the goals and objectives previously defined. The final category, audit methodology, includes the choices available in determining how to conduct the on-site audit. The key elements included in these three categories are discussed in some detail below.

Program Objectives

Companies undertake an environmental audit program for any of a variety of purposes. These program objectives often compete and conflict in terms of the role of the audit team, the audit methodology, and the type of audit reporting required. An audit program may have different purposes, all legitimate, but no company is likely to be able to devote the resources required to fulfill all, or even most, of them. Although most established audit programs have set forth, and often documented, objectives, they differ by the driving force behind the program, by the role the audit program plays and the corporation's overall approach to environmental management, by the degree of compliance verification, and by the level of involvement of different functions within the organization. Program objectives commonly found include:

- *Management assurance.* Assurance to top management and/or the board of directors that operations are consistent with good practice, that systems are in place and operating, and that legal and ethical responsibilities are being met. Providing management assurance usually requires a determination of the facility compliance status and an effective means of reporting this information to management.

- *Compliance assistance.* Helping local (facility) management to understand and interpret regulatory requirements, company policies and guidelines, and perhaps good practices; and helping to identify compliance problems and actions that should be taken. Compliance assistance tends to focus on identifying and correcting problems rather than on determining and reporting to management on compliance status.

- *Risk assessment.* Identification of conditions that may have an adverse impact on the company, assessment of the risks associated with the hazardous conditions identified, and determination of what actions are necessary to control these risks.

- *Optimization of resources.* Identification of current and anticipated costs, recommendations for reducing these costs, and identification of potential longer-term savings which can be accrued. Optimizing resources tends to focus on environmental cost savings and other economies available to the corporation.

Audit programs fitting any of the objectives described briefly above are most often conducted as an environmental management tool. Nevertheless, companies sometimes choose to shield the program under attorney-client privilege or work-product doctrine in order to attempt to keep the audit results confidential.

Some elements are common to all audit programs, regardless of the stated objective. For example, in each program the audit team conducts a field assessment, gathers information, analyzes the information, makes judgments about the status of the facility, and reports the results to some level of management. Yet with these similarities come a number of important differences. An audit program designed primarily to assist facility management is likely to have a significantly different character from one designed primarily to provide assurance to top management that facility operations are in compliance. In the first case the audit team may act as counselors or advisors providing staff assistance. As such, they typically say, "We're here to help you," and they behave that way. Their primary mission during the audit is to identify and correct (or at least take the initial steps toward correcting) problems. In the second case the auditors will probably act more as detectives. Here the primary purpose of the audit team is to determine and report on compliance status.

Frequently, companies want to accomplish all the goals listed above. The questions then become, How are the conflicting goals and objectives going to be attained, and what role should the audit program play? Whatever the primary objective of an environmental audit program, a number of questions emerge relating to program characteristics.

Program Characteristics

In designing an audit program to fulfill the goals and objectives that have been defined, those charged with developing or managing the program must make a number of program design choices. At this point it is important to distinguish between structural design elements relating to the environmental audit program and those relating to the approach, conduct, and methodology used for an individual audit. This section considers program design issues; issues relating to audit methodology are explored in the next section. The program design issues considered include organizational status, program boundaries, staffing, and confidentiality and reporting.

Organizational status

The organizational status of the environmental audit function is directly related to management goals and expectations. The audit function may report to the internal auditing department or to the corporate environmental affairs department. A company may choose the internal auditing department if it places a particularly strong emphasis on an independent view and established auditing techniques; if the emphasis is on the building and strengthening of the environmental management system, it will put the environmental auditing function in the corporate environmental affairs department.

The issue of objectivity is critical in selecting the organizational position of the audit program. There are often two conflicting goals: the desire to have the audit team fully objective and independent of the organizational setting that is being audited and the desire to have effective communication and efficient follow-up of audit findings.

If the decision is made to have the audit function housed in the environmental affairs department, additional choices must be made. Generally speaking, the environmental affairs function involves development of policies and guidelines and day-to-day management of environmental hazards. The questions become the following: Should auditing be a separate unit within the department, independent from the staff responsible for day-to-day environmental management and oversight? Or should auditing be one of several activities performed by the environmental staff? If the purpose of the program is to provide management with independent verification of compliance status and corresponding assurances, the first arrangement makes more sense. If the purpose of the program is to assist facility management, the second may be preferred.

Program boundaries

The boundaries of the environmental audit program need to be clearly defined in terms of what should be included within the scope of the audit and how much evidence is enough to fulfill program goals.

The scope of the audit program can be considered from organizational, geographical, locational, functional, and compliance perspectives. Organizational boundaries depend on corporate culture, business-unit reporting relationships, and organizational structure. Geographical boundaries relate to state or regional, national, or international scope. Locational boundaries refer to what is included in an audit (e.g., just what is within the plant boundaries or also off-site disposal sites, local residences, etc.). Functional boundaries relate to the specific environmental, health, or safety discipline being audited (e.g., pollution control, industrial hygiene, occupational safety, medical, product safety, or loss prevention). Compliance boundaries define the standards against which the facility is measured. These commonly include federal, state, and local laws and regulations and may or may not include corporate policies or "good environmental practices."

In determining how much evidence is enough to fulfill program goals, management must choose whether to include all facilities, all product lines at a given facility, and all environmental areas (air, water, solid waste, etc.). In addition, each company must decide how often and in what level of detail each facility is to be audited. These decisions must be made in the context of environmental risk, in which those charged with program design recognize that material harm can be caused by a single permutation of the facility operation.

Arriving at the optimal boundaries for an environmental auditing program can be a long and complicated process, because management generally would like to see more items included in the program than available resources will allow. For example, a company may have enough resources to conduct a detailed audit of the air, water, and hazardous-waste activities within the physical boundaries of twenty facilities per year, yet there may be important reasons to want to include other functional areas, such as occupational health and safety, and to extend the audit beyond the plant boundaries to include transportation activities, off-site manufacturers, and old dump sites. Decisions must be made regarding the activities which must be included within the scope of the audit program.

Staffing

In deciding how to staff the environmental audit program, management is often faced with a dilemma. From the perspective of objectivity, the most credible auditors are often the least desirable to management (e.g., outside consultant, lawyer) while the most desirable are often the least credible (e.g., the manager of the audited plant). Finding the appropriate mix of technical expertise, regulatory expertise, plant experience, audit-technique expertise, and independence is a challenging process for each organization setting up an audit program. Possible audit team members might include environmental specialists, plant managers, process engineers, lawyers, analytical chemists, internal auditors, outside consultants, and toxicologists.

It is important to select team members who bring appropriate training and experience to bear on the specific facility being audited. Most (if not all) environmental audit teams have expertise in technical areas, knowledge of environmental regulations, and plant experience. Nevertheless, programs differ in staff-selection methods, team size, degree of independence, use of internal vs. external resources, and auditing expertise.

The critical staffing choices that must be made relate directly to the program goals. If independence is a crucial aspect of the program, the choices might include using team members who bear no organizational relationship to the facility being audited, using an outside consultant as a member of the audit team, or having the team leader (if not the entire team) represent an independent activity, such as internal auditing. If an important aspect of the program is to educate middle management in the intricacies of environmental management, rotation of the team members can be built into the staffing formula. Likewise, the desire for audit-to-audit consistency must be balanced with available resources in deciding whether to have part-time or full-time auditors. This final choice often depends at least in part upon the size of the company and the number of audits to be conducted.

Confidentiality and reporting

Audit reports provide appropriate linkages for audit findings and observations, so that management can determine what, if any, actions are required. Within this broad objective, the report purpose is to provide management information, initiate corrective action, and provide documentary evidence.

An important consideration in audit program design is how to address the legal issues involved with documented audit findings. An adverse report which has been buried in the files and not otherwise acted upon constitutes what is commonly known as the "smoking gun." Companies differ in how they decide to manage the smoking-gun risk, even if their program objectives are similar. All companies believe that appropriate and timely follow-up of identified deficiencies is paramount. Some handle this by issuing enough copies of the report to facilitate the follow-up process; others insist, in the interest of confidentiality, that only one or two copies be prepared and all working papers be destroyed.

In balancing the risks and opportunities associated with audit reporting, most companies have the overall goal of clear and appropriate disclosure. The report format and content depend on the varying needs of different parties. In addition, most, if not all, programs have clearly established reporting relationships, provide feedback to facility management at the conclusion of the audit, and have different levels of reporting, depending upon the severity of the problem. Companies differ in how high up in the organization the reports go, the content and specificity of the audit report, and the formality of response required.

Audit Methodology

After design decisions have been made about what to include in the audit, who will conduct the audit, and where the audit results will be reported, the program designer can finally address the question, How are we going to conduct the audit? There is a temptation to conduct the audit before completely designing the audit program, particularly as more audit protocols, checklists, and guidelines become available.

Decisions about program boundaries, staffing, and reporting will clearly influence the audit design, but many options remain. Specific audit design choices relate to facility orientation, audit evidence, and documentation and reporting. The decisions made on these audit design options will markedly influence the content and quality of the audit.

Facility orientation

In responding to the question, How are we going to conduct the audit? the team leader's initial task is to gather the background information and perspective needed to develop an initial plan for gathering audit evidence. Developing an understanding of the facility processes, internal controls, and compliance parameters generally requires, as a first step, gathering information related to plant processes and products, applicable requirements, plant organization and responsibilities, and current and past problems. In gathering this information, most audit teams set aside time to review background information before beginning the formal part of the audit and have an introductory meeting with plant management.

While the general approach to orientation and familiarization is similar in most companies with established audit programs, the specific methods vary considerably. In some cases plant management provides information to the audit team leader in advance of the audit. In other cases the team leader makes an advance visit to the facility in order to collect necessary information. A third option is for the audit team to spend a portion of the initial day of the audit obtaining information from plant staff. Regardless of the way in which the audit team becomes familiar with the plant, the purpose of the initial audit plan is to guide the auditor through a series of activities so that the review is thorough and appropriate.

Facility orientation suggests also the need to develop an understanding of the facility's environmental processes, performance, management control systems, risk identification and evaluation process, staff, and organization. The audit team must be familiar with the systems in place before system effectiveness can be tested and verified.

In developing an understanding of internal controls, most companies with established audit programs interview facility staff and review a variety of documents. Despite these common activities, a variety of approaches to understanding internal controls are found. Choices must be made regarding the effort the audit team will devote to this step before proceeding to systems testing and verification. There is a natural tendency to form an opinion about the compliance status or the appropriateness of the management system before a complete understanding of the system is developed. A second choice relates to the extent to which this understanding is documented. Some companies choose not to document a description of the systems, while others devote considerable time to this task. Choices must also be made regarding the method used to document the auditors' understanding of internal controls. One option is to have detailed written descriptions in working papers; another is to develop diagrammatic descriptions or sketches.

Audit evidence

Audit evidence forms the basis on which the team determines compliance with present laws, regulations, and corporate policies, and it aids the team in assessing the plant's overall ability to deal with future environmental concerns. The first choice to be made in gathering audit evidence often is the following: Given what we know about the facility, where do we focus our resources? One approach is to formally assess the strengths and weaknesses of the management control systems. Here the auditor looks at the soundness of the system design and the effectiveness with which that design is implemented. The types of indicators of sound control that an auditor might look for include clearly defined responsibilities, capable personnel, documentation, and internal verification. However, many audit teams informally assess the strengths and weaknesses of the internal control systems as they gain an understanding of those systems. Within the typical time limits of an audit, it is difficult to "step back" from the plant operations and critically assess the strengths and weaknesses of the facility's approach to environmental compliance management.

In gathering evidence, most companies use some combination of formal checklists, guidelines, protocols or questionnaires, and informal discussions and observations. The purpose of the formal documents is to guide the auditor through the process of gathering evidence. The choices that must be made include the kinds of evidence needed, the amount of evidence to gather, and the role of the audit protocol or guide.

In response to the question, What kinds of audit evidence do we need? the answer involves an appropriate balance of inquiry, observation, and verification. Inquiry includes both formal and informal questions; observation includes a physical examination; and verification involves a wide variety of activities to increase confidence in audit evidence. While many audit programs focus on inquiry and observation, many of the more advanced programs focus on the overall management system (including management as well as engineered controls) and perform system tests (retracing data, verifying paper trails, etc.) to ascertain that the system performs as intended.

The choice of how much audit evidence is enough is faced by team members constantly during the audit. For example, if a team member reviewing temporary storage of hazardous-waste containers finds that four of the first ten containers looked at have storage dates more than 90 days old, should the auditor go ahead and look at all the remaining drums, or is the evidence from the admittedly small sample sufficient?

Companies differ as to the role of the audit protocol or guide. For example, one company may desire to have a protocol which lists all audit procedures which are appropriate, while a second company chooses to use the protocol as a general guideline for the audit team, to which items can be added as appropriate. Likewise, some companies use a questionnaire as the primary audit tool; it can include straight yes or no answers, short descriptions to support those answers, or even numerical ratings. Other companies use a questionnaire as a preliminary tool to develop an understanding of the procedures in place and use a protocol to guide the auditor through verification and testing.

Documentation and reporting

The final group of audit design choices relates to the documentation and reporting of audit findings. One issue is, How much detail does the audit team need to substantiate audit findings? Some programs require detailed, organized working papers which document the steps the auditor went through and the rationale for the conclusions reached. Other programs require simply a yes or no answer, perhaps with some limited explanation.

Near the completion of the audit, the team generally evaluates and integrates the audit findings and observations of each team member and determines their ultimate disposition. Depending on the goals of the program, some items may require reporting to corporate management and further follow-up; others may require only the attention of the plant manager. Most companies evaluate audit findings by having one or more team meetings during which each team member describes his or her observations. In addition, many companies have a closeout meeting with plant management to review the results of the audit before leaving the site.

Companies differ in their approach to summarizing audit findings. One example of an area in which choices must be made is what supporting examples to include in the summary document: Should all deficiencies noted be listed, or only examples of the type of deficiencies that relate to a specific aspect of the audit? Choices must also be made about reporting audit findings. Within the reporting framework designed for the audit program, the key mission for the audit team is to ensure clear and appropriate disclosure of all audit findings and observations. Choices must be made for each element of the audit regarding the extent of information and level of detail to be included in the audit documentation.

SORTING OUT THE CHOICES

It should be evident from this brief examination of the variety of forces that work to shape an environmental auditing program that there is no one best way to proceed. Environmental auditing is a new endeavor, for which generally accepted standards have not yet been developed. For a given corporation and its unique culture, many audit program designs are possible, differing in purpose, in approach, and in outcome. Yet from the diversity available, a pattern of sensible choices emerges, just as to the native Bostonian the logic behind the pattern of streets on the downtown peninsula emerges.

In developing a strategy for achieving management's expectations in the most efficient and effective manner, one must consider a number of important steps. First, it is critical to identify the primary concerns of top management and the specific role auditing should play in addressing those concerns. It is important to find answers to such questions as the following: What is management's view of the principal purpose of the program? To whom is the program ultimately responsible? What is the minimum acceptable output of the program?

A second step is to understand and pay attention to the context in which the program will operate. Should it operate as policeman or watchdog? Counselor or advisor? Troubleshooter? Detective? Pioneer? Clues for defining the context may come from the role of analogous staff units, from management attitudes regarding efforts that go beyond required compliance, and from the manner in which audit program performance is likely to be assessed.

Third, after identifying the primary concerns of top management and understanding the context within which the audit program will operate, the next step is to develop, review, or revise explicit program goals and objectives. These objectives should be as concrete as possible and should define what the program is to achieve over the long term (3 to 5 years), what the near-term objectives (12 to 18 months) are, and what the output of the individual audit should be.

The fourth step is to define linkages and overlapping responsibilities with other programs, to optimize the effectiveness of the audit program. The audit program will generally interact with other parts of the organization in data gathering, site selection, staffing, action planning and follow-up, and the dissemination of lessons learned.

The fifth step is to design the program in a way that responds to the established goals. When the relation of the audit program to other parts of the organization is defined, program characteristics and audit methodology can be developed that both fit the culture of the company and fulfill the program goals and objectives. In developing the program characteristics, it is important to pay attention to potential barriers to implementing or improving the program. Frequent communication with all appropriate levels of the organization can minimize these barriers.

In one sense, the development of an environmental auditing program is a process of trial and error in which you move forward by developing your own experience. Yet, while some stumbling and refocusing is inevitable, by paying close attention to management's expectations and alternative audit techniques, it is possible to sort through the seeming maze of choices to find the "shortest path to the Common."

Managing Environmental Data by Computer

William C. Hope

Sun Information Services

After a dozen years of the environmental movement in the United States, it is possible to say that few, if any, corporations are untouched by the thousands of regulations written during this period that govern the release of pollutants into the environment. So completely do these regulations permeate current business activity that no corporation can plan effectively without considering the cost of complying with them. Yet however great the cost of compliance, the cost of noncompliance can be even greater. Nothing can tarnish the image—and the balance sheet—of a corporation more than to be known as a polluter of the environment.

Consequently management frequently asks for reports on a corporation's compliance with environmental regulations. Compiling such a report can be a difficult if not impossible task, considering the amount of data collected for each facility within most companies and the number of reports already mandated by specific regulations. Those responsible for corporate environmental compliance need to get on top of this huge flow of information and stay there without being swamped by paperwork. As a result, many environmental managers are turning to computers to store the mountains of environmental data and to prepare environmental compliance reports for management and for federal and state agencies. Such environmental information management systems (IMS) also can be used to aid implementation of a company's environmental control program, store data, and print reports on everything from permit status to air and water emissions and waste disposal.

ENVIRONMENTAL INFORMATION MANAGEMENT SYSTEM

At the heart of the information management system is an environmental data base, a collection of both descriptive and routinely monitored data, from which reports are prepared. Descriptive data, which are usually static, can be used to describe a facility, a stack, or a water outfall. As an example, one could determine from descriptive data on a National Pollution Discharge Elimination System (NPDES) outfall that NPDES source number 001 is the plant wastewater discharge, using primary and secondary treatment prior to discharging into the Mississippi River. Monitored data, which change with time, are usually used to determine compliance with portions of the various regulations. Data collected from water outfalls, process stacks, and manifests are examples of monitored data. Throughout the IMS these two types of data work together to provide meaningful reports.

All data entered into the data base are associated with a facility (e.g., chemical plant, manufacturing plant). Each facility is associated with a division, which in turn relates to the corporation. This hierarchical structure allows for reports to be prepared for a single facility or to be summarized for a division.

An additional benefit from this data-base structure is that each facility can enter its own data (descriptive and monitored) and generate its own reports, with no impact on other facilities using the data base. Corporate environmental staff then can review environmental data from all facilities within the division or corporation.

The data base will consist of several files, each storing related data on a particular subject, much like a filing cabinet with several drawers for water data, air data, spills, etc. Each file will contain several data fields in which the actual data are entered, stored, and then reported from. As an example, in a file for environmental permits, a data field for "agency" would store the name of the agency that issued each permit.

This chapter describes several data files that should be included in an environmental IMS, along with the benefits that reports from each file can provide to environmental management.

TYPES OF DATA FILES

Environmental Permits

Several data fields can be established within this file to describe all environmental permits for a facility, e.g., operating and construction permits, NPDES permits, and Resource Conservation and Recovery Act (RCRA) permits. Information describing the permit as well as the issuing agency help to establish the permit file. See Table 1 for an expanded listing of the data fields for all files described in this chapter.

Reports generated from this file can be a valuable aid to management. An environmental manager who is responsible for hundreds of permits for several facilities can prepare a report each month listing all permits that will expire within 180 days (Table 2). This report is then mailed to all facilities as a reminder to renew any permits that will be expiring soon. Another report would list all water permits for the company (Table 3). If a particular facility does not appear on this report, the first question asked would be, Should they have a water permit? Bringing up this question may avoid a later compliance problem.

Water Data

Within this file all data collected from the laboratory on the water quality of NPDES and publicly owned treatment works (POTW) outfalls can be stored. Information describing the physical characteristics of the source as well as the monitored data for all parameters are stored in the water file.

Several reports can be prepared to indicate the compliance or non-compliance of each source for a facility. A comparison between the monitored data and the established permit limits (from the permit file) can provide a historical summary of the compliance status for each source (Table 4).

A second type of report available would analyze the water data for significant trends. Graphs of the monthly maximum, minimum, or average amount of any parameter can indicate upward or downward trends in the data (Figure 1). Yet another report that can be a real time saver is the discharge-monitoring report that must be submitted to state or federal agencies on a monthly or quarterly basis (Table 5).

Air Emissions

The air file can be subdivided into information on hydrocarbon storage tanks and data from boiler and heater stacks. If reports on the amount

TABLE 1 Data Fields for Selected Files

Permits	
Permit number	Date renewed
Permit name	NPDES source number
Type of permit (air, water, spill, waste)	Source name
Issuing agency	Parameter [biological oxygen demand
Agency contact, address, telephone	(BOD), chemical oxygen demand
number	(COD), etc.]
Date issued	Sample type and frequency
Date expired	Concentration and quantity limits

Water	
NPDES or POTW source number	Treatment (biological, primary)
Source name	Sample date
Source type (cooling water, wastewater)	Parameter tested
Receiving stream	Amount and units

Air	
Tanks:	Stacks:
Tank number	Stack number
Tank type (floating roof, fixed roof)	Stack type (boiled, heater)
Product stored	Stack height and diameter
Product vapor pressure	Air flow
Tank location	Exit gas temperature
Volume	Size (million Btu/h)
Diameter	Date monitored
Height	Fuel type and amount burned
Emission factors*	Sulfur content
Color	
Seal type	
Date constructed	

Solid waste	
Waste reference file:	Handler reference file:
Waste number	EPA identification number
DOT hazard class	Handler type (transporter, disposer)
EPA waste number	Company name, contact, address,
Waste name	telephone number
Waste type (hazardous, nonhazard-	State identification number
ous)	
Density	
Special handling methods	
Cleanup procedures	
Reportable quantity	

TABLE 1   Data Fields for Selected Files (*Continued*)

Manifest	
Manifest number	Waste amount and units
Date generated, transported, disposed	Number and type of containers
Date returned to generator	Generator, transporter, and disposer
Waste number	

PCB equipment	
Equipment number	Owner
Equipment type (transformer, capacitor)	Date installed and labeled
	Date removed from service
Volume	Date inspected
Concentration	Date disposed of
Location of equipment	Disposer

Environmental events	
Event number	Violation date
Event type (spill, inspection, etc.)	Amount spilled
Event date	Material spilled
Date resolved	Agency involved
Event cause and corrective action	Date fined and amount paid
Type of violation received (administrative order, notice of violation)	Comments

*Factors from *Compilation of Emission Factors*, 3d ed., U.S. Environmental Protection Agency, no. AP-42, August 1977, pp. 4.3-1 to 4.3-17.

of hydrocarbon emissions from storage tanks are expected, the data fields within the tank file must conform to the requirements from EPA publication AP-42 section 4. This document, which lists many emission factors for several industries, contains the formulas and tables needed to calculate emissions from storage tanks and, utilizing a second file for stacks, to calculate the five conventional pollutants [SO_2, oxides of nitrogen (NO_x), particulates, hydrocarbons, and CO] from boilers and heaters.

From the air data, reports can be generated that list descriptive features of tanks and stacks (Table 6). Many states require an annual report to be submitted listing all the information necessary to calculate emissions from stacks and tanks. Any reports from the air files should be formatted to satisfy the state requirements for emission data surveys.

Additional reports can be prepared that will calculate and summarize emissions from both storage tanks and stacks (Table 7). The air file and the associated reports will prove invaluable when negotiating permits for new construction.

TABLE 2 Permit Expiration Report

```
                        THE ABC CHEMICAL CO.
                         EXPIRATION REPORT
                             FOR SMI-1

              PERMITS WITH LESS THAN 180 DAYS UNTIL EXPIRATION
                          DATE: 01/08/82
```

FACILITY	PERMIT NUMBER	PERMIT TYPE	EFFECTIVE DATE	EXPIRATION DATE	REVISION DATE	DAYS UNTIL EXPIRATION
SMITHFIELD	PA-11096	SPCC	12/30/79	12/30/81	6/29/81	EXPIRED
SMITHFIELD	PA-2121	AIR	4/15/79	1/15/81	6/23/80	EXPIRED
SMITHFIELD	PA-224	AIR	5/17/80	1/01/81	2/01/81	EXPIRED
SMITHFIELD	PA-2289	WATER	4/23/79	1/23/81	6/23/80	EXPIRED
SMITHFIELD	PA-291	AIR	5/15/80	2/15/82	11/15/81	38
SMITHFIELD	PA-9898	AIR	12/14/79	12/24/81	6/16/81	EXPIRED

TABLE 3   Water Permit Report

```
                            THE ABC CHEMICAL CO.
                         WATER PERMITS FOR SMITHFIELD

                             DATE: 01/08/82


      FACILITY              PERMIT                               PERMIT
       NAME                 NUMBER        AGENCY                  NAME
      --------              ------        ------                  ------
      SMITHFIELD            PA-2289       STATE DEPT OF ENV RES.  NPDES
```

TABLE 4   Monthly Noncompliance Summary Report

```
                            THE ABC CHEMICAL CO.
                    MONTHLY NON-COMPLIANCE SUMMARY REPORT
                                 BY SOURCE
                                 FOR SMI-1
                           FROM 01/81 TO 7/81

                             DATE: 09/03/81
```

SOURCE	MONTH	1	2	3	4	5	6	7
001	MONTHLY EXCURSIONS	0	0	0	0	0	0	0
	DAILY EXCURSIONS	0	0	2	0	2	0	0
	NUMBER OF SAMPLES	12	12	12	12	15	12	12
	% DAILY EXCURSIONS	0	0	17	0	13	0	0
002	MONTHLY EXCURSIONS	0	0	0	0	0	0	0
	DAILY EXCURSIONS	5	3	4	4	2	2	4
	NUMBER OF SAMPLES	10	8	8	8	10	8	8
	% DAILY EXCURSIONS	50	38	50	50	20	25	50
003	MONTHLY EXCURSIONS	0	0	0	0	0	0	0
	DAILY EXCURSIONS	1	2	0	1	2	0	1
	NUMBER OF SAMPLES	10	8	8	8	10	8	8
	% DAILY EXCURSIONS	10	25	0	13	20	0	13

Solid and Hazardous Waste

Within the broad category of waste disposal, three files can be established. The first one stores information on all wastes generated by a company; the second contains a list of all waste transporters, disposers, and contractors used throughout the country. On-line access to these first two files can form the basis for decisions on emergency cleanup. As an example, if a truckload of hazardous waste is spilled in transport, an environmental manager would have instant access to special handling instructions for the waste, along with a list of all contractors and disposers used by the company in the state where the spill took place.

The third file is for data from manifests—the government-required documents that must accompany each shipment of hazardous waste

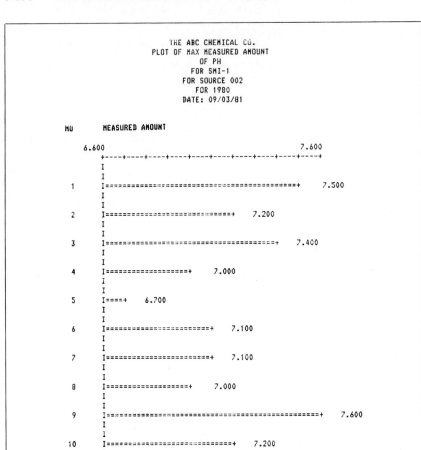

FIG. 1   Plot of maximum pH

from a generator's property. From the manifest, the dates, waste amounts, shippers, and disposers are entered into the manifest file. Waste shipments for on-site disposal should also be entered. From these data, reports can be generated to indicate which manifests have not been returned to the generator by the disposer and how many days have elapsed (Table 8). The RCRA requires that manifests be returned within 35 days. Another valuable report is a summation of the amount of each waste material sent to each treatment, storage, or disposal facility (Table 9). This report, previously required by RCRA, is now required by many states either quarterly or annually.

TABLE 5 Monitoring Report

```
                        THE ABC CHEMICAL CO.
                         MONITORING REPORT
                        BY MONTH FOR YEAR 1981

                         OUTFALL NUMBER: 100
                 TRMT PLT EFFL    TO: HOOK CREEK
                         DATE: 09/03/81
```

MONTH	PARAMETER	MAXIMUM VALUE	MINIMUM VALUE	AVERAGE VALUE	DAILY PERMIT EXCURSIONS	MONTHLY PERMIT EXCURSIONS	NO. TIMES SAMPLED
5	AMMONIA	3.000	1.800	2.360	0		5
	BOD	84.400	50.100	67.020	1	*	5
	CHROMIUM-T	.099	.082	.091	0		5
	CHROMIUM-6	.007	.003	.005	0		5
	OIL+GREASE	99.000	10.100	62.620	4	*	5
	PH	10.800	2.230	7.142	9		31
	PHENOL	8.300	1.900	5.240	5	*	5
	SULFIDE	.800	.300	.560	4	*	5
	TEMP-F	101.000	80.000	87.065	0		31
	TS-SOLIDS	195.000	121.000	163.600	2	*	5

TABLE 6 Stacks Descriptive Information Report

```
                      THE ABC CHEMCAL CO.

                STACKS DESCRIPTIVE INFORMATION

            FOR CHA-1       - CHARLESTON
```

STACK NUMBER	NAME	LOCATION	STACK HEIGHT (FT)	STACK VELOCITY (FT/MIN)	SIZE MILLION BTU/HR	TEMPERATURE (DEG F)
DESULF	DESULF HEATER	12 PLANT	80.0	1509	20.0	680
FC	FC HEATER	12 PLANT	175.0	1636	130.0	575
FF	FF HEATER	12 PLANT	80.0	2234	44.0	585
H-04	NO 04 HEATER	17 PLANT	90.0	1791	191.5	560
H-05	NO 05 HEATER	17 PLANT	90.0	1861	56.2	560
H-101	NO 101 HEATER	17 PLANT	102.0	1653	190.5	600
H-102	NO 102 HEATER	17 PLANT	102.0	1479	86.8	560
H-103	NO 103 HEATER	17 PLANT	71.0	1634	86.8	560
H-104	NO 104 HEATER	17 PLANT	91.0	975	20.8	560
H-3	NO 3 HEATER	17 PLANT	66.0	1719	38.2	600
HT-1	CRUDE H-1	8C PLANT	110.0	991	54.0	560
HT-2	VACUUM H-2	8C PLANT	110.0	902	37.8	540
HT-3	CRUDE H-3	8C PLANT	110.0	1734	25.6	560
HT-4	NO 4 HEATER	17 PLANT	66.0	1497	24.1	570
HY-1	HYDRO UNIT	8C PLANT	110.0	1614	26.1	999
LF	LF HEATER	12 PLANT	100.0	510	90.0	580
NIA	NIA HEATER	12 PLANT	88.0	717	39.6	635
NIB	NIB HEATER	12 PLANT	88.0	698	39.6	605
NO-1	NO 1 HEATER	12 PLANT	100.0	1261	43.2	535
NO-2	NO 2 HEATER	12 PLANT	100.0	1261	43.2	535
N2	N2 HEATER	12 PLANT	88.0	674	39.6	570
PIA	PIA HEATER	12 PLANT	67.0	839	12.0	580
RC	RC HEATER	12 PLANT	175.0	1547	153.0	625
RECY	RECYCLE	12 PLANT	175.0	971	120.0	410
VAC	VAC HEATER	12 PLANT	121.0	1008	56.0	625

TABLE 7   Monthly Stacks Emissions Report

THE ABC CHEMICAL CO.

MONTHLY STACKS EMISSIONS REPORT
FOR MONTH 1 1981
FOR CHARLESTON   ABC COMPANY

STACK GAS COMPONENTS ** BASED ON ACTUAL SULFUR **
(POUNDS/MONTH)

STACK NUMBER	NAME	FUEL	SO2	NO	CO	HC	TSP
HT-1	CRUDE H-1	RESID6	5,582.49	4,320.00	360.00	72.00	567.10
HT-2	VACUUM H-2	RESID6	5,428.26	4,200.00	350.00	70.00	551.40
HT-3	CRUDE H-3	RESID6	5,816.22	4,500.00	375.00	75.00	590.80
HY-1	HYDRO UNIT	RESID6	5,743.08	4,440.00	370.00	74.00	583.20
LF	LF HEATER	RESID6	5,197.71	4,020.00	335.00	67.00	527.90
NIB	NIB HEATER	RESID6	5,582.49	4,320.00	360.00	72.00	567.10
NO-1	NO 1 HEATER	RESID6	6,360.00	4,920.00	410.00	82.00	646.00
NO-2	NO 2 HEATER	RESID6	5,582.49	4,320.00	360.00	72.00	567.10
N2	N2 HEATER	RESID6	5,274.03	4,080.00	340.00	68.00	535.70
RECY	RECYCLE	RESID6	5,353.53	4,140.00	345.00	69.00	543.70

One large oil company found it difficult to monitor the waste-disposal practices for many remote facilities. Who transports our waste? Where is it disposed of? How much do we generate? Answers to these questions were available after all manifests were entered into an information management system.

PCB Equipment

This file is designed to store information and print reports on equipment contaminated with polychlorinated biphenyls (PCBs). Data are entered to create an inventory of all company-owned transformers, capacitors, and miscellaneous containers. Reports can then be prepared that list the status of each piece of equipment (in service, in storage, etc.). These reports should be designed to satisfy the requirement of the Toxic Substances Control Act (Table 10) for an annual report that summarizes the past year's activity concerning PCB-contaminated equipment.

TABLE 8 List of Manifests Not Returned

THE ABC CHEMICAL CO.

LIST OF MANIFESTS NOT RETURNED

SMITHFIELD ABC COMPANY

DATE: 09/03/81

MANIFEST NUMBER	WASTE DESCRIPTION	AMOUNT		CONTAINER		DATE TRANSPORTED	TRANSPORTER	DISPOSER	DAYS OUTSTANDING
8000	BUNDLE CLEANING SL.	11.0	G	2	D	8/01/81	COUNTY	CHEMDUMP	33
8001	LEADED TANK BOTTOMS	527.0	G	1	VT	8/03/81	MORTON	CHEMDUMP	31
8002	DAF FLOAT	796.6	G	1	VT	8/05/81	MARV	GREENFARM	29
8003	LEADED TANK BOTTOMS	527.0	G	1	VT	8/07/81	MORTON	CHEMDUMP	27
8004	CYANIDE WASTE	11.0	G	2	D	8/09/81	MORTON	CHEMDUMP	25
	POTASSIUM CYANIDE	16.5	G	3	D				
	PCB WASTE	5.5	G	1	D	8/09/81	MORTON	CHEMDUMP	25
8005	LEADED TANK BOTTOMS	527.0	G	1	VT	8/11/81	MARV	GREENFARM	23
8006	DAF FLOAT	768.7	G	1	VT	8/13/81	MORTON	CHEMDUMP	21
8007	CONTAMINATED DIRT	2.4	CY	1	ROC	8/15/81	MORTON	GREENFARM	19
8008	FILTER CAKE	1,578.9	P	1	ROC	8/17/81	MORTON	CHEMDUMP	17
8009	FILTER CAKE	1,538.7	P	1	ROC	8/19/81	MARV	CHEMDUMP	15
8010	FILTER CAKE	1,512.3	P	1	ROC	8/21/81	MORTON	CHEMDUMP	13

TABLE 9   Annual Waste Report

THE ABC CHEMICAL CO.

ANNUAL WASTE REPORT

FOR SMITHFIELD   - (PA9845948594498)

FROM MONTH 1 TO 12 IN 1981

DISPOSER CHEMDUMP   - (TX3540935965000)

DATE: 09/03/81

COMPANY WASTE NUMBER	COMPANY WASTE NAME	DOT CLASS	EPA ID	AMOUNT	UNITS LBS/TONS	NUMBER OF SHIPMENTS
CAKE	FILTER CAKE	09	D001	37,208.40	P	24
CS1	BUNDLE CLEANING SL.	08	K050	761.20	P	8
CYAN	CYANIDE WASTE	07	D089	596.31	P	5
DC11	POTASSIUM CYANIDE	02	P098	376.20	P	4
OS1	DAF FLOAT	08	K048	51,152.07	P	8
PCBX	PCB WASTE	09	1212	403.59	P	6
TB1	LEADED TANK BOTTOMS	08	K052	92,662.50	P	16
POSITION PAPER NOW						

Environmental Events

While the previously described files collect data for one specific regulatory area, the events file crosses essentially all regulations. Although the definition of an environmental event may vary in different companies, some common events are oil spills, hazardous-substance spills, water noncompliance, air violations, manifests outstanding, and inspections. For each event, the cause, corrective action, type of violation, and amount fined are entered. Data fields should also be provided for additional comments to be entered by facility employees. These data then create a kind of environmental diary for all events at a facility.

One large chemical company uses this file as a cornerstone for an annual environmental audit. By reviewing the frequency, cause, and corrective action for various events, a corporate environmental manager can identify facilities that represent an environmental liability to the company. As an example, if a report of all spills for a particular facility (Table 11) indicates many spills caused by faulty dock operations, this would indicate to a corporate manager the need to train dock operators on proper loading and unloading methods. Another valuable report would be a summation of the dollar value of all environmental fines paid (Table 12).

TABLE 10   Containers—In-Service Report

```
                              COMPANY TITLE

                      CONTAINERS--IN SERVICE REPORT
                             FOR CHICAGO

                           DATE: 01/08/82


PCB ITEM                          DATE    DATE                QUANTITY
NUMBER    TYPE         FORM       INSTALLED LABELED  LOCATION    KG
--------  ----         --------   --------- -------  --------  --------
DR-01     MISC. CONTAINERS  DIELECTRIC     1/30/78  1/23/81  MAINT ROOM      26.2
DR-02     MISC. CONTAINERS  DIELECTRIC     2/20/79  2/23/81  SWITCH RM       26.2
DR-03     MISC. CONTAINERS  DIELECTRIC     3/20/79  3/23/81  NO 5 SUBSTATION 15.7
DR-04     MISC. CONTAINERS  DIELECTRIC     4/10/78  4/10/81  DELAWARE AVENUE 20.9
DR-05     MISC. CONTAINERS  DIELECTRIC     1/18/80  5/23/81  FIN. PROD ROOM  26.2
DR-06     MISC. CONTAINERS  DIELECTRIC     2/18/80  1/23/81  FIN. PROD ROOM  26.2
DR-07     MISC. CONTAINERS  DRAINED FL     4/11/81  9/23/81  STORAGE AREA   157.2
DR-08     MISC. CONTAINERS  DRAINED FL     4/11/80  3/23/81  STORAGE AREA   262.0
DR-09     MISC. CONTAINERS  DIELECTRIC     1/12/78  1/12/81  NO 7 SUBSTATION 20.9
DR-10     MISC. CONTAINERS  DRAINED FLUID  2/12/78  5/12/81  NO 3 SUBSTATION 183.4
DR-11     MISC. CONTAINERS  DIELECTRIC     1/12/78   ----    12 PLANT OFF    513.4

*TOTAL CHICAGO
                                                                1278.3


   TOTAL                                                        1278.3



SUMMARY
-------
FOR CHICAGO
BARRELS.............. 0
DRUMS................ 0
MISC. CONTAINERS..... 11
ALL CONTAINERS....... 11

FOR COMPANY TITLE
BARRELS.............. 0
DRUMS................ 0
MISC. CONTAINERS..... 11
ALL CONTAINERS....... 11
```

Other files can be established to complete the environmental data base. Files for groundwater monitoring, fugitive emissions, and RCRA employee training will create an IMS that captures the greater part of the data used by both facility and corporate environmental employees.

MANAGING DATA

An environmental IMS cannot replace existing environmental auditing programs. The system allows those persons responsible for the audit to focus on the true environmental issues facing the company; time is not spent collecting and organizing data for an annual environmental re-

TABLE 11 Spill Report

```
                              THE ABC CHEMICAL CO.

                                 SPILL REPORT
                                 FOR YEAR 1981

                               DATE: 09/03/81


          EVENT EVENT                                                      VIOLATION FINED   PAID
FACILITY  NO.   DATE   MATERIAL SPILLED   AMOUNT  UNITS  AGENCY            TYPE    AMOUNT  AMOUNT
-------   ----- -----  ----------------   ------  -----  ------            ------  ------  ------
CHI-1     481  1/18/81 CRUDE OIL          150.0 BBLS     U.S. COAST GUARD  NOV     4000    4000
          1181 3/19/81 SOLVENT              6.0 G        ILLINOIS EPA      NOV        0       0
          1281 4/01/81 SULFURIC ACID       41.0 G        ILLINOIS EPA      NOV        0       0


TOTAL                                                                             4000    4000
-----


VIOLATION TYPES

AO=ADMINISTRATIVE ORDER
CIVIL=CIVIL ACTION
CRIMINAL=CRIMINAL ACTION
NOV=NOTICE OF VIOLATION
OTHER=OTHER
```

TABLE 12   Fines Report

```
                   THE ABC CHEMICAL CO.

                       FINES REPORT
                  SUMMARY OF FINES RECEIVED
                   FOR CHI-1       FACILITY
                 FROM MONTH 01 TO MONTH 6 1981

                       DATE: 09/03/81
```

EVENT TYPE	EVENT NO.	EVENT DESCRIPTION	EVENT DATE	AMOUNT FINED	AMOUNT PAID	DATE RESOLVED
NOCOM	781	SOURCE 001	2/14/81	25000	25000	2/14/81
SPILL	481	CRUDE OIL SPILL TANK 36	1/18/81	4000	4000	3/21/81
TOTAL				29000	29000	

```
-----
EVENT TYPES

AIRVIOL=AIR VIOLATIONS
EXPIRE=PERMIT EXPIRED
INSPECT=INSPECTION
MANOUT=MANIFESTS OUTSTANDING
MISC=MISCELLANEOUS EVENTS
NOCOM=NONCOMPLIANCE
```

port. Managers can review reports from all files and note any potential problem areas, which are then followed up with specific questions to local environmental employees.

The most widely recognized benefit of installing an IMS is the efficient storage and retrieval of myriad data; other benefits are a reduction of the time and cost of preparing regulatory reports and the ability to instantly access environmental data.

Computer systems similar to the one described in this chapter are available in one of two ways. The system can be designed and programmed using in-house resources. The overriding advantage of this approach is that the system will be custom-fitted to a company's needs. But, like the custom-tailored suit, it costs more and takes a long time to get. Estimated costs to develop in-house systems range from $250,000 to $1 million. The minimum time for completion and implementation is 18 months.

The other approach to obtaining an environmental IMS is to purchase or lease a software package. The system will cost less and be available almost instantly but will not be designed to exactly fit a company's needs. The following are critical questions to be answered when purchasing a software package: (1) Is it proven—has it been debugged? (2) How good is the documentation? (3) How will the package be supported?

Once the system is available, the initial data entries can require a significant amount of time. Depending on the amount of historical monitored data to be entered and the number of files used, the time required for start-up can vary from 6 weeks to 6 months. By collecting all the necessary data for one file at a time, a company can phase into the system at a manageable pace. Although the initial work can be a burden, system users can feel satisfied that the data, once entered, will always be instantly accessible in an organized format.

A NOTE
OF
CAUTION

Protecting the Confidentiality of Your Audit

Stuart E. Eizenstat
Robert E. Litan
Powell, Goldstein, Frazer & Murphy

The concepts discussed in this handbook are, with the exception of those reviewed in this chapter, applicable to environmental auditing generally. For purposes of this chapter, however, it is necessary to distinguish between two broad categories of environmental audits: those conducted pursuant to an Environmental Protection Agency (EPA) environmental audit program and those conducted by private parties on their own initiative. At this juncture, the EPA is considering the creation of a self-auditing program which almost certainly would require substantial disclosure of the results of each audit. Whether such a program will eventually be proposed and, if it is, whether it will be ultimately adopted are thus far unclear.

Regardless of how the EPA chooses to act in this area, certain firms may find it in their best interests to conduct regular environmental audits on a *voluntary* basis. Audits can be useful not only in minimizing enforcement difficulties with environmental authorities but in ascertaining, and then reducing, costs of complying with environmental standards. Corporations have little incentive, however, to conduct such audits unless they have reasonable assurance that the information generated during the course of the audit will be kept confidential and outside the reach of the legal discovery process; otherwise the information produced could damage sensitive business relationships, harm the company's competitive position, expose the firm to legal liability, and impair its public image. In short, the voluntary environmental audit is not likely to be a useful management tool or to lead to improvements in private-sector compliance efforts unless firms can be assured that their findings will be protected from ultimate disclosure.

This chapter discusses the two principal legal doctrines that are available for preserving the confidentiality of corporate information and preventing its discovery in subsequent litigation: (1) the attorney-client privilege and (2) the work-product doctrine.[1] On the basis of a review of the legal privileges in each of these areas, this chapter also attempts to develop a set of guidelines to assist corporate managers in protecting, to the maximum extent possible, the information generated during the course of an internal environmental audit.

THE ATTORNEY-CLIENT PRIVILEGE

The attorney-client privilege protects communications exchanged between lawyers and their clients in the course of representation from being revealed during discovery or at trial. Once established, the privilege is absolute, and no showing of need by the opposition will pierce it. It is vital to understand that neither the attorney-client privilege nor the work-product doctrine (discussed next) prevents parties to litigation from obtaining access to *primary* sources of information. A firm cannot shield itself behind the attorney-client privilege when asked about a fact that was communicated to counsel. It is only what is said to the lawyer, the communication itself, that is privileged.

As generally understood, the attorney-client privilege will be successful in cloaking certain corporate documents and materials with privilege where four critical elements are present:

1. The communication at issue must have been made during the course of or as part of advice given by an attorney acting in that capacity.[2]
2. The communication must be between attorney and client. As discussed below, exactly which persons in a corporation are considered to be clients has been a controversial and, until recently, an unsettled matter.
3. The communication must be made and treated in a confidential manner, that is, with regard for its confidentiality.[3]
4. The privilege itself can be waived through voluntary disclosure by the holder of the privilege, for example, if any person deemed to be

a client voluntarily testifies about a document for which the privilege is claimed. Some courts have held that waiver occurs even when the disclosure is inadvertent.[4]

Control Group Test

Although these principles are relatively straightforward, much controversy surrounded the scope of the privilege in the corporate context. In 1981, the Supreme Court settled an important and long-standing disagreement among lower courts concerning the application of the attorney-client privilege to different groups of individuals within a corporation. Up to that time, a number of courts restricted the privilege solely to communications between the lawyers for a corporation and that corporation's "control group"—individuals with sufficient authority to make decisions or changes on behalf of the corporation. This test proved difficult to apply, because the line between the control group and the rest of the corporation was naturally—and quite frequently—difficult to draw.

In *Upjohn v. United States*,[5] however, the Supreme Court specifically rejected the narrow control-group test, although it did not provide blanket protection under every circumstance for communications between any corporate employee and a lawyer. The *Upjohn* holding is of great significance in formulating confidentiality guidelines for environmental audits, not only because it represents the latest Supreme Court pronouncement on the scope of the attorney-client privilege, but also because the facts at issue in *Upjohn* bear a striking resemblance to situations typically presented by environmental audits.

In *Upjohn*, the dispute centered on an internal investigation pursued by outside counsel retained by the corporation's general counsel following consultation with the board of directors. As part of the investigation, counsel circulated a questionnaire among foreign managers. Subsequently, Upjohn voluntarily filed a report with various government agencies based on this investigation. The Internal Revenue Service then commenced an investigation which resulted in a summons demanding production of the questionnaires. The corporation resisted the move, asserting, as defenses, the attorney-client privilege and work product doctrine.

The lower courts ordered Upjohn to comply with the summons, on the ground that the employees who had responded to the questionnaire were outside the control group and therefore not clients whose communications would be protected by the privilege. The Supreme Court reversed. Specifically, the Court rejected outright the control-group test, with its narrow emphasis on rank and authority of corporate employees.

Instead, the Court focused on the particular procedure at issue and the nature of the communication involved in upholding Upjohn's claim to the privilege. Although the Court refused to announce a set of rules to govern the application of the privilege in future cases, it mentioned five specific attributes of the communcations elicited by the Upjohn questionnaire that were critical to its decision: the Upjohn communications were made:

1. By Upjohn employees to counsel for Upjohn acting as such
2. At the direction of corporate superiors
3. In order to secure legal advice from counsel
4. Concerning matters within the scope of the employee's duties
5. By employees who were sufficiently aware that they were being questioned so that the corporation could obtain legal advice

Since *Upjohn*, other courts have adhered to its case-by-case approach for determining the application of the attorney-client privilege in the corporate context. For example, in *Baxter Travenol Laboratories, Inc. v. Lemay*,[6] the federal court followed *Upjohn* closely because the operative factors in the two cases were virtually the same. Although the communications at issue in *Baxter* did not specifically concern matters within the scope of the employees' duties, the court upheld the privilege, reasoning that the *Upjohn* decision was intended to protect the *process* of communication, not merely a particular communicator or topic of communication. In a later case, a state court was presented with similar facts but utilized the *Upjohn* standards to arrive at an opposite result. In *Leer v. Chicago, M., St. P. and Pacific Ry.*,[7] the Minnesota Supreme Court decided that during the course of corporate investigations, communications to counsel by an employee who was a witness to an accident were not protected. The *Leer* court relied on *Upjohn* in holding that protected communications must be within the scope of the employee's duties.

A more recent decision in this area, *Consolidation Coal Company v. Bucyrus-Erie Company*,[8] however, departed somewhat from the *Upjohn* formula. In this case, the Supreme Court of Illinois retained the control group test—explicitly rejected by the *Upjohn* court—as a standard for measuring the application of the attorney-client privilege. The Illinois court reasoned that because *Upjohn* provided no specific standard to replace the control group test, it was compelled to continue to apply that test. Moreover, the court expanded the control group itself to include some employees who served in an advisory role to top management.

The Illinois Supreme Court's ruling in *Consolidation Coal* appears to be ill-founded. Firms interested in conducting environmental audits would be well advised to devise procedures to ensure that corporate communications adhere as closely as possible to the five factors specified in *Upjohn*, in order to maximize the legal protection accorded to information developed through their audits.

THE WORK-PRODUCT DOCTRINE

Corporate information may also be protected from disclosure under the work-product doctrine. First announced by the Supreme Court in *Hickman v. Taylor*[9] and included in the Federal Rules of Civil Procedure as Rule 26(b)(3), this doctrine provides qualified protection for the mental impressions, files, and memoranda prepared by or for a lawyer in "anticipation of litigation or for trial." The doctrine stems from the belief that a lawyer charged with the duty of protecting his clients' interests needs a "certain degree of privacy, free from unnecessary intrusion by opposing parties and their counsel."[10] It is important to note, however, that although the work-product doctrine may prevent access to documents maintained in *counsel's* files, it will not preclude access by the same party to *corporate* files in the course of normal litigation discovery to obtain the original documents.

More specifically, the protection afforded by the work-product doctrine is substantially more limited than that provided by the attorney-client privilege in two respects. First, the doctrine applies only to materials prepared "in anticipation of litigation." Second, the protection itself is qualified, since it may be overcome by a showing of "substantial need" of the materials and "undue hardship" in obtaining equivalent information from other sources.[11] Nevertheless, the doctrine may provide additional protection in certain cases—over and above that provided by the attorney-client privilege—when litigation is a distinct possibility, because it does not require communications to have been made solely between an attorney and his or her client.

The Effect of the Upjohn Decision

Indeed, the *Upjohn* decision, which addressed both the scope of the attorney-client privilege and the work-product doctrine, expanded the protection provided by the doctrine by restricting the scope of each of its two limitations. First, the Supreme Court addressed the government's argument that, whether or not the information at issue was prepared in anticipation of litigation, the government had made a showing of need sufficient to overcome the qualified protection. Although the Court did not decide precisely what degree of need an opposing party is required to show in order to overcome a party's claim to protection, it held that something more than a simple showing of substantial need or inability to obtain the equivalent material without undue hardship is necessary before a court will order otherwise-protected information to be disclosed.

The second expansive aspect of *Upjohn*'s work-product holding relates to the anticipation of litigation requirement. The fact that the Court upheld the application of the doctrine, even though there were no proceedings (actual, contemplated, or threatened) against Upjohn by the government when the materials in question were prepared, suggests that the Court construed the anticipation of litigation requirement very broadly. To the extent that the Court's view governs later situations, it would appear that a remote possibility of future litigation could be sufficient to accord work-product protection to certain material.

The mixed signals given by the lower courts on the scope of the anticipation of litigation requirement, however, suggest that some caution in this area is warranted. In *In re Grand Jury Investigation*,[12] the Third Circuit found the prospect of litigation in that case to be sufficiently real to mandate work-product protection for questionnaires and interview memoranda, since (1) the investigation concerned suspected criminal violations (and there was evidence that illicit payments had been made by corporate officers) and (2) the Securities and Exchange Commission had begun a number of actions for injunctions against companies that had allegedly engaged in transactions similar to those suspected by the SEC audit committee in the case. By contrast, the Fifth Circuit has held that materials generated by an attorney who prepared tax returns were not within the work-product doctrine simply because of the possibility that the IRS might challenge the return at a later date.[13] In that case, the IRS served an investigatory summons on an attorney, requiring him to produce documents and give testimony relating to his client's tax liability. The court concluded that while litigation need not necessarily be imminent, the motivating purpose behind the creation of the document must be to assist in possible litigation.

In sum, the outer limits of the work-product doctrine have yet to be defined. Nevertheless, the doctrine can help plug certain gaps in the protective shield provided by the attorney-client privilege. For example, the work-product doctrine may be of help in protecting documents and interviews conducted with persons outside the corporate structure, who ordinarily are not protected under the attorney-client privilege. Similarly, communications lacking some or all of the *Upjohn* factors required for the attorney-client privilege might nevertheless find protection under the work-product doctrine.

With respect to information developed in an environmental audit, the critical test will be whether legal action can reasonably be anticipated.

This will be clearest, of course, where enforcement has been threatened. Most courts should also find litigation to be anticipated where the company has previously been involved in similar enforcement proceedings or if the agency has a well-known record for taking enforcement action on the specific regulations with which the company must comply. Even if regulatory agencies such as EPA have not established enforcement records in particular areas, a good case can often be made that enforcement litigation is certainly possible—which may at least satisfy some (but certainly not all) courts under the broader standards of *Upjohn*.

MAINTAINING CONFIDENTIALITY OF INFORMATION DEVELOPED IN AN INTERNAL ENVIRONMENTAL AUDIT

Although no court decision has yet analyzed the confidentiality of an environmental audit, the foregoing legal principles that have been invoked to protect corporate information provide a useful framework for structuring an environmental audit in a manner that will maximize protection from disclosure of information generated during the course of the audit. Specifically, the attorney-client privilege and the work-product doctrine affect four critical aspects of the audit: (1) who should conduct it, (2) which materials will be protected from disclosure, (3) what steps must be taken to ensure confidentiality, and (4) which procedures will guard against waiver of any legal protection that may exist.

Who Should Conduct the Audit?

The fact that the attorney-client privilege and work-product doctrine grant special protection to communications made by and to attorneys dictates that environmental audits performed outside of an EPA-authorized program should be conducted through counsel. Courts have consistently concluded that if management conducts an internal corporate investigation, there is no basis for any claim of privilege or confidentiality.[14] Similarly, if a consultant or nonlegal independent contractor performs an internal investigation without supervision of counsel, the results will be subject to discovery.[15]

From the vantage point of the attorney-client privilege, protection is likely to be strongest where outside counsel is in charge of the investigation. Although participation of in-house counsel certainly offers a substantial degree of protection, there is always the risk that courts will view claims of privilege advanced from in house with suspicion. *Handgards Inc. v. Johnson*[16] expressed concern that otherwise the office of house counsel could "be converted into a privileged sanctuary for corporate records with relative ease."

There are practical reasons as well for appointing outside counsel to conduct the audit. Internal corporate investigations are often surrounded by controversy and suspicion and by their nature may give rise to some friction among employees, managers, directors, officers, and house counsel. An investigation conducted by house counsel may mar the amicable relationship between house counsel and line managers and corporate employees. This friction can be minimized if all corporate employees understand that the investigation is being directed from outside the corporation.

Whichever counsel is chosen to supervise the audit, a series of additional steps should be taken to safeguard the information that is subsequently generated.

First, a high-level executive within the corporation should direct that an audit be undertaken by counsel, acting in his legal capacity. There should be a written memorandum providing such direction, which should be carefully phrased so as to emphasize that the object of the investigation is to develop a factual foundation for obtaining legal advice.

Second, the memorandum should make clear that the information to be developed by the audit is confidential and should authorize counsel to take all reasonably necessary steps to ensure that confidentiality.

Third, the added protections of the work-product doctrine should be kept in mind by mentioning in the memorandum that litigation is anticipated and asserting the basis for that belief. In addition, the courts have repeatedly made clear that parties seeking discovery will have more difficulty in obtaining material reflecting the "mental impressions, conclusions, opinions or legal theories" of counsel[17] than in obtaining other documents and materials. It may therefore be desirable to conduct portions of the audit through oral interviews.[18] Work-product claims (in addition to any available under the attorney-client privilege) may be strengthened where the information acquired during the course of an audit is recorded in counsel's own notes rather than in material supplied directly by corporate employees.

Which Communications Will Be Protected?

Not all communications made during an audit by or through counsel may receive the same degree of protection from ultimate discovery. In particular, companies must be aware of differences in protection between information produced and communicated by corporate employees and by third parties.

Corporate employees

In rejecting the control-group test that formerly determined who was and was not covered under the attorney-client privilege, the *Upjohn* decision extended the protection of the privilege to potentially *any employee* of the corporation who possesses information necessary to the completion of an internal investigation such as an environmental audit. Nevertheless, corporations are advised to take certain steps to ensure that the communications of their employees to counsel will be covered under the privilege.

First, the memorandum directing counsel to conduct the audit should explicitly grant the counsel authority to obtain all necessary information related to the audit from any corporate employee—managerial or nonmanagerial. In addition, the resolution should authorize the use of outside consultants (discussed further below) where such assistance is deemed useful in collecting and analyzing relevant data.

Second, companies would profit from developing and adhering to a policy for situations in which, as part of or an outgrowth of the audit, corporate employees seek legal advice from counsel on behalf of the corporation. The employee in such a situation should advise counsel of the situation, identify the nature of the advice sought, and identify the employees who are privy to the information. Counsel should then make arrangements to secure the information directly. When an authorized employee has information which may be needed by counsel in order to advise the corporation, the employee should contact counsel directly. In that case, only counsel, and no other authorized employee, should be contacted; otherwise the attorney-client privilege may be jeopardized.

Outside parties

It is likely that in many cases the attorneys conducting the environmental audit will greatly benefit from the assistance of outside environmental experts and related support staff. Once counsel determines the need for outside experts, counsel should explain to all such experts that they are assisting in delivering legal advice to the company. This explanation can take the form of a memorandum from counsel outlining three points: (1) asking the expert to perform the necessary project, (2) advising that this project is necessary in order to provide legal advice for the company, and (3) requesting that the information gathered or studied by the experts should be maintained in confidence and disclosed only to counsel. If the assistance is to be rendered by a consultant, the above three factors should also be spelled out in the contract between the parties. Further, any information or correspondence regarding other nonconfidential parts of the agreement, such as billings, should be kept separate from the text of the confidential project.

Provided that the company is careful to adhere to the foregoing guidelines, the prospects are good that, as long as the activities of the consultant are supervised and directed by counsel, communications and information generated by such third parties will be brought within the scope of the privilege. Several appellate courts have, in fact, expanded the attorney-client privilege to include certain communications in addition to those between clients and counsel. In *United States v. Kovel*,[19] the court recognized that the privilege can attach to reports of third parties made at the request of the attorney or the client, where the purpose of the report is to put information obtained from the client in usable form. There, an accountant who worked for a law firm sat in on a client's conversation with attorneys to aid in preparation of the client's defense. When the accountant was subpoened by a grand jury to answer questions regarding the conversation, the trial court held that these communications came within the purview of the privilege and did not compel the accountant to answer; the role of the accountant was held analogous to that of a translator who puts the client's information into terms the attorney can use effectively.

This decision also sanctioned assistance by a lawyer's support staff, such as secretaries or legal assistants, as being made in furtherance of professional legal services and, consequently, within the privilege. Other cases have followed the same reasoning in other contexts, for example, by applying the privilege to a psychiatrist hired by the defense to aid in preparation of an insanity defense.[20]

At least one court, however, has recently declined to extend the privilege to that portion of a corporate internal investigation prepared by a third party. In *FTC v. TRW, Inc.*, cited above, the District of Columbia Circuit dismissed company arguments that the documents at issue were entitled to protection because the documents were prepared by a specialized consultant and that the purpose of the study was to put technical information into a form that lawyers could understand. Although the court acknowledged that there was a basis in law for protection granted to third parties performing such a role, it held that the burden of establishing the privilege is on the claimant and that the company had not met its burden. *FTC v. TRW* shows that a high standard of evidence may be required by some courts before the attorney-client privilege will be extended to include third parties.

The cases involving the assistance of third parties in the context of internal corporate investigations raise a tangential, but conceivably significant, set of issues related to the use of accountants. Although environmental audits are geared predominantly toward a company's compliance with existing regulations, a company may want to include as part of the audit an examination of certain accounting-related aspects of its compliance effort. For example, the company may desire to ascertain with greater specifity the cost of all or part of its existing compliance effort, that of an enhanced effort, and that which might be required if certain environmental rules were changed. Any or all such information could be useful to the company's internal management and to those in the company charged with responding to federal-agency rule-making initiatives.

To the extent that the generation of such accounting and financial data is deemed desirable, companies should be aware of the strong governmental policy fostering the disclosure of such reports and the federal courts' reluctance to find an "accountant-client" privilege. As early as 1971, the Securities and Exchange Commission issued rules requiring general disclosure of material information when future compliance with environmental regulations necessitates material capital outlays. These rules have been amended over the years to include more information and presently require disclosure of all costs of compliance with federal, state, and local environmental regulations in effect.[21]

Furthermore, at least one circuit has recently declined to extend any privilege to an accountant retained by an attorney in anticipation of potential litigation.[22] In that case, the court reasoned that the accountant's worksheets in question were based on business records that would probably have been discoverable, and that they neither embodied communications between the attorney and client nor contained the attorney's mental impressions. Although some states, such as Pennsylvania, statutorily provide for an accountant-client privilege, even this state-created privilege might not survive a challenge in federal court.

In short, the only method for acquiring protection for accounting-related aspects of an environmental audit, in the light of these federal court and government policies, is, following *Kovel*, to direct that the accountant perform only such tasks as will allow him or her to be characterized properly as a "translator" for counsel. Companies should, however, be mindful of the public policy favoring disclosure of such information and that, accordingly, financial information contained in or developed as part of the audit may be susceptible to disclosure through legal or regulatory channels.

Steps to Maintain Confidentiality

Even if the foregoing requisites for protection have been met, a corporation must take certain precautions to ensure that confidentiality of key documents and information is maintained; otherwise legal protection, particularly that afforded under the attorney-client privilege, will be lost. At a minimum, corporations should make every effort to adhere to the five factors outlined in *Upjohn* as critical to the claim of privilege. Beyond this, however, counsel should take steps to develop clear procedures and guidelines for maintaining confidentiality. For example, all communications to counsel related to the audit should be labeled "privileged and confidential" (as should those from counsel to client) and should be addressed to counsel in his or her legal capacity. Any claim to privilege will be further bolstered by keeping all such communications in separate and clearly marked files, segregated from information and documents routinely used in conducting day-to-day affairs of the company.

Guarding against Waiver of Legal Protection

Finally, whatever protection may be afforded by the attorney-client privilege will be deemed waived if the information covered by the privilege has been voluntarily disclosed by any person found to be a client or, potentially, any corporate employee under the expanded application of the *Upjohn* decision. To guard against such waivers—particularly inadvertent voluntary disclosures—counsel must take steps to ensure that only those corporate employees who must know the results of the audit are kept informed. While there may be no foolproof way to guard against inadvertent disclosure of critical information by those employees who must give—but not necessarily receive—information from counsel, the corporation can make clear to all its employees the importance of maintaining the confidentiality of information furnished during the course of the audit.

CONCLUSION

Although no case describes the precise circumstances under which an environmental audit will be protected, there is precedent for protecting intracorporate investigations under the attorney-client privilege and the work-product doctrine. On the basis of the Supreme Court's latest ruling in *Upjohn* and other recent court decisions, this chapter has outlined certain steps a corporation might take to maximize its protection from discovery of confidential information generated during the course of an audit, including:

- The appointment of outside counsel to manage the audit
- The preparation of a memorandum directing that an audit be conducted and describing the role of counsel, corporate employees, and outside consultants

- The establishment of procedures to ensure that confidentiality of information is maintained and that applicable legal protections are not waived

1. The Federal Rules of Civil Procedure accord qualified protection to "trade secrets" but require a party seeking such protection to move for a protective order that such information not be disclosed at all or be disclosed in a designated way (e.g., permitting inspection only by attorneys at court chambers), Fed. R. Civ. P. 26(b)(3). Courts have discretion as to whether to grant all or part of such a request, which must be balanced against the well-established judicial policy favoring disclosure. Another privilege which has been recognized by some courts as protecting internal corporate investigation is the "public interest privilege." This privilege rests on the theory that candid corporate self-evaluations are in the public interest and should therefore be encouraged by protecting all relevant documents. It has been applied in a number of different contexts, such as malpractice actions and private discrimination suits, but the case law is divided as to its application. The courts appear to be especially reluctant to apply the privilege where the documents in question have been sought by a governmental agency.

2. *United States v. United Shoe Machinery Corp.*, 89 F.Supp. 357, 358–60 (D. Mass. 1950).

3. *See*, e.g., *Diversified Industries, Inc. v. Meredith*, 572 F.2d 596 (8th Cir. 1978) (en banc).

4. *See*, e.g., *In re Grand Jury Investigation of Ocean Transportation*, 604 F.2d 674 (D.C. Cir.), *cert. denied*, 444 U.S. 915 (1979).

5. 449 U.S. 383 (1981).

6. 89 FRD 410 (S.D. Ohio 1981).

7. 303 N.W. 2d 305 (1981).

8. No. 54742 (Ill. Jan. 11, 1982).

9. 329 U.S. 495 (1947).

10. 329 U.S. at 510.

11. Fed. R. Civ. P. 26(b)(3).

12. 599 F. 2d 1224 (3d Cir. 1979).

13. *United States v. Davis*, 636 F.2d 1028 (5th Cir. 1981).

14. *In re Grand Jury Subpoena*, 599 F.2d 504 (2d Cir. 1979).

15. *United States v. Nobles*, 422 U.S. 225 (1975); *FTC v. TRW, Inc.*, 628 F.2d 207 (D.C. Cir. 1980).

16. 69 F.R.D. 451 (N.D. Cal. 1975).

17. Fed. R. Civ. P. 26(b)(3).

18. *See*, e.g., *Duplan Corp. v. Moulinage et Retorderie de Chavanoz*, 509 F.2d 730 (4th Cir. 1974), *cert. denied*, 420 U.S. 997 (1975); *In re Grand Jury Investigation, supra*.

19. 296 F.2d 918 (2d Cir. 1961).

20. *United States v. Alvarez*, 519 F.2d 1036 (3d Cir. 1975).

21. *In re U.S. Steel Corporation*, Securities Exchange Act Release No. 16223 (Sept. 27, 1979), reaffirmed the SEC's intent to enforce compliance with its rules requiring disclosure of material environmental information where regulatory compliance may require significant capital outlays or otherwise materially affect the corporation.

22. *In re Grand Jury Proceedings*, 658 F.2d 782 (10th Cir. 1981).

How to Size up Your Audit Program

J. Ladd Greeno
Gilbert S. Hedstrom

Center for Environmental Assurance
Arthur D. Little, Inc.

I n recent years there has been increased interest in corporate programs to monitor and audit the effectiveness of environmental, safety, and health activities at the plant level. To accomplish this, many corporations are embracing the concept of environmental auditing with considerable zeal. More and more companies have come to see audit programs as an excellent managerial tool to help keep abreast of the environmental compliance status and/or environmental performance at the plant level and to show "due diligence."

While many companies are conducting environmental audits, few seem to be approaching it in exactly the same way. Generally accepted environmental auditing principles, procedures, or standards simply do not exist, nor are they likely to exist for quite some time. Because environmental auditing is still in a relatively embryonic state, companies find it especially difficult to determine how far they should go in developing an audit program or even to judge how far they have gone. Thus, as more companies make a new and specific commitment to auditing their environmental status, it is only appropriate to ask what constitutes an effective and suitable audit program.

This chapter describes some benchmarks for reviewing and evaluating the design of an environmental audit program. While the fundamentals for designing and conducting an effective audit program are beginning to take shape, the options are, and are likely to remain, manifold.

PROGRAM GOALS AND OBJECTIVES

The audit program should have a clearly defined purpose and explicit objectives. Time and again, we have found a strong and obvious relationship between the clarity of program goals and the effectiveness of the audit program.

Not only must the audit team have a clear understanding of its expected role, but all the various constituencies of the audit program must understand the nature of the auditing effort. These constituencies typically include those members of management (and/or the board of directors) who receive program reports and corresponding assurances; the corporate and divisional environmental staff who have staff responsibilities for helping line management to meet desired levels of performance and correct deficiencies discovered in audits; and management of the audited facilities. These groups must have a shared understanding of the mission of the audit program.

In examining the effectiveness of your audit program, begin with an in-depth review and critical examination of the program's goals and objectives. Ask yourself the following four questions:

Has the nature or mission of the environmental auditing effort been defined explicitly, accurately, and realistically?

Just what is the auditing program aiming to accomplish? The objectives should be realistic, given the program's resources and the general state of the art of environmental auditing. To judge whether they are realistic, first develop as explicit a statement as possible of the desired outcomes of a specific audit and then ask yourself whether the audit, as now designed, consistently generates sufficient proof to support and document the achievement of the desired outcomes. For example, a program with the purpose of verifying compliance should, in fact, examine and verify the actual compliance status for enough situations to be representative of the time period under review. If the purpose of the audit is to verify the compliance status for the past 12 months, the audit must look at more than today's (or even this week's) compliance situation. Similarly, a program to examine environmental management systems should critically review those systems and not just the resulting compliance status.

Are the audit goals and objectives appropriate to the situation?

Explicit definition of goals and objectives is not sufficient; they must also be appropriate to the organizational context in which the program will operate. Being appropriate means that they take into consideration the needs and expectations of the board of directors and corporate officers; the corporation's culture, values, and norms and overall environmental management philosophy; and the general state of the art of environmental auditing. Each has important implications for a corporation's audit program.

Corporate management needs to be assured that environmental activities throughout the company are being conducted in accordance with applicable laws and regulations and corporate policies and guidelines. Management generally wants to hear "good news" in environmental areas, be aware of "bad news," and know that problems are being attended to at appropriate managerial levels. Finally, corporate management typically wants sufficient detail to ensure that it will not be caught uninformed or without adequate knowledge of real problems and the remedial actions undertaken to alleviate them.

Board members have the obligation, on behalf of the stockholders, to inquire about and receive information on the performance of the organization. They want answers to questions such as:

- Does our environmental management program compare favorably with other companies' programs?
- What standards are used in making this judgment?
- Do environmental matters have a material impact on the corporation?
- Are we in compliance with federal, state, and local laws and regulations?

Board members generally want assurances that environmental problems are adequately managed—i.e., they want a clean bill of health. If they cannot be so assured, they need to hear that management is addressing and resolving environmental problems in a way that benefits the corporation financially and in terms of public image. In evaluating your program's objectives, ask yourself to what extent the program fulfills the needs of corporate officers and board members. Is the primary thrust of the program in line with management expectations and needs?

Consideration of the corporation's culture, values, and norms and its overall environmental management philosophy is a second factor in determining whether the audit program goals are appropriate. In general, the overall thrust and character of the corporate environmental management system are highly influenced by the desires and needs of the board and the chief executive officer. The goals of the audit program should be congruent with and supportive of the overall environmental management approach. For example, in situations where the primary purpose of the corporate environmental management system is to anticipate and solve problems, the audit may focus on the process for identifying potential problems. However, in corporations where the overall environmental philosophy is to manage for compliance, the audit's objectives are likely to be tied more directly to a checklist of regulations and policies, focusing on verification of the compliance status in order to provide feedback to corporate management on the performance of the environmental compliance management system. In evaluating your audit-program goals, ask yourself to what extent environmental auditing supports overall corporate environmental management goals. Does the audit program do all that it should (or could) to support corporate environmental affairs goals? Is the audit program appropriate for this organization?

Unlike the first two elements of appropriateness, the general state of the art of environmental auditing is pretty much outside the control of any one corporation. Accordingly, you will also have to look outside your corporation in evaluating the appropriateness of your audit goals. What is the state of the art of environmental auditing? Does your program accomplish all that it might? (If not, are shortfalls the result of a conscious decision?) On the other hand, might the program promise or imply more than it can deliver (e.g., certification of compliance), given the current state of the art?

Have the program goals and objectives been communicated effectively to all concerned?

It is important for what is often a diverse group of individuals to have a common understanding of the nature and goals of the audit effort. Top management should be familiar with the capabilities and limitations of the audit program. Plant management should understand program goals well enough to ensure that the audits of their facilities present a fair and accurate picture of facility performance consistent with corporate goals. It is imperative that audit team members clearly understand both the program's overall mandate and their individual accountabilities.

A formal policy statement for the audit program is one means of minimizing ambiguity about the nature of the audit program. A policy statement approved at the proper level not only defines the activities of the program but also provides evidence of top management support.

Have audit accountabilities been clearly defined?

In addition to defining the program's purpose, it is also important to clearly define and delineate the various responsibilities and account-abilities for carrying out the audit program. Responsibilities for oversee-ing, supervising, and carrying out the audit program should be clearly defined and communicated to all concerned. (For example, the presi-dent, corporate counsel, environmental management, operating man-agement, and audit team members need to be informed.) Likewise, it is important to define and establish responsibilities for reporting, review-ing, and following up on audit findings.

AUDIT APPROACH AND METHODOLOGY

The term "environmental auditing" can be used to describe a wide range of environmental monitoring and review programs. Auditing, for some companies, refers to an *assessment* of, or expert opinion on, the presence or potential of environmental hazards and the effectiveness of control measures and management systems. Other companies may include a verification or testing component designed to determine or confirm that policies and procedures are being properly followed.

In evaluating the appropriateness of your approach to auditing, ask yourself the following two questions:

Do your audit procedures and techniques facilitate a review that is congruent with program goals and objectives?

Are there explicit instructions and procedures prescribing how the audit work is to be performed and its quality controlled? Audit protocols are one way of providing guidance to the audit team in its collection of evidence. Typically, the protocol is a written plan that includes a list of specific audit procedures to be used to gather evidence. In programs with ad hoc or rotating teams, as well as in larger programs where the size of the auditing staff makes if difficult to achieve consistency, the protocol, or formal audit guide, can be particularly useful in building consistency into the audit.

In order to consistently achieve audit results that meet management's expectations, audit protocols should not only outline the topics to be included in the review but also specify the nature of the examination and the depth of review that is desired for each topic. Environmental auditing protocols typically provide direction and guidance about the type and extent of inquiry, observation, and verification required. In larger programs, a comprehensive, up-to-date audit manual containing internal standards and procedures as well as overall program philosophy can be especially helpful in achieving the desired level of consistency.

Audit protocols should be kept up to date. They should reflect current audit techniques used in the audit program and relevant regulatory requirements as well as corporate guidelines that are to be considered in the audit. Formal audit protocols can be used to control and monitor the activities of the audit program. Work completed during each audit should reasonably correlate with the company's standard audit practices; all modifications or deviations from the company's standard practices should be so noted.

Is sufficient evidence generated and recorded during the audit to support findings in a manner consistent with program goals?

As discussed previously, the nature of the examination should match management's expectations for the audit. If management expects a verification of compliance status, the protocol should specify what steps constitute an appropriate review consistent with the objective. Similarly, if management desires a confirmation that corporate policies and procedures are adhered to and that management systems are in place and functioning to assure compliance, the audit must not only review the current compliance status but also critically examine the systems in place to manage compliance.

Sufficient evidence to support all audit findings or conclusions should be generated during the audit. Equally important, audit records should document the audit procedures followed, the verification tests performed, the information obtained, and the findings reported. Audit documentation should be designed to meet the particular circumstances and needs of the program. While the specific format, quantity, and content of the documentation may vary considerably according to program goals, the audit working papers should permit reasonable identification of the work done by the audit team.

To ensure that the evidence is collected and documented properly by team members, provision should be made for supervision and review of audit work by the person responsible for carrying out the audit program. In some cases this review may take on the flavor of a quality-assurance review. Both the audit team members and company management should have confidence that the audit is in fact accomplishing what it set out to do.

AUDIT TEAM STAFFING

The quality of the audit program is a direct result of the competence, training, expertise, and proficiency of the personnel assigned to conduct the audit. Here two questions are critical:

Is audit program staffing consistent with program goals?

Five aspects of audit-program staffing are important. First, what is the purpose of the audit? Who wants it conducted and why? What staffing requirements are implied by the goals and objectives of the audit? For example, verification of compliance requires a team that is knowledgeable in both compliance requirements and verification techniques.

Second, must any special staffing requirements be met because of program needs for reliability and credibility? To whom will the audit results be reported? The needs and expectations of the recipients of the audit report can provide important insights into staffing requirements. For example, reports that will be provided to (or discussed with) outside directors or others outside the corporate management structure may suggest greater need for independence in the audit staffing.

Third, is the audit staff large enough to provide the audit coverage desired by management? Program objectives calling for comprehensive audits of all facilities on a periodic basis will, of necessity, require substantially greater staffing resources than a program based on audits of a selected sample of facilities. Audit staff size is influenced by the total number of facilities within a corporation and the extent of audit coverage desired.

Fourth, staffing may have to take into account the program's needs for continuity and personnel commitment. Should assignment to the audit team be on a full-time basis, or is a part-time or collateral basis more suitable? Where strong audit-to-audit continuity and team commitment to the auditor's role are important, it is desirable to have as near a full-time assignment as possible.

Fifth, the staffing scheme should take into account not only the nature and importance of assigned responsibilities but also the degree of objectivity.

Lastly, environmental auditors should be free of organizational pressures or bias that may limit or otherwise affect their objectivity in conducting the audit, evaluating results, or reporting findings.

Does the audit team have the necessary training and experience needed to conduct the audit?

Audits should be performed by personnel with technical training and proficiency in auditing commensurate with the audit scope and complexity and the special nature of the facility to be audited. A dilemma in determining the appropriate balance of the team is that often the most credible auditors from the point of view of the board or the general public (outside consultants, corporate auditors, corporate lawyers, corporate environmental managers) are the least desired by facility management, and the most desired auditors from the point of view of the facility (plant staff or the plant manager) are the least credible to corporate management or the public. Ideally, the audit team would include experts in regulatory requirements, relevant environmental control technologies, manufacturing operations and processes, legal considerations, management systems, scientific disciplines needed to identify potential hazards, and state-of-the-art understanding of the environmental management practices of peer companies and facilities.

Clearly, no single person or even small group of persons is likely to satisfy all these needs. Moreover, the size of the environmental staff assigned to the audited facility or the number of facility staff knowledgeable about environmental aspects of the facility's activities may place an upper limit on the size of the audit team. An especially small facility staff may prevent effective utilization of a large team. Thus compromises are likely to be required in staffing the audit team. The exact number on the team should be consistent with the scope and desired depth of review of the audit.

The specific areas in which specialized expertise is needed will depend to a large extent on the charter or mission of the audit program. However, in addition to the various expertise and disciplines identified above, the audit team *must* have the appropriate audit training and competence to perform the audit required by the program objectives.

It is our experience that specialized training in auditing methods and techniques (such as methods of examining, questioning, evaluating, and documenting specific audit procedures) can be crucial. Such training is needed to ensure that the audit examination is both consistent with company objectives and in conformity with the state of the art of environmental auditing, so that audit resources are used in a manner that maximizes the effectiveness of the audit and the reliability of its findings.

The need for and value of expertise in auditing methods and procedures cannot be overemphasized. We have often observed that novices in auditing, as a result of lack of understanding of or unfamiliarity with audit procedures, fail to conduct a proper investigation in terms of their own program's goals and then issue a report of audit findings which is not fully supported by evidence developed during the audit. Nothing can be more destructive to the long-term health of the audit program than the generation of erroneous or otherwise misleading information.

REPORTING AUDIT FINDINGS AND RESULTS

Environmental auditing reports and records are designed to provide management with information about environmental compliance, initiate corrective actions, and document the results of the audit program. A number of potentially complex issues are involved in assessing whether reporting of individual audit findings and overall program performance are appropriate. They can be summed up in three questions:

Have formal reporting relationships between the audit program and various levels of management been established and specified?

It is important that the audit team, the audited organization, the environmental staff, legal counsel, and corporate management all have a clear and shared understanding of what is to be reported, when, to whom, and for what purpose(s); otherwise the audit program is seriously vulnerable to, above all, misunderstandings that can contribute to inappropriate action or to a lack of action.

One way to avoid this problem is to ensure that the appropriate detail is consistently reported throughout the management organization. For example, top management generally needs to know that the program is functioning in accordance with goals, plans, and budgets and to be aware of any findings which could have a material effect on the corporation. Operating management needs timely information on all substantive findings and exceptions, in order to ensure that deficiencies are corrected. Environmental management also needs to know of all substantive findings and exceptions, in order to both assist operating management in correcting specific deficiencies and incorporate the implications of audit findings in various policies, procedures, guidelines, and other communications or training activities. Managers and supervisors of the facility or other organization undergoing the audit want and need to know of *all* deficiencies as soon as they are identified. Additionally, they want to be assured that reporting to upper management will not unfairly reflect on their organization.

In evaluating your program's reporting relationships, also examine whether reporting responsibilities have been specified for audit findings that may require outside disclosure under one or more existing regulatory frameworks. In most cases, corporate counsel will play a major role in determining what, if anything, must be disclosed outside the corporation and how such a disclosure will be made. The audit program's external reporting relationships should be clearly specified and understood by all concerned.

Are audit reports timely and concise, and do they clearly and appropriately disclose audit findings to their addressees?

Each audit should result in a timely, concise, and understandable report. The audit report describes the audit scope, the general nature of the examination, the time period under review, the auditor(s) who conducted the audit, and the findings. We believe that the reporting format should focus on the facts and that, if any opinions or recommendations are to be included, they should be isolated and clearly identified as such. (The basic program goals should provide specific clues about the overall appropriateness of including audit opinions or recommendations in the formal report.) Such a separation of facts and recommendations can enhance the acceptability of the report and avoid confusion arising out of recommendations or opinions that are questioned, disputed, or flatly rejected.

We believe that the benefits of a consistently applied, standardized reporting format far outweigh the disadvantages. If your reporting formats vary from one audit to the next, ask yourself whether the changes and deviations contribute more than they detract from achievement of an understandable, concise report. Remember also that differences in wording and/or style may misleadingly indicate or subtly communicate unintended messages about the significance of one audit's findings relative to another's.

Lastly, one must consider the appropriateness of the reporting medium. Reporting of audit findings can be oral, written, or some combination of the two. Oral reporting does not raise the "smoking gun" paper-trail liability concerns that are often associated with written reports. However, in terms of documenting audit results, ensuring clear and concise communications, and providing a foundation for corrective action and follow-up, oral reporting can have serious shortcomings.

One benchmark for evaluating your current reporting approach is to ask whether other comparable (nonenvironmental) information is generally reported in a similar manner to management. If management is used to receiving detailed written reports on minor events and only oral reports on more serious situations, then such an approach may be highly appropriate. Conversely, if your management expects greater detail and documentation as the significance of a matter increases, substantive findings should be reported and documented in written reports.

Do audit findings receive appropriate consideration and follow-up?

It is not sufficient that audit findings result in a more accurate picture of the environmental status on the part of management. The identified deficiencies must receive prompt consideration, action planning, and follow-up. Procedures should be established to provide for regular reporting of audit findings, routine review of all audit reports, prompt corrective action in all situations where it is deemed appropriate, and appropriate steps taken to avoid any similar discrepancies elsewhere within the company. These procedures should be communicated to and understood by all those concerned with the audit and its follow-up.

THE REAL TEST IS IN THE RESULTS

The ultimate test of any environmental auditing program is not in the elegance of its design but in the results it produces. On the basis of the results of some of the more sophisticated environmental auditing programs, we believe that a soundly designed environmental auditing program, adequately staffed and effectively implemented, should result in (or at least help bring about):

- Environmental audits that produce an accurate understanding of the current environmental status of the plant, division, or company and clearly identify potential concerns within the scope of the audit
- Audit findings that are routinely reported to appropriate levels of management and that lead to timely correction of noted discrepancies and adoption of steps to avoid repeat or similar occurrences both at the audited facility and elsewhere within the corporation
- Audit results that are borne out over time, without subsequent discovery of significant "surprises" or recurring patterns of shortcomings in environmental performance
- Management recognition that environmental conditions are better known and understood as a result of the audit program
- Increased confidence by management that the environmental activities of the company are in good order

- An environmental audit program that has not only the support but also the confidence of top management

One final caution: This chapter has been prepared at a time when auditing standards and procedures are only beginning to emerge. As widely accepted environmental auditing standards come into being (and we believe that it is only a matter of time before they do), the ability to measure audit performance will sharpen and improve, as will the criteria against which environmental audits will be measured. This chapter basically serves as a first step in that measurement process rather than as the final examination.

The View From Washington

The Responsibility of Regulators

Karen Blumenfeld
Mark Haddad
Office of Policy and Resource Management
U.S. Environmental Protection Agency

E nvironmental auditing is a private-sector initiative that has potential benefits not only for industry but for the environment and government as well. This chapter describes the efforts of a federal regulatory body—the Environmental Protection Agency (EPA)—to stimulate environmental auditing and enhance its public benefits without bridling its effectiveness or private benefits. The term "environmental auditing" refers here to a set of methodological procedures used by a firm to verify its facilities' compliance with legal requirements and corporate policies and to correct problems that are found.

Two things need to be said at the outset about the development of EPA's response to environmental auditing. First, it is an iterative process. Even as this chapter is written, the agency's response is evolving to meet emerging concerns. Second, the process is unlike the traditional regulatory process. It is characterized by three attributes: (1) it involves no rule making and has no preconceived regulatory assumptions; (2) it encourages collaboration and is deliberately open to industry, environmental groups, and any other interested parties; and (3) it builds on corporate expertise and acknowledges "real world" operating experience. While it is not yet clear what EPA's ultimate response to environ-

This paper reflects only the views of the authors and not those of the U.S. Environmental Protection Agency or any other government agency.

mental auditing will be, a process is in place to develop and share information about auditing with industry and the public and to lay the groundwork for cooperation and innovative approaches to compliance.

The following sections cover the period from August 1981 to January 1983. The first explains why the government has a potential stake in the continued growth and spread of environmental auditing. The second discusses several responses to environmental auditing which the agency has considered and has attempted, in varying degrees, to implement. The third section summarizes some conclusions drawn from this experience that are potentially relevant not only to environmental auditing but to the development of regulatory alternatives in general.

WHY EPA IS INTERESTED IN ENVIRONMENTAL AUDITING

EPA is interested in environmental auditing because it seems to represent an unusual convergence of private and public interest. While environmental auditing is developing in large part for good business reasons—e.g., to assure corporate management that its facilities are in compliance with legal and company requirements, to assist facility managers in understanding and complying with those requirements, to avoid tort liability, to identify financial savings, and/or to improve the company's public image—it clearly can serve the public interest as well.

State and federal regulatory agencies face increasing strains which threaten to impair their ability to oversee compliance with environmental requirements. Budgets are being cut severely, and at the same time new regulatory programs for control of toxic substances and hazardous waste and the Superfund cleanup program create additional responsibilities. In the maturing air and water pollution-control programs, enforcement is becoming more complex as the focus shifts from assuring initial installation of pollution-control equipment to assuring compliance on an ongoing basis. Regulatory agencies are looking for novel approaches to fulfill their public mandates under the strain of fewer resources accompanied by more diverse and complex responsibilities.

One such approach would involve government stimulation of private-sector environmental auditing programs. While auditing programs do not obviate the need for government oversight, they can substantially enhance firms' environmental compliance and potentially supplement government enforcement. There are four reasons in particular why EPA believes it is important to encourage the spread of auditing.

Enhancement of Corporate Responsibility

First, EPA is interested in strengthening the internal systems that firms devise to ensure compliance with environmental regulations when the government is not around. Environmental auditing affirms a company's responsiveness to the existence of environmental regulations. By starting an auditing program, a firm takes a significant step away from a purely defensive, reactive posture toward regulation. It is a step that can enhance corporate environmental responsibility in two significant ways.

First, the existence of an audit program signals to the firm's staff that senior management is committed to complying with environmental regulations. Staff members know that the company's general counsel ordinarily would not permit a team to poke around company facilities looking for problems unless management were clearly committed to responding. In practice, this means that the identification of environmental problems may be encouraged rather than dampened by management. Second, an audit program strengthens the cadre of professionals within the organization who have a stake in the firm's environmental status and whose professional rewards are based on environmental performance rather than on production or financial outcomes alone. This is significant, because people—and the inherent limits of human wisdom and skills—may be as important to a firm's environmental performance as technology.

Auditing does not guarantee that a company will respond to every compliance problem identified. Even if a firm is aware of a problem, it may choose not to respond because it has other priorities, because the problem creates a low environmental risk, or because the risk of being caught or penalized appears small. But because auditing builds on internal systems, it can achieve what externally imposed regulation and enforcement cannot: it can institutionalize corporate responsibility by strengthening the internal procedures and incentives that promote compliance as part of normal business activity.

Day-to-Day Compliance

The second reason for EPA's interest in auditing is that it offers a way to address a long-term problem now facing EPA and state agencies: how to achieve and monitor day-to-day compliance with regulations with a lean budget, a small number of inspectors, and a desire to minimize the paperwork burden on industry.

In the 1970s, environmental enforcement consisted primarily of ensuring the initial installation of pollution-control equipment as mandated by the Clean Air Act and Clean Water Act. Initial compliance is no longer a sufficient measure of whether a company is meeting the goals of the air and water acts, however. Now that most of the mandated equipment is installed, federal and state agencies are growing increasingly concerned about the daily operation and maintenance of this equipment.[1] Since day-to-day compliance relies heavily on daily work practices and management procedures—which are difficult to verify through periodic conventional inspections—federal and/or state agencies may eventually need to develop new standards and inspection techniques to address the problems of day-to-day compliance.

One alternative or supplement to mandatory operating standards and permit programs could be to build on the existing in-house procedures that firms devise to assure corporate management that adequate compliance and risk-management procedures are being observed at operating facilities. Such an approach could capitalize on and reinforce operating expertise, rather than impose controls generated entirely by regulators. If firms with sound audit programs prove more apt to be in compliance over the long run than comparable firms lacking such programs, then such voluntary in-house management programs might be recognized as a legitimate alternative or supplement to emerging mandatory state or federal operating requirements.

Enforcement Targeting

The third reason for EPA's interest in environmental auditing grows out of the second. If the government were able to recognize auditing programs as a legitimate means of assuring compliance, substantial improvements could be made in enforcement targeting. The existence of sound audit programs could be used by regulators to differentiate more precisely and reliably than they now do between likely compliers and noncompliers. Regulators could thus target scarce enforcement resources where they are needed most, with some assurance that nontarget companies had adequate procedures in place to assure ongoing compliance.

From Confrontation to Cooperation with Responsible Firms

A strategy that acknowledges responsible firms' environmental performance has long-term potential for improving relations between government and industry. Reducing unnecessary public-private confrontation is the fourth reason for EPA's interest in environmental auditing.

Traditional adversary relations are not necessarily conducive to the achievement of regulatory objectives. In the regulation development process, for example, adversarial standoffs may produce rigid requirements that encourage segments of industry to comply with the letter rather than the spirit of the law and to delay compliance until the last possible moment.[2]

In the enforcement process too, traditional adversary relations can be damaging. Industry is not a monolith; some companies are clearly more environmentally responsible than others. An enforcement regime that punishes violations of the law but fails to acknowledge active corporate efforts to assure compliance may discourage some companies from undertaking environmental auditing, for fear that information developed routinely as part of an audit may be used against them.

One way to counteract this effect would be for the government to provide mechanisms that acknowledge the extra compliance efforts made by responsible firms. Such an approach could serve to reduce existing disincentives for firms to establish auditing programs, publicly acknowledge firms that voluntarily develop audit programs to assure compliance when the government is not around, and produce a more balanced agency posture in which enforcement success is defined not only as litigation and victory over recalcitrant noncompliers but also as acknowledgment and encouragement of affirmative environmental management.

Any approach involving cooperation with members of the regulated community, even with responsible firms, could be construed by some as EPA's "capture" by industry. Capture is not the only alternative to purely adversary relations, however. In concert with an effective program of regulatory development, oversight, and enforcement, there seems to be ample room for greater public and private cooperation in addressing problems with nonregulatory as well as regulatory solutions.

The development of private-sector environmental auditing presents government and industry with an unusual opportunity to work together to solve compliance problems of mutual interest. Two caveats should be noted here. First, this collaboration does not mean exclusion of the public and the environmental community. To the contrary, any collaboration between government and industry must include the public if it is to be viable and credible. Second, collaboration does not mean that a vigorous government enforcement program will become unnecessary. Indeed, EPA's aggressive enforcement of regulations in the 1970s probably contributed to the development of environmental auditing. A strong, continued enforcement presence can ensure not only that pressure is maintained on likely noncompliers but that responsible firms continue to be motivated to maintain rigorous internal audit programs.

EPA'S RESPONSES TO ENVIRONMENTAL AUDITING

Environmental auditing as a corporate initiative plainly has much to recommend it. As described in the previous section, there are a number of compelling reasons why EPA would want to promote it. When the agency first began to explore environmental auditing, however, it was not immediately apparent what, if any, response the agency should make. EPA could have chosen to do nothing. By late 1981, however, the agency decided to act, and several factors contributed to this decision.

First, as a response to regulation, environmental auditing represented a valuable tool for assuring ongoing compliance. The agency acknowledged that even an army of inspectors could not accomplish as much as a comprehensive internal compliance program regularly checked, or audited, by company personnel.

Another reason not to ignore private auditing was that its future was not necesarily assured. As the transition to the Reagan administration took place, considerable doubt was expressed in the business press and elsewhere about EPA's intention to develop and enforce environmental regulations. Industry's desire to retain or establish audit programs might decline if it perceived little immediate threat of government regulation or enforcement. A faltering economy added another reason for concern: as profits diminished, programs such as auditing, which do not contribute directly to production, were likely to receive more hostile corporate scrutiny. EPA support of environmental auditing might help bolster the position of audit managers within corporations and strengthen industry's perceptions about the long-range potential of environmental auditing to improve environmental management and compliance with legal requirements.

The Decision Not to Mandate Auditing

EPA initially considered a traditional regulatory path—requiring auditing. There was some precedent for this. The Nuclear Regulatory Commission requires nuclear power plants to meet a set of management and organization guidelines in order to obtain an operating license. Environmental auditing was stressed by the Securities and Exchange Commission in settlements with Occidental Petroleum Corporation, United States Steel Corporation, and Allied Corporation. EPA needed at least to consider this regulatory, or mandatory, approach, though it rejected mandatory environmental auditing for several reasons described below.

Limits of command and control

First, traditional command-and-control regulation is not always the most appropriate response to a given problem. The inherent limits of such regulation—its inflexibility with regard to specific firms and industries, the difficulty of developing uniform standards and regulations, and the need to back such regulations with credible enforcement procedures—were particularly constraining in the case of auditing, which focuses on management procedures rather than end-of-pipe compliance. Moreover, firms that did not have the management commitment to develop environmental audit procedures voluntarily seemed unlikely to establish meaningful, effective programs under compulsion.

Diversity

Second, the brief five or six years of private-sector auditing activity has spawned a wide variety of programs which would be difficult to regulate in a uniform way. The goals of these programs vary significantly. Some are designed specifically to reduce the risk of expensive and potentially embarrassing incidents such as major oil spills, hazardous-waste leaching, or visible and prolonged emissions violations. Others focus on ongoing regulatory compliance as well. Still others stress paperwork, using audits to verify the accuracy of all reports made to local, state, and federal officials.

The audit process varies, too. Some firms employ a central team of auditors, others staff the audit teams with a variety of company personnel. Frequency of plant visits varies, as do internal reporting procedures. Firms with more centralized philosophies usually give corporate management greater direct control over the audit than do firms with decentralized structures.

One attribute is common to all programs: each serves the interest of the company that has established it. Auditors and the corporate managers to whom they report appear zealously committed to their own programs. "This is the way we do it," said one audit manager. "It might not suit anybody else, but it suits us, and we don't want to change it."

Enforceability and legal questions

Any audit regulations would have to accommodate not only the inevitable diversity of corporate structures and management styles but also the need for enforceable requirements. It is one thing to require a company to perform a host of oversight activities; it is another to create a credible government system to monitor such oversight and detect and enforce violations of audit procedures. For companies to treat new audit requirements seriously, EPA would need to train regional and state inspectors in ways of "auditing the auditors."

Designing audit regulations that were conducive to EPA oversight but did not require extensive examination of company files, prolonged visits to company headquarters and plants, and additional company paperwork would be difficult. Moreover, given the shortage of state and federal inspectors, a new inspection and enforcement program might exacerbate the very manpower problems auditing was supposed to help solve. In addition to these challenges, it was not clear to what extent EPA had authority to regulate management practices under the enforcement provisions of its statutes.

The Voluntary-Incentives Approach

Instead of mandating auditing, EPA decided to explore whether EPA and the states could offer industry incentives to encourage the establishment and upgrading of internal environmental auditing programs. These incentives could be offered within a structured federal and state program, initially in one or two interested pilot states, on a voluntary basis. They could be available to interested firms with good compliance records who were committed to establishing and/or maintaining reliable audit programs. No company would be required to establish an audit program, but those which chose to participate and which met specified standards could qualify for certain incentives from EPA and participating states.

Through an incentives program, EPA and the states could recognize formally and publicly that environmental auditing programs were environmentally and socially responsible, could begin developing a compliance policy that used scarce enforcement resources more efficiently, and could encourage companies to take affirmative steps to ensure compliance instead of focusing exclusively on penalizing those found not to be in compliance.

This proposed incentives program was dubbed the "voluntary approach." It was based on EPA's recognition that (1) auditing had much to recommend it to industry even apart from any incentives EPA or states might offer; and (2) a voluntary program which provided modest acknowledgment for starting or upgrading audit programs could accelerate the spread of auditing and increase environmental benefits accordingly, at relatively little cost to EPA and participating industry.

The proposed incentives which EPA and interested states might provide included less frequent inspections, reduced reporting or record-keeping requirements, accelerated permit review and renewal, and waiver or suspension of penalties for reportable violations which the company had discovered and promptly reported and corrected. With these incentives would come general recognition (perhaps formalized with a certificate) that the company was an exemplary environmental actor. This could be valuable in demonstrating to senior management, the board of directors, stockholders, the general public, and possibly the courts the good-faith effort the company was making to comply with environmental requirements.

In return, the company would agree to establish and/or maintain an audit program which demonstrated top management support, an audit manager or team independent of production responsibilities, a structured program with written audit procedures, a system for reporting audit findings to senior management, and a corrective-action program. The acceptability of these elements would be judged by flexible evaluation criteria to be developed by the agency and states, with comment from industry and the public.

Implementation

In the proposed incentives program, EPA and one or two states interested in piloting the program, together with industry and environmental groups in those states, would draw up criteria for a company's eligibility and continued participation in the program. They would also agree on the incentives to be provided by the state and EPA to participating companies. Once the guidelines were established, a pilot program of 1 to 3 years would begin.

To participate in the program, a firm (in a pilot state) would indicate its interest by contacting the state environmental department. The state would review the company's compliance history and audit program. If the state approved, it would affirm the approval formally and adjust inspections, reporting requirements, and enforcement priorities accordingly. The firm's chief executive officer would be responsible for certifying to the state annually the continued existence of the audit program and any significant changes. The state would reserve its right to inspect the company's facilities and to take action, such as disqualification from the program or levying fines, if the results of an inspection so warranted.

Advantages

The chief advantage of the proposed incentives approach was that it would remove one of the major disincentives many companies see to instituting an audit program. A significant number of firms are reluctant to establish audit programs for fear of discovering and documenting compliance problems that were previously unidentified by EPA or the state. The government's policy toward firms that uncover evidence of their own noncompliance is unstated, but many fear it would be negative. The potentially perverse result is that the government's enforcement program could serve to discourage firms from doing the very housecleaning that would lead to improved environmental performance. A program of incentives, in which firms that audited their facilities ordinarily would not be penalized for the problems they uncovered as long as those problems were promptly reported (if required) and corrected, could help redress this.

The proposed program would also allow EPA and the states to shift scarce inspection and enforcement resources away from those plants and companies less apt to be in violation, while providing some assurance that as government surveillance decreased, ongoing auditing procedures were in place to oversee compliance. Meanwhile, those resources could be used to inspect target facilities more frequently and more thoroughly.

Such an incentives program might also accelerate the spread of auditing to companies which might otherwise not adopt or take longer to adopt auditing programs. It would bring to companies' attention an attainable standard of responsible compliance management, together with incentives to achieve it (and the prospect of perhaps greater surveillance if they did not).

Finally, by choosing to develop an internal audit program, a company would be able to take advantage of less intrusive and less adversarial relations with the government and also to help lay the groundwork for a solution to the problem of assuring day-to-day compliance which did not involve the development of new regulations or the hiring of new inspectors.

Results

The voluntary approach was discussed and debated at numerous informal sessions with EPA program and regional staffs and state environmental officials as well as in a variety of formal settings such as regulatory conferences and industry, trade association, chamber of commerce, and environmental group meetings.

The incentives approach elicited both enthusiasm and concern. It stimulated increased state and industry interest in auditing even as it became clear that the incentives approach itself was too ambitious to implement in the near term.

States to which the idea was presented initially reacted with some caution. Already strapped by constricting budgets and overextended staff, they were reluctant to pursue any new initiative which was outside the traditional regulatory framework. One state simply did not have the resources to commit to a nonregulatory initiative. Another was experimenting with a program in which operating permits would be written for individual plants, stipulating procedures which the permit holder had to follow to properly operate its plants' air-pollution control equipment. In effect, the state was planning to require procedures at the plant level that would achieve day-to-day compliance, although it would leave unaddressed the issue of how compliance with those procedures would be achieved or enforced.

Several states were interested in pursuing with EPA the possibilities of an incentives approach. They wanted to study further the types of auditing programs that had been developed in the private sector, the relation of auditing practices to ultimate compliance, and the advisability of offering incentives to industry to pursue auditing versus simply publicizing and encouraging the practice of auditing. EPA agreed to work with these states, at their request, as described in more detail later.

Environmental groups were primarily concerned with declining government attention to traditional enforcement. They did not object to EPA or states encouraging the practice of environmental auditing, but they did not want to endorse a program which could lead to a reduction in enforcement strength. They felt that before EPA or the states devoted attention to a program such as environmental auditing, existing enforcement should be buttressed.

Industry reaction was mixed. Many firms were willing to share information about their programs and to comment in detail on various informal agency proposals. Some applauded the initiative and volunteered to become pilot firms should a trial program materialize. But many were troubled by some or all of the following issues.

Those with well-established audit programs in place were invariably proud of and satisfied with their programs. They stressed repeatedly their belief that a company's audit program is inevitably tailored to fit that particular company. Participating in a federal and state auditing program might require adjusting their own procedures, which many firms were reluctant to do. Much of the debate, therefore, revolved around whether criteria for evaluating the acceptability of a firm's audit program could be made general enough to admit firms with highly effective though structurally diverse audit programs, yet specific enough to exclude companies whose programs were unlikely to be effective.

Some firms were skeptical about the very process of developing any criteria, no matter how general, for any government program, even if it was voluntary. These firms saw the development of criteria as the first step down a slippery slope that would ultimately lead to regulations mandating detailed management practices. To these firms, it was just a matter of time before the program became mandatory, rigid, and intrusive.

Some firms saw the incentives approach as a legitimate alternative to more traditional regulatory solutions to emerging compliance-assurance problems but were unenthusiastic about the incentives EPA proposed. For example, several argued that neither the public nor the government would find credible an enforcement program which waived inspections at certain facilities. Moreover, since inspections are already infrequent at most facilities, a reduction in frequency would have little meaning. Thus elimination of inspections was not a desirable incentive, and reduction of inspections was not a meaningful one. Other proposed incentives designed to reduce bureaucratic delay and red tape were not without interest to companies but seemed insufficient to galvanize active industry support.

A final concern which industry frequently expressed concerned the confidentiality of in-house audit reports. Environmental auditing can create a paper trail documenting a firm's awareness of its compliance problems. While such a paper trail may help a firm demonstrate to a judge due diligence in correcting these problems, it may also identify problems which would probably go undetected by the government and the public. Firms with audit programs were concerned that if the government or environmental groups chose to publicize and act on the audit findings, companies which had brought their own problems to light would be compromised, while their competitors who had not performed audits would escape adverse publicity.

EPA's proposed program never intended to require submission of companies' audit reports. What the confidentiality concern underscored, however, was the potentially perverse logic at the core of an enforcement regime that punishes violations of law but fails to acknowledge active corporate efforts to assure compliance. The agency's enforcement posture—largely through its silence on the issue—seemed to discourage some firms from taking the kind of positive action that would improve compliance. In this sense, the proposed incentives program could have been at least a partial solution to the confidentiality problem.

The incentives approach was abandoned by EPA partly as a response to the concerns expressed by states, environmental groups, and industry. These concerns had underscored the importance of addressing certain fundamental issues before structuring any government response to environmental auditing. For example, more information needed to be developed concerning how auditing programs worked in practice and how they ultimately contributed to a firm's compliance performance.

Beyond resolving these threshold policy and implementation issues,

EPA would have to find better ways of expressing its ideas to industry and the public. To make a voluntary, structured approach attractive to industry, EPA and the states would need to provide more information and more certainty about their intentions regarding the voluntary and flexible nature of the program. At the same time, to make the approach credible to both environmental groups and industry, a stronger concomitant enforcement program was a prerequisite. The milder the threat of enforcement, the less credible a cooperative government and industry program would be to the public and the less likely industry would be to perceive a need to initiate an audit program or to ask that an existing program be officially recognized by the government.

Current Thinking

Notwithstanding the problems associated with the incentives approach, the original reasons for exploring environmental auditing—to encourage companies to internalize affirmative environmental management, to secure better compliance over time, to obtain maximum use of scarce government resources, and to reduce needless public-private confrontation—remain valid. But it appears that environmental auditing is too new, too fluid, and too diverse to support a structured, programmatic approach. The challenge is to stimulate environmental auditing in less formal and perhaps more productive ways.

Various approaches have been proposed, discussed, and modified. Any approach that the government adopts must be both responsive to industry and responsible to the public. It should encourage companies to begin auditing programs without threatening those which already have programs in place; and it should enable federal and state agencies to get a better understanding of auditing practices and their potential benefits.

EPA's current thinking, which will undoubtedly continue to evolve after this handbook is published, calls for three interrelated initiatives: endorsement, analysis, and assistance. In this mode, EPA is acting as catalyst rather than as lead for joint public and private approaches.

- *Endorsement* Endorsement refers to EPA's public support for environmental auditing. High-level endorsement is reinforced by visible agency activities such as acting as a clearinghouse on auditing practices to help companies learn from one another; conducting workshops on auditing; showcasing individual audit programs that could serve as models; and continuing to develop networks of interested businesses, environmental groups, various state agencies, professional and trade associations, academics, and others. This public recognition through endorsement of environmental auditing should help accelerate private initiatives.

- *Analysis* At the same time, EPA is developing an analytic base on which to build future activities. This involves surveys and evaluations of audit programs, exploration of the benefits of environmental auditing, research into alternative government strategies for stimulating private initiatives, and other analyses. Since lack of sufficient data and information contributed to the agency's change of course, such analysis is particularly important for reducing uncertainties about the possibilities and limitations of joint public and private auditing approaches.

- *Assistance* In the meantime, the analyses described above will feed into EPA's assistance to states and companies interested in exploring joint public and private auditing approaches. The agency is providing needed suport to various initiatives in a number of states. EPA assistance should stimulate states to develop approaches that suit local needs and that can serve as experiments to demonstrate different strategies for public-private interaction.

At the crux of the current approach is the belief that without structuring a formal program, EPA can advance the same long-run goals without the immediate risks of a formal program. Using this three-pronged approach, the agency can continue to encourage and accelerate private auditing; work in a longer time frame to permit problems to be resolved incrementally; collaborate with interested firms, environmental groups, and others to address policy issues of mutual concern; develop a better empirical understanding of private-sector auditing; support states seeking to use auditing to solve specific, rather than global, regulatory problems; observe and evaluate different auditing strategies in those states; and develop recommendations based on experience.

The chief advantages of this approach are that it allows time for the affected parties to work through problems and reduce uncertainties gradually as data and experience are developed, and it facilitates a cooperative learning environment in which decisions can be integrated with operating experiences and disparate groups can work together collaboratively. EPA's current environmental auditing approach could represent a second generation of EPA decision making in which traditional rule making and public notice and comment are supplemented by procedures designed to harness public, government, and industry cooperation to resolve environmental problems of mutual concern.[3]

CONCLUSIONS

What conclusions can be drawn about EPA's efforts to stimulate a private-sector initiative and enhance its public benefits without bridling its effectiveness or private benefits?

Public Benefits

To analyze whether EPA has helped enhance the public benefits of environmental auditing, it is useful to distinguish between public benefits in a broad sense, i.e., benefits to the public at large, and public benefits more narrowly defined, i.e., direct benefits to the public sector (government). The agency's environmental auditing activities during the early 1980s probably contributed more to the former than to the latter. Although it should be noted that any assessment of benefits in this context is largely qualitative, nonetheless it seems fair to say that by establishing a framework for long-range dialogue, research, development of alternative approaches, and clarification of common objectives and interests, EPA helped lay the groundwork for the spread of environmental auditing, regardless of how the agency ultimately responds.

In general, the spread of auditing should serve the broad public interest by increasing corporate responsibility for compliance. This, in turn, could be expected to contribute to three publicly beneficial outcomes: increased likelihood that environmental problems will be identified in a timely way through comprehensive, periodic in-house audits of a firm's facilities; increased likelihood that identified environmental problems will be resolved, owing to the formal reporting and follow-up procedures that characterize most sound audit programs; and increased likelihood that the remedial actions taken will be effective if audit programs continue to be driven by top management support, which fosters effective problem identification and resolution.

In terms of achieving specific objectives for the government, the agency's early goals are only partially met as of this writing. There is no structured, centralized government program in place that would enable regulators formally to use environmental auditing to better target scarce enforcement resources. Some states, however, are beginning to experiment with auditing programs.

In the meantime, the process of debate and dialogue has, in our estimation, served to improve relations between EPA and responsible firms and to foster constructive dialogue without casting formal solutions in concrete. The process has served both to help EPA and the states learn from industry's operating experiences and to enable EPA and state personnel to convey to industry their ideas and concerns vis-à-vis environmental management.

Effectiveness and Private Benefits

Whether EPA has thwarted, enhanced, or had no impact on the effectiveness of corporate audit programs is unknown at this time. The agency's clearly expressed interest in environmental auditing has probably impelled a number of corporate managers to examine their audit programs to make sure they are operating adequately and to explore ways of upgrading their programs. On the other hand, one can imagine a scenario in which a handful of companies, in response to EPA's activity, might have decreased their firm's written audit trails or made their records so secret as to reduce operating managers' access to information that could help improve compliance. On balance, however, EPA expects its continued efforts to contribute to an increase in the overall effectiveness of environmental auditing by promoting a better understanding of what environmental auditing is and how it seems to work best for different firms and industries.

Substantial evidence also suggests that EPA has not thwarted the private benefits of environmental auditing. Despite the expression of numerous industry concerns about EPA's involvement in environmental auditing, the evidence suggests that environmental auditing is here to stay. Five years ago, few published works on environmental auditing were available. Today, a growing body of knowledge is being disseminated through public seminars, articles, issue papers, and books such as this one. The marketplace is at work.

Environmental auditing champions can be found in industry, state and federal agencies, and trade, professional, and other associations. A broad constituency for environmental auditing is emerging. At the same time, environmental auditing is beginning to take on the characteristics of a profession: there is a growing body of literature, underlying and competing theories, available training, and a set of practitioners and tools. At least one professional association is contemplating certifying environmental auditors.

If companies did not think environmental auditing continued to make good business sense, their interest—and hence the market in auditing—would drop off. There seems to be no evidence of such a drop, however.

On Developing Regulatory Alternatives

In the course of EPA's efforts to stimulate environmental auditing, the agency developed some insights into how regulatory alternatives might be best advanced. Following is a brief summary of a few of them.

Barriers to new ideas

First, there is probably more to hinder than facilitate the adoption of new ideas concerning regulatory alternatives. EPA encountered substantial resistance to its ideas about how regulators might build on private auditing, even though a number of people both inside and outside the agency agreed that the concepts made sense in principle. Few were comfortable constructing a program from the ground up. A frustrated lawyer once lamented: "Just give us a finished proposal; we can't respond to all these pie-in-the-sky ideas." The status quo seems to be a powerful competitor to new ideas; they are best pursued by taking small steps first.

Second, a balance needs to be achieved between the early sharing of ideas and sufficient development of those ideas in advance so that misunderstandings are minimized. Boldly putting forth new ideas for discussion was useful, both because it stimulated immediate feedback and because it demonstrated the agency's openness in debating these ideas. But because EPA's proposals seemed at the same time both radical and incomplete, they were understandably threatening. Industry speculation about what EPA really intended was difficult to quell without a fully structured proposal. Agency skepticism and environmentalists' concerns about "another agency giveaway" were difficult to counter in the absence of hard data demonstrating environmental, economic, and resource benefits. When ideas are still in the formative stage, it is easy to assume that they may develop in a direction contrary to one's interests.

Finally, a regulatory alternative that builds on a newly developing private initiative faces an added challenge. The diversity of corporate programs and the diversity of needs that give rise to them make extremely difficult the development of standard evaluation criteria. Companies have not yet developed a consensus on how an audit program should best be structured, and they have not yet reached agreement on how to deal with regulators. Government agencies can try to hasten the development of consistent practices in a newly developing field, but if EPA's experience is any indication, they are likely to encounter powerful resistance at the outset.

Hurdling the barriers

Despite these barriers, several key factors seemed to help advance the agency's proposals. The first factor was the existence of champions. There are environmental auditors in numerous corporations who have a stake in advancing their profession and who, having a few years of experience under their belts, are in a position to do so. Some of these people have been champions for environmental auditing outside their firms as well as inside. They have advanced environmental auditing concepts and techniques at conferences, in trade associations, and in professional organizations; and they provide both legitimacy and impetus for private auditing, as well as precedent for dialogue with the government and the public.

A related factor that helped advance EPA's activities was the development of networks. Though EPA did not initiate these networks, its activities probably helped stimulate their development. Various groups generated informal and formal networks to address emerging private-sector auditing issues as well as issues related to EPA's activities. A number of major trade associations developed environmental auditing work groups whose activities have spawned surveys, workshops, conferences, and issue papers. In 1982 an informal ad hoc group representing a number of interests was formed to address environmental auditing. By early 1983 the group had named itself the Environmental Auditing Roundtable and was committed to meeting periodically to address topical issues in the field.

These peer networks serve to advance environmental auditing in several important ways. They legitimize dialogue with regulators; they advance the state of the art by providing a forum for information exchange; they help spread environmental auditing practices; and they offer support for environmental auditing champions, who do not always receive full support for their ideas within their own corporations.

Beyond the Battleground

It strikes us that environmental auditing represents a true convergence of public and private interest. Though this convergence is not currently formalized, it will undoubtedly provide a basis for continued exploration and debate. As two perceptive observers of the regulatory process have noted, "The social responsibility of the regulators, in the end, must be not simply to impose controls, but to activate and draw upon the conscience and talents of those they seek to regulate."[4] Environmental auditing offers an opportunity to stimulate industry expertise rather than coerce it and to harness private ingenuity for public benefit. In the context of the regulatory battleground, environmental auditing offers a new, constructive role for government—one that involves neither confrontation nor capture.

1. A 1981 study conducted by EPA and the Council on Environmental Quality highlighted the problem of assuring day-to-day compliance. It indicated that of 180 major air sources studied, 70 percent believed to be in compliance actually experienced substantial intermittent excursions above allowable emission levels. The study found

that for the average source, actual emissions exceeded allowable emissions by an average of 25 percent. The study concluded that roughly one-third of those excess emissions could have been avoided with proper operation and maintenance procedures.

2. For a description of the way past adversary relations can perpetuate and expand future ones in the regulatory process, see Robert B. Reich, "Regulation by Confrontation or Negotiation," *Harvard Business Review* (May–June 1981).

3. A growing body of literature suggests that if environmental regulation is to be effective in the coming decades, it will have to conform to a new generation of rule-making styles and procedures. The new process would involve corporations, government agencies, and the public in cooperative planning designed to promote mutual learning and understanding about environmental consequences. See, for example, Gregory Daneke, "Planning vs. Regulation: An Alternative Future for Environmental Protection," in *The Environmental Professional*, 4(3):213–218 (1982).

4. Eugene Bardach and Robert A. Kagan, *Going by the Book: The Problem of Regulatory Unreasonableness*. Temple University Press, Philadelphia, 1982, p. 323.

Environmental Auditing as a Management Information System

John Palmisano

New Reforms Project
U.S. Environmental Protection Agency

Quality-assurance and quality-control activities are integrated into many production processes. Modern managers need information on how well a plant or production unit performs and the implications of previous and current performance. As a result of this ever-growing need, plant operations that may have seemed tangential to profit and loss are now being monitored for a variety of good business reasons.

Food-processing firms, for instance, have developed sophisticated management information systems to detect variations in quality and portion size. Because such reliable, self-correcting quality-assurance systems have been developed, the Department of Agriculture has allowed select firms to self-certify compliance with applicable regulations. Other regulatory agencies have tied reporting and other requirements to a firm's capability at the plant to identify, correct, and report varying states of compliance with federal and state regulations. The success of internal compliance assurance and self-auditing systems in achieving and maintaining compliance may provide environmental regulators with better ways to reach pollution-control objectives.

This article reflects the views of the author and not necessarily that of the U.S. Environmental Protection Agency or any other governmental agency.

Environmental auditing is the evaluation of a firm's compliance-assurance activities. During the last few years, the U.S. Environmental Protection Agency (EPA) has been investigating the benefits to firms, the environment, and regulatory agencies which may accrue from large-scale private-sector adoption of this management concept.

This chapter advances the notion that environmental auditing is one of many management information systems (MIS) which the modern corporation should develop and summarizes the evolution of environmental auditing as a complement and/or supplement to regulatory activities.

WHAT IS ENVIRONMENTAL AUDITING?

During the last 5 years, the concepts of compliance assurance and environmental auditing have captured the attention of progressive environmental professionals and corporate managers. Interest in these concepts stems from the desire to proactively, not reactively, deal with environmental problems—to anticipate and prevent environmental catastrophes which could damage the economic health and public image of the company.

Compliance assurance is defined as a systematic way of determining, attaining, and maintaining compliance with applicable environmental rules and regulations. Environmental auditing, then, is a vital component of an effective compliance-assurance program. It provides a systematic, independent method of verifying that the firm's compliance-assurance system is working as intended.

Environmental auditing not only determines a company's compliance with relevant federal, state, and local environmental regulations; it also provides the firm with information (not just statistical data) on which environmental decisions and planning can be based. Companies may vary in their approach to environmental audits; they do not vary in their need for information from which they can determine the best course of action to meet both today's and tomorrow's regulatory requirements.

The environmental audit is also a form of protection against findings of noncompliance. By undertaking periodic reviews of compliance, firms are better equipped to correct procedures which could result in noncompliance and better able to minimize the cost and trouble that result when regulators identify noncompliance. If an enforcement action is undertaken, the information necessary to remedy the problem is at hand and the company may be better able to protect corporate officials from legal proceedings. Without an auditing system and the organized data base it produces, a period of confusion ensues after a serious enforcement action which further disrupts normal business activities.

It seems obvious that environmental auditing, like compliance-assurance activities, is an important part of responsible corporate management. Furthermore, a company's use of its auditing system will become more sophisticated as the auditing becomes integrated with other planning and evaluation functions.

As an overall corporate policy, compliance assurance operates horizontally in the organization. It provides a framework within which all facilities operate. Although each plant must comply with different regulations, each must adhere to corporate policy and maintain compliance with all applicable regulations. Environmental auditing, on the other hand, functions vertically, transmitting information from different levels of the organization upward for review and use in decision making by upper management.

While the primary objective of environmental auditing programs was originally to assure chief executive officers (CEOs) that their firms were in compliance with local, state, and federal environmental regulations as well as corporate environmental policy, the goals have broadened to encompass a wide variety of management interests. For example, an increasingly important objective is to warn management of environmental risks which might arise from nascent toxic-waste problems and Superfund regulations. In general, a firm that has adopted a compliance-assurance program as a management tool has a system which covers air, water, and solid-waste problems. Successful programs may also tie in with either occupational-safety or loss-prevention programs.

To meet regulatory requirements, a firm can select from a set of compliance techniques, each having different cost and risk characteristics. Stockholder and senior-management needs drive the development of compliance assurance and environmental auditing, for example, information on compliance at a given emission point. The compliance-evaluation activities are intended to assure successively higher levels of corporate hierarchy that the corporation is responsibly conducting its business. Auditing does this by capturing data on compliance and producing useful information for each corporate level—namely, plant managers, planners, corporate decision makers, and stockholders. Each group has different concerns, so the same data may be used to generate different kinds of information. These MIS provide CEOs and other corporate managers with environmental compliance data which can be used to complement MIS data obtained from financial, strategic planning, and other areas of the corporation to improve overall corporate decision making.

EPA is continuing to explore the means by which regulators can build on private-sector auditing to reduce the overall burden that environmental regulations place on industry and regulators. For example, one scenario EPA may consider would allow firms with sound compliance-assurance and auditing programs to self-certify to assure compliance over time with government regulations. Self-certification is a means by which regulated companies assume greater responsibility for compliance activities, with a corresponding reduction in government intervention.

ENVIRONMENTAL AUDITING AS A MANAGEMENT INFORMATION SYSTEM

Most corporations use an MIS to provide corporate managers and planners with a range of data on how the company is performing with respect to budgets, sales targets, changes in inventory, long-term goals, etc. This information allows them to assess corporate performance against projected milestones, identify problems, and make decisions regarding future activities for the firm. Environmental auditing can be viewed as an MIS that provides management with specific data on how the firm is performing with respect to both externally established environmental requirements and internally established environmental objectives and policies.

Integrating Environmental MIS with Other Corporate MIS

For environmental auditing to be an effective MIS, it should be part of an overall corporate compliance-assurance program. The compliance-assurance program sets priorities for the corporation as a whole with respect to environmental performance. The audit then becomes the tool for evaluating the performance of specific plants and activities with respect to the overall compliance-assurance program.

Keep in mind the following rules when planning a compliance-assurance and environmental auditing program:

1. Compliance-assurance planning is part of an overall corporate strategic plan and flows from decisions made by senior management.
2. Compliance-assurance planning relates to decisions regarding product and plant design as well as operation of production facilities and environmental control activities.
3. Compliance-assurance planning is a fluid process; the way the system behaves will change over time with feedback regarding the rele-

vance and need for certain compliance-assurance procedures. The program must be flexible enough to change in response to changing corporate needs and priorities and new regulatory requirements.

4. The audit, or monitoring and reporting, function is the key element of compliance-assurance planning. This aspect of the system ensures that all necessary information is collected, verified, put in the proper format, and reported to either the appropriate part of the corporation or an outside regulatory agency.

5. An audit system will change over time. All systems evolve. Auditing activities, whether initiated in house or by consultants, will evolve to higher levels of sophistication. Auditing programs, therefore, should be developed with an understanding that uses and demands on the system will mature.

Key Elements of an Environmental Audit Program

Key elements of the auditing process include clearly defined objectives, established criteria for selecting auditing targets, definition of specific reporting protocols, staffing and training of the auditing team, and both inspection routine and actual inspection.

Clearly defined objectives and priorities are an essential part of any MIS; an effective environmental audit program will have clearly defined goals. From those goals flow the methods for evaluating program success, as well as a description of the relations between individuals in the auditing system. Individual plant audits may have different goals, depending on the situation, perceived risks, regulatory developments, corporate resources, etc. The audit program works by marrying the needs of the specific audit with the information needs of various corporate users. Users of the auditing system include plant foremen, plant managers, environmental auditors, quality-control specialists, accountants, and corporate attorneys. Uses include keeping the CEO out of jail, minimizing expenditures on pollution control, promoting quality control, reducing trouble with regulators, enhancing the corporate image, promoting integration of environmental planning in the corporation, and identifying and characterizing the extent of corporate liability due to regulatory requirements.

After defining the needs of corporate users, auditing protocols and auditing targets must be identified. There must be criteria for selecting the specific facilities, products, or environmental control processes and procedures that are targeted for audit. For example, selection criteria can be based on information obtained from previous audits, facility compliance reports, expectations regarding future performance, perceived risk, resource availability, or outside complaints.

Specific reporting requirements and data-gathering and data-quality-assurance procedures must be developed. Routinized reporting ensures that data are reported in an internally consistent manner and that appropriate levels of management receive the data or information relevant to their function.

Staffing and staff training must be appropriate to the audit objectives. Dollars to support these programs do not come from the "good fairy"; they must be appropriated and their use planned. Manuals and training materials must be developed for the audit staff and members of the auditing system, and the training process itself must be developed.

Eventually the audit team goes out to the field for the on-site inspection. The inspection team reviews plant activities to verify the existence and operation of compliance-assurance activities in conformance with appropriate procedures, evaluates compliance monitoring, the effectiveness of responses to emergency environmental episodes, and adherence to compliance-reporting requirements. Merely identifying problems is not enough. There must be feedback to assure auditors that problem areas are being addressed, and good compliance-assurance programs (and their managers) must be rewarded.

ENVIRONMENTAL AUDITING AS A REGULATORY CONCEPT

EPA believes that private-sector environmental compliance assurance and auditing provide an opportunity for developing compliance regulatory reform. Simple logic dictates that as the private sector assumes greater responsibility for ensuring compliance with environmental regulations, the public-sector role could diminish. However, for this to become a reality, EPA would need to be assured of the acceptability and integrity of the private programs, i.e., the agency would need to establish characteristics of effective private-sector compliance-assurance programs.

In addition, companies would need assurance that these programs would not work to their disadvantage and that EPA would not use them to increase, rather than reduce, the regulatory burden.

As the agency has discovered, these issues are not easily resolved. The agency has considered several approaches in developing this reform over the last 2 years. The current position is more laissez faire than some of the previous approaches, but it may prove more workable and acceptable in the long run. The sections that follow describe the history of the agency's efforts to develop environmental auditing into an effective reform.

Initial Approach: Use of Third-Party Auditors

Environmental auditing as a regulatory concept developed first with the Council on Environmental Quality (CEQ) proposal to use licensed water pollution auditors to assist EPA and state agencies in ensuring compliance under the water-permitting program. The proposal was subsequently expanded to encompass all mediums of pollution.

The CEQ proposal to use third-party auditors was based on the assumptions that it is increasingly difficult to ensure compliance as the regulatory focus shifts from mandating initial investment in pollution-control equipment to ensuring compliance over time; that the growth in the number of pollutants, pollutant sources, and rules may overwhelm the resources available to adequately monitor emissions and effluents; that the high cost of monitoring prevents EPA and the states from inspecting enough sources themselves to ensure adequate compliance with regulations; and that the quality of self-monitoring data varies widely.

The proposed auditing concept was to be modeled after other nongovernmental licensing functions such as that of certified public accountants. Under CEQ's proposal, certified environmental auditors would be engaged by the discharger to oversee compliance monitoring and certify that the firm did or did not meet the applicable requirements. Laboratories also would be certified, and an auditor would contract with a laboratory to conduct sampling and analysis. The perceived advantages of this program were:

- Monitoring would be done in a systematic way and with greater accuracy than before, and the costs of monitoring would be borne by the polluters, not the public.

- The auditing program could adjust to the growing compliance-assurance problems in ways which traditional enforcement activities fail to do; also, states would have information on compliance gathered in standardized ways by professionals. Furthermore, data generated would be consistent across the country.

- As a consequence of the above, enforcement activities at the national and local level could be better targeted.

This initial program design garnered only a handful of supporters. Critics of the proposal stressed the high cost to EPA of creating, licensing, and overseeing these private-sector auditors, the high cost to firms of paying for the increased surveillance, and the problems of keeping data confidential and third-party auditors impartial. Except by a few enthusiasts, the proposal was soundly rejected.

Second Approach: Incentives for Self-Certification

In the spring of 1981, EPA's policy office undertook a study of how firms could use insurance as a complement or supplement to direct regulation. That study revealed few opportunities for using insurance alone to leverage regulator resources. At that time, insurance companies were leery about becoming both insurer and quasi regulator of their clients. In fact (or at least, from anecdotes), insurance underwriters did not support waste-disposal requirements which would have required many firms to secure nonsudden liability insurance. At one of the meetings to review the progress of the insurance study, it was observed that the use of audits alone, as part of the underwriter's plant review, promoted greater compliance with environmental regulation. EPA then began a review of what was known about environmental auditing, how use of private-sector auditing might evolve into a form of self-certification, and what might be the benefits to various interest groups.

The first model that seemed to make sense was the self-certification model employed by the Internal Revenue Service. The IRS could send an agent to each taxpayer to review the taxpayer's records and file a return. Instead, a system of self-certification and the use of certified (and uncertified) experts, together with the judicious use of auditing, has become the foundation of the federal and state income tax system. CPAs (and other professionals) carry insurance to protect themselves against suit from clients, while taxpayers choosing a lower-cost way of complying (doing their taxes themselves) "self-insure" against penalties which may result from noncompliance with the tax code. It was thought that a similar system could be developed which would reduce reliance on the federal government's efforts to control pollution.

This system of self-certification of compliance was based on the dual notion of auditing and auditors. It was believed that merely employing auditing procedures would be a cost-effective way of enhancing compliance, but in order to secure maximum regulatory benefit from these activities, regulators would want a professional group (with narrow interests) to authenticate the auditing results. The process of environmental auditing would, or so it was and is believed, inexorably lead to professionalization of what had been a loose confederation of auditors. With the inclusion of a bonding, or insurance, component, checks and balances seemed sufficient to protect the interests of firms, regulators, and the environment. Instead of using the threat of EPA or state enforcement as the main compliance tool, the mainstay of compliance would be the environmental auditors, who would verify a firm's compliance with applicable regulations.

Checks and balances were thought to be ensured. Since firms were already dependent on insurance in complying with many regulatory requirements, improved compliance would result from developing auditing programs, and premiums could decrease for "good actors" as the actuarial data base developed. A professional group of auditors would serve their best interest by developing standards more rigorous than EPA could ever promulgate, and the auditors would be experience-rated by insurers who provide malpractice and professional liability insurance to the auditors. EPA would not have to take an active role in licensing auditors, and auditors would not need to be third parties. This system seemed to have something for everyone.

Upon further inspection it was realized that this model of self-certification was based on some naive notions as to how environmental auditing was practiced, the nature of EPA's enforcement activities, and how such a system would be implemented; and the proposal was rejected.

What grew out of the rejection of the proposal was a process of refinement through which EPA has tried to identify means by which regulators can blend the private-sector interest in getting better and less costly compliance management with ways that regulators can better ensure compliance. During the winter of 1981–1982, EPA's focus again changed.

Everyone seemed to agree that self-auditing was good for industry and good for the environment. Because it was good for the environment, it could be assumed to be good for regulators. It seemed logical to conclude that EPA should promote adoption of auditing by more and more firms. What could, or should, EPA do to encourage firms to implement good environmental auditing systems?

During this period EPA developed what has been called the "incentive-based" approach. The thrust of this inquiry was to define potential incentives available to EPA which would encourage firms to adopt auditing systems. Contact between staff working on this project and regulators, auditors, and interested parties increased at a rapid rate, and many comments were received as to what EPA should do. Response to the incentive-based approach was mixed. While some industry spokesmen wanted EPA to be actively involved in the evolution of auditing, others wanted no EPA presence at all. Environmentalists and regulators were unenthusiastic. But there continued to be agreement from all quarters that auditing provided benefits to firms and improved environmental outcomes. There was agreement that EPA should promote auditing but disagreement as to how this should be done.

Surveys conducted by various trade associations confirmed that interest in auditing ran high. In a survey conducted by the Edison Electric Institute, half the responding utilities stated that they would or might participate in a structured EPA auditing program, and over half said they had auditing programs or would develop them within 2 years. So, with support for private-sector auditing high and support for a direct EPA role low, EPA again reconsidered its approach.

EPA's Current Position

Rather than use third-party auditors or self-certification and incentive approaches, the EPA is now considering less structured ways of achieving these goals. During the fall of 1982, EPA expressed its then-current position on environmental auditing, comprising three interrelated aspects—endorsement, analysis, and assistance. It is believed that activity in all these areas can promote many of the benefits characteristic of previous program designs without their associated implementations problems.

Endorsement

EPA will continue to publicly support private-sector auditing efforts and will not restrict its endorsement to rhetoric. To encourage wider adoption by industry, EPA will act as a clearinghouse on auditing practices; participate in periodic workshops to transfer auditing information to potential users; showcase or highlight individual environmental auditing programs that can serve as good models; and continue to work with the network of corporate auditors, professionals standards organizations, and environmental liability insurance underwriters, as well as trade associations and state agencies.

Analysis

EPA will continue to study elements of compliance assurance and auditing, benefits to various interest groups, benefits to the environment, and characteristics of good auditing programs. This study should not only result in an improved understanding of enforcement activities but will connect with other compliance-related studies focused on water-pollution and air-pollution regulatory reforms.

Assistance

EPA will continue to provide susbstantial assistance to interested states and firms, as it is already doing with five eastern states. EPA will support states or industry groups that want to pursue specific approaches to promote auditing. Without being heavy-handed, EPA will encourage and learn from hands-on experience at trying to implement auditing-based programs.

This research agenda should identify alternatives to new mandatory reporting, monitoring, and inspection requirements, and the research and outreach should result in maintaining the current momentum. EPA, other regulators, environmentalists, and industry will know much more about environmental auditing by the end of 1983. Furthermore, the research has inherent value because it will permit program evaluators to better understand how and under what conditions performance auditing can be used to complement regulatory activities.

SELF-CERTIFICATION AND REGULATORY AGENCIES

Several efforts have been made to develop a process of self-certification to reduce regulatory lag and disputes, the costs of regulation, and the amount and kinds of information gathered and passed to regulators. The Securities and Exchange Commission changed its role from that of a direct regulator to a manager of regulatory activities when it changed the rules governing broker/dealer organizations in 1975; these organizations now self-regulate, with SEC auditing compliance with rules and regulations. By placing greater reliance on industry quality-control systems, the Coast Guard eliminated factory inspection of lifesaving equipment and is phasing in a system of third-party auditors.

The U.S. Department of Agriculture (USDA) allows meat processors to adopt programs which relieve the firms of constant USDA inspection. In the early part of this century, Congress recognized a need for a regulatory inspection program that would assure safe and wholesome meat and meat products. Legislation was therefore enacted and a program developed that was based on the needs of the public at that time: government inspectors were stationed at packinghouses to sort out and inspect certain livestock, carcasses, and parts of carcasses. The inspectors also were responsible for inspecting manufacturing facilities for processed meats. This regulatory inspection program proved effective in fulfilling the regulatory objectives of the USDA at that time. Even though every piece of retail meat or sausage was not inspected, every animal and its carcass and parts were inspected, as were certain production processes.

After the Second World War, national economic growth, advancing technologies, competition, and social changes caused a significant evolution in the nature and type of meat and meat products prepared and marketed. During this time regulatory activities remained essentially unchanged. As additional inspectors were hired to meet the growth in the meat-packing and processing industry, the inspection program began to rely on laboratory analyses to confirm the wholesomeness of finished products. The laboratory analyses, however, were used primarily as a check on the inspection program rather than as a substitute for the USDA program.

During this same period modernized plants began to specialize in slaughtering, canning, and processing hams, sausage, and meat. Consumer demands changed, and so did food-processing technology. With these developments came a need for effective production control—generally called quality control. Thus firms no longer relied only on USDA inspectors for product control; managers found that adopting their own quality-control systems was cost-effective and could be an efficient means for ensuring compliance with USDA's regulatory requirements.

On August 15, 1980, USDA amended the federal meat-inspection and poultry-inspection regulations to permit a meat or poultry establishment to develop and submit quality-control plans for evaluation by USDA; if approved, the firm could self-certify compliance with applicable federal regulations which had previously been enforced by on-site government inspections.

As of April 1, 1982, 55 plants had implemented voluntary quality-control programs. The cost to establish a self-certification program has been $2000 to $3000 per plant and record keeping has been held to less than 2 hours a day, while direct benefits have ranged from $200 to $30,000 a year. The federal government also is relieved of unnecessary administrative headaches. Lastly, firms can display a special logo on products made in facilities which have a self-certification program. The program is young, but all accounts suggest it is a cost-effective reform which benefits both consumers and industry.

A second, but more limited, application of self-certification is EPA's reform which allows pesticide manufacturers to self-certify the efficacy of pesticides undergoing registration by the Office of Pesticides Program (OPP). The efficacy-waiver reform grew out of congressional review of the Federal Insecticide, Fungicide, and Rodenticide Act (FIFRA). The review, aimed at streamlining pesticide regulation, resulted in Congress's granting the EPA administrator authority to determine whether and under what circumstances review of a registrant's proof of effectiveness is needed as part of the registration process.

The approach adopted by OPP to implement this authority was to waive all efficacy-data requirements for a few classes of pesticide use and to take a wait-and-see attitude with respect to nonwaived classes. For the most part, however, efficacy data were already being waived for products that did not pose public health concerns.

The waiver experiment had three goals. The first was to eliminate the thousands of person-hours per year spent on data review which seemingly did not produce public health benefits. The second was to speed up the registration of pesticides and promote the climate for innovation in the agricultural chemical industry. Lastly, the experience generated from this regulatory experiment was to serve as precedent for similar reforms in OPP or elsewhere.

Complete information for use in an evaluation of the efficacy-waiver program is currently unavailable. Anecdotal information suggests that the reform did not result in any environmental loss and resources were turned to use on more important regulatory activities. The waiver has recently been extended to cover more products.

USDA's self-certification program was more ambitious than OPP's. These two approaches are at opposite ends of a continuum—the efficacy waiver is a limited application of self-certification, while USDA's self-auditing program is probably as ambitious as regulatory reform can be. One can imagine a reform program which would pass all pesticide-registration activities to the private sector; laboratories could be certified to register pesticides (for limited use or wide use) if those laboratories had, for example, a $10 million surety bond backing up any potential claims from injured parties and a certification from EPA that the laboratory complied with accepted testing and evaluation protocols. EPA would periodically check laboratory records to certify compliance with accepted procedures for registering pesticides. The point is, self-certification programs can be narrow or broad, and they can grow from narrow to broad.

THE FUTURE OF ENVIRONMENTAL AUDITING AS A REFORM

Environmental auditing presents a rare opportunity for pursuing private and public goals. There is much to be gained from developing compliance reforms based on private-sector environmental auditing. The public would benefit as private-sector environmental auditing began to help regulators achieve more efficient use of resources. An effective reform could allow a significant reduction in EPA and state-agency compliance monitoring and enforcement activities. Environmental auditing might also enhance environmental quality in the long run, because firms with auditing programs develop the tools to check compliance and to assess and improve the firm's environmental performance over time. In the short run, such programs allow firms to promptly identify and correct many more noncompliance problems than would be detected by government inspectors.

There are also numerous benefits to the private sector from performing environmental auditing. First, environmental auditing can improve economic viability. Better integration of environmental (pollution-control) management with other management functions such as financial planning, production planning, and quality control permits more efficient business decisions to be made, because firms that include residuals management as part of their strategic planning can better determine which raw materials and production processes will be most cost-effective overall. In addition, auditing procedures yield compliance and operating data that allow management to take maximum advantage of opportunities, such as emissions "bubbling" and trading, which can generate profits as well as limit costs.

Second, evaluation of compliance with federal, state, and local regulations allows firms to assess risks associated with identified but unmanaged hazards, avoid tort liability, and prevent environmental surprises.

Third, environmental auditing is a socially responsible initiative which improves a firm's public image as well as its government relations. Improved government relations can result in reduced government oversight, reduced penalties and reporting requirements, and the potential for fast-track permit changes and additional regulatory flexibility.

Finally, environmental auditing might be evaluated by regulators as more feasible and cost-effective than mandatory reporting, monitoring, and inspection requirements.

Environmental auditing as a way for the private sector to verify compliance is a reality. Many firms have adopted this management concept; many are actively considering adoption of such programs and will join the hundreds of firms believed to have environmental-assurance or compliance monitoring in place.

The development of auditing systems is another step toward the second generation of relationships between regulators and industry that will be needed as monitoring and measuring technologies (hardware) become cheaper and compliance assurance and regulatory programs (software) mature. The information on how best to control pollution will always reside in the private sector, and regulators will continue to seek ways to use some of that information. Some reforms, such as EPA's emissions-trading policy, encourage firms to use their information in pursuit of cost savings. Other reforms are under development which will utilize private-sector motivations—cost or time savings—as an incentive to reach compliance with a regulatory requirement. Channeling private-sector interests to achieve a regulatory objective is becoming more and more common, especially within EPA. It is reasonable that, over time, regulators and industry will find ways to shift a greater burden of compliance to the private sector.

The evolution of environmental auditing into a regulatory reform is not yet complete. The process, however, has begun. Experience with other reforms, such as emissions trading, suggests that auditing is a promising area for substantive reform but that resolution of the many implementation issues will take time. The program which ultimately evolves may differ substantially from those approaches which EPA has considered to date. But whatever program results from the ongoing debate and analysis, if it provides a better, more cost-effective way of ensuring day-to-day compliance, it will serve the needs of regulators, industry, and the public.

Index

About the Editor in Chief

L. Lee Harrison has degrees in civil engineering and journalism and has written about environmental regulation since the beginning of the environmental era in the early 1970s. After working for two years as an engineer at Bechtel Corporation, he wrote for McGraw-Hill's *Construction Methods and Equipment* magazine, covering aspects of new environmental laws as they related to construction. He later worked for McGraw-Hill *World News*, covering environmental and business topics in Alaska, and he also wrote about business and the environment for McGraw-Hill's *Electrical Week* newsletter. Most recently he served as environment editor for McGraw-Hill's *Chemical Week* magazine. Other publications for which he has written include *The New York Times*, *Europe Magazine*, and his own publication, the *Environmental Audit Letter*.